THE NEW CAMBRIDGE SHAKESPEARE

GENERAL EDITOR
Brian Gibbons, *University of Münster*

ASSOCIATE GENERAL EDITOR
A. R. Braunmuller, *University of California, Los Angeles*

From the publication of the first volumes in 1984 the General Editor of the New Cambridge Shakespeare was Philip Brockbank and the Associate General Editors were Brian Gibbons and Robin Hood. From 1990 to 1994 the General Editor was Brian Gibbons and the Associate General Editors were A. R. Braunmuller and Robin Hood.

PERICLES, PRINCE OF TYRE

Over the last two decades there has been a resurgence of theatrical interest in Shakespeare's *Pericles*, which has been rescued from comparative neglect and is now frequently performed. This development is charted in the Introduction to this edition, which differs radically from any other currently available. Doreen DelVecchio and Antony Hammond reject the current orthodoxies: that the text is seriously corrupt and that the play is of divided authorship. They show how the 1609 quarto has features in common with the first quarto of *King Lear*, now widely regarded as being based on Shakespeare's manuscript. Likewise they regard the arguments concerning divided authorship as unproven and misleading. Instead they show the play to be a unified aesthetic experience. The result is a view of *Pericles* far more enthusiastic than that of other editors.

THE NEW CAMBRIDGE SHAKESPEARE

All's Well That Ends Well, edited by Russell Fraser
Antony and Cleopatra, edited by David Bevington
The Comedy of Errors, edited by T. S. Dorsch
Hamlet, edited by Philip Edwards
Julius Caesar, edited by Marvin Spevack
King Edward III, edited by Giorgio Melchiori
The First Part of King Henry IV, edited by Herbert and Judith Weil
The Second Part of King Henry IV, edited by Giorgio Melchiori
King Henry V, edited by Andrew Gurr
The First Part of King Henry VI, edited by Michael Hattaway
The Second Part of King Henry VI, edited by Michael Hattaway
The Third Part of King Henry VI, edited by Michael Hattaway
King Henry VIII, edited by John Margeson
King John, edited by L. A. Beaurline
King Lear, edited by Jay L. Halio
King Richard II, edited by Andrew Gurr
Macbeth, edited by A. R. Braunmuller
Measure for Measure, edited by Brian Gibbons
The Merchant of Venice, edited by M. M. Mahood
The Merry Wives of Windsor, edited by David Crane
A Midsummer Night's Dream, edited by R. A. Foakes
Much Ado About Nothing, edited by F. H. Mares
Othello, edited by Norman Sanders
Pericles, edited by Doreen DelVecchio and Antony Hammond
The Poems, edited by John Roe
Romeo and Juliet, edited by G. Blakemore Evans
The Sonnets, edited by G. Blakemore Evans
The Taming of the Shrew, edited by Ann Thompson
Titus Andronicus, edited by Alan Hughes
Twelfth Night, edited by Elizabeth Story Donno
The Two Gentlemen of Verona, edited by Kurt Schlueter

THE EARLY QUARTOS
The First Quarto of King Lear, edited by Jay L. Halio
The First Quarto of King Richard III, edited by Peter Davison

PERICLES, PRINCE OF TYRE

Edited by
DOREEN DELVECCHIO
Assistant Professor of Drama, McMaster University

ANTONY HAMMOND
Professor of Drama and English, McMaster University

PUBLISHED BY THE PRESS SYNDICATE OF THE UNIVERSITY OF CAMBRIDGE
The Pitt Building, Trumpington Street, Cambridge CB2 1RP, United Kingdom

CAMBRIDGE UNIVERSITY PRESS
The Edinburgh Building, Cambridge CB2 2RU, United Kingdom
40 West 20th Street, New York, NY 10011-4211, USA
10 Stamford Road, Oakleigh, Melbourne 3166, Australia

First published 1998

Printed in the United Kingdom at the University Press, Cambridge

Typeset in Ehrhardt [BT]

A catalogue record for this book is available from the British Library

Library of Congress cataloguing in publication data

Shakespeare, William, 1564–1616.
(Pericles)
Pericles, Prince of Tyre / edited by Doreen DelVecchio, Antony Hammond.
 p. cm. – (New Cambridge Shakespeare)
Includes bibliographical references.
ISBN 0 521 22907 3 (hardback) – ISBN 0 521 29710 9 (paperback)
 1. Princes – Lebanon – Tyre – Drama. I. DelVecchio, Doreen. II. Hammond,
Antony. III. Title. IV. Series: Shakespeare, William, – 1564–1616. Works. 1984.
Cambridge University Press.
PB2830. A2D45 1998
822.3′3 – dc21 97-1358 CIP

ISBN 0 521 22907 3 hardback
ISBN 0 521 29710 9 paperback

CONTENTS

ILLUSTRATIONS

PREFACE AND ACKNOWLEDGEMENTS

When we first proposed editing *Pericles* for the New Cambridge Shakespeare, our enthusiasm for it had been fired by a flawed but generally remarkably successful production at the Stratford Festival in Ontario. Though both of us had been teaching Shakespeare at McMaster University, in neither of our courses had *Pericles* played a large role. It was something of an overwhelming experience for us, then, to find it as stunningly successful a play for the stage as the Stratford production proved. This led us to propose to 'break a lance' for it in our edition, and so we began our work from a radically different point of view from that of many editors of the play, whose first reaction to the task seems to have been 'Oh, dear'. Because our mind-set was enthusiastic, we found ourselves questioning the received view of the 1609 quarto as essentially corrupt, and far less convinced than most of our colleagues about the theory that the play was a work of collaboration. We feel pleased that our several years' work on the play has dulled neither our conviction of its dramatic and literary merits, nor our suspicion of the hostile and disintegrative views of its text.

Our edition, we feel, should therefore begin with a mandatory Government Health Warning: THIS EDITION OF *PERICLES* MAY BE HARMFUL TO YOUR PREJUDICES. We have done what no other editor has done: we have tried to trust the text and to respect the integrity of the play. As a consequence, our edition differs in hundreds of readings from other editions on the market, and we hope it will prove a refreshing change.

We have incurred some pleasant debts in the course of our work. First and greatest, we owe much to the wit and wisdom of Professor A. R. Braunmuller, the most generous, conscientious, and helpful of General Editors. Brian Gibbons, General Editor of the series has likewise been most helpful, and we would also like to record our appreciation of the care and support of Sarah Stanton and the CUP publishing team. We express gratitude to that most civilised research library, the Shakespeare Centre in Stratford-upon-Avon, and especially to Sylvia Morris there. We are grateful to the Royal National Theatre for help with the photographs of their production, and to the Archive of the Stratford Festival in Ontario for permitting us to see the videotapes of their productions. Professor Ann Savage of the English Department at McMaster University was enormously helpful to us on the thorny matter of the archaisms in Gower's language. We also are most obliged to Verena Bühler of the Englisches Seminar, Universität Zürich for assisting us to obtain a microfilm of the unique Zürich copy of Wilkins's *Painfull Aduentures*. Antony Hammond records his gratitude to Trevor Howard-Hill for inviting him to read a paper to the Society for Textual Scholarship on 'The perils of *Pericles*', and to the Arts Research Board of McMaster University for their partial funding of his visit to New York.

ABBREVIATIONS AND CONVENTIONS

Shakespeare's plays, when cited in this edition, are abbreviated in a style modified slightly from that used in the *Harvard Concordance to Shakespeare*. Other editions of Shakespeare are abbreviated under the editor's surname (Malone, Hoeniger) unless they are the work of more than one editor; in such cases an abbreviated series name is used (Cam., Oxford). When more than one edition by the same editor is cited, the later editions are identified by a superscript numeral (Rowe²). All quotations from Shakespeare, except those from *Pericles*, use the text and lineation of *The Riverside Shakespeare*, text ed. G. Blakemore Evans, 1974.

1. Shakespeare's plays

Ado	*Much Ado About Nothing*
Ant.	*Antony and Cleopatra*
AWW	*All's Well That Ends Well*
AYLI	*As You Like It*
Cor.	*Coriolanus*
Cym.	*Cymbeline*
Err.	*The Comedy of Errors*
Ham.	*Hamlet*
1H4	*The First Part of King Henry the Fourth*
2H4	*The Second Part of King Henry the Fourth*
H5	*King Henry the Fifth*
1H6	*The First Part of King Henry the Sixth*
2H6	*The Second Part of King Henry the Sixth*
3H6	*The Third Part of King Henry the Sixth*
H8	*King Henry the Eighth*
JC	*Julius Caesar*
John	*King John*
LLL	*Love's Labour's Lost*
Lear	*King Lear*
Mac.	*Macbeth*
MM	*Measure for Measure*
MND	*Midsummer Night's Dream*
MV	*The Merchant of Venice*
Oth.	*Othello*
Per.	*Pericles*
R2	*King Richard the Second*
R3	*King Richard the Third*
Rom.	*Romeo and Juliet*
Shr.	*The Taming of the Shrew*
STM	*Sir Thomas More*
Temp.	*The Tempest*
TGV	*The Two Gentlemen of Verona*
Tim.	*Timon of Athens*

Tit.	*Titus Andronicus*
TN	*Twelfth Night*
TNK	*The Two Noble Kinsmen*
Tro.	*Troilus and Cressida*
Wiv.	*The Merry Wives of Windsor*
WT	*The Winter's Tale*

2. Editions, adaptations, works of reference, and periodicals

Abbott	E. A. Abbott, *A Shakespearian Grammar*, rev. edn, 1870 (references are to numbered paragraphs)
Alexander	*William Shakespeare: The Complete Works*, ed. Peter Alexander, 1951
Anatomy	Northrop Frye, *Anatomy of Criticism*, 1957
Arber	*A Transcript of the Registers of the Company of Stationers of London 1554–1640 A. D.*, ed. Edward Arber, 1875–1894
BCP	The Book of Common Prayer
Boswell	*The Plays and Poems of William Shakespeare*, ed. James Boswell, 21 vols., 1821
Bullen	*The Works of William Shakespeare*, ed. A. H. Bullen, 10 vols., 1904–7
Bullough	*Narrative and Dramatic Sources of Shakespeare*, ed. Geoffrey Bullough, 8 vols., vol. VI, 1966
c.	*circa*
Cam.	*The Works of William Shakespeare*, ed. W. G. Clark, J. Glover, and W. A. Wright, 10 vols., 1863–8 (The Cambridge Shakespeare)
CA	John Gower, *Confessio Amantis*, Book VIII (in Bullough, pp. 375–423)
Collier	*The Works of William Shakespeare*, ed. J. P. Collier, 9 vols., 1844, 1842–53
Collier²	*The Plays of William Shakespeare*, ed. J. P. Collier, 8 vols., 1853
Companion	Stanley Wells and Gary Taylor, *William Shakespeare: A Textual Companion*, 1987
conj.	conjectured
corr.	corrected
Crown	G. Wilson Knight, *The Crown of Life* [1947] 1948
Deighton	*Pericles*, ed. K. Deighton, 1907 (first Arden Shakespeare)
Delius	*Shakspere's Werke*, ed. Nicolaus Delius, 7 vols., 1854–61
Dent	R. W. Dent, *Shakespeare's Proverbial Language: An Index*, 1981
Dryden	*The Works of John Dryden*, ed. E. N. Hooker *et al.*, 1956–
Dyce	*The Works of William Shakespeare*, ed. Alexander Dyce, 6 vols., 1857
edn	edition
Edwards	*Pericles Prince of Tyre*, ed. Philip Edwards, 1976 (New Penguin Shakespeare)
Ellacombe	Henry Ellacombe, *The Plant-Lore and Garden Craft of Shakespeare*, 1884
ELR	*English Literary Renaissance*
Ewbank	Inga-Stina Ewbank: ' "My name is Marina": the language of recognition', in Philip Edwards, Inga-Stina Ewbank, G. K. Hunter (eds.) *Shakespeare's Styles: Essays in Honour of Kenneth Muir*, 1980, pp. 111–30.

F3	*Mr. William Shakespear's Comedies, Histories, and Tragedies*, 1663–4 (Third Folio)
F4	*Mr. William Shakespear's Comedies, Histories, and Tragedies*, 1685 (Fourth Folio)
Falconer	Alexander Frederick Falconer, *Shakespeare and the Sea*, 1964
Farmer	Richard Farmer, *An Essay on the Learning of Shakespeare*, 1767
Globe	*The Works of William Shakespeare*, ed. W. G. Clark and W. A. Wright, 1864 (the Globe edition)
Herford and Simpson	C. H. Herford and Percy Simpson, *Ben Jonson*, 11 vols., 1925–52
Hoeniger	*Pericles*, ed. F. D. Hoeniger, 1963 (Arden Shakespeare)
Hudson	*The Works of Shakespeare*, ed. H. N. Hudson, 11 vols., 1851–6
Knight	*Comedies, Histories, Tragedies and Poems of William Shakespeare*, ed. Charles Knight, 12 vols., 1842–4
Last Phase	Derek Traversi, *Shakespeare: The Last Phase*, 1955
Long	John H. Long, *Shakespeare's Use of Music: The Final Comedies*, 1961
Lucr.	William Shakespeare, *The Rape of Lucrece* (in Riverside)
Malone	*Supplement* to the Johnson–Steevens *Plays of William Shakespeare* 1778, ed. E. Malone, 1780
Malone²	*The Plays and Poems of William Shakespeare*, ed. E. Malone, 10 vols., 1790
Marlowe	*The Complete Works of Christopher Marlowe*, ed. Fredson Bowers, 2nd edn, 1981
Mason	J. M. Mason, *Comments on the Last Edition of Shakespeare's Plays*, 1785, rev. edn, 1807
National 1994	The (Royal) National Theatre, London production of 1994
Natural Perspective	Northrop Frye, *A Natural Perspective: The Development of Shakespearean Comedy and Romance*, 1965
N&Q	*Notes and Queries*
NCS	New Cambridge Shakespeare
NS	*Pericles*, ed. J. C. Maxwell, 1956 (The New Shakespeare)
NT	The New Testament
Onions	C. T. Onions, *A Shakespeare Glossary*, 1911, rev. edn, 1953
OED	*The Oxford English Dictionary on Compact Disc*. Second edn, ed. J. A. Simpson and E. S. C. Weiner, 1992
Oxford	*William Shakespeare: The Complete Works, Original-Spelling Edition*, ed. Stanley Wells and Gary Taylor, 1986
PA	George Wilkins, *The Painfull Aduentures of Pericles Prince of Tyre*, 1608
PBSA	*Papers of the Bibliographical Society of America*
Percy	Bishop Thomas Percy, who contributed a number of conjectured readings to the Steevens editions
Peterson	Douglas L. Peterson, *Time, Tide and Tempest: A Study of Shakespeare's Romances*, 1973
PPA	Laurence Twine, *The Patterne of Painefull Adventures*, *c.* 1594, rpt 1607 (in Bullough, pp. 423–82)
Q, Q1	*The Late, and much admired Play, Called Pericles, Prince of Tyre*, 1609 (STC 22334) (first quarto)
Q2	*The Late, and much admired Play, Called Pericles, Prince of Tyre*, 1609 (STC 22335) (second quarto)

Q3	*The Late, and much admired Play, Called Pericles, Prince of Tyre*, 1611 (STC 22336) (third quarto)
Q4	*The Late, and much admired Play, Called Pericles, Prince of Tyre*, 1619 (STC 26101) (fourth quarto)
Q5	*The Late, and much admired Play, Called Pericles, Prince of Tyre*, 1630 (STC 22337) (fifth quarto)
Q6	*The Late, and much admired Play, Called Pericles, Prince of Tyre*, 1635 (STC 22339) (sixth quarto)
r	recto (the right-hand page when a book is opened)
Ridley	*Pericles*, ed. M. R. Ridley, 1935 (New Temple Shakespeare)
Riverside	*The Riverside Shakespeare*, text ed. G. Blakemore Evans, 1974
Round	*Pericles*, ed. P. Z. Round, 1890
Rowe	*The Works of Mr. William Shakespear*, ed. Nicholas Rowe, 6 vols., 1709
Rowe²	*The Works of Mr. William Shakespear*, ed. Nicholas Rowe, 6 vols., 1709
Rowe³	*The Works of Mr. William Shakespear*, ed. Nicholas Rowe, 9 vols., 1714
RSC 1947	Royal Shakespeare Company production of 1947
RSC 1958	Royal Shakespeare Company production of 1958
RSC 1969	Royal Shakespeare Company production of 1969
RSC 1979	Royal Shakespeare Company production of 1979
RSC 1989	Royal Shakespeare Company production of 1989
RES	*Review of English Studies*
Scott-Giles	C. W. Scott-Giles, *Shakespeare's Heraldry*, 1950
Schanzer	*Pericles*, ed. Ernest Schanzer, 1965 (Signet Shakespeare)
Schmidt	Alexander Schmidt, *Shakespeare Lexicon: A Complete Dictionary*, 4th edn, 2 vols., 1923
SD	stage direction
Sewell	*The Works of Shakespear*, ed. George Sewell, 9 vols., 1728 (revised from Pope's edn)
SH	speech heading
sig.	signature(s) (printer's indications of the ordering of pages in early modern books, used here where page-numbers do not exist, or occasionally for bibliographical reasons)
Singer	*Dramatic Works of William Shakespeare*, ed. Samuel W. Singer, 1826
Sisson	*William Shakespeare: The Complete Works*, ed. Charles J. Sisson, 1954
Son.	William Shakespeare, *Sonnets* (in Riverside)
SQ	*Shakespeare Quarterly*
S.Sur.	*Shakespeare Survey*
Staunton	*The Plays of Shakespeare*, ed. Howard Staunton, 3 vols., 1858–60
STC	*A Short-Title Catalogue of Books Printed in England, Scotland, & Ireland and of the English Books Printed Abroad 1475–1640*. First compiled by A. W. Pollard and G. R. Redgrave. Second edition, revised and enlarged, begun by W. A. Jackson and F. S. Ferguson, completed by Katherine F. Pantzer, 3 vols., 1986, 1976, 1991
Steevens	*The Plays of William Shakspeare*, ed. Samuel Johnson, George Steevens, and Isaac Reed, 10 vols., 1785
subst.	substantively

sv	*sub verbum* (Latin for 'under the word' used in dictionary citations)
Theobald MS	Unpublished marginalia by L. Theobald, in copies of Q4 (Folger Shakespeare Library) and Q6 (University of Pennsylvania)
Stratford 1973	The Stratford (Shakespeare) Festival, Ontario, Canada production of 1973
Stratford 1986	The Stratford (Shakespeare) Festival, Ontario, Canada production of 1986
Tilley	Morris Palmer Tilley, *A Dictionary of Proverbs in England in the Sixteenth and Seventeenth Centuries*, 1950 (references are to numbered proverbs)
Tonson	*Pericles Prince of Tyre*, pub. J. Tonson, 1734
Tyrwhitt	Thomas Tyrwhitt, *Observations and Conjectures upon some Passages of Shakespeare*, 1766
uncorr.	uncorrected
v	verso (the left-hand page when a book is opened)
Ven.	William Shakespeare, *Venus and Adonis* (in Riverside)
Walker	W. S. Walker, *A Critical Examination of the Text of Shakespeare*, 3 vols., 1860
Williams	Gordon Williams, *A Dictionary of Sexual Language and Imagery in Shakespearean and Stuart Literature*, 3 vols., 1994
Yale	*Pericles*, ed. A. R. Bellinger, 1925 (Yale Shakespeare)
Young	Alan R. Young, 'A note on the tournament impresas in *Pericles*', *SQ* 4 (1985), 453–6

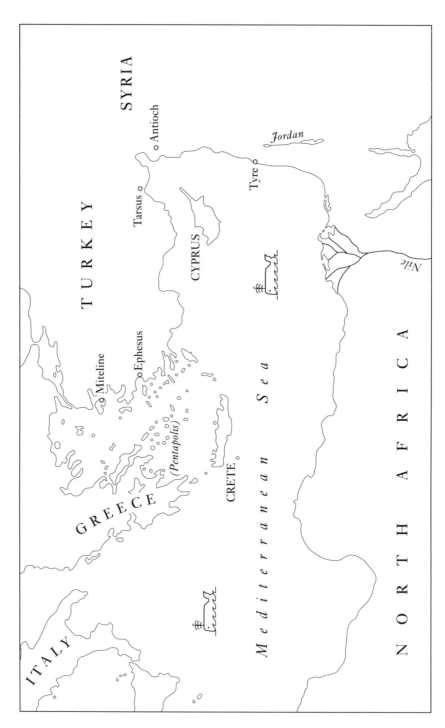

1   Map of the eastern Mediterranean

INTRODUCTION

Date

Pericles cannot be later than 1608, since on 20 May of that year it was entered in the Stationers' Register. There is no terminal date in the other direction. It was seen by Zorzi Giustinian, who was Venetian ambassador between 5 January 1606 and 23 November 1608, in the company of the French ambassador de la Boderie and his wife (who seems not to have been in England before April 1607). Since Giustinian paid admission, the performance must have been a public one; and since the theatres were closed by plague from April to December 1607 and again in the summer and autumn of 1608, some time during the first six months of 1608 seems plausible, though it does not follow that the play was new when he saw it.[1] It has been suggested that the use of Guicchiardine as Chorus in Barnabe Barnes's *The Devil's Charter* influenced the treatment of Gower in *Pericles*, but the resemblances between the two are slight (see p. 35 n.). Barnes's play was performed by the King's Men at court on Candlemas night (2 February) 1607, and therefore presumably was first publicly performed late in 1606 (the quarto was not entered on the Stationers' Register until 16 October 1607, but being a King's Men's play, it is not out of the question that Shakespeare may have known it on stage). The choruses in *The Travailes of the Three English Brothers* (by John Day, William Rowley, and George Wilkins) bear some similarities to those in *Pericles*. This play was entered on 29 June 1607; it was a topical piece, and may well have been published shortly after it was performed (the title page declares 'As it is now play'd' by the Queen's Men), and it was successful enough to attract a satirical reference in *The Knight of the Burning Pestle*.[2] There is general agreement that *Pericles* predates the other romances, but by how much no one can say. While it remains possible that *Pericles* was both written and produced in the busy year 1606, it seems likelier that it was written in 1607 and first performed early in 1608.

Sources

The sources and analogues of fairy-tales and legends tend to reach back in time for their generation, and grow in various directions throughout their narrative travels in different countries, either by word of mouth or in written form. In this way, tracing the sources of *Pericles* over distance and time bears a resemblance to the journeys of the hero in the play. The story of *Pericles* originated in Hellenistic antiquity in the Greek romance of Apollonius of Tyre and, after all sorts of metamorphoses, attained its final

---

[1] See E. K. Chambers, *William Shakespeare: A Study of Facts and Problems*, 1930, II, 335.
[2] See 4.1.27–30 (in *The Dramatic Works in the Beaumont and Fletcher Canon*, general ed. Fredson Bowers, 1966, I, 64). The first performance of *The Knight* is usually dated 1607 on the basis of this allusion.

statement in Shakespeare's play in the seventeenth century.[1] Like the histories of
Xenophon, Heliodorus, and Iamblichus, the original story exhibits the familiar characteristics of the Greek sophistic romance: sea-storms, pirates, apparent death,
dreams, and reunited lovers – the very fabric of adventure in Shakespeare's last plays.

The survival and popularity of the Apollonius of Tyre story is attested by a number
of Greek and a hundred Latin manuscripts surviving from the Middle Ages, as well as
by the number of adaptations and translations produced, including one in Anglo-
Saxon (dating from the eleventh century; the only romance in Anglo-Saxon literature
and the first of all known vernacular versions), and one in Middle English (early
fifteenth century).[2] In the twelfth century Godfrey of Viterbo included it in his Latin
Pantheon, or Universal Chronicle (written *c.* 1186 and first printed in 1559). By the
fourteenth century the story entered the famous collection of fictitious moralising
stories, the *Gesta Romanorum* (the 153rd story), in which much is made of wanderings,
searches, sufferings in the brothel, and riddles to be solved; riddles asked not only by
Antiochus but also by the maid in an effort to relieve her ailing father. It is clear that
the story became disseminated in vernacular versions throughout Europe from the
eleventh century onwards: Italy, Russia, Hungary, Bohemia, Norway, Iceland, Den-
mark, the Netherlands, Germany, France, and Spain.[3]

Despite the story's enduring fame, Chaucer's Man of Law refers unflatteringly to
its features of rape and incest as unsuitable subjects for an author:

> (Of swiche cursed stories I sey fy!).
> Or ellis of Tyro Appollonious,
> How that the cursed kyng Antiochus
> Birafte his doghter of hir maydenhede,

---

[1] For the full history of the story see A. H. Smyth, *Shakespeare's Pericles and Apollonius of Tyre*, 1898:
'Shakespeare's *Pericles of Tyre* is the most singular example in Elizabethan literature of a consistent
copying of a venerable and far-travelled story. The Apollonius saga, from which it is wholly drawn, is
known to nearly every language of Europe, and persists through more than a thousand years, flourishing
in extraordinary popularity', p. 5. See also S. Singer, *Apollonius von Tyrus*, 1895; E. Klebs, *Die Erzählung
von Apollonius aus Tyrus*, 1899. For a comprehensive survey and reprint of the major sources, see
Bullough.

[2] The Anglo-Saxon version is a prose fragment (the MS. is in Corpus Christi College, Cambridge) which
contains the story as far as the betrothal of Apollonius to Aroestrates' daughter, their reunion in the
Temple of Diana, and the marriage of their daughter Tharsia to Athenagoras. The Middle English
fragment (in the Bodleian Library, Oxford) is in rhymed verse (144 lines) and relates Apollonius' narrative
in the Temple. Both works have been edited by J. Raith in *Die alt- und mitttelenglischen Apollonius-
Bruchstücke*, 1956.

[3] In Italy the story appears in a fourteenth-century MS.; a version in *ottava rima* was published frequently
between 1486 and 1692. In Germany Heinrich von Neustadt wrote a verse version in 20,893 lines in the
fourteenth century; Heinrich Steinhöwel wrote a prose history in the fifteenth century (printed in 1471).
In the Netherlands the story appeared in the translations of the *Gesta Romanorum* from 1481 onwards and
was separately published in 1493. In France the story was known by the troubadours and was assimilated
into the cycle of Charlemagne; a prose version appeared *c.* 1480; F. de Belleforest retold the story from the
Gesta Romanorum in his *Histoires Tragiques* in 1595. In Spain there were vernacular MSS.; Juan de
Timoneda printed a version from the *Gesta Romanorum* in 1576. As Bullough has pointed out, 'a few
coincidences with other versions suggest that the dramatist knew some folklore version of the tale
unknown to us. "Perillie" is a name assumed by Apollonius in a French MS. in Vienna [MS. 3428, Wiener
Hofbibliothek]; Cerimon's helper Philemon . . . is called Philominus in von Neustadt's poem; and in a
Greek poem on the story printed in the sixteenth century there is a tournament at Pentapolis' (p. 355).

That is so horrible a tale for to rede,
Whan he hir threw upon the pavement.
And therefore he, of ful avysement,
Nolde nevere write in none of his sermons
Of swiche unkynde abhomynacions . . .[1]

His views were not shared by Chaucer's contemporary and friend, John Gower
(?1330–1408) who retold the full story from Viterbo's *Pantheon* in Book VIII of his
Confessio Amantis (1390s); Shakespeare knew early in his career of Gower's work, and
probably drew from its version of the reunion in the Temple of Diana for the conclusion of *The Comedy of Errors*. Gower is one of the two major sources of *Pericles*.

The popularity of the tale grew throughout the Renaissance with the publication of
a scholarly edition of the early romance,[2] new adaptations, and translations. The first
printed English version appeared in 1502 when Wynkyn de Worde published a prose
romance, *Kynge Apollyn of Thyre*, translated by Robert Copland from a French
romance derived from the *Gesta Romanorum*.[3] Shakespeare's second major source for
the play was a novel by Laurence Twine, *The Patterne of Painefull Adventures* (c. 1594,
reprinted 1607), which draws upon a French translation of the Latin *Gesta* for its
version of the story.

Both Gower's *Confessio Amantis* and Twine's *Patterne of Painefull Adventures* are
generally recognised to be the primary sources for the play, which draws material from
one or other in a fashion that suggests Shakespeare the scholar consulting the open
pages of these books during composition. It was Gower, however, who exercised the
greater influence on the dramatist.[4]

GOWER

The *Confessio Amantis*, finished not later than 1393, contains 141 stories in its 33,000
lines of octosyllabic couplets.[5] Gower is not much read these days except by medieval-
ists, yet C. S. Lewis, in his *Allegory of Love*, declared him 'almost Chaucer's equal as
a craftsman'. While conceding that 'architectonics were not the strong point of the

[1] *The Man of Law's Tale*, lines 80–8, in *Works* ed. F. N. Robinson, 1957.
[2] Velserius' *Historia Apollonii regis Tyrii* in M. Welser, *Narratio Eorum Quae Contigerunt Apollonio Tyrio*,
1595.
[3] Other translations of the *Gesta* were published at intervals in the sixteenth century, but did not include the
Apollonius story.
[4] There are two possible lesser sources or analogues worth mention. Sir Philip Sidney, in Books I–III of his
Arcadia (1590), recounts the adventures of Pyrocles who, like Pericles, undergoes sea-storms and shipwreck; he is provided with clothing by two shepherds, rescued by pirates, adopts a disguise for love of
Philoclea; and his friend Musidorus finds a suit of armour belonging to his cousin. When Pyrocles believes
Philoclea dead he is visited by a woman who rebukes his excessive grief; angered, he attempts to strike her
only to discover that she is really Philoclea. Events such as these strongly suggest that Sidney was recalling
a version of the Apollonius story, but are not enough to confirm that Shakespeare borrowed from the
Arcadia. Marina's situation in the brothel has an analogue in *The Orator* (1596, Declamation 53), a
translation by L. Piot from the French of Alexandre van den Busche, which ultimately derived from
Seneca the Elder's *Controversia*. The story tells of the triumph of chastity in the adventures of a nun who
is captured by pirates and sold to a brothel where she withstands temptation.
[5] First printed by Caxton in 1483, and by Berthelette in 1532 (reprinted 1554; the edition probably used by
Shakespeare).

2 Genius and Amans, from Gower's *Confessio Amantis*, British Library MS. Egerton 1991 fol. 7ᵛ

Middle Ages', Lewis goes on to praise Gower for 'a concern for form and unity which is rare at any time, and which, in the fourteenth century in England, entitles him to the highest praise'. Lewis also defends Gower's 'plain style' in poetry, and praises his ability to sustain narrative movement ('What he sees is movement, not groups and scenes, but actions and events').[1] The entire poem is the confession of a lover, Amans, to Genius, a priest of Venus, who helps Amans examine his conscience by telling him

[1] *The Allegory of Love: A Study in Medieval Tradition*, 1936, pp. 222, 198–9, 206. Lewis further comments that 'Ships and the sea, indeed, are always good in Gower' (p. 207), a comment apposite in view of the poem's relationship to *Per*.

stories of behaviour and fortune in love (see illustration 2, p. 4). The theme of Book VIII
(3,172 lines) is 'unlawful love' and its chief narrative illustration is the story of
'Apollinus the Prince of Tyr' (taking up 1,785 lines), used to warn Amans against the
evils of incestuous lust as exemplified in Antiochus and his daughter. This narrator
and his obvious enjoyment of storytelling surely suggested to Shakespeare the Chorus,
Gower, whose resurrected spirit presents the dramatisation of the story throughout
the course of the play. Like Genius in the *Confessio*, Gower is Shakespeare's ancient
storyteller, shaping and giving life to the dramatic experience for the audience by
engaging the help of their imagination. The whole concept of narration, of telling a
story with a beginning, a middle, and an end, proceeding in intricate stages and
leisurely description, was utilised by Shakespeare as the structural basis for *Pericles*
(see pp. 27–36).

From Gower Shakespeare derived most of the names of characters and places.[1]
Likewise certain passages are freely paraphrased from the source, like the riddle in
1.1.65–72, the letter found in Thaisa's coffin at 3.2.67–74, the first part of Marina's
epitaph at 4.4.34–7, and several lines from each of the five choruses.[2] Shakespeare also
took from the *Confessio* the basic outline of the story and the order of events in the plot
while adapting and omitting from it to suit the requirements of a play. A glance at the
play's differences from Gower helps to shed light on Shakespeare's working method
with his sources during composition.

In Gower, Antiochus' daughter and her situation are initially described in a sympa-
thetic light, and the story of Antiochus' incest before Apollonius' arrival is given more
treatment than it receives in the play. There is nothing in Gower which resembles 1.2;
Hellicanus is introduced much later and has a brief and unimportant role. Thaliard
leaves Tyre having discovered its people are in mourning because of the disappearance
of their prince, and returns to Antioch where the king eventually abandons any notion
of killing or pursuing Apollonius; these events are reshaped and compressed into
Thaliard's meeting with the Lords of Tyre in 1.3. Gower has only one fisherman and
therefore nothing which corresponds with the lively comedy of 2.1.

There is no tournament scene in Gower, though the young men of Pentapolim play
athletic games at which Apollonius excels. At the banquet Apollonius distinguishes
himself with his harp-playing and is given the post of music teacher to the princess
(unnamed in the source); in the play Pericles' skill in music is referred to by Simonides
in 2.5.[3] Where Shakespeare has three Knights sue in person for Thaisa's hand in 2.5,
Gower has a lengthy description of the process in which three suitors write their bills
of intention and are subsequently dismissed with the daughter's written refusal of
them in favour of Apollonius. There is no equivalent in the play to the Queen of
Pentapolim, who in Gower is instrumental in consenting to the marriage between her
daughter and the Prince of Tyre, and the description of the marriage feast itself is

[1] See Notes to the List of Characters for details of the characters' names and place-names as they appear in
the play and the sources.
[2] See Commentary for paraphrases and word-borrowings.
[3] See Textual Analysis, p. 209.

much condensed in the play. In Gower it is Apollonius who has a coffin made for his wife and Cerimon himself who finds it on the seashore.

Much of the material of Act 4 appears in Gower in outline form; Theophilus (Leonine) is reluctant to kill the young Thaise (Marina in the play), and nothing suggests the antagonistic argument between Cleon and Dioniza in 4.3. The brothel scenes are extended in the play with much colour and additional characters: in Gower there is no female bawd, only the master of the brothel (Leonin) and his servant (who corresponds to Boult); Athenagoras (Lysimachus in the play) never appears in the brothel and is introduced only at the point when he sees Apollonius' ship on the day of Neptune's festival when he meets Thaise for the first time; he is allowed to speak to Apollonius but is not successful in soliciting a response from the ailing king. Most significantly, the great recognition scene between father and daughter, which in Shakespeare is carefully constructed and builds to the climax of the play, in Gower occupies only a few lines. The play omits the marriage and accompanying feast in Miteline between Athenagoras and Thaise.

Where Shakespeare ends the play with the reunion of the family in Ephesus, and has Pericles tie up loose ends by announcing his plans concerning future events (5.3.75–8), Gower has everyone travel back to Tyre where Athenagoras and Thaise are made king and queen; he then has Apollonius and his wife set off for Tharse (Tarsus) to seek revenge on Stranguilio (Cleon) and his wife. Yet another journey brings Apollonius and his wife to Pentapolim where they rule for the rest of their days. In general the most dramatically effective scenes in the play are either not in Gower or are only present in rudimentary form: the comic turn of the Fishermen, the ritualistic and chivalric presentation of the Knights' tournament, the unique perspective of the low-life in the brothel scenes, the drawn-out intensity of the recognition scene between Pericles and Marina.

Gower's intentions are strictly moral; he expounds them in his conclusion to his story about 'What is to love in good manere, / And what to love in other wise'.[1] Shakespeare's play encompasses not only that but much more. Gower's hero goes on many journeys and experiences various adventures along the way, but the journeys are simply a travelogue, a process of going from one place to the next. In Shakespeare the journeys are elevated metaphorically to a towering significance: the journey of the hero through the archetypal rhythms of birth, life, death, and rebirth, in a sea which is not merely a body of water under his ship but the fecundating emblem of these rhythms.

TWINE

Laurence Twine's novel *The Patterne of Painefull Adventures* was entered on the Stationers' Register in 1576 and is extant in two editions, one undated but published about 1594, and reprinted in 1607 (mistakenly ascribed to Thomas Twine, Laurence's

---

[1] In both Gower and Twine the intentions of the authors are simply expressed and reiterated throughout their stories: Gower is interested in the eventual rewards bestowed on the good, and the punishment meted out to the bad; Twine is chiefly concerned with the vagaries of fortune.

brother), but it is not possible to determine which edition Shakespeare used.[1] The novel contains in its twenty-four chapters, as the title page tells us,

the most excellent, pleasant and variable Historie of the strange accidents that befell unto Prince Apollonius, the Lady Lucina his wife, and Tharsia his daughter. Wherein the uncertaintie of this world, and the fickle state of mans life are lively described.

Though in general the dramatist depended more on Gower than on Twine, Twine's influence is particularly evident in the fourth act of the play, especially as it concerns Athanagoras (Lysimachus), who has a much more prominent role in Twine than in Gower. Theophilus (Leonine in the play) lurks nearby as Tharsia (Marina) is abducted by the pirates, and then goes to tell Dionisiades (Dioniza) that the girl is dead (4.1). Twine does not confine the scenes in Machilenta (Miteline) to the brothel as Shakespeare does, but includes the street scenes where Tharsia is sold in the market, and is paraded through the public to attract custom: in the play this material is made the subject of discussion among the bawds within the brothel itself (4.2). In Tarsus, Stranguilio (Cleon) deplores his wife's evil deed in an extended diatribe (4.3).

Athanagoras, who comes to the brothel disguised (4.5), intends to be Tharsia's first client but is moved with compassion (more so because he has a daughter himself, an awkward fact the play understandably omits) when she tells him her history and reveals her identity: in the play Lysimachus is unaware of Marina's presence in the brothel, is a bachelor, and does not hear Marina's true story until he is made aware of it in Act 5. Another converted client receives the same 'divinity preached there'; he and Athanagoras enjoy the discomfiture of the 'many which went in and gave their mony, and came foorth againe weeping' which corresponds somewhat to the conversation of the converted gentlemen at the beginning of 4.5, and Boult's declaration that 'we'll have no more gentlemen driven away' (4.5.118–19). Since Athanagoras has heard Tharsia's story in detail, he is more instrumental in bringing Apollonius and Tharsia together than he is in the play. In dramatically appropriate fashion, Shakespeare reserves the discovery of the father–daughter relationship for the recognition scene. Like Gower, Twine goes on beyond the point where the play ends to record Apollonius' completed history: yet more travelling, seeking acts of revenge, rewarding past kindnesses, issuing pardons, sorting out kingdoms and who will rule them, having another child; all this sees Apollonius into his eighty-fourth year.

It is clear that Shakespeare decided to end *his* story on the note of concord which is established by reunited familial bonds, a recurrent theme in the late plays. Perhaps more than anything else, Twine suggested to Shakespeare the broader scope for the brothel scenes which in Twine make up a lively and sometimes humorous section of

---

[1] As Hoeniger has remarked in his Arden edition, 'the edition of 1607 may have been the immediate cause for the play, or the play may have been the immediate cause for it. As Twine's novel is an indirect translation of the story in the *Gesta Romanorum*, some passages in the play that appear to be derived from Twine may in fact come from a different source', p. xvi. Whatever the chronology it seems that the subject of Pericles was unusually topical in 1607–8, especially since the play occasioned the subsequent publication of George Wilkins's novel, *The Painfull Aduentures of Pericles Prince of Tyre* in 1608 (see 'Authorship', pp. 9–14).

the larger story. Tharsia's role, which is more prominent in Twine than in Gower, is amplified in the play in terms of the daughter's significance to the father: the familial bond rather than the characters' relationship itself receives the dramatic focus.

Previous editors have allowed their low estimate of the play to obscure the true novelty of the dramatist's use of his source material. Hoeniger believed that

the playwright of *Pericles* followed, on the whole, the outlines of his story – a very undramatic story at that! – more closely than was Shakespeare's usual custom in romantic comedy or tragicomedy.[1]

J. C. Maxwell in his New Shakespeare edition maintained that

the plotter follows a complicated episodic narrative in a fashion unparalleled in Shakespeare, and makes very little attempt to adapt it to the requirements of drama, though the introduction of Gower reflects a certain sense of the difficulties involved. It might be said that it is only by means of a deliberately naïve transcription that this fantastic and often irrational narrative could be put on the stage at all . . . If it was Shakespeare who first dramatized the story, all we can say is that he used a method he never used before or after.[2]

Rather than seeing Gower's and Twine's works as sprawling narratives incompatible with the stage and the requirements of drama, it is preferable to credit Shakespeare with a new insight into the handling of his sources for dramatic purposes. Although of course he took from Gower and Twine the elements of the story, perhaps their most instrumental influence on him was the potential he found there for presenting narrative as a dramatic form. This is different from a play telling a story; all plays tell a story in one way or another. What Shakespeare dramatises in *Pericles* is *the storytelling process itself*. Maxwell is right to say it is a method he never used before or after; he is wrong to imply it is dramatically naïve and theatrically unsuccessful.

Authorship

The first quarto of *Pericles* is in no doubt about the authorship of the play: it roundly declares that the work 'hath been diuers and sundry times acted by his Maiesties Seruants, at the Globe on the Banck-side. By William Shakespeare'. Unfortunately, other printed plays of the period grandly but fraudulently make the same claims.[3] No word of protest arose at the time at the attribution, but the play was not included in the first collected edition of Shakespeare's plays, the First Folio of 1623. Though it was included in the Third and Fourth Folios (1663–4 and 1685), and in Rowe's pioneering editions (1709 and following), most of the important editions of the eighteenth century omit it. Doubts as to the actual relationship between Shakespeare and the play seem to have arisen somewhat more than a hundred years after it was first performed and

---

[1] Hoeniger, p. xvi.
[2] NS, pp. xiii–xiv.
[3] Both *The London Prodigall* (1605, STC 22333) and *A Yorkshire Tragedy* (1608, STC 22340) are likewise claimed on their title pages to be by Shakespeare and to have been performed by the King's Men. Scholars have overwhelmingly rejected the attributions to Shakespeare. Neither publication seems to have aroused any objection at the time; perhaps the King's Men could afford to take a lofty attitude to such matters, or perhaps they thought any publicity good.

printed. George Lillo's adaptation of *Pericles* as *Marina* (1738) includes a Prologue
that calls the play 'unequal', complains of its 'rude wild scenes', but holds that
Shakespeare's 'bright inimitable lines' are to be found therein. (It should be remembered that almost all the adapters of Shakespeare from the Restoration on have
defended their vandalism with similar excuses.) The opinion that Shakespeare was the
reviser or re-toucher of someone else's play, then, is very much a child of eighteenth-
century critical Bardolatry. Curiously, rather than being challenged by subsequent
critical scholarship, it has survived and hardened into dogma.[1]

The play's absence from the First Folio has often been taken as an indication of
doubts about its authenticity on the part of Heminge and Condell (the members of the
King's Men responsible for its compilation); but they included in that collection plays
which Shakespeare wrote in collaboration with other dramatists (such as *Henry VIII*
and to a lesser extent *Macbeth*) and excluded others that Shakespeare wrote either on
his own (*Love's Labour's Won*) or in collaboration (*Cardenio* and *The Two Noble
Kinsmen*). The notion, then, that Heminge and Condell might have stayed their hands
on *Pericles* because they knew it to be collaborative is hard to sustain.

The reason collaboration has been suspected is the widespread perception that there
is a change in the style of the play after Act 2. The characteristic style of the first two
acts is a leisurely and formal use of verse, often rhyming couplets, interrupted by the
lively prose scene of the Fishermen (2.1). At the beginning of Act 3, a much more
intensely poetic language begins to inform the play, especially 3.1 and most of 5.1 and
5.3; besides, the scenes in the brothel (4.2 and 4.5) are written in very agile and
confident prose. When disintegration was fashionable, it seemed to many a reasonable
inference that Shakespeare wrote the second half of the play (adding 'touches' to
the first half) and that the celebrated author, Another Hand, composed at least Acts 1
and 2.

It would be pointless to rehearse the various theories that have been advanced and
names that have been put forward concerning this putative collaboration (so far as we
know, no one has dared to suggest Jonson).[2] H. Dugdale Sykes first made out a
plausible case for George Wilkins, in 1919.[3] In our time Wilkins has become the
preferred collaborator, beating off all other comers; and though we have the gravest
doubts that Wilkins had anything to do with *Pericles*, in view of his popularity in the
co-author stakes it seems only fair to summarise what is known of him, and the
arguments put forward in his favour.

---

[1] Barbara Everett, in the programme note for the National 1994 production, trots out all the clichés: 'the
Quarto *Pericles* is formidably badly written . . . its language moves from the untalented to the nonsensical.
And yet there are even in the problematical first two acts touches which may be called Shakespearian
. . . substantial masses in the last three acts are not only Shakespearian but wonderful . . . Shakespeare
picked up, or was presented with, an old play of little merit . . . [or] Shakespeare worked with an actual
if clearly dim collaborator from the beginning', etc., etc. 'Touches' has a nicely antique ring; though
she concedes that 'the collaborative case has always had grave flaws' on the grounds that 'no Elizabethan
playwright who we know writes badly enough for *Pericles*'. For our view of the play's language, see
pp. 36–51.
[2] See Hoeniger pp. lii–lxiii for a full, though misguided, survey.
[3] See his *Sidelights on Shakespeare*, pp. 143–204.

Happily, a good deal of light, much of it unflattering, has been shed on Wilkins by the researches of Roger Prior, to which the following account is indebted.[1] Wilkins (born *c.* 1576) was a minor writer who collaborated with William Rowley and John Day in *The Travailes of the Three English Brothers* (1607), wrote a play of his own called *The Miseries of Inforst Mariage* (STC 25635) and a pamphlet, *Three Miseries of Barbary* (both 1607) among other minor things. The *Three English Brothers* was performed by Queen Anne's Men; his *Miseries of Inforst Mariage*, rather surprisingly, by the King's.[2] He also published a novella called *The Painfull Aduentures of Pericles Prince of Tyre*, based on the play, which was printed in 1608 (see Textual Analysis, pp. 197–210 for details).

This book makes no claim to be the work of the author of the play. Its title page declares that it is 'the true History of the Play of *Pericles*, as it was lately presented by the worthy and ancient Poet *John Gower*', a claim reiterated at the end of the Argument on A3ʳ: 'Onely intreating the Reader to receive this Historie in the same maner as it was under the habite of auncient *Gower* the famous English Poet, by the Kings Maiesties Players excellently presented'.[3] It is evident that the novella is indeed a recollection of the performed play, with additional material taken verbatim from Twine's novel of nearly identical title (*The Patterne of Painefull Adventures* – see 'Sources', pp. 6–8.).

By profession, Wilkins was a victualler (i.e. an innkeeper) who lived in Cow Cross, hard by the present Farringdon station, and who made a regular series of appearances before the Middlesex Sessions between 1610 and 1618. He may have been the 'George Wilkens, Poett' recorded as the father of a son whose birth is included in the register of St Giles Cripplegate, 11 February 1605.

Wilkins also made a deposition in the Belott–Mountjoy suit of 1612, in which Shakespeare was a witness.[4] In 1604 Shakespeare 'laye in the house' of, i.e. lodged with, Christopher Mountjoy on the corner of Muggle and Silver Streets in Cripplegate, close to St Giles. According to Wilkins's deposition in the suit, Belott and his wife lived in one of the 'Chambers' in Wilkins's inn after their marriage. There is nothing whatever in the depositions made at the trial to suggest that Shakespeare was acquainted with Wilkins. Nor is there anything that makes it impossible, for Shakespeare deposed he had known the families for about ten years, Wilkins had known them for seven.

The fact that seems pretty well to clinch the connection between Wilkins the victualler and Wilkins the author arises from one of the nastiest cases for which Wilkins was arraigned: that of March 1611, when he was accused of 'abusinge one Randall Borkes and kikkinge a woman on the Belly which was then greate with childe'

---

[1] See 'The life of George Wilkins', *S. Sur.* 25 (1972), 137–52.

[2] Equally surprisingly, this bad play went through three subsequent editions: it was probably therefore also popular on stage.

[3] The sole evidence to connect Wilkins with the book consists of a dedicatory leaf present in one of the two surviving copies, the Zürich (not in the British Library's) with Wilkins's name attached. There seems no reason to challenge the identification, though the coyness of both title page and Argument are worthy of note.

[4] See E. K. Chambers, *William Shakespeare*, 90–5.

(Prior, p. 144). Two men stood guarantor for this charming offender, one of whom was Henry Gosson of St Lawrence Poultney, gentleman, the same Henry Gosson who had published the first edition of the play *Pericles*, and who published Wilkins's booklet, *Three Miseries of Barbary*.

It is very difficult to resist the obvious conclusion that Wilkins had, in the first decade of the century, attempted to make a career as a writer, during which time he had become acquainted with Gosson. After his hopes in this direction had been dashed, his career took a much uglier turn, but apparently Gosson was still prepared to bail him. There is no evidence for thinking that the fact that both Wilkins and Shakespeare knew the Belott–Mountjoy families is anything more than a coincidence.[1] Wilkins was reported as dead in a Sessions record of 2 October 1618.

The Oxford Shakespeare has made the strongest claims possible that the author of the first nine scenes of *Pericles* was George Wilkins.[2] Insofar as this attribution is based on statistical evidence, it is fresh, interesting, and open to challenge by better evidence. Insofar as it still rests on subjective impression, it adds nothing to the case.

At this point it is necessary to say outright that we do not regard the stylistic differences in the play (which have often been exaggerated) as in any way conclusive evidence of collaboration.[3] The dramatic function of the verse and prose of a play must be considered very carefully in its dramaturgical context, rather than in stylistic literary isolation (see 'The Play', pp. 36–51). There are other plays by Shakespeare which use different styles for different dramatic purposes.

Consider *Measure for Measure*, which begins as a grittily realistic play of personal moral dilemmas that would have pleased Stanislavsky, only to modulate into a folk-tale conclusion, with appropriate change in the style of writing. The different languages used in the histories, notably in *King John* and *Henry V*, bear contemplation in this regard, as do the multiple languages of some of the comedies, most particularly *A Midsummer Night's Dream* and *Love's Labour's Lost*. Closer to *Pericles* in date, *The Winter's Tale* also has a radical stylistic change in Act 4; indeed, any play which contains complex stylistics invites disintegration to those so minded. To the retort that nothing in any of these plays is so poorly written as is much of the first scenes of *Pericles*, the only reply is that literary taste, especially as regards theatrical verse, is an uncertain arbiter, and that the early scenes of *Pericles* have been proved both to harmonise with the later scenes and to work well on stage, the only real court of appeal. Nor is the division of the play into two halves anything like as absolute as some have maintained. 3.2 contains some language as awkward and flat as anything in the earlier scenes, and 4.3 some language as grammatically contorted as that in the most tortuous of the previous scenes (2.4).

---

[1] Prior's biographical researches deserve the utmost respect, but his attempts to link the older George Wilkins's lifestyle with the material in his works are purely fanciful (pp. 149–51). See p. 10, n. 1.
[2] See *Companion*, especially pp. 80–8, 130–1, 556–60; and see also MacD. P. Jackson, 'Rhyming in *Pericles*: more evidence of dual authorship', *Studies in Bibliography*, 1993, 239–49, especially his note 7, p. 240, which gives a helpful list of recent publications. Jackson's Oxford edition of the play is forthcoming.
[3] There has always been a sort of minority party that has rejected the collaborative theory out of hand. See, for example, Karen Csengeri, 'William Shakespeare, sole author of *Pericles*', *English Studies*, 1990, 230–43.

Turning from subjective opinion to that which has been promoted as a more 'scientific' test of authorship, one finds that there has been much excitement over, and interest in, the possible information that may be derived from computerised statistical analysis of 'stylometry' and 'function words'.[1] The Oxford Shakespeare, reviewing the evidence, comments that in its lineation, metrics, and element of verbal repetition, *Pericles* is 'significantly abnormal' by relation to any Shakespearean norm. This assertion is supported in part by the statistical tables in the section on 'The canon and chronology of Shakespeare's plays', especially *Companion*, pp. 80–108. Oxford also presents a limited but interesting statistical test of 'function words', which confirms that the disputed scenes of *Pericles* are anomalous: they employ two linguistic usages that differ significantly from the Shakespearean norm. This is indeed a useful, but not (in our judgement) necessarily an incontestable, indicator of divided authorship, since it is by no means proven that an author cannot deliberately write in a different style that might produce such abnormal results. Much more refinement needs to be brought to statistical analysis of elements of usage and style before it can claim certainty; doubtless this will happen as computers get faster and more sophisticated, and programmers learn from their early fumbles.[2]

Naturally, much of the statistical evidence presented in the Oxford Shakespeare is applied gleefully by the editors in support of their revival of the practice of disintegration.[3] They declare

The function-word test distinguishes with remarkable clarity between the two shares of both *Timon of Athens* and *Pericles*. In both plays, the share assigned to Shakespeare by other tests does not contain a single figure in excess of two [standard statistical] variations . . . the first nine scenes of *Pericles* contain one figure in excess of three (3.76) [the word is 'to'] and another of two ['by'].[4]

'By', however, is 'anomalous' also in *Macbeth* and in the 'Shakespearean' portions of *Two Noble Kinsmen* and *Henry VIII*; in the latter, 'to' runs to 2.54 standard statistical deviations. Mathematicians will know whether to be overwhelmed by this evidence; we find it both interesting and inconclusive.[5]

[1] For stylometry, see for instance Andrew Morton, *Literary Detection*, 1978. Function words (articles, adverbs, conjunctions, prepositions etc.) occur with sufficient frequency and are not so subject to the vagaries of compositional spelling and punctuation that they are entirely unreliable as evidence. They were first used by F. Mosteller and D. Wallace to distinguish Alexander Hamilton from James Madison (see *Inference and Disputed Authorship: The Federalist*, 1964), and have come to be the statistical tool of preference in current enquiry. However, it is worth remembering how certain compositor-determination by statistical analysis was thought to be in the 1960s, and as how much more doubtful it is now regarded.

[2] There are many good true stories of the inadequacy of much early computer-based analysis. In his *Arcadia* Tom Stoppard invents an entertaining one: 'by comparing sentence structures and so forth, this chap showed that there was a ninety per cent chance that the story had indeed been written by the same person as *Women in Love*. To my inexpressible joy, one of your maths mob was able to show that on the same statistical basis there was a ninety per cent chance that Lawrence also wrote the *Just William* books and much of the previous evening's *Brighton and Hove Argus*' (*Arcadia*, 1993, p. 19).

[3] They claim to have established, through statistical analysis of function words, that *Tim.*, *Tit.*, *Mac.*, and *1H6* join *Per.*, *H8* (or *All is True*, as Oxford will have it), and *TNK* as Shakespeare's collaborative plays.

[4] Two other words also approach the magical 2 standard statistical deviations: 'no' and 'with' (both 1.99).

[5] It may, indeed, turn out to be a tool more adapted to literary studies than to determination of authorship. Could the prevalence of the word 'no' in the first scenes of *Per.* be an element in the creation of the dismal, negative dramatic atmosphere that pervades these scenes?

Perhaps the most persuasive case so far made for Wilkins is MacD. P. Jackson's study of rhymes.[1] He shows that, of the 145 rhymes in *Pericles* Acts 1 and 2, 58 are shared with Wilkins's *Miseries of Inforst Marriage*, and that this percentage (40 per cent) is immensely greater both than that for the second half of the play (13 shared of 128 rhymes, 10.2 per cent) and for any other Shakespearean work (the nearest in frequency of rhymes shared with Wilkins is *Measure for Measure*, 11 of 46 rhymes, or 23.9 per cent, followed by *Romeo and Juliet*, 55 of 254, 21.7 per cent). Even if the whole of *Pericles* is taken, the numbers (71 shared rhymes of 273) give 26 per cent, higher than any other Shakespearean work. Jackson's conclusions are fairly and moderately stated:

> The results are very difficult to explain without resort to a theory of dual authorship ... Nor does the theory that the style of *Pericles* 1–2 results from Shakespeare's conscious attempts at archaism provide a satisfactory explanation of the data. If attempts at archaism were responsible for the prevalence of rhyme links with *Miseries*, the links should be predominantly with the Gower choruses, which deliberately imitate Gower's medieval rhymes. But of the 58 rhyme links with *Miseries* in *Pericles* 1–2, 46 occur within the dialogue ... and only 23 within the Gower choruses.   (p. 246)

Persuasive indeed, but it seems to us that the anomaly, involving as it does a relatively small number of items (in statistical terms), is not beyond the bounds of coincidence. It should be remembered that in law, the difference between counsel's plausible case and the judge's conviction is the jury's 'reasonable doubt'.[2]

In summary, we think the evidence so far collected, though undeniably persuasive, falls short of carrying complete conviction of either proposition: that the composition of *Pericles* was shared, or that the secret sharer was George Wilkins. No one has been able to put forward a convincing reason why Shakespeare should have attempted a collaboration with so junior and inexperienced a partner as Wilkins, *especially* if Wilkins was such a bad author as his champions maintain. Neither has any convincing explanation been given for the alternative hypothesis, that Shakespeare revised a complete script by Wilkins, but revised it so unenthusiastically that the first half of the play should remain so bad as the disintegrators insist it to be. Nor do those pressing the theory of collaboration give fair weight to the overall coherence of design in the play.[3] It would also appear anomalous that there are so few verbal links between *Pericles* and *The Miseries of Inforst Marriage*, even allowing for the different subject-matter and style of the two plays.[4]

---

[1] See p. 11, n. 2.
[2] A recent contributor to the debate is Jonathan Hope, in his *The Authorship of Shakespeare's Plays: A Socio-linguistic Study* (1994). His examination of the use of auxiliary 'do' and what he calls 'relative markers' does little to strengthen the Wilkinsites' case (pp. 106–13).
[3] See 'The Play', pp. 27–78. Jackson, with scrupulous fairness, concedes 'Whatever the extent and nature of Wilkins's participation in the play, its overall design, though unusual, seems Shakespearian' ('Rhyming in *Pericles*', p. 248 n.).
[4] *Miseries* is Wilkins's sole unaided drama. His share in the *Three English Brothers* has never been established by any reliable method: see Robin Jeffs's reprint of A. H. Bullen's edition of Day (London 1963), p. xix. There are a few lines in *Miseries* which make one think of *Pericles*: 'The murther of a creature, equald heauen / In her Creation (D2ᵛ; cf. 4.3.6–9); 'Thus I am left like Sea-tost-Marriners, / My Fortunes being no more then my distresse, / Vpon what shore soeuer I am driuen' (D3ʳ; cf. various phrases in 2.1, 2.3); and, the closest: 'And all are pleas'd / *All*. We are / *Scar*. Then if all these bee so, / I am new wed so ends

Whatever the rights and wrongs of the authorship debate, the argument has had the unfortunate consequence of linking the merits of the play with its authorship. In other words, the implication is that if *Pericles* were proved to be collaborative, somehow this would make it a worse play than if it were proved to be Shakespeare's unaided work. This, of course, is absurd. It has, however, an unfortunate corollary that *is* true: if someone were to prove *Pericles* to be the unaided work of Wilkins, or any other insignificant 'dramataster', it would be neither so frequently performed nor so frequently published as it is at present, protected by the Shakespearean aura. Though it is many years since Barthes proclaimed the death of the author, authorial celebrity is still a significant factor in the evaluation of artistic merit and theatrical viability.

This preposterous heresy is only too evident in the grotesque and immoral world of art-dealing, where a painting's 'value' may depreciate from £50 million to 50p should 'experts' 'prove' it to be a 'fake'. It has had relatively little to do with theatre, *except* for the case of Shakespeare in Anglo-Saxon countries, where the Bard's name has been used as a drawing-card since the eighteenth century. What would a theatrical company do should it be proved that the first nine scenes of *Pericles* (or *Hamlet*, or whatever) be by Wilkins, or John Smith? Omit them? No company, one hopes, would be so insane.[1] Banish the play from the repertory when experience has shown that it plays nobly? No company, let us hope, would be so blind to its own interests. The 'authorship' of (say) *Gone With the Wind* has no bearing on the continued success of that movie: the public, rightly, enjoys the film for itself.

It may seem a belabouring of the obvious to say that a play, any play, is *ipso facto* a work of collaboration. Actors, and other theatrical professionals, must collaborate with the author to get the play staged; and then the collaboration of the audience in attending a performance is pretty essential too. Many dramatists (such as Tom Stoppard) rejoice in this kind of collaboration; others (like Harold Pinter) resist it, but only up to a point. As everyone knows, the play performed will not be identical with any script written by the author. Scripts get adapted and modified in the process of production, a fact which not even the most controlling author (e.g. Richard Wagner) was ever able to overcome. The text of a printed play is a summary version of *one stage* in this process; nothing more. Yet it is a version of the whole: it must be taken as a unity, since that is how it will be presented upon the stage.

From this point of view it matters very little to an acting company who wrote the words they are learning to deliver: what matters is making theatrical sense of them. It should be an editor's task to make as good sense as possible out of the words in our

---

old marryage woe, / And in your eies so louingly being wed, / We hope your hands will bring vs to our bed (K4ᵛ, cf. 2.5.88–91, using the same rhyme). More than one explanation is possible for these parallels, one being that Shakespeare, an active sharer in the King's Men in 1606/7, surely saw *Miseries* either in rehearsal or performance, and his retentive memory gleaned a few ears from Wilkins's chaff.

[1] Reality, intruding, dashes such hopes: in 1947 the RSC omitted the first act of *Per.*, grandly informing the public, 'In this presentation, the producer has omitted the first act, being in agreement with the general academic view that it is irrelevant and not the work of William Shakespeare.' Apart from meanly blaming academic opinion for this decision, the statement provokes chicken-and-egg questions: would the act suddenly become relevant if it were by Shakespeare?

script for the reader. Who wrote them is an interesting *but fundamentally irrelevant* aspect of the process of reading and comprehension. For all these reasons, we have regarded the entire 'authorship debate' concerning *Pericles* as something that wrong-fully and almost frivolously turns the reader's attention away from the text to non-textual side issues. We as editors don't really care who wrote *Pericles* (though we do believe it to be the product of a single creative imagination): we really care that it is, in the Oxford editors' words, 'a masterpiece'.[1]

Performance and reception

SEVENTEENTH CENTURY

From the beginning *Pericles* has been a play that has divided opinion. It is evident that it was a popular play on stage, and this success surely was at least in part owing to the opportunities it (like the other romances) offered for theatrical spectacle and musical embellishment. The implications for staging found in the quarto text are quite elabo-rate, though often ambiguous. Many of them are discussed in the Commentary, but this is a good place to remark on their scope.

The opening scene, with the grim display of severed heads, is one. Act 2 presents many challenges for staging, such as the location of King Simonides and Thaisa during the parade of the Knights and presentation of the impresas (2.2), and how exactly the stage was disposed for that scene. The royal party 'withdraws' at the end of the scene while the tilting takes place *offstage* and the main stage is set for the banquet in 2.3, an elaborate scene requiring torches and pages, and later music and dancing, all of which entail use of the maximum resources of the company. Unless 2.4 takes place on the upper stage (for which there is no evidence), there must also be a busy clearing of the banquet before the scene can take place.

Storms in the Elizabethan theatre were often accompanied by 'effects', of which the cannon-ball for thunder, fireworks for lightning, and some way of simulating wind sound were the commonest. In as tempestuous a play as *Pericles*, such effects were almost certainly used in 3.0–3.1, and probably also in 2.0–2.1. The staging of 3.1, however, demands the abandonment of all naturalistic criteria (which few editors seem capable of), so that the main stage becomes the deck of the ship, and the stage doors may be taken to lead below deck. Any attempt to use the stage otherwise would place the actors in a huddle upstage in what is plainly the 'biggest' scene in the play.

More elaborate staging occurs in 3.2, the sudden safe haven of Cerimon's house after the howling of the storm just ended, where in Thaisa's revival many properties are called for by Cerimon (and presumably supplied) and use is made of music. The disposition of the coffin on the stage is a bit of a puzzle, for its contents would be invisible to those in the yard unless it were raised and tilted, which seems unlikely.

There are more lively scenes in Act 4 such as the melodramatic frustration of Leonine's attempt to murder Marina by the Pirates' apparently instantaneous appear-ance and disappearance, and the sudden transition into the Miteline brothel; sand-

[1] *Companion*, p. 559.

wiched between the two brothel scenes is the scene at Tarsus, and the visual display of Marina's tomb there, Pericles' mimed passion, and donning of sackcloth. The scenic requirements of Act 5 are complex, but probably best resolved by staging it like 3.1, with the main stage the deck of the ship, and the doors leading either to the ship's rail, or below decks, or both; this is the only scene in the play which seems to mandate use of a discovery space, though it would come in handy elsewhere (e.g. 4.4). The music of the spheres (played, no doubt, from the musicians' gallery) and the theophany of Diana comprise the single most spectacular scenic element in the play, though there is ample opportunity to make Diana's temple in the final scene a splendid tableau.

Companies in recent years who have staged the play in large, well-equipped theatres (RSC 1958, Stratford 1973 and 1986, National 1994) have seized upon all these opportunities, and invented many more (no director, apparently, can resist staging the Knights' joust between 2.2 and 2.3, even though the quarto is very careful to leave it out). We may confidently assume that the sharers at the Globe[1] seized with equal enthusiasm upon the play's scenographic potential, though as usual there are no useful eye-witness accounts.[2]

Early references to *Pericles* are mainly complimentary. The very rare pamphlet *Pimlyco. Or, Runne Red-Cap. Tis a mad world at Hogsdon* (1609, STC 19936) is influenced by the play, since it involves a tribute to Skelton, and refers to 'learned *Gower*' on B2[r]; the reference to *Pericles* occurs on C1[r]:

> Amazde I stood to see a Crowd
> Of *Ciuill Throats* stretchd out so lowd:
> (As at a *New-play*) all the *Roomes*
> Did swarme with *Gentiles* mixt with *Groomes*.
> So that I truly thought, all *These*
> Came to see *Shore*, or *Pericles*.[3]

The Prologue to *The Hogge Hath Lost His Pearl* optimistically concludes:

> *And if it proue so happy as to please,*
> *Weele say tis fortunat like* Pericles.[4]

The views of the contrary party emerged presently. Ben Jonson, much disgruntled at the failure of his play *The New Inn*, attacked contemporary popular theatrical taste in the poem, 'The just indignation of the author . . .' (sometimes known as 'Ode to Himself', written in 1629 and appended to the printed text of his play). He singled *Pericles* out for particular condemnation:

---

[1] There is a commonly held view that the scenographic characteristics of the last plays imply that they were originally written for the Blackfriars. But *Per.*, which shares these characteristics, is too early for the Blackfriars; as the title page of the quarto makes clear, it was a Globe play. This casts doubt on the whole theory.

[2] Hoeniger, p. lxvi, quotes a letter from Sir Gerald Herbert, with its account of a court performance of *Per.* on 20 May 1619, but Herbert was much more interested in the fancy banquet than the play; the only useful information is that the long interval was taken after Act 2.

[3] '*Shore*' is perhaps the lost play by Chettle and Day performed by Worcester's Men in 1603, about Jane Shore, King Edward IV's celebrated mistress.

[4] A3[v] (STC 23658). The play was seen by Sir Henry Wotton on 21 February 1613.

> No doubt some mouldy tale,
>   Like *Pericles*; and stale
> As the Shrieves crusts, and nasty as his fish-
>   scraps, out of every dish,
> Thrown forth, and rak't into the common tub   (lines 21–5)[1]

This poem was by no means Jonson's only diatribe against the kind of play he took *Pericles* to be, and the kind of play which was attracting audiences in droves, while they slighted what he regarded as his own more serious work. The best-known such attack is found in the Prologue to *Every Man in his Humour* (not printed in the first edition of 1601; included with the Folio of 1616):

> He rather prays, you will be pleased to see
> One such today as other plays should be;
> Where neither *Chorus* wafts you ore the seas;
> Nor creaking throne comes downe, the boyes to please;
> Nor nimble squibbe is seene, to make afear'd
> The gentlewomen; nor roul'd bullet heard
> To say, it thunders; nor tempestuous drumme
> Rumbles, to tell you when the storme doth come   (lines 13–20)

The tenor of this objection lies against abuses of the unities, and against the use of what we now call special effects. Jonson believed Shakespeare, by abusing principled dramaturgy in this way, to be belittling the dramatist's profession.[2] He returned to the fray in the Induction to *Bartholomew Fair*, where the 'author' declares 'Hee is loth to make Nature afraid in his *Playes*, like those that beget *Tales, Tempests,* and such like *Drolleries*' (lines 128–30). Jonson's attitude towards dramaturgy has served as a stick to beat *Pericles* with ever since.[3]

How long *Pericles* stayed in the King's Men's repertory is anyone's guess, but the continuing production of quarto editions suggests it remained popular. Two references suggest that its reputation as a successful play remained high even after the closure of the theatres. The first occurs in Samuel Sheppard's *The times Displayed* (1646); it is in the sixth sestiad which, unlike the others (which are religious debates), is a lament by Apollo on the degenerate state of poetry:

> See him whose Tragick Sceans *EURIPIDES*
> Doth equal, and with *SOPHOCLES* we may
> Compare great *SHAKESPEAR ARISTOPHANES*
> Never like him, his Fancy could display,
> Witness [t]he Prince of *Tyre*, his Pericles,
> His sweet and his to be admired lay
> He wrote of lustful *Tarquins* rape shews he
> Did understand the depth of Poesie.[4]

---

[1] The 'common tub' consisted of the unattractive leftovers from City feasts, collected for the poor.

[2] The date of this Prologue is in dispute; Herford and Simpson believe it to have been written during or shortly after the War of the Theatres, but there is no external evidence for this, and it might well express Jonson's mature dislike of the romances.

[3] Most recently in Benedict Nightingale's review of the National 1994 production, which follows the grand tradition of theatre reviewing in berating *Pericles*' plot for its lack of realism (*The Times*, 23 May 1994).

[4] Stanza 9, p. 22 (C3ᵛ).

To be sure, this is a literary, not a theatrical, appreciation: though Sheppard began his literary life as Jonson's amanuensis in 1606, this is clearly an old man's literary retrospective (there is, for instance, no mention of the closing of the theatres).

A much more interesting, because often misrepresented, reference is found in John Tatham's prefatory poem to Brome's *A Joviall Crew* (1652):

> There is a Faction (Friend) in Town, that cries,
> Down with the *Dagon-Poet, Johnson* dies.
> His works were too elaborate, not fit
> To come within the Verge, or face of *Wit.*
> *Beaumont* and *Fletcher* (they say) perhaps, might
> Passe (well) for currant Coin, in a dark night:
> But *Shakespeare* the *Plebean* Driller, was
> Founder'd in's *Pericles*, and must not pass.
> And so, at all men flie, that have but been
> Thought worthy of Applause: therefore, their spleen.   (A4ᵛ)

The whole poem is quite clever, as such things go, attacking the malice of those that condemn 'the Beams that warm'd you, and the Stage'. If the two lines about Shakespeare are taken out of context, they appear condemnatory; in context, the implication is clear: *Pericles* was considered by Tatham a success.

But the climate was about to change. Downes says *Pericles* was acted at the Cock-pit in Drury Lane, by Rhodes's company, with Betterton in the title role, in the 1659–60 season.[1] Following this the play's long theatrical neglect began.[2] A modified version of Jonson's view prevailed: changing literary and theatrical fashion found romance plots and subjects outmoded;[3] and by the time Romanticism might have restored interest in *Pericles*, at least for its spectacular aspects, its virtue had been sullied by the doubts concerning its authorship.

NINETEENTH CENTURY

Samuel Phelps's production at Sadler's Wells in 1854, which ran for fifty-five performances, was a grand tribute to Victorian scenography. Phelps, normally a purist in his productions, cut Gower, all references to incest, and the brothel scenes; but according to the critic of the *Athenaeum*, the scenery was 'several years in preparation, and the immediate expense of the production is scarcely less than 1,000 *l*.[4] *The Times* treated the venture sardonically:

Not a single opportunity is missed for hanging on a wondrous picture or group that shall hide the paucity of the dramatic interest. When Pericles is thrown upon the sands, it is with the very best of rolling seas . . . when the storm afterwards rocks his vessel, it rocks in real earnest, and spectators of delicate stomachs may have uneasy reminiscences . . . An admirably equipped

---

[1] *Roscius Anglicanus, or an Historical Review of the Stage*, 1708, p. 18.
[2] Broken only by the three performances of Lillo's *Marina* in 1738.
[3] Not that the other romances did better: *WT* was not performed; *Cym.*, adapted by D'Urfey, was given twice. Only *Temp.*, first adapted by Davenant and Dryden, and subsequently further humiliated by Shadwell, and Webberised into a musical, was a roaring success.
[4] 21 October 1854. A thousand pounds in 1854 would have been the equivalent of perhaps £250,000 today.

3 Marina's tomb (Act 4, Scene 4), in Nugent Monck's 1947 production at the Shakespeare Memorial Theatre

Diana, with her car in the clouds, orders his course to her sacred city, to which he is conducted by a moving panorama of excellently-painted coast scenery. The interior of the temple, where the colossal figure of the many-breasted goddess stands in all its glory amid gloriously attired votaries, is the last 'bang' of the general magnificence.

However, 'the personages in general do little else than walk on and walk off the stage, without betraying or exciting an emotion'.[1] The last English production before the twentieth century was the bizarre Coleman farrago at Stratford-upon-Avon. The veteran Coleman had produced his own revised script of *Pericles*, and the hard-pressed Benson in a weak moment gave Coleman permission to produce it, and only ten days in which to do so. The results were catastrophic.[2]

TWENTIETH-CENTURY SPECTACLE

The twentieth century has seen the revival of the play's fortunes: a slow, hesitant revival which nonetheless has led to productions of *Pericles* having these days become a quite common theatrical event.[3] The Royal Shakespeare Company's 1947 production was a relic of an earlier age; director Nugent Monck omitted the first act, on the grounds that 'it is irrelevant and not the work of William Shakespeare', a curious portmanteau judgement. Barry Jackson's scenes were likewise old-fashioned (see illustration 3, p. 19). In 1958 Tony Richardson directed a more complete version, in which Gower (Edric Connor) became a calypso singer; Richard Johnson played Pericles, Geraldine McEwan, Marina, and a young Edward de Souza, Lysimachus. The design was by Loudon Sainthill (illustration 4, p. 21).

Unfortunately, all productions since then by the major companies have treated *Pericles* as a lame-duck text, and both rearranged it and Wilkinsised it in varying degrees.[4] The last main-stage production at Stratford-upon-Avon was Terry Hands's in 1969, designed by John Bradley, which featured an unchanging bare stage dominated by a hanging dodecahedron which puzzled all reviewers, and very sixties-ish costuming, or lack thereof (see illustration 5, p. 22). Emrys James played Gower as a Welsh bard, (illustration 6, p. 23), but the most unusual feature of the casting was the doubling of Thaisa and Marina by Susan Fleetwood. This peculiar idea necessitated the use of another actress for Marina in the final scene, and provoked an objection from Harold Hobson. By returning Fleetwood to Thaisa's part in the final scene, and by not attempting to age her, he wrote, the impression was given 'that Pericles is in danger of misbehaving with his own child. So the play appears to have come full circle,

[1] 16 October 1854.
[2] J. C. Trewin has a very entertaining account of it in his *Benson and the Bensonians* (1960), pp. 115–19.
[3] No attempt is being made here to record all productions of the play. Productions in translation, and many professional, as well as semi-professional and amateur productions (with one exception), are necessarily and deliberately excluded. Details of many of these can be found in *Shakespeare Around the Globe: A Guide to Notable Postwar Revivals*, ed. Samuel L. Leiter, 1986, pp. 555–67; and in vol. XXI of Gale's *Shakespearean Criticism* series (1991).
[4] In his chapter on *Pericles*, Roger Warren (*Staging Shakespeare's Late Plays*, 1990) provides an overview, often in fascinating detail, of the RSC 1969 and 1989 and Stratford 1986 productions, but his missionary view of the Oxford adaptation colours and distorts many of his statements and all of his opinions.

4   Gower as calypso singer (Edric Connor) in Tony Richardson's 1958 production at the Shakespeare Memorial Theatre

5   Pericles and Thaisa (Ian Richardson and Susan Fleetwood) begin their dance (Act 2, Scene 3) in Terry Hands's 1969 production at the Royal Shakespeare Theatre

and to finish where it began, in incest. This is clean contrary to what I understand to be Mr Hands's intention.'[1]

Jean Gascon directed *Pericles* for the Shakespeare Festival (as it was then called) of Stratford, Ontario, in 1973, in a production that one reviewer not given to unnecessary enthusiasm called 'superlative theatre, and an illumination of the play that came as a revelation . . . not conflicting with one's own response to the written text, but making one aware that, by comparison, that response was meager and imaginatively under-nourished'.[2] Nicholas Pennell was much admired as Pericles, as was Edward Atienza's voice-over Gower; whilst Leslie Hurry's storybook costumes also met with approval. In retrospect, however, it can be seen, even for its own time, to have been an old-fashioned production.

Arguably the best large-scale production of the play in recent years has been that at Stratford, Ontario in 1986. Director Richard Ouzounian clearly regarded the work with enthusiasm and, aided by an excellent cast, caught much of the play's appeal both as fairy-tale and as profound myth; all this despite the intrusion of some of the Oxford

---

[1] *Sunday Times*, 6 April 1969. No theatrical judgement, however sane, can 'scape whipping. Warren contrives to argue that incest 'is a possibility raised by the text itself, a danger narrowly averted' (p. 233). This seemingly incredible misprision arises from a doggedly post-modern misreading of 5.1.190 (see Commentary).

[2] Berners W. Jackson, 'Shakespeare at Stratford, Ontario, 1973', *SQ* 24 (1973), 408.

6   Gower (Emrys James) as a Welsh bard in Terry Hands's 1969 production at the Royal Shakespeare Theatre

adaptation's fantasies. Like Tony Richardson, he emphasised Gower's otherness geographically and culturally: Renée Rogers belted out the choruses in pop – soul fashion, nearly becoming the star of the show in the process.[1] The resources of Guthrie's famous stage were often used to excellent advantage, as for instance when Pericles was cast upon the angry shore in Pentapolis, hurtling up from the vomitorium as if cast by a gigantic wave. Geraint Wyn Davies, as Pericles, contrived a more convincing progression from naïve youth to exhausted age than any other recent exponent, and the central scenes (2.2 and 2.3) were deftly handled, thanks to the excellent acting of Goldie Semple as Thaisa, and the wonderfully old-King-Cole-style Simonides of the inimitable William Needles.[2]

MINIMALISM

The tradition of spectacular production has thus been given every opportunity. The play works equally well, however, in more restrained or economical settings: it does

[1] It is curious that no director has attempted to do the obvious, that is to show Gower as a familiar figure from the past, a celebrated storyteller whose speech and looks are of a previous age.
[2] It is most regrettable that the absurd conditions imposed by Canadian Equity and endorsed by the Stratford Archive make it impossible to include photographs of this remarkable production.

not depend upon expensive sets and prodigies from the audiovisual departments to make its effect. Ron Daniels made his début with the Royal Shakespeare Company by directing it in 1979 at The Other Place, a carefully minimalist production, which was liked by reviewers in direct proportion to their dislike of *The Merry Wives of Windsor* on the main stage; Peter McEnery was much admired as Pericles. More recently, the Swan was in 1989 the venue for another directorial début, David Thacker's. This modest production, vaguely Georgian in costuming, reverted to 1958's idea of a West Indian Gower (Rudolph Walker), without the calypso music; he carried and referred to a big book, and remained on stage throughout.[1] Nigel Terry played a measured Pericles; many reviewers took objection to Cerimon's being played by a woman (Helen Blatch), a practice which seems now to have become inevitable. This is the only RSC production to have an archival videotape; it is a scandal that the tape is so poor that only a handful of brightly lit scenes can be made out at all: a twentieth-century equivalent of a 'bad quarto'.[2]

A remarkable student production (professionally directed: Mimi Mekler) by the joint Erindale–Sheridan Theatre and Drama Studies programme of the University of Toronto at Erindale showed how the minimalist approach can be carried to a surprisingly successful extreme (1993). The tiny, wingless theatre, and the small cast (eleven) were treated as opportunities for theatrical inventiveness, rather than as limitations. Cuts were relatively few: more of the text was retained, and in the original order, than in any of the professional productions described here. The small cast of course entailed elaborate doubling; the only actor who did not double was the Pericles. The set was a bare stage with one corner curtained off, with a raised platform, to become scenes 'within'. A cloth backdrop became a wall with the heads of the unsuccessful princes in 1.1 (leaning against it from behind, the actors seemed like bas-reliefs). The director's best ideas came in the Pentapolis scenes, the fairy-tale comic centre of the play, which Mekler treated admirably as a series of children's play-acting games. So, the rusty armour in 2.1 was a mesh gown with tin can tops sewn into it, which looked funny until all the Knights appeared so clad; their shields were dustbin lids, and their procession before Simonides and Thaisa joked up with swingy music; the combats were included, the funniest being when Pericles and a Knight shook hands, and then made their forefingers their swords. The brothel scenes were aided by the addition of two girls acting as tarts most suspicious of the unwanted newcomer; the appearance of the 'disguised' Lysimachus in a huge crow-beaked mask reduced the cast to hysterics. The sexual politics of the last Cleon–Dioniza scene were emphasised by having them in bed, with Dioniza using her sexuality to overcome Cleon's feeble moral resistance: a nice idea in juxtaposition with the brothel. All in all, this was a remarkable achieve-

[1] A useful caution against over-reliance on reviews emerges here: Michael Coveney (*Financial Times*, 14 September 1989) condemned Walker as 'haltingly half-comprehensible'; Michael Billington (*Guardian*, same date) says he articulated beautifully. Billington was right: the videotape confirms it.

[2] The tape of Stratford 1986 is equally frustrating, in a different way: for a vast chunk of the play the sound track is audible, but the video picture has disappeared in a jumble of mistracking. A plague on both their houses.

ment, considering the limitations of the forces involved.[1] Perhaps *Pericles*' future fortunes lie in directions such as these.

NATIONAL 1994

Curiously, the National (now Royal National) Theatre had not mounted *Pericles* until Phyllida Lloyd's production at the Olivier Theatre, May 1994. And certainly, this, the most recent staging of the play at the time of writing, gives cause for thinking that minimalism is the better choice. The production has become notorious for its cost (shades of Phelps) and for its problems with stage technology, which caused the cancellation of the first preview, and its opening without a dress rehearsal. A useful account of the production has been published[2] which, besides chronicling some of the difficulties, is helpfully illustrated.

The production epitomised the difficulties that the current approach to main-stage productions of the classics blunders into. It is assumed that today's visually oriented audiences, brought up on blockbuster movies and musicals, will tolerate classical theatre only if it is produced in a spectacular fashion. The technical facilities of modern theatres make directors feel obliged to use them (the tilting revolve in the Olivier was the cause of much of Lloyd's misery), and since for all sorts of practical reasons the cast has very little time to accustom themselves to their costumes, the lighting, and other technical aspects, the traditional ecology of the theatre – that it is a place for acting – is once more threatened, as it was in the worst days of nineteenth-century pictorialism. The play becomes the excuse for the display of technological gee-whizzery, rather than the technology's being placed at the service of the play. It is a sad tale, apologetically documented by Reynolds (see p. 25, n. 2).

The production earned mixed reviews and smallish audiences. Michael Billington rightly complained that Lloyd's emphasis on dance and music left the language undervalued, and that 'propulsive narrative is too often sacrificed to arresting detail' (*Guardian Weekly*, 26 June 1994). Others were referring to it as *Pericles – the Musical*; Benedict Nightingale in *The Times* (23 May 1994) gave a full, and devastating, description of all the visual effects in language recalling his predecessor's report on Phelps, 140 years before. However, despite the difficulties created by the staging, by some very strange costuming, and by the interpolation of some perfectly gratuitous 'production numbers', such as the roaring twenties musical interlude beginning the brothel scene, the performance had all sorts of genuine theatrical imagination. The use of simultaneous staging, especially of 3.3 and 3.4, was imaginative (illustration 7, p. 26), and at last there was a real theophany (illustration 8, p. 26). Though generally under-cast, there were some good performances, most especially Henry Goodman's audience-engaging, charming Gower. But overall, Lloyd's was as much an *adaptation* of the play as Lillo's, Phelps's, or Coleman's.

---

[1] It seems to have shared many features with Ultz's production for the Theatre Royal, Stratford East (1983): see Leiter, *Shakespeare Around the Globe*, p. 557.

[2] Peter Reynolds's *Pericles: Text Into Performance*, published by the Education Department of the National Theatre (undated, but obviously 1994).

7 Simultaneous staging in Act 3 in Phyllida Lloyd's production, Royal National Theatre, 1994

8 The theophany in Act 5, Scene 1 in Phyllida Lloyd's production, Royal National Theatre, 1994

Clearly, the ecological balance between acting and *mise-en-scène* has swung to an extreme at present; it's time for another Jonson (or Guthrie, or Peter Brook) to give everyone what for, and begin the return swing.

The play

THE CHORUS: SOME MOULDY TALE

Ben Jonson's dismissal of *Pericles* as 'some mouldy tale'[1] was celebrated, and frequently quoted. Dryden also included *Pericles* among those plays 'made up of some ridiculous, incoherent story'.[2] Whilst not sharing these great writers' disapprobation, we believe that Jonson and Dryden were absolutely right in their focus on the play as an old 'tale' and as a 'story'. The use of Gower as Chorus makes Shakespeare's dramaturgy clear: he is presenting a dramatic action in the something old–something borrowed tradition of storytelling: 'To sing a song that old was sung, / From ashes, ancient Gower is come' (Prologue 1–2). Gower's entry is a reincarnation of the poet two hundred years after his death, as well as a step back to the style and manners of that distant time. Any honest appreciation of the play will have to begin by admitting and exploring Gower's overriding influence as *Pericles*' presenter.[3]

It is the *author of the play's story himself* who speaks first: representing the voice of authority, the resurrected figure[4] is that of the artist who appears at the beginning of each act, not merely a character in the play, but as the poet–artist through whom Shakespeare shapes the story and unifies the action. The voice of the dead poet, then, is the dramatist's chief structural device, a cue and inspiration taken from his sources, as Gower and Twine depended on older sources before them. In the *Confessio Amantis* Gower recalls the twelfth-century *Pantheon* (the version behind his story) as 'a cronike in daies gone', and recounts his tale 'as the cronike telleth' and from what the 'olde

---

[1] In the poem, 'The just indignation of the author', appended to the printed text of *The New Inn*; discussed pp. 16–17.

[2] *Defence of the Epilogue*, in *Works*, XI, 206. Dryden's neo-classical principles were naturally outraged by the dramaturgy of this, and other Shakespeare plays; besides, Dryden apparently believed *Per.* to have been Shakespeare's first. His Epilogue to the nineteen-year-old Charles Davenant's *Circe*, premiered on 12 May 1677, declares: '*Shakespear*'s own Muse his *Pericles* first bore, / The Prince of *Tyre* was older than the *Moore*' (lines 16–17; *Works*, I, 158). (The implication is that Davenant's work would likewise improve.) It is not known upon what Dryden based this opinion.

[3] Gary Taylor, in an essay in *Shakespeare Reshaped 1606–1623*, 1993, on what he calls the 'structure of performance', establishes beyond any reasonable doubt that (a) *pace* G. K. Hunter, professional plays in the adult companies did not have act-breaks in the performances in the 1592–c. 1610 period (it was, however, not unusual to have a 'Chorus' or 'presenter' to mark the internal, literary five-act structure) and (b) that from 1616 the evidence of printed texts *and* MSS., both theatrical and otherwise, suggests that plays did indeed have act-intervals. He further shows that the childrens' companies before 1600 *did* have intervals, and that the acquisition of the Blackfriars was the key event in introducing intervals into adult plays. *Per.* was certainly written before the King's Men's acquisition of the Blackfriars, and therefore conforms to the older convention.

[4] Gower's 'resurrection' to act as Chorus dramatically anticipates the various resurrections that are found in the last plays, where one who is thought dead is in reality alive: Marina, Thaisa (*Per.*), Imogen, Guiderius, Arviragus (*Cym.*), Perdita, Hermione (*WT*), Ferdinand (*Temp.*).

9   Gower's tomb and monument in Southwark Cathedral

bokes seyne'.¹ For his version of the story in *The Patterne of Painefull Adventures* Twine points back to the fourteenth-century *Gesta Romanorum* 'of which historie this is but a small abstract, promising if ever the whole chance to come into my hands, to set it forth with all fidelitie, diligence, and expedition'.² Shakespeare's Gower in coming to 'tell you what mine authors say' (Prologue 20) thus embodies the long tradition of storytellers who perpetuated the survival of the tale through time and the human imagination. It is highly likely that Shakespeare had seen Gower's monument in what is now Southwark Cathedral: on top of the tomb is the recumbent statue of the poet, his head pillowed on his books (see illustration 9, p. 28).

Gathered together as members of the audience at the feet of the storyteller, we are continually reminded that what we are watching and hearing is Gower's own story come to life; he stands 'in th'gaps, to teach you / The stages of our story' (4.4.8–9), and what he relates is said 'For certain in our story' (4.0.19) and as 'our story says' (5.0.2). Gower is the authority of literary tradition itself whose function as the story-telling poet, as Northrop Frye said, is 'primarily to remember'.³ His act of memory is a testament to the story's worthiness, since it has induced Gower to reassume 'man's infirmities' (Prologue 3), and offer his narrative as a burning taper giving his audience light. As the rhythms of memory and time are defined by the seasons and man's rituals, so too has the story played its part in a collective remembrance: it 'hath been sung at festivals, / On ember-eves and holy days' (5–6) and 'lords and ladies in their lives / Have read it for restoratives' (7–8). Even if 'wit's more ripe' in these 'latter times' (11–12), it would be a mistake and a denial of the past (indeed of time) should the audience dismiss the presentation of the story simply for its antique familiarity and its old-fashioned language: '*Et bonum quo antiquius eo melius*' Gower reminds us (10) and perhaps one might add, Shakespeare too.⁴

Gower's language in the choruses is that of a pseudo-medieval past, the dramatist's revival of obsolete style along with its dead poet. By accepting Gower's 'rhymes', so removed from what is local, current, and specialised in the drama of the day, the

---

¹ Berthelette's dedication to the 1554 edition of *CA* draws the reader's attention to the worth of old authors and their language: 'There is to my dome no man, but that he maie by readinge of this warke get right great knowlage, as well for the understandynge of many and diuers auctours, whose reasons, sayenges, and histories are translated in to this warke, as for the pleintie of englishe wordes and vulgars, beside the furtherance of the life to vertue . . .' (quoted in Hoeniger, p. xiv–xv).

² Quoted in Bullough, p. 481. Even the hero in Twine is a storyteller who 'applied his vacant time to his booke, and hee wrote the whole storie and discourse of his owne life and adventures at large, the which he caused to be written foorth in two large volumes, whereof he sent one to the Temple of Diana at Ephesus, and placed the other in his owne library' (*ibid.*).

³ *Anatomy*, p. 56.

⁴ Except perhaps in *H8*, there is a sense in the last plays that Shakespeare was going back to origins, in retrieving and reviving past literary traditions. Plots are based on fable, and contain much folklore, as well as the conventions of fairy-tale in plays which can be seen as re-creating old stories with the feeling of the familiar about them. *Per.* was not Shakespeare's last venture into the archaic past to rework material for his plays; *TNK* bases its story on Chaucer's 'Knight's Tale', and *WT* insists on its likeness to old tales and ballads. Frye held that 'the effect of these archaizing tendencies in Shakespeare is to establish contact with a universal and world-wide dramatic tradition . . . and works toward uncovering a primeval dramatic structure that practically anything in the shape of a human audience can respond to', *Natural Perspective*, p. 58.

Pericles   [*30*]

audience is engaged in linguistic time-travel of a sort, one which makes the narrative a kind of magic-carpet ride to exotic places in the archaic past. Stylistic eccentricities, archaic expressions[1] enclosed in sing-song octosyllabic lines, rhyming couplets of iambic tetrameters, openly admitted as the 'lame feet of [Gower's] rhyme' (4.0.48), are deliberately employed in an artificial style which serves a dramatic purpose. His language differentiates him from the characters of the play; they are his creations brought to life from the pages of his story and therefore speak with a different and more immediate reality.

In a sense, the language of the choruses helps to emphasise Gower's presence as something partially outside the play, creating the boundaries of stilted convention and artifice out of which the heightened significance and lifelike truth of the events emerge by contrast. If the early choruses are more consciously archaic and irregular in their versification, the later ones suffer a sea-change as the play progresses to its climax in the recognition scene. Octosyllabic couplets with four stresses evolve into a five-stress rhythm (4.0), and ultimately give way to alternately rhyming iambic pentameters in quatrains (5.0). The transformation of Gower's verse to more familiar structures is a linguistic pointer to the way the story itself evolves from quaint fairy-tale to the intensity of immediate dramatic experience. As the characters emerge from their trials, and the happy-ever-after ending approaches, the chorus returns to its original style for the last few pages of the narrator's story: 'Now our sands are almost run, / More a little, and then dumb' (5.2.1–2). Gower's language is also a condition of the play's articulation of mythic archetypes in fairy-tale form: to tell an old story of heroic adventure, love, loss, birth, death, and rebirth, requires the voice of the dead poets in the sense that T. S. Eliot described, using 'last year's words' and 'last year's language'; the 'next year's words [that] await another voice'[2] are defined by Shakespeare's dramatic art which transforms the ancient narrative into a living and palpable experience. Archetypes are not new or modish, which is precisely their point; they are by definition timeless, and when great art employs them, as Shakespeare does in his last period, archaic language can be seen not as the 'mould' on the tale but as a condition of the *fons et origo* of all archetypes that are transmitted and passed on in story form.

Resurrecting old-fashioned verse to suit his dramatic purpose was not new to Shakespeare: the plays-within-the-play in *Love's Labour's Lost*, *A Midsummer Night's Dream*, and *Hamlet* employ older forms and structures of language to distinguish them from their contexts. J. M. Nosworthy remarks that euphuism is found in Brutus' Forum speech in *Julius Caesar*; that the bleeding Sergeant in *Macbeth* is Senecan in style; and that the Leonati in *Cymbeline* speak in rhyming fourteeners, a style current during Shakespeare's early career.[3] There are better examples: Don Armado in *Love's Labour's Lost* is a more complete euphuist than Brutus, for example; there is more

---

[1] A few examples only here (though the choruses are full of them): 'he spoken can' (2.0.12), 'to killen' (20), 'perishen' (35), 'Ne . . . escapend' (36), 'y-slackèd' (3.0.1), 'Y-ravishèd' (35).
[2] 'Little Gidding', lines 120–1.
[3] Arden edn of *Cym.*, pp. xxxv–xxxvi. In the vision scene, Nosworthy maintains, Shakespeare 'is reaching far back to a style current during his apprenticeship and employing it for a new and specific purpose', p. xxxvi.

Senecanism in *Richard III*; pastiche Petrarchanism is important in *Romeo and Juliet* and so on. Though *Pericles* makes more use of an extended archaic style than any other Shakespearean play, the very contrivance and artifice serves as a reminder that the truest poetry is the most feigning. As the language of Gower's first speech makes clear, the audience will have to surrender their sophisticated notions of dramatic speech, and in this way be guided and open to a recollection of their older, imaginative responses. To achieve this requires the audience to take the advice Theseus offers to Hippolyta: 'The best in this kind are but shadows; and/the worst are no worse, if imagination amend them' (*MND* 5.1.211–12).

One of Gower's chief functions as storyteller is to appeal to the audience's imagination, never letting them forget that their responses are necessary to the story's presentation, in fact to its very existence on the stage. Gower may will this story into life, controlling the characters and the events, but it is the audience who must accept it. This is entirely appropriate: in order to tell a story and to present it, the narrator must have willing and participating auditors and viewers (the story is after all recalled to 'glad your ear and please your eyes', Prologue 4). Their act of will and their participation lie exclusively in the realm of their imagination.

Gower's appeals to the imagination are consistent, pervasive, and integral to the play's narrative structure. They fall into various categories such as direct appeal for the audience's assistance:

And time that is so briefly spent
With your fine fancies quaintly eche . . .   (3.0.12–13)

            – think this pilot thought –
So, with his steerage, shall your thoughts groan
To fetch his daughter home, who first is gone.   (4.4.18–20)

That you aptly will suppose . . .   (5.2.5)

The interim, pray you, all confound.   (5.2.14)

Some are with reference to stage representation:

In your imagination hold
This stage the ship, upon whose deck
The sea-tossed Pericles appears to speak.   (3.0.58–60)

Others serve by focussing on the whereabouts of the characters:

Imagine Pericles arrived at Tyre . . .   (4.0.1)

Now to Marina bend your mind,
Whom our fast-growing scene must find
At Tarsus . . .   (4.0.5–7)

      And to her father turn our thoughts again
Where we left him on the sea.   (5.0.12–13)

      Suppose him now at anchor.   (5.0.16)

In your supposing once more put your sight:
    Of heavy Pericles, think this his bark,

Where what is done in action – more, if might –
　　Shall be discovered; please you sit and hark.　　　　　　　　(5.0.21–4)

At Ephesus the temple see,
Our king and all his company.
That he can hither come so soon,
Is by your fancies' thankful doom.　　　　　　　　　　　　　(5.2.17–20)

Another focus is on actions yet to come:

　　　　　The unborn event
I do commend to your content;
Only I carried wingèd time
Post on the lame feet of my rhyme,
Which never could I so convey
Unless your thoughts went on my way.　　　　　　　　　　　(4.0.45–50)

Lastly, there are those that deal with travel in distance and time:

Thus time we waste, and long leagues make short,
Sail seas in cockles, have and wish but for't,
Making to take your imagination
From bourn to bourn, region to region.
By you being pardoned we commit no crime
To use one language in each several clime
Where our scenes seem to live.　　　　　　　　　　　　　　(4.4.1–7)

　　　think you now are all in Miteline.　　　　　　　　　　(4.4.51)

By these appeals, the audience is urged to become co-creators of the story, and the more they use their imagination, the better the resulting play will be: true of all theatre, of course.

Not content solely with guiding the productive participation of the audience's imagination, Gower finds it necessary also to nudge their alertness: 'Be quiet then, as men should be' (2.0.5), 'Be attent' (3.0.11), 'learn of me' (4.4.8), 'you bear in mind' (4.4.14), 'Now please you wit' (4.4.31), 'Patience then' (4.4.50), 'sit and hark' (5.0.24). He makes promises to the audience and verifies their experiences: 'Here have you seen' (2.0.1), 'I'll show you' (2.0.7), 'What's dumb in show I'll plain with speech' (3.0.14), 'See how belief may suffer by foul show' (4.4.23), 'you have heard', 'In Pericles, his queen and daughter seen', 'may you well descry' (Epilogue 1, 3, 7). The close relationship thus established between audience and presenter is so designed that entry into the processional narrative of the story is as easy as Alice's passage through the looking-glass. However impossible or improbable things may appear, however swiftly we are taken from place to place over a period of many years, Gower's confident control of the narrative shapes the play, securing our faith and trust in return.

With the help of the audience's imagination, and what they can confirm with their eyes and ears, Gower can surmount time as well as create dimensions of it. 'Ancient' Gower transcends the past by his appearance in present time while evoking a tale which recedes even further into a distant past. His storytelling choruses and the scenes which enact them thus present two alternating dimensions of time, attested to and shared by the audience simultaneously. The tale itself contains a history which works by its own clock, as the stages of the story process chronologically in terms of past, present, and future throughout the many years in the events of the characters' lives. One might add the final dimension of time which contains the play within the 'two hours' traffic of our stage' (*Rom.* Prologue 12).

Explaining the action, filling the gaps in time, providing moral commentary, are only a part (and perhaps a conventional part as far as choruses go) of the intricate structure of narrative in Gower's storytelling. Its primary effect is continually to impress upon the audience the dramatic process of narrative itself, which is not confined to Gower's appearances, but also spills over into the play, making itself felt as an important aspect of the action. Storytellers and narrative texts of various kinds permeate the play, giving an overwhelming impression of the centrality of narrative. The following list, though not exhaustive, suggests their pervasiveness: Antiochus' riddle tells a cryptic story of sorts (1.1.65–72); relating information we already know, Pericles recounts his venture in Antioch to Hellicanus (1.2.69–94); Cleon describes the situation in Tarsus by 'relating tales of others' grief' (1.4.2–51); the three stylised dumb shows[1] enact their silent stories; each of the Knights' impresas presents visual and textual narratives which are read and interpreted by Thaisa and Simonides (2.2); Antiochus' incest is revisited yet again in Hellicanus' account of the king's death as told to Escanes (2.4.1–12); the letter in Thaisa's coffin tells the story of her identity (3.2.67–74); as she has learned of the events surrounding the night of her birth from Lychorida, Marina retells the story to Leonine (4.1.51–63); the reading of Marina's epitaph represents Dioniza's false tale of the girl's death (4.4.34–43); Lysimachus, wanting to know 'at large' the cause of Pericles' sorrow, is promised by Hellicanus to 'recount' it to him (5.1.57–8).

By saturating the play thus far with narrative devices and thereby attuning the audience's ear to and perception of narrative technique, Shakespeare has carefully prepared the way for their increased significance in bringing about the resolution. The recognition of father and daughter is a result of a storytelling process, the piecing together of a history's narrative strands, which creates a new reality for both characters. Their exchanges are shaped and enhanced continually by a lexicon of narrative: 'If I should tell my history' (5.1.114), 'in the reporting' (115), 'Prithee speak' (115), 'Thy relation to points' (120), 'Didst thou not say' (123), 'Report thy parentage. I think thou saidst' (126), 'Some such thing I said' (129), 'Tell thy story' (131), 'Re-

---

[1] The dumb shows at 2.0.16, 3.0.14, 4.4.22 are visual narratives, another way of telling a story in the manner described by Alonso in *Temp.*:

> I cannot too much muse
> Such shapes, such gesture, and such sound expressing
> (Although they want the use of tongue) a kind
> Of excellent dumb discourse. (3.3.36–9)

In addition, all three dumb shows contain literal texts or narratives which require the act of reading: in the first two Pericles receives news-bearing letters, in the third he is shown Marina's tomb and presumably reads the epitaph. For a discussion of Shakespeare's use of dumb shows see Dieter Mehl, *The Elizabethan Dumb Show: The History of a Dramatic Convention*, 1965.

count, I do beseech thee' (138), 'I will end here' (149), 'speak on' (152), 'as my good nurse / Lychorida hath oft delivered' (156-7), 'I'll hear you more / To th'bottom of your story, and never interrupt you' (161-2), 'I will believe you by the syllable / Of what you shall deliver' (164-5), 'Tell me' (195, 200), 'as in / The rest you said' (200-1), 'she shall tell thee all' (211), 'Tell him o'er point by point' (220). As a confirmation of his joy, Pericles simply retells the story: 'Thou that wast born at sea, buried at Tarsus, / And found at sea again' (191-92).

After father and daughter are reunited the play reaches its conclusion of concord through yet further narrative structures and their permutations. The entire family is reunited in Ephesus as a consequence of Diana's bidding Pericles to 'reveal', to 'tell' aspects of his history and to 'give them repetition to the life' 'before the people all' (5.1.235-41), which Pericles does in yet another iteration of past events (5.3.1-12). Thaisa responds to Pericles' narrative in a phrase which stands out for its resonance, sounding the thematic core of the play's story in terms of its mythic rhythm: 'Did you not name a tempest, a birth, and death?' (5.3.31). Familial bonds are reunited, confirmed, and verified through explications which weave the narrative strands in 'retellings': Cerimon assuages Pericles' doubts by recounting the events of Thaisa's recovery (5.3.18-23); he 'can from first to last resolve' Pericles' questions (57) and 'deliver / How this dead queen re-lives' (59-60). His story will guarantee 'No needful thing omitted' (64), a promise for the after-play narrative when the happy parties will be gathered 'To hear the rest untold' (80).

The narrative art employed as part of the play's miraculous conclusion is not abstruse: like all storytelling, it simply involves the sharing of the word, the passing-on of language which, when appropriately delivered at the right moment, can unlock knowledge and allow miracles to seem even more wondrous. In this respect Shakespeare has added his own manner of *telling* to Gower's and to that of every other teller of the tale before him, in a new creation of dramatic narrative. The centrality of narrative to the play makes it clear that the song Gower comes to sing is not the 'mouldy tale' that Jonson described, but the 'new joy' which can be found in old stories retold on the stage.[1] By appearing eight times in the course of the play, Gower ensures the lasting impression of this effect.

Shakespeare uses the device of the Chorus quite frequently, but never to the same extent, nor with the same structural importance as he does in *Pericles*. Gower appears more frequently than any other Chorus in Shakespeare. *Henry V* is next with six; in *2 Henry IV* the Prologue presents 'Rumour painted full of tongues'; the Chorus in *Romeo and Juliet* speaks a sonnet before Acts 1 and 2; *Troilus and Cressida* is presented by the 'Prologue in armour'; Time appears as the Chorus before Act 4 in *The Winter's*

---

[1] A similar sentiment occurs in *TNK*, 'If the tale we have told / (For 'tis no other) any way content ye / (For to that honest purpose it was meant ye)', Epilogue 12-14. However, its most profound expression is in *WT*, where the fairy-tale wonder of the miraculous is defined in terms of narrative: 'Such a deal of wonder is broken out within this hour that ballad-makers cannot be able to express it' (5.2.23-5); 'This news, which is call'd true, is so like an old tale, that the verity of it is strong suspicion' (5.2.27-9); 'Like an old tale still' (5.2.61); 'That she is living, / Were it but told you, should be hooted at / Like an old tale' (5.3.115-17).

Tale; Prologue and Epilogue are delivered by a Chorus in *Henry VIII*. Analogues of the device of Gower outside Shakespeare can be found in Barnabe Barnes's *The Devil's Charter* (probably 1606), and in *The Travailes of the Three English Brothers* (1607) collaboratively by John Day, William Rowley, and George Wilkins. In Barnes's play Guicchiardine (the Italian historian, author of the play's source) appears as Prologue, 'sent downe' by the Muse to present the tragedy; unlike Gower, he confines himself to filling the play's plot, and speaks in contemporary idiom. In *The Travailes* the Chorus is the allegorical figure of Fame, whose language, especially in its appeals to the audience's imagination, suggests Gower more strongly. However, it is more likely that the source was *Henry V*. Since the date of *Pericles* cannot be absolutely established, it is possible that both these plays influenced *Pericles*; and also possible (though less likely) that the influence went the other way.[1]

Clearly, however, Gower in *Pericles* has a closer affinity with the Chorus in *Henry V* than with any other Chorus or presenter. Both speak a Prologue and Epilogue, and appear before each act. Like Gower, the Chorus of *Henry V* is the presenter of the play, an interpreter of the events who narrates parts of the action and assists the audience in their imaginary travels as they follow Henry's army from place to place over the periods of time involved in the action. Both Choruses ask for the audience's acceptance and their judgement on the ensuing performance, and both stand in the interim of events by explaining what has passed. Gower 'stands in th'gaps to teach ... / The stages' of the story; similarly the Chorus in *Henry V* asks if he may 'prompt' those that 'have not read the story' (5.0.1–2). Like Gower, he develops a close familiarity with the audience in his numerous appeals to their imagination (even more frequently than Gower; there are about twenty of them). However, the structural use of the Chorus in *Henry V* is clearly ironical and subversive, quite the reverse of the dramatic condition of Gower in *Pericles*.[2]

In his developing relationship with the audience, Gower delivers what he promises, never confounding audience expectation nor frustrating the essential employment of their imagination. The audience's faith and trust in him (and more important, in his presentation of the story) are thus secured, because faith and trust are necessary adjuncts to the reception of mythic truth which is shaped by art. 'It is requir'd / You do awake your faith', says Paulina in *The Winter's Tale* (5.3.94–5): as Leontes must open himself to the truth in art of Hermione's statue and her miraculous resurrection, so too must the audience of *Pericles* accept the truth that the resurrected artist comes to tell.[3]

---

[1] See 'Date', p. 1; and also see Hoeniger's detailed discussion, pp. xxi–xxiii.

[2] It is impossible here to examine the nature of the choruses in *H5* in detail. See Andrew Gurr (ed.) *Henry V* (NCS, 1992), pp. 6–16, and Antony Hammond, ' "It must be your imagination then": the Prologue and the plural text in *Henry V* and elsewhere', in John W. Mahon and Thomas A. Pendleton (eds.), *Fanned and Winnowed Opinions*, 1987, pp. 133–50. It is important, however, to stress that the Chorus is a character in the play and is not literally apologizing on the author's behalf for the inadequacies of his company – this is a trope in the Chorus's tenor of contradiction. Gower, on the other hand, while still a character in a play and as such not necessarily speaking for the author, is endued with the kind of authority that is implied by the fact that Gower *is* an author.

[3] As Frye has pointed out, this kind of faith 'is what we should call imaginative faith, but this imaginative faith is something much more positive than any mere suspension of disbelief, however willing' (*Natural Perspective*, p. 19).

Although usually dismissed as a quaint device of inferior and unsophisticated dramatic quality, the choruses in *Pericles* tell us more about Shakespeare's linguistic treatment, dramatic narratology, structural organisation,[1] and awareness of the audience than anything he ever attempted with a Chorus before or after.

LANGUAGE AND STYLE

The dismissal of *Pericles*' integrity on the basis of style and language has fuelled debate on the play's authorship,[2] and influenced its publication and performance. The chorus of critical disapprobation seems, on examination, to be unjustly weighted and narrow in perception, and has attained the condition of Holy Writ more through excess of repetition than by its intrinsic merit. George Lillo, in his Prologue to *Marina* (1738), encapsulates a judgement of the play that, amazingly, still persists today:

> We dare not charge the whole unequal play
> Of Pericles on him [Shakespeare]; yet let us say,
> As gold though mix'd with baser matter shines,
> So do his bright inimitable lines
> Throughout those rude wild scenes distinguish'd stand,
> And shew he touch'd them with no sparing hand.

The current view is still typified by Hoeniger's strictures in his Arden edition:

> its most pronounced and bewildering feature is the extreme unevenness in the literary quality of its language. For stiffness and triteness of verse most of the scenes of Acts I and II, and some in the later acts, afford no equal elsewhere in Shakespeare. On the other hand, some parts in Acts III and V are of the highest order. (Hoeniger, p. xxviii)

Hoeniger speaks for the majority of present-day critics in his complaints that the first two acts of the play contain a 'general low level' of versification, 'humdrum', in a 'jog-trot rhythm'; only the dialogue of the Fishermen provides a 'pleasant interlude in the mediocre verse-drama'. The second half of the play does not escape censure either:

> the writing of the later acts continues to be markedly uneven. Some scenes, especially III. iv, seem flat and undistinguishable. There are still many botched-up lines, and some passages are quite as bad as the worst of Acts I and II. (Hoeniger, pp. xxix–xxx)

More recently, the Oxford editors are even more magisterial: 'We believe that no textual theory can make it credible that Shakespeare wrote the bulk of the first nine scenes.'[3] Partly, these opinions arise from doubts concerning the authorship of Acts 1 and 2; partly they are the *consequence* of deciding that Acts 1 and 2 were written by someone other than Shakespeare. The circularity of this process seems obvious: 'This

---

[1] The internal coherence of the play is served by Gower's choruses and maintained even in the Epilogue. As G. Wilson Knight observed, 'nothing is here forgotten: Antiochus's wickedness, Pericles' relief of famine, the crime of Dionyza and Cleon, all are exactly remembered long after their purpose in the narrative sequence has been fulfilled; from first to last the Gower speeches have the whole action in mind; the various imagistic correspondences, cutting across divergences of style, knit the narrative into a unity' (*Crown*, p. 75).
[2] See 'Authorship', pp. 8–15.
[3] *Companion*, p. 557.

piece of verse is very bad – Shakespeare couldn't have written it – the play was therefore written collaboratively – the work of the collaborator was inferior – the collaborator wrote this piece of verse – it is therefore bad.' A great deal of the verse of Acts 1 and 2 has been condemned by this self-fulfilling process; it seems, these days, a perverse, old-fashioned, and unproductive way of discussing dramatic language. Its implied hieratic elitism has very often led to the omission in performance of vast chunks of Acts 1 and 2 – thereby depriving critics and audiences of the opportunity of having demonstrated to them that, as a dramatic experience, a full-text *Pericles* works extremely well in the theatre.[1]

The misdirected and tempest-tossed journeys of the plot are emblematised by the language. What begins awkward and linguistically disappointing is made sharp, keen, vigorous, and finally intensely moving, paralleling the pattern of trials and tribulations Pericles goes through. No other Shakespearean play follows this pattern exactly, but there are suggestive similarities in *Richard II*, where the rhyme-laden formality of the opening scenes leads to increasing profundity and eloquence on Richard's part. Some of the reasons why *Pericles* succeeds on stage are precisely because of its language and the way language shapes the dramatic action within distinctive styles.

As we have shown, Gower's speeches reveal a self-conscious awareness of the special uses of narrative language in presenting a story that comes to life on stage. On occasion, he also provides a reminder that language, and being attuned to its capabilities, are a way into the play: to 'accept my rhymes', as Gower says (Prologue 12), is to accept his invitation to appreciate the play's linguistic variety. The 'lame feet' of his 'rhyme' is an ironic apology, designed to inspire the audience's linguistic as well as their dramatic imagination: 'never could I so convey, / Unless your thoughts went on my way' (4.0.48–50). Obviously, he may be forgiven for using 'one language in each several clime / Where our scenes seems to live' (4.4.6–7),[2] but in this lies an essential clue to the way language distinguishes the different worlds and environments in *Pericles*, as well as the play's different dramatic actions. As the episodic scenes shift their locations and focus of concern, so too the ear becomes attuned to the shifting verbal structures. Antioch, Tyre, Tarsus, Pentapolis, Ephesus, Miteline, each have their own mood, tone, and atmosphere: a kind of *tinta* in the Verdian sense which colours the various worlds through which the hero travels on his spiritual journey. Further, the environments within these different exotic places provide a dimension to

---

[1] Hoeniger came to accept the play's theatrical integrity, unfortunately subsequent to the publication of his edition: 'Because large parts of the play, particularly its first two acts, seem to critical readers so obviously defective and crude, both in style and dramaturgy, we may be surprised by the evidence that in Shakespeare's own time and for a generation after, the play was highly popular . . . Yet it does seem strange . . . that a work which appears so dismally written and undramatic in its first two acts could experience such a success on stage . . . This new knowledge of how well the whole play works in the theatre should make us reflect on whether the traditional negative explanations that seek to account for the marked incongruity in quality of the play's scenes are at all convincing . . . the early scenes work much better in the theatre than critical-minded readers of the text have assumed', 'Gower and Shakespeare in *Pericles*', *SQ* 33 (1982), 461–79.

[2] The jovial element in Gower was nicely caught at this point in National 1994 when the polyglot cast began to chatter in various languages. 'One language', Gower insisted. '¡Si, hombre, el espanol!' declared someone; 'No: Este es el Royal National Theatre, Londres. One language!', Gower retorted.

the language of the characters who inhabit them: the royal courts of Antiochus, Pericles, and Simonides; the famine-stricken Tarsus ruled by Cleon and Dioniza; the Pentapoline seashore where toiling fishermen conduct their daily routine; the serene refuge of Cerimon's dwelling; the Miteline brothel with all its colour; Marina's tomb; the Temple of Diana; and of course there are the shipboard scenes where the sea has its own special *tinta* as well.

The strangeness and variety of these locations along with their relevant dramatic actions[1] suggest that an 'unevenness' in literary style is not undesirable, but a dramatically appropriate form of expression: its unevenness *is* its style. If the earlier acts have been distinguished because of their unrefined versification and linguistic simplicity, this seems more by way of design than by incompetence. Pericles' journey begins with a simple first step into the world of fairy-tale artifice and progresses through the more difficult and purgatorial stages of spiritual growth, a progression mirrored in the play's style and language culminating in the sublimity of the recognition scene. In the structure of the play the initial style of elementary artifice is slowly transfigured into a dramatic language immediate and moving in its intensity, made all the more so because of its growth from humbler origins. R. S. White describes this transition as the 'shift of gear in poetic concentration and intensity' which is 'part of the process of lifting the play into a higher realm'.[2]

The opening scene in Antioch has the formal quality of the 'once upon a time' beginning, as recognisable in its features as any pop-up page in a picture-book. In only 171 lines of dialogue the love-quest, the danger involved, the evil transgressions of the wicked father, the hero's ordeal, his escape, and the murder plot, are all swiftly conveyed because of their stock conventionality: a quality facilitated and shared by the language, appropriately illustrating how the medium can be the message. That this partakes of the 'trite verse' and 'jog-trot rhythm' that Hoeniger condemns is not detrimental to the dramatic purpose, but rather serves it.[3] In this environment, where we find the hero *in medias res* in a fairy-tale situation, all we need to know about Pericles is immediately defined by the language of folkloric heroism:

> I have, Antiochus, and with a soul
> Emboldened with the glory of her praise,
> Think death no hazard in this enterprise. (1.1.3–5)

> Like a bold champion I assume the lists
> Nor ask advice of any other thought
> But faithfulness and courage. (1.1.62–4)

Antiochus' Daughter does not even have a name (let alone a 'character' which defines her – she speaks only two lines); it is enough that she represents the love-quest. A

---

[1] For Twine these features of the story were attractive attributes, which he offered to the delectation of his patron in the dedication of *PPA*: '*that this worke would be the welcommer unto you, especially considering the delectable varietie, and the often changes and chances contained in this present historie, which cannot but much stirre up the mind and sences unto sundry affection*', Bullough, p. 424.

[2] '*Let Wonder Seem Familiar*': *Endings in Shakespeare's Romance Vision*, 1985, p. 118.

[3] A conclusion Knight came to: 'after a number of re-readings one begins to suspect some especial purpose in the passages of stilted verse', *Crown*, p. 33.

10 'As yon grim looks do testify' (Prologue 40); a conjectural reconstruction of Act 1, Scene 1, by
C. Walter Hodges

primitive danger hangs about this quest, conveyed in the imagery of forbidden fruit,
Hesperidean gardens, and serpents that surround the Daughter. Pericles' adventure is
to undertake the ancient riddle-game, itself a linguistic convention of folklore but here
with a triple ramification: the riddle reveals Antiochus' secret rather than concealing
it; if Pericles solves it, he will lose his life; if he fails to solve it, he will also lose his life.

11   A conjectural reconstruction of the original staging of the theophany by C. Walter Hodges. Note that the staging described in the text is slightly different from the illustration

12   Rachel Kempson as Dioniza, showing what a Wicked Queen should look like, in Tony Richardson's 1958 production at the Shakespeare Memorial Theatre, Stratford-upon-Avon

In Frye's astute phrase, 'the logic is that of the Arabian Nights',[1] but it is also the dramatist's way of enjoying the transparency of the convention itself (its construction in sing-song rhymes and rhythms are charming in their effect). When Pericles hears

[1] *Natural Perspective*, p. 32.

Marina's riddle in the last act, the convention, by contrast with its previous use, is endued with infinitely greater profundity both in its language and dramatic function:

> No, nor of any shores,
> Yet I was mortally brought forth and am
> No other than I appear.
>
> (5.1.98–100)[1]

The entire action in Antioch is thus ironically distanced by language to keep the audience in a frame of mind appropriate to the kind of story the play is telling for the first two acts. The verse, however 'trite', does duty in conveying the drama: the hero's hairbreadth escape, for example, is delivered in gnomic rhyming couplets, as close as the language of the action ever comes to that of Gower's choruses:

> Antioch farewell: for wisdom sees, those men
> Blush not in actions blacker than the night,
> Will show no course to keep them from the light.
> One sin, I know, another doth provoke:
> Murder's as near to lust as flame to smoke;
>
> .   .   .
>
> Then lest my life be cropped, to keep you clear,
> By flight I'll shun the danger which I fear.
>
> (1.1.135–43)

The language of 1.2 and 1.4 is snarled out of simplicity for dramatic purposes. In 1.2, Pericles' perplexities – contrary to fairy-tale expectations, Antiochus turns out to be a particularly nasty villain, and the Daughter not as advertised – create his confusion, and his subsequent indecision – am I in the right play? – is figured in his tormented verse. Likewise, in 1.4, Cleon's long litany of tribulation is contorted by his impotence, his refusal or inability to govern his country properly. Pericles' sudden appearance at the end of the scene brings linguistic as well as nutritional relief.

Ruled by benign joviality, Simonides' court, in contrast, has a lighter atmosphere suited to a birthday feast, and the winning of the fair damsel; but here too Pericles finds himself in the world of the love-quest itself within the bounds of folk-tale artifice. Triumphs, knights, tilting, and victory feast are the very stuff of chivalric action found in any antique story. This air of ceremonial ritual is heightened by the formal awareness of the verse:

> for princes are
> A model which heaven makes like to itself.
> As jewels lose their glory if neglected,
> So princes their renowns if not respected.
> 'Tis now your honour, daughter, to entertain
> The labour of each knight in his device.
>
> (2.2.10–15)

The ritual atmosphere is further enhanced by the elaborate scene of the Knights' progress, in which scenography and the linguistic artifice of the Latin mottos (and one in semi-Spanish) combine in a stately display. Act 2 is a mirror image of the first in terms of love-quest and trial, father and daughter, the honour-seeking hero, but in

---

[1] Both riddles are apt for comparison since each has conception and birth for a focus.

13 The impresa scene (Act 2, Scene 2): Thaisa (Sally Edwards) on the stairs between upper and lower stage, Simonides (Russell Dixon) enthroned aloft, in David Thacker's 1989 production at the Swan Theatre, Stratford-upon-Avon

action its moral opposite: Antioch brings the knight to dismay, Pentapolis to triumph. Nonetheless both acts represent a contrived world in strict fairy-tale style in which evil, goodness, danger, love, adventure, and heroism play their accustomed archetypal roles. In Antioch and Pentapolis action is more literary than lifelike, an effect achieved not by 'bad' verse but by a language suited to archetypal conventions.[1]

The Latin of the Knights' impresas is one of many special uses of language which add to the strange variety of tongues and actions found in *Pericles*. The colourful prose of the Fishermen (2.1) is written in the idiom of a local dialect (not Greek, of course, but peculiarly English). Appropriately, their language uses a diction derived from their occupation as they discuss 'the fenny subject of the sea' by which Pericles learns that even 'fishers' can 'tell the infirmities of men' (2.1.45–6), a moral Pericles draws from the Fishermen's idiosyncratic use of language.

The other prose scenes are those set in the brothel (4.2, 4.5), which make a striking contrast with the language of the Fishermen. No one would call them 'honest'; the low-life grittiness and humour of their idiom, which reveal a more extended and vibrant use of specialised language (recalling similar scenes in *Measure for Measure*) are emblematic both of their surroundings and their attitude to life: almost every phrase can be seen to derive from the localised world of the stews.[2] Languages clash in the environment of the brothel as the bawds find it difficult to understand Marina's use of words; she does not belong in the brothel and therefore speaks a different language:

BOULT Worse and worse mistress, she has here spoken holy words to the Lord Lysimachus.
BAWD Oh abominable.

(4.5.121–3)

MARINA Hark, hark you gods.
BAWD She conjures!

(4.5.133–4)

Marina's 'virginal fencing', the twists of meaning she gives to the words spoken to her, keeps both the Bawd and Lysimachus for a time in a state of frustrated bewilderment (4.5.49–71). It is Marina's language that converts the visiting Gentlemen and Lysimachus to better ways: 'I did not think / Thou couldst have spoke so well, ne'er dreamed thou couldst' (4.5.94–5). Her skill, Lysimachus believes, will 'win some words' of the ailing Pericles and so bring about his recovery.

The language of the sea or the use of sea terms is another idiom of the play, so pervasive that it provides a separate textual layer of meaning which imposes a unity on the whole work. Whether spoken by the Sailors as part of their own precise and technical vocabulary, or part of the speech of other characters, the precisely used language of the sea permeates the action[3] and intensifies the poetic resonance of key moments:

---

[1] Both matter and manner of the first two acts of the play owe much to *The Faerie Queene*, especially with regard to Spenser's redefinition for his own time of the concepts of chivalric quest and combat and the archaic language in which these may be expressed.

[2] In these scenes we have retained much of Q's ungrammatical but vivid punctuation. It seemed absurd to regularise the bawds into conventional modern syntactical punctuation, when that in Q caught their run-on style of speech so well.

[3] As Falconer has observed, 'only a detailed glossary could do justice to the extent and accuracy of his use of sea terms'; Shakespeare is 'at ease in an idiom unknown to most and his scope and precision can be adequately illustrated only in an analytical glossary': pp. xiii, 149.

this fresh new seafarer . . .   (3.1.42)

Where for a monument upon thy bones,
The air-remaining lamps, the belching whale,
And humming water must o'erwhelm thy corpse,
Lying with simple shells.   (3.1.61–4)

                              Called Marina,
For I was born at sea.   (5.1.153–4)

Give me a gash, put me to present pain,
Lest this great sea of joys rushing upon me
O'erbear the shores of my mortality,
And drown me with their sweetness . . .   (5.1.186–9).

Differing languages in specific verbal constructs are also evident in the changes that are constantly being rung by the play's linguistic fabric: the speaking or swearing of oaths;[1] Pericles' ceremonial benediction given to the newborn child (3.1.28–38); his 'priestly farewell' spoken over Thaisa's body (3.1.56–64); the letter found in Thaisa's coffin (3.2.67–74); the neo-Arcadian language of Marina's visit to Lychorida's grave (4.1.13–17); Dioniza's epitaph for Marina (4.4.34–43); the commands of the goddess in the vision (5.1.232–41); Pericles' public speech in Ephesus (5.3.1–12). All these by their specific functions interject a different sound and style into the linguistic texture. The choruses also inhabit a linguistic domain all their own. Blank verse, verse which rhymes in couplets or in alternating lines, tetrameters and pentameters, irregular verse lines, the shifts into distinctive prose, distinctive languages and idioms, are all part of the undulating rhythm of the work as a whole. The dramatist is using verbal alchemy of various kinds in order to conjure the sundry worlds and actions of his story.

By virtue of this variety, the recognition scene stands out all the more for its pure and moving simplicity of expression. No matter how strange, distant, geographically varied, and improbable (as manifest in language and style) the play has been hitherto, the recognition inhabits that higher realm of action that has stillness and wonder at its core. Yet because the scene asks its protagonist to accept the impossible, it dramatises a task of greater difficulty than any he had undertaken in the role of romantic hero. All he must do to undertake the task is to listen and to have faith in words. The naturalistic verbal structure of simple question and answer between father and daughter discloses identity and achieves a sense of awe as the miraculous truth is slowly revealed:

MARINA My name is Marina.   (5.1.139)

PERICLES And wherefore called Marina?
MARINA   Called Marina,
            For I was born at sea.   (5.1.153–4)

    MARINA Is it no more to be your daughter than
            To say my mother's name was Thaisa?   (5.1.204–5)

---

[1] There are many oaths spoken or referred to in the play: 1.2.119–20, 1.3.6–7, 1.4.99–103, 2.5.10–11, 3.3.20–4, 3.3.26–8, 3.4.10–11, 4.1.1, 4.1.67–8, 4.1.88, 4.1.95, 4.3.49, 4.4.27–8, 4.4.42–3.

Simply to 'name', and thereby, through language, to achieve the impossible, exceeds any effect attained hitherto by the most elaborate and artificial verbal constructs, as Thaisa also recognises: 'Did you not name a tempest, a birth, and death?' (5.3.31). Like Cordelia's 'No cause, no cause' (*Lear* 4.7.74), the language of recognition is one of few key words and tentative silences.

Inga-Stina Ewbank has analysed the verbal dynamism of the recognition scene:

As [Pericles] elaborates, feature by feature, on the similarity he senses, the remembered past merges with the perceived actuality, until the image of the wife who 'was' and that of the daughter who 'might have been' dissolve, as the use of the present tense shows, onto the girl before him, 'who starves the ears she feeds / And makes them hungry the more she gives them speech. / Where do you live?' If we note the echo here of several earlier Shakespearian passages, notably Enobarbus's description of Cleopatra, we should also note that this is the only instance where the 'appetites' left unsated are for more and more 'speech'. Marina's being is still held in her words; the miracle which they have barely begun to suggest can only be approached by words, in the form of simple questions: 'Where do you live?' . . . The dynamism of the scene – that which keeps it moving forward – is the pull between, on the one hand, Pericles' urge to hear and know more and more facts of Marina's life and, on the other, her awareness that these facts are, by normal standards, incredible.[1]

Yet the facts of the story here uncovered are truer than any fiction, despite their seeming improbabilities. As the contrived fiction of the first part of the play is mirrored in its language and versification, the higher truth of the recognition scene is reflected in simple utterances of great evocative power that are capable of transforming incredible fictions into necessary truths. Its effect depends on the contrast with all the play's other languages and styles.

On another level, an examination of the play's imagery also vindicates its integrity in a way which has been given little attention. It is an accepted characteristic of the last plays that they do not contain the same density and continuity of imagery, charged with symbolic meaning, as that found in Shakespeare's other plays. W. H. Clemen argues that we could not understand the significance and import of a tragedy like *King Lear* or *Macbeth* 'without a proper understanding of its image-patterns. This cannot be said with like emphasis of the romances.'[2] To say this is to say no more than that Shakespeare was writing a different kind of play in the last stage of his career, for which his previous use of images was inappropriate. And although Caroline Spurgeon maintained that '*Pericles* alone of the romances has no sign of any running "motif" or continuity of picture or thought in the imagery',[3] image-patterns, image clusters, running motifs, continuity of picture *do* in fact have a presence throughout the play. Their emphasis is more generalised than in previous plays; they form a matrix of recurring ideas which serve the broader concerns of the play in their mythic scope.

[1] Ewbank, p. 119. Ewbank's opinion that *Ant.* predates *Per.* is not universally shared (though we agree), but it scarcely affects her argument.
[2] *The Development of Shakespeare's Imagery*, 1951, p. 180.
[3] *Shakespeare's Imagery and What it Tells Us*, 1935 (rpt 1968), p. 291. Spurgeon offers this as a 'fact sufficient in itself to throw grave doubts on [the play's] authorship'. The present discussion focusses on the consistency of the play's imagery as a task worthy in itself rather than as evidence of authorship, while we accept, with Spurgeon and with Edward A. Armstrong, that 'no two poets employ the same image clusters' (*Shakespeare's Imagination*, 1946, p. 184).

It is no surprise that the image or motif of conception and birth should be found most frequently in the play; over thirty instances through all five acts.[1] Gower, of course, sounds the note early, reminding the audience that they are people 'born in those latter times' (Prologue 11). The conception of Antiochus' Daughter is a recalled memory in which the gods had 'knit in her their best perfections' (1.1.9–12), yet a truer picture is painted in the riddle with images that associate birth with destruction and animal appetite. In keeping with the incestuous relationship, the first scene associates the 'womb' with death (108–9), a place which 'breeds' poison (134). His experience in Antioch gives rise to Pericles' melancholy thoughts, which are likened to children who 'have their first conception by misdread' (1.2.12). His unfortunate pursuit of the glorious beauty from 'whence an issue I might propagate' (1.2.72) has disappointed his hope to provide heirs who are 'arms to princes and bring joys to subjects' (1.2.73). On a more optimistic note, the occasion of Thaisa's birthday provides the setting in which Pericles wins her hand; she is 'beauty's child, whom nature gat / For men to see' (2.2.6–7). Marina's conception is blessed by Hymen, whereby a 'babe is moulded' (3.0.11); she is the creation of excellence, a good turn bestowed by nature who 'framed this piece' (4.2.112–13). Her birth, however, is Thaisa's 'travail' (3.0.52), the 'terrible child-bed' (3.1.56) and 'bearing time' (3.4.6) in the midst of the storm where the babe is offered to Pericles as 'this piece of [his] dead queen' (3.1.17). Heralded 'from the womb' in a 'blusterous birth', so 'chiding a nativity', the newborn child greets the world not as a 'prince's child' but as 'this fresh new seafarer' at the beginning of her life's journey and trials (3.1.29–35, 42): named Marina 'for she was born at sea' (3.3.13); left with Cleon and Dioniza in order to receive the princely training 'that she may be mannered as she is born' (16). Cleon's vow, that reaches to the 'end of [his] generation' (24), is juxtaposed with Pericles' vows to conceive no more heirs (28).

The juxtaposition of birth and death is found not only in the storm of the third act, but manifests itself with increasing frequency: Gower describes the attempt on Marina's life as the 'pregnant instrument of wrath' and the 'unborn event' (4.0.44–5); over Lychorida's grave, Marina laments being 'born in a tempest when [her] mother died' (4.1.18); she speaks to her would-be murderer in descriptions which recall the beginning of life: 'When I was born the wind was north . . . When was this? / When I was born' (4.1.51–7); Marina's epitaph describes her as '*Thetis' birth-child*' (4.4.41) who has been bestowed upon the heavens.

That the play has a running motif and a continuity of thought centred on birth is beyond question. It takes on an increased, evocative power in the last act where it assumes a place in the language of recognition. That which awakens the silent Pericles and makes a 'battery through his defend parts' (5.1.42) is Marina's talk of her 'derivation', how time has rooted out her 'parentage' (5.1.85, 87). When he looks at her, it is the image of the dead mother and the daughter who might have been that he sees. The vision before him, however, was 'mortally brought forth' (5.1.99). As father and

---

[1] The word 'born' has its highest frequency in the romances: it occurs 12 times in *Per.*; 11 in *Cym.*; 14 in *WT*.

daughter approach mutual discovery their exchanges are intensified with the language of birth – phrases which express the pull of familial bonds rooted in their genesis. These fall into three main categories; first those that deal with pregnancy and birth:

I am great with woe, and shall deliver weeping.   (5.1.101)

I will believe you by the syllable
Of what you shall deliver . . .   (164–5)

                          O come hither,
Thou that begetst him that did thee beget,
Thou that wast born at sea, buried at Tarsus,
And found at sea again . . .   (189–92)

The second group deals with family:

What were thy friends?   (122, 136)

                    . . . thou camst
From good descending?   (124–5)

Report thy parentage.   (126)

Thirdly, a group is concerned with parentage, and naming after birth:

                    . . . where were you born?
And wherefore called Marina?
                         Called Marina,
For I was born at sea.
                    At sea, what mother?
My mother was the daughter of a king, who died
The minute I was born, as my good nurse
Lychorida hath oft delivered weeping.   (152–7)

Thaisa was my mother, who did end
The minute I began.   (206–7)

The man who 'for this three months hath not spoken / To anyone, nor taken sustenance' (5.1.22–3) emerges from living death and withdrawal from the world as a man reborn. His rebirth is a condition of his redemption achieved by a faith which accepts the resurrected Marina. The child who was given life by the father in turn 'begets' the parent. The verbal paradox is emblematic of the mystery and wonder which resides at the core of all miracles. As Inga-Stina Ewbank so beautifully explains it, 'the words, in their particular order, speak the miracle . . . The miracle lies latent in what is happening, but it is born to us through what is spoken.'[1] In the second recognition, when mother meets daughter for the first time, the sense of the miraculous is again emphasised through the bonds that are made at the moment of birth and owned for ever:

PERICLES Look who kneels here: flesh of thy flesh, Thaisa,
               Thy burden at the sea, and called Marina,
               For she was yielded there.
THAISA [*Raises and embraces her*] Blest, and mine own.   (5.3.43–5)

---

[1] Ewbank, p. 126.

The last plays' preoccupation with birth as one of the great archetypal human myths is announced with its first extended treatment in the language of *Pericles*.

A second image-pattern or running motif, as far as we know never noticed before, occurs throughout the play; it involves food, the process of eating; feeding, satiation, and regurgitation. Pericles desires to 'taste the fruit', the 'golden fruit' represented by the Daughter of Antiochus (1.1.22, 29). She is the viper that 'feed[s] on mother's flesh' (65–6), reiterated as 'an eater of her mother's flesh', and a serpent who feeds on flowers yet breeds poison (131–4). Pericles' melancholy thoughts have 'after-nourishment' by too much care (1.2.13). Cleon describes at length the famine in Tarsus in terms of want, food, hunger, the famished, a city of former plenty whose tables were stored full 'not so much to feed on as delight' (1.4.30), savouring palates which must reinvent the sensation of taste, mothers who are ready to eat their children, so 'sharp are hunger's teeth' (1.4.46); their present state of destitution is contrasted with those cities which taste of 'plenty's cup' in their 'superfluous riots' (1.4.53–5). Pericles' ship in his mission of succour is described as something gorged, not with the bloody veins of the Trojan horse, but 'stuffed' with corn to make bread (1.4.91–3).

The image of the honey-eating drone occurs twice (2.0.18, 2.1.43–4) as an emblem of the abuse of authority and social injustice. The Fishermen's comment on society's economic and social imbalances is given in terms of the powerful who devour the less fortunate: the fishes live in the sea 'as men do a-land, the great ones eat up the little ones', (2.1.26–8); rich misers are compared by the First Fisherman 'as to a whale: ''a plays and tumbles, driving the poor fry before him, and at last devours them all at a mouthful' (2.1.28–30); such whales 'never leave gaping till they swallowed the whole parish, church, steeple, bells, and all' (2.1.31–2). The Third Fisherman in the role of sexton declares that if such a whale had swallowed him, he would have 'kept such a jangling of the bells that he should never have left till he cast bells, steeple, church, and parish up again' (2.1.38–40). The image of regurgitation continues in the Fishermen's dialogue as a desire to 'purge the land' of injustice (2.1.43), and with every repetition of the word 'cast'. The Fourth Knight's impresa expresses love as food (2.2.34; translated, it means 'Who feeds me extinguishes me'), and both Thaisa's and Simonides' nervous giddiness at the victory feast translates into a lack of appetite for food. Her food is 'unsavoury' and she rather wishes Pericles her 'meat'; Simonides cannot eat if he does not think of Pericles (2.3.28–31). Pericles is praised for the 'sweet music' which has 'never better fed' the ear (2.5.26).

The north wind 'disgorges such a tempest forth' (3.0.48), and the 'belching whale' inhabits the sea (3.1.62). The sea is a great repository of things which it feeds on and casts up again: the shipwrecked Pericles, his armour, Thaisa's coffin.[1] For Cerimon the process is benevolent: 'If the sea's stomach be o'ercharged with gold, / 'Tis a good constraint of fortune it belches upon us' (3.2.53–4). Like Pericles who fed Tarsus with his corn, Cerimon provides sustenance for those in need, calling for 'fire and meat for these poor men' (3.2.3). Only a few lines earlier at the end of the previous scene

---

[1] In Marina's epitaph, Thetis, the sea-nymph, is said to have '*swallowed some part a'th'earth*' (4.4.39).

Pericles alters his course for Tyre so that the newborn babe may have 'careful nursing' in Tarsus (3.1.79).

In the Miteline brothel the images of food and eating serve to characterise sensual pleasure and its consequence in deadly corruption. The diseased prostitutes have turned men into 'roast-meat for worms' (4.2.19–20); according to the Bawd, in Marina's new occupation 'men must feed' her as well as 'stir [her] up' (73). She is likened to a good cut of meat; since Boult has 'bargained for the joint' he may 'cut a morsel off the spit' (104–6); though her 'peevish chastity' is 'not worth a breakfast' (4.5.113) she is nonetheless a 'dish of chastity with rosemary and bays' for Boult to feed on (136–7). The kind of 'food' or sustenance the world of the brothel offers 'is such as hath been belched on by infected lungs' (149–50).

Having been a provider of much-needed food in the past, Pericles not only starves himself of nourishment, but also of human company and the sound of the spoken word.[1] In 'sorrow all devoured' (4.4.25) Pericles, who 'hath not spoken / To anyone, nor taken sustenance, / But to prorogue his grief' (5.1.22–4), now becomes the recipient of a different kind of much-needed food, in which satiation is not a sin of appetite but the desired effect of spiritual nourishment: Marina 'starves the ears she feeds / And makes them hungry the more she gives them speech' (107–8); the more she speaks the more Pericles returns to life.

The breaking of bread in communion and celebration is the essential nature of a feast, and feasts are referred to or presented in the play five times: when Hellicanus extends a courtly welcome to Thaliard (1.3.38) and when Pericles relieves the famine-stricken Tarsus (1.4.105); when the Fishermen offer their hospitality to the ship-wrecked Pericles in sharing their home where 'we'll have flesh for all day, fish for fasting-days and more, or puddings and flap-jacks' (2.1.74–5); the onstage banquet in Simonides' court (2.3) where mirth, food, and drink reflect the cohesion and good will of men; the opening of the third chorus in which the effects of 'this most pompous marriage feast' are felt by the 'o'er-fed breast' (3.0.3–4).[2]

This discussion of food as a consistent and widely diffused image-pattern in the play reveals that, like the language of birth, food takes its place in the play's larger construct of myth. As Frye declares, food, drink, bread, and wine in the structure of a quest-romance mean fertility; a quest-romance (like *Pericles*) represents the 'victory of

---

[1] Even those on board the royal ship seem to be suffering something similar to the king's predicament but in a more literal, and minor sense. Though they are 'not destitute for want / But weary for the staleness' (5.1.52–3), Hellicanus asks for provision that will refresh and therefore renew. In this respect the ship represents a microcosm of a larger emotional state of being (the request is seconded by Pericles at 248–50). Another facet of these requests for food is the essential act of charity which responds out of a sense of human obligation – a point not lost on Lysimachus:

> Oh sir, a courtesy,
> Which if we should deny, the most just God
> For every graff would send a caterpillar,
> And so inflict our province ...
> (5.1.53–6)

The image of the plant-eating caterpillar and its devastating effects recalls the famine of Tarsus and how Pericles' act of charity restored that city.

[2] Another reference to a marriage celebration (that of Marina and Lysimachus) is made at 5.3.76.

fertility over the waste land',[1] in which the fullness of charity, love, and spiritual renewal conquer their destitute opposites.

There are other recurring image-patterns and running motifs in *Pericles*; too many for detailed discussion here, but worth cursory and perhaps stimulating mention. The word 'breath' is frequently used as a substitute for the act of speaking, or invoked as an image of life and the living.[2] Burial or the act of burial forms a recurring thought; so does the frequent use of the words 'casket', 'tomb', 'grave', 'chest', 'coffin', 'coffer', 'hearse'.[3] There are over twenty-five instances of 'eyes', 'tears', 'weeping',[4] which generate an emotional momentum throughout the action; jewels[5] are used to describe royal attributes, eyes, and chastity, as well as forming part of the contents in Thaisa's coffin; there is also an evocative use of the word 'wonder' especially when it is applied to a daughter (Antiochus' Daughter, Thaisa, Marina).[6]

The point of this discussion has been to show first, that the various styles of the play reflect a coherent dramatic purpose in a way that a traditional 'literary' evaluation has overlooked; and second, that despite the play's linguistic variety, there are key image-strands running through it which further enhance its theatrical coherence.

ROMANCE: THE DIFFERENT WORLD OF THE LAST PLAYS

Although Shakespeare's last plays are usually classified as 'romances', and though the word was long in existence before Shakespeare wrote, as Stanley Wells points out 'it occurs in none of his writings. The Elizabethans generally found little use for it, and so far as I know it was never used to describe a play.'[7] To the compilers of the First Folio, 'romance' was not a descriptive category for any of Shakespeare's plays: *The Winter's Tale* and *The Tempest* appeared among the 'comedies', and *Cymbeline* with the 'tragedies'. As Polonius' blather over his list of play-types (*Ham.* 2.2.396–400) confirms, the use of labels to describe dramatic genre can create confusion and absurdity. For Sir Philip Sidney, as for many more recent critics, romance's improbability and remoteness from reality formed the basis of his famous attack on the plays of his time which violated the neo-classical unities:

For where the Stage should alway represent but one place, and the uttermoste time presupposed in it, should bee both by *Aristotles* precept, and common reason, but one day; there is both manie dayes and many places, inartificially imagined . . . where you shall have *Asia* of the one side, and *Affricke* of the other, and so manie other under Kingdomes, that the Player when he comes in, must ever begin with telling where he is, or else the tale will not be conceived. Now you shall

---

[1] *Anatomy*, p. 193. Its most obvious emblem is the famine-stricken Tarsus which is relieved by the food Pericles brings.

[2] 1.1.47, 1.1.100, 1.1.161, 1.4.15, 1.4.20, 2.1.6, 2.3.95, 2.4.28, 3.2.90–2.

[3] 1.4.50, 2.1.71, 2.4.12, 3.1.59–60, 3.2.71, 5.1.160, 191, 5.3.41; 1.1.78, 1.2.5, 2.1.10, 2.3.45, 2.4.30, 3.1.66–7, 70, 3.2.48–50, 3.4.2, 4.3.41, 5.3.21.

[4] 1.1.100, 1.4.14, 20, 52, 55, 85, 88, 2.3.24, 3.1.38, 3.2.95–9, 3.3.38, 4.1.11, 40, 77, 4.2.96, 4.4.26, 5.1.96, 101, 157, 173, 181, 184, 5.3.35.

[5] 2.1.142, 2.2.12, 2.3.35, 2.4.53, 3.1.66, 3.2.96–8, 3.4.1, 4.5.140, 5.1.106, 5.3.22.

[6] 1.2.74, 1.4.26, 2.2.7, 2.3.60, 3.2.93, 3.3.7, 4.0.11.

[7] 'Shakespeare and romance' in D. J. Palmer (ed.), *Shakespeare's Later Comedies: An Anthology of Modern Criticism*, 1971, p. 117.

have three Ladies walke to gather flowers, and then we must beleeve the stage to be a garden. By
and by we heare newes of shipwrack in the same place, then we are too blame if we accept it not
for a Rock . . . Now of time, they are much more liberall. For ordinarie it is, that two yoong
Princes fall in love, after many traverses she is got with childe, delivered of a faire boy: he is lost,
groweth a man, falleth in love, and is readie to get another childe, and all this in two houres
space: which howe absurd it is in sence, even sence may imagine . . .[1]

This diatribe long predates *Pericles* or any other of Shakespeare's last plays, but his
hostile views were still current (especially in Jonson). Certainly, what Sidney says
applies to *Pericles*, and actually provides a way of entry into the kind of dramatic world
the romances inhabit.

Prose and verse romances were cultural commonplaces in the Middle Ages and
Renaissance, culminating in such English extremes as Spenser's immense *Faerie
Queene* or Nashe's *Unfortunate Traveller*. They share recognisable characteristics,
listed by Sidney as reasons for their theatrical unsuitability; the style may be high or
vulgar, the theme profound or scurrilous. While Shakespeare's last plays fit into this
category, they have a dimension which sets them apart from romance as normally
described. Towards the end of his career Shakespeare's dramatic imagination seemed
occupied with a quality of human experience that transcends the boundaries of comedy and tragedy in a vision of the world where verisimilitude plays little or no
importance. The common characteristics of the last plays have been well discussed
elsewhere.[2] In the remote and improbable world of romance the most profound human
experiences are shaped into the articulating myths of human existence: birth, love,
suffering, loss and finding, death, time, reconciliation and restoration, resurrection
and redemption. Shakespeare's preoccupation with these myths reveals in varying
degrees the ascendancy of spirit over literal sense, whereby the re-enactment of the
incredible compels belief. The impression received by the audience – as if the action
is in the world but not of it – is part of the strangeness created in the romances, a
strangeness that leads ultimately to understanding in the recognition of higher truths.
The happy endings, the idealised worlds thus miraculously created, are not an escape
from reality but images of life as it strives to be. Invert the postulates of Sidney's attack
and they more than accurately depict what the romances accomplish by means of
remoteness and improbability beyond what 'even sence may imagine'. The appeal to
the sense of wonder which the last plays make is, precisely, to arrive at the familiar and
know it for the first time. 'To sing a song that old was sung' (Prologue 1) is perhaps the
best way of seeing the last plays as a return to origins and the rediscovery of eternal
truths. Although their presentation involves revisiting the past, the great myths are
shown in these plays to be necessary (in the philosophers' sense), not contingent upon
the plot: they are truths that must and will reveal themselves, never mind the circum-

---

[1] *The Defence of Poesie*, in Albert Feuillerat (ed.), *Philip Sidney, Prose Works*, 1963, III, 38. Of course, as Frye
observed, once the postulates of romance have been established there are no rules of probability violated,
Anatomy, p. 33.
[2] The shared characteristics of *Per.*, *Cym.*, *WT*, and *Temp.* are discussed in Hoeniger pp. lxxi–lxxiv, and
J. H. P Pafford's Arden edition of *WT*, 1963, pp. xxxvii–l.

stances.¹ The recognition scene of *Pericles*, the recovery of Cymbeline's three children, Hermione's 'statue' coming to life, and the 'brave new world' (*Temp.* 5.1.183), seen for the first time through the eyes of Miranda's wonder, are the manifestations of intense realities: the means by which the numinous is made evident, and the invisible, palpable.

Finally, a caution. The idea, frequently expressed, that Shakespeare was 'experimenting' in new dramatic forms in his last plays, while true, is misleading in two respects. First, it undervalues the extent to which all Shakespeare's plays – indeed, all great works of art – are experimental. Great artists, though they may use the same subjects, do not repeat themselves. Secondly, there is a faintly supercilious way the term 'experimental' tends to be used, that implies some of these 'experiments' are failures, an impression we are decidedly anxious *not* to give.

PERICLES: 'THE PATTERN OF PAINFUL ADVENTURES'
To speak of 'characterisation' in *Pericles* in the traditional sense is to set off in a wrong direction, to miss the larger, more symbolic aspect of romance that has little use for complex and ambiguous personalities: Pericles is not Prince Hamlet. In the world of *Pericles* the heroes are valiant, the heroines virtuous and beautiful, the villains villainous, the gods and fortune powerful and omniscient. Moral action and character are pictures of simplicity like pieces on a black and white chess board, and the vagaries in the fortunes of the hero are resolved on the level of symbolic and thematic action rather than on the level of plot and character. As Eliot said, the writer has 'seen through the dramatic action of men into a spiritual action which transcends it'.² The episodic nature of the play, the ebb and flow of good and bad fortune, produce a pattern of multiple adventures through which the meaning of Pericles' life attains fulfilment.

As advertised on the title page of Twine's novel, the story's merit lies, like any good romance, in 'the patterne of painefull adventures', the 'variable historie of the strange accidents', the 'uncertaintie of this world and the fickle state of mans life'. In Shakespeare these 'patterns' take on a profounder meaning than the simple catalogue of mutability or the vagaries of fortune. Like the rhythms of the sea which they imitate, the rhythms of Pericles' spiritual journey flow from love to loss, birth to death, loss to restoration, resurrection to rebirth and final redemption. By virtue of his patience and endurance throughout his pilgrim's progress from youth to age, Pericles loses a mite but gains the mountain.

The hero, first seen at the height of his adventurous love-quest, is soon disillusioned by Antiochus' incest and tyranny which both malign the worthiness of the enterprise and endanger his life. This first low point (or ebb) in his life leaves him in a melancholy

¹ Julian Barnes, in his novel *A History of the World in 10½ Chapters*, 1989, caught this concept admirably: 'the point is this: not that myth refers us back to some original event which has been fancifully transcribed as it passed through the collective memory, but that it refers us forward to something that will happen, that must happen. Myth will become reality, however sceptical we might be', p. 181.
² Quoted from an unpublished lecture in Kenneth Muir, *Shakespeare as Collaborator*, 1960, p. 83.

state, not only because of the threat Antiochus poses to Tyre, which necessitates his flight, but also because the purpose of his quest has not been realised: to provide for the succession. This importance of the heir to the prince, the child to the father, does not receive its fullest realisation until Pericles attains true love in Thaisa. In his present state of fear and melancholy Pericles is advised 'To bear with patience' (1.2.64), a quality he will increasingly assume throughout the course of his trials.[1] His next appearance, in Tarsus, is as the leader of a miraculous relief mission whose corn-bearing ships are a beacon not of war, but of charity that restores life to the dying. His mission to Tarsus is a quest, seeking to give and asking for nothing in return except what men owe to each other by human obligation: 'We do not look for reverence, but for love' (1.4.97), a fair description of the quest of his entire life's journey.

Gower's chorus at the beginning of the second Act helpfully crystallises the character of the action unfolding for the hero: Pericles is a man who must pass 'necessity', one of 'those [who] in troubles reign' (2.0.6, 7). In flight once again he suffers shipwreck and loss of everything, 'Till fortune, tired with doing bad, / Threw him ashore to give him glad' (37–8). This is the second low point ('ebb') in his fortunes, worse in degree than the first because it leaves him bereft of friends, stranded on a strange shore as what King Lear, in his encounter with the tempest, calls a poor naked wretch, the figure of 'unaccommodated man' (*Lear* 3.4.28 and 106). Unlike Lear, however, Pericles does not denounce the storm but yields to it with patient forbearance:

> Yet cease your ire, you angry stars of heaven!
> Wind, rain, and thunder, remember earthly man
> Is but a substance that must yield to you,
> And I, as fits my nature, do obey you.
>
>   .   .   .
>
> And having thrown him from your watery grave,
> Here to have death in peace is all he'll crave.   (2.1.1–11)

Pericles here offers to accept death as an easy way out of his trials, but like the blinded Gloucester in *King Lear* he must live on and through endurance earn his particular end. Fortune, who has sported with Pericles like a ball on the sea's tennis-court, nonetheless bestows the opportunity for his rescue in the form of the three Fishermen. As unaccommodated man, Pericles learns that the first necessity of the human condition is love; the man 'that never used to beg' (2.1.58) and whose act of charity saved Tarsus must now depend on the charity of the Fishermen who gladly feed, clothe, and shelter him. The second happy consequence of his shipwreck, despite all fortune's 'crosses' (2.1.109), is the restoration of his armour, a symbol of his lineage which the sea returns to him as if from beyond the grave in memory of his father.[2] With these

---

[1] The audience too is exhorted by Gower to have patience, and in this way is encouraged to bear with Pericles as he learns to bear his trials.

[2] The armour, and the recollection of his father, is a somewhat anomalous episode in the play. Great stress is placed on both in this scene, and the importance of his father recurs in 2.3, but neither is mentioned previously or subsequently.

blessings fortune adds another, that he has arrived at the opportune moment to woo Thaisa. But things have changed since Antioch. Pericles' wooing of Thaisa is

characterized not by daring and aspiration (as was the other) but by a profound humility and crowned with unexpected success. We are watching something like a parable of human fortune, with strong moral import at every turn.[1]

Despite the 'dejected state wherein he is' (2.2.46), Pericles places his hopes in the fortune that Thaisa's love represents; his motto *In hac spe vivo* is an expression, not of chivalric ambition as are the other Knights' impresas, but of a simple faith in the love that gives life. Fittingly, the fruition of his fortunes is the birth of his child.

No sooner does Antiochus' threat disappear and everyone is set for a joyful return to Tyre than a second storm at sea imposes a yet severer trial for Pericles to endure. The death of his wife in childbirth provokes Pericles to demand an explanation from the gods: 'Why do you make us love your goodly gifts / And snatch them straight away?' (3.1.23–4). But to know the will of the gods is a process which (if ever successful) requires the effect of both time and patience. Twice the latter word is repeated by Lychorida: 'Patience, good sir, do not assist the storm', 'Patience, good sir, even for this charge' (3.1.19, 27). His trial is the simultaneous experience of both central human mysteries, birth and death, events which appropriately occur at the centre of the play. The griefs of his tempest – his loss of his wife, the child's loss of its mother – are translated into ritual by the priestly farewell at burial and benediction of the newborn. In this scene the pattern of his painful adventures suddenly assumes much larger dimensions than anything he has had to endure before.

Though his 'shakes of fortune' haunt him mortally (3.3.6), Pericles' response to tragic experience is resignation to a purpose yet to be comprehended:

> We cannot but obey the powers above us;
> Could I rage and roar as doth the sea she lies in,
> Yet the end must be as 'tis.   (3.3.10–12)

By vowing to conceive no more heirs, he imposes a condition of spiritual bereavement upon himself (and one contrary to his princely responsibility; see pp. 65–71); there will be no more births to come, save his own rebirth. Many years later, fortune's last blow deprives him of his daughter, 'all his life's delight' (4.4.12). Convinced by Marina's tomb and the feigned grief of Cleon and Dioniza that his child is dead, Pericles suffers a '*mighty passion*' and '*lamentation*' which devours him (4.4.22 SD.4). By representing this moment in dumb show, the play gains the effect of a grief inexpressible in words: a resignation to tears, and a stripping of outward royalty for the humility of sackcloth. The figure Gower evokes is that of a purgatorial mendicant who, by his vows 'Never to wash his face nor cut his hairs' (4.4.28), withdraws from the normality of the world into a hermit's silence. Marina's death means more than the loss of a child, a human being (severe though that loss is in itself); to the Renaissance, procreation emblematised immortality and the defeat of time (the theme of many of Shakespeare's

---

[1] *Crown*, p. 52.

sonnets): 'now that she is dead Pericles has nothing to give meaning and shape to time'.¹ It is the lowest ebb of his life, yet again he is able to endure:

> He bears
> A tempest which his mortal vessel tears,
> And yet he rides it out. (4.4.29–31)

This pattern of Pericles' painful adventures creates a picture of abiding patience and resignation, but it has been widely complained of on the grounds that it makes him appear merely passive, and therefore undramatic.² In the world of romance, patience and readiness to endure are themselves actions of the highest order, different in degree from the choices taken by characters in the comedies and tragedies. To choose patience and endurance, and thereby to accept suffering without demanding comprehension, requires willing and willed spiritual submission; the stress of doing so is great, and is itself active. Submission in this sense is not easy, but the road to redemption never is. Hermione consciously understands that 'this action I now go on / Is for my better grace' (*WT* 2.1.121–2); patience is an important 'action' found in varying degrees in all the last plays where transcendence is achieved through endurance.

Unlike Shakespeare's tragic heroes, and his other romance characters, Pericles is essentially a man without fault, a good person who does not deserve the degree of suffering and loss he experiences, but this does not make him any the less interesting.³ Uniquely among the romances, there is no initial sin in *Pericles* which can somehow be linked to, or account for, the ensuing suffering.⁴ Like the 'pattern of all patience' that Lear hopes but fails to be, Pericles succeeds, by being more like Job, sacred because he is both cursed and blessed. The human vessel chosen for chastisement must be worthy of the suffering so imposed, but that worthiness must also be proven over time. Patience then may be defined as a continual active choice of acceptance and resignation: 'We cannot but obey the powers above us' (3.3.10). Such resignation, however, is never the final word since it serves a larger purpose, described by Derek Traversi as the 'necessary prelude to the restoration of harmony made potentially richer by exposure to adversity'.⁵ Indeed, Pericles' new-found joy in the last act is felt more intensely as a result of his long tribulations, a purpose given to the action which the god in *Cymbeline* explains: 'Whom best I love, I cross; to make my gift, / The more delay'd, delighted.' (5.4.101–2).

---

¹ Peterson, p. 95.
² Hoeniger's objections (pp. lxxx and lxxxv) are typical.
³ Aristotle objected that seeing such a person falling into misery is not tragic, but morally shocking (*The Poetics*, 52b28). But of course the redemptive element, essential to the romances, does not figure largely in Aristotelian theory.
⁴ Posthumus' unjust banishment and Imogen's imprisonment in *Cym.*; Leontes' transgression of jealousy and injustice in *WT*; Antonio's usurpation of Prospero's dukedom in *Temp.* Arguments which try to suggest that Pericles is somehow tainted by the sin of Antiochus' Daughter, for which he must suffer in expiation (Knight, *Crown*, p. 38), or that Pericles' family undergoes trial because Thaisa breaks her vow to Diana (2.5.9–11) (Kenneth Muir in *Shakespeare as Collaborator*, 1960, pp. 80–1) can only be called grotesque.
⁵ *Last Phase*, p. 32.

Endurance and patience in *Pericles* are sounding notes shared between the two strangers that are father and daughter, and expressed by both in the pattern of their painful adventures:

> She speaks, my lord, that may be hath endured
> A grief might equal yours, if both were justly weighed.   (5.1.82–3)

> If thine, considered, prove the thousandth part
> Of my endurance, thou art a man, and I
> Have suffered like a girl. Yet thou dost look
> Like Patience, gazing on kings' graves, and smiling
> Extremity out of act.   (132–6)

The patience expressed in the face of his child encourages Pericles to overcome his own apparent tragic situation; but his excitement must still be tempered with patience, required of him yet this last time before the final recognition:

> MARINA   Patience good sir, or here I'll cease.
> PERICLES   Nay I'll be patient . . .   (142–3)

As in the storm at sea which forced Pericles to confront simultaneously the mysteries of birth and death, and birth in death, so those same mysteries, spiritually transfigured on the placid Miteline seashore, are now bestowed upon him as a saving grace.[1] Marina's resurrection[2] redeems Pericles from a living spiritual death by his own rebirth. The grief-stricken king who began the scene in sackcloth, barely living in a world of isolation, silence, and self-deprivation, reawakens in fresh garments to a life and world which are beyond the normal senses.[3] Having endured the rites of passage through darkness, he is allowed a beatific revelation of the divinity which shapes our ends in the music of the spheres and the theophany of Diana. The point is clear: only through trial and suffering can the door to joy be opened; without them, it would not be joy.

The rewards of suffering and patience are his recovery of Marina, and hers of him; and the reward of his obedience to Diana gives him back Thaisa. By not seeking revenge on Cleon and Dioniza, Pericles, like Prospero, chooses the 'rarer action' appropriate in one who has suffered and learned so much.[4] His final adventure to Ephesus is thus the completion of a pattern of resignation, a submission to things beyond understanding that he has revealed throughout the play. The final reunion of

---

[1] Even extreme ecstasy must be endured; the 'great sea of joys rushing upon' (5.1.187) him is similar to Gloucester's experience in death, whose heart ''Twixt two extremes of passion, joy and grief, / Burst smilingly' (*Lear* 5.3.199–200).

[2] See p. 77.

[3] The metonymic significance of disrobing and re-robing is paralleled in *Lear*: Lear 'does not cast off his clothes in order to discover his humanity, as is sometimes claimed, for the finding of himself involves the restoration of proper clothing, and when he is comforted by Cordelia, the first thing done for him is to "put fresh garments on him" (4.7.21)', R. A. Foakes, *Hamlet versus Lear: Cultural Politics and Shakespeare's Art*, 1993, p. 197.

[4] See *Temp.* 5.1.25–8: 'Though with their high wrongs I am strook to th'quick, / Yet, with my nobler reason, 'gainst my fury / Do I take part. The rarer action is / In virtue than in vengeance', and compare *AYLI* 4.3.128: 'But kindness, nobler ever than revenge . . .'

14 The resuscitation of Thaisa (Act 3, Scene 2) in Ron Daniels's 1979 production at The Other Place, Stratford-upon-Avon: Clyde Pollitt as Cerimon, Emily Richard as Thaisa

the family, the miraculous happy ending of harmony created, is more a comment on the past and an attitude to suffering than a condition of the future. Extreme ecstasy, like suffering, must also be endured:

> This, this! No more, you gods, your present kindness
> Makes my past miseries sports; you shall do well
> That on the touching of her lips I may melt,
> And no more be seen.
>   (5.3.37–40)

Such is the 'great sea of joys' (5.1.187) that nearly overwhelms mortality, an affirmation of the spirit that transcends the actions of men at the conclusion of a play where the audience too, with *their* 'patience evermore attending', is rewarded with the 'New joy' that waits on them.[1]

JOURNEYS

'Of all fictions', remarks Frye, 'the marvellous journey is the one formula that is never exhausted.'[2] *Pericles* is readily appreciated in terms of its parabolic action (so appropriate to Gower's fantastic narrative) represented by the physical and spiritual journeys that the characters make throughout the play. Nowhere else in Shakespeare's plays is

[1] Epilogue 17–18.
[2] *Anatomy*, p. 57.

there so much travel to so many places whereby life is symbolically represented as a process of journey on the map of the human heart, and no other Shakespearean hero travels so extensively as Pericles. The pattern of Pericles' adventures is represented by the journeyings in which the most profound human experiences are realised.

Movement from one place to another in Shakespeare's plays is usually a symbolic action. In the comedies, characters move into a heightened, 'other' place and return altered in the creation of a new social order, as they do in the green worlds of *As You Like It* and *A Midsummer Night's Dream*; and places like Belmont (*The Merchant of Venice*) and Illyria (*Twelfth Night*) afford a different context of experience which may provide escape from harsher realities. In the tragedies, a movement of the action from one location to another, as from Venice to Cyprus in *Othello*, may provide a context for the tragic event, or alteration in point of view as occurs with Hamlet's return from England. *Antony and Cleopatra* presents the most extended treatment of place-as-metaphor in the dizzying alternation of scenes between Egypt and Rome and the dialectic of two opposed world views. Beginning with *Antony and Cleopatra*, and continuing through *Coriolanus*, *Timon of Athens*, and the romances, the last stage of Shakespeare's career seems to be marked with an intense interest in geography, specifically the geography of antiquity which evokes the cradle of civilisation in the plays' Mediterranean locations: Rome, Egypt, Athens, Greece, Sicily; even Prospero's island is arrived at by way of Tunis, a place recalled in terms of the *Aeneid*. The map in *Pericles* is both geography and spiritual journey in an antique time where man's civilised origins are rooted.

From Antioch where the play begins, to Ephesus where it ends, the characters find themselves in constant transit not only between one location and another, but also between the moral extremes of action such as are represented by the physical worlds which begin and end the play: the Ephesian environment is as opposite to Antioch as Pericles' love is to Antiochus' incest. The emphasis the play places on travel and distance intensifies the vagaries of the many journeys which ultimately lead to the Temple of Diana where all that has been lost is finally restored.

The very first journey represented in the play is announced in the second line of the Prologue with Gower's own arrival from a distant past, but there are so many more that scarcely a scene goes by without someone arriving or leaving to go somewhere else, or without some reference to travel. No sooner is Pericles introduced in Antioch than the scene ends with his escape and Thaliard's hot pursuit to Tyre. Once in Tyre Pericles makes preparation for his ships' departure (1.2.49), and is advised by Hellicanus that the best solution for his problems is to 'go travel for a while' (1.2.105): an ironic understatement considering the subsequent events! Pericles 'intends' his travel to Tarsus and the scene ends with an impression of distance in the travelling letters between two countries.[1]

By the beginning of the second Act Pericles' fortunes so far can be measured in the leagues of the sea from Antioch to Tyre, from Tyre to Tarsus, and to the shores of

---

[1] Travelling messengers bring letters from Tyre to Tarsus (2.0.16 SD.3) and to Pentapolis (3.0.14 SD.3) which precipitate Pericles' departure from both places.

Pentapolis, where the image of converging distances and travel is reinforced by the Knights who have come from Sparta, Macedon, Antioch, Tyre, and two other un-specified places.[1] Back in Tyre, Hellicanus finds himself appeasing the disquieted Lords: ever the travel agent, Hellicanus suggests a chivalric journey: 'Go search like nobles, like noble subjects, / And in your search spend your adventurous worth' (2.4.50–1). As the Knights do so, the play progresses in ever-widening circles of travel incorporating greater distances that seem to include the expanse of the globe itself:

> By many a dearne and painful perch
> Of Pericles the careful search,
> By the four opposing coigns
> Which the world together joins,
> Is made with all due diligence
> That horse and sail and high expense
> Can stead the quest.   (3.0.15–21)

Inversely proportional to Pericles' fortunes, the whole concept of journey in the play now takes on a larger dimension. The image of the whole world as landscape for the quest is emblematic of Pericles' journey in the sea of life which takes away Thaisa and gives him Marina in the storm of Act 3. Even the storm is large enough to encompass 'both heaven and hell' (3.1.2). As a 'fresh new seafarer' (3.1.42) Marina's first role in life is that of voyager: her first course as prince's child is altered, and she begins to endure the vicissitudes of her life. Thaisa also becomes a solitary voyager, separated from all she knows and loves by her ostensible death; miraculously, the chest in which she is thrown overboard performs more as a seaworthy vessel than as a coffin settling to the bottom of the sea. Complete with 'passport' (3.2.65), her entry into Ephesus brings her journey in the play to an apparent close.

Once Pericles leaves Tarsus his family becomes effectively separated into three in both distance and time; Gower urges the audience to keep straight and separate the strands of voyages thus far completed. Pericles remains in Tyre; Thaisa, unbeknownst to Pericles, is alive in Ephesus; Marina grows up in Tarsus and is carried off by pirates to Miteline. Pericles' next journey ends at Marina's tomb, where he is made to believe that his entire family is irretrievably lost to him. He 'Leaves Tarsus and again embarks' (4.4.27): in terms of journey the play so far is never in stasis.

The state of ignorance of each other's existence in which the characters live is a necessary element towards achieving the emotional burden of resolution reached at the end of all these travels, reached not by human plans and knowledge, but by a benign fortune which 'brings in some boats that are not steer'd' (*Cym.* 4.3.46):

> Let Pericles believe his daughter's dead,
> And bear his courses to be orderèd
> By Lady Fortune . . .   (4.4.46–8)

---

[1] A similar effect is achieved with the continental flavour of the clients 'of all complexions' who frequent the Miteline brothel: the Transylvanian (4.2.18), the Spaniard (4.2.80), and the French knight, Monsieur Verollus (4.2.83). The array of nationalities is a source of good commerce, a point not lost on Boult: 'if we had of every nation a traveller, we should lodge them with this sign' (4.2.91–2).

Driven by the winds, Pericles' ship comes to rest at anchor at Miteline where his daughter lives; more than just a place on a map, it is a port of call which gives meaning to his entire life's journey. Appropriately, the recognition takes place on a calm sea, in the environment of symbol: the place of Marina's birth, which now witnesses the rebirth of her father, represents a point of arrival which not only looks forward in time, but more important, reaches back to origins and the beginning of all things that give shape to time. In terms of human experience and wonder, father and daughter arrive where they started and 'know the place for the first time' (T. S. Eliot, 'Little Gidding', line 244). On a ship that does not move, the greatest journey is thus travelled in an instant's recognition. All roads ultimately lead not to Rome but to Ephesus, the gathering point to which all the play's journeys gravitate. That human journeying should culminate in a vision of restoration and concord, achieved after so much tempest and travel, is an affirmation of the mythic concept of journey's fortunate conclusion.[1] The audience participates in the journeys, thanks to Gower's reminder that their imagination, like ships, sail from 'bourn to bourn, region to region', travelling to 'each several clime', making short the 'long leagues' of the story's own journey in the theatre (4.4.1–6). The 'pilot' whose 'steerage' (18, 19) guides the audience's course of journey is not only Gower but their willing thoughts as well, which also enable them to participate in the final great moment of harmony.

THE SEA AND TEMPEST

As an active agent in plots involving sea voyages and shipwrecks, and as a recurring image and symbol, the sea's evocative scope is immense in its suggestiveness. It is not hard to understand why the sea had such an emblematic significance in the Renaissance; its inherent potential to represent the great antitheses in nature and life served dramatists and poets well. The sea is never far away in *Pericles*, either in the literal sense or in its symbolic associations: to ignore it is to miss the play altogether.[2] The ever-changing nature and rhythms of the sea in both tempest and calm, cruelty and kindness, reflect the human voyage through life in its severest tribulations and consummate joys.

Pericles' trials are first and always defined by, or expressed in terms of, the chaos of tempest. The sea's menacing effect is threaded throughout the language even before the first storm in the play. The first tempest wrecks Pericles' ship, swallows his possessions and drowns his men, leaving him destitute on the Pentapoline shore. The second tempest, because more devastating than the first, is given a more elaborate prelude in Gower's chorus (3.0.44–50) and is represented on stage (unlike the first which was only described (2.0.27–34)). Its cataclysmic force is such that Pericles' cries, insignificant amidst this 'great vast' (3.1.1), only assist the storm. With the apparent

---

[1] The many journeys in the play provide an emblem for the random and episodic quality of life but nonetheless lead to a point where life's deeper continuities are realised and given coherence. Peterson made a similar point, p. 80.

[2] For a discussion of the symbolic use of the sea in Shakespeare, see G. Wilson Knight, *The Shakespearian Tempest*, 1953, p. 218, and Peterson. In Knight's view, 'to analyse the tempests in *Pericles* would be to analyse the whole play'.

death of Thaisa and the 'blusterous' (3.1.29) birth of Marina, this tempest, as Pericles concedes, 'hath done to me the worst' (3.1.41). The 'watery grave' (2.1.10) that Pericles escapes in Pentapolis now becomes Thaisa's monument. The 'wayward seas' (4.4.10) bring Pericles to Tarsus and to Marina's tomb; his next voyage brings Pericles to bear a 'tempest which his mortal vessel tears' (4.4.30).

The sea is no more favourable to Marina than to her father. Her birth in a tempest robs her of her mother; her journey through life seems to her 'as a lasting storm' (4.1.19), in which the only account she has of her father is in terms of the tempest's violence (4.1.52–63).

In its negative aspects the sea thus threatens, destroys, and separates with the cruelty of indifference and the formless chaos of random fortune. But for everything which the sea destroys and takes away, an antithetical rhythm is also part of its tides: the sea provides, restores, and unites in actions which reverse the withdrawal of fortune's favours; his winning of Thaisa and conception of an heir are the best gifts of fortune which the first tempest bestows on Pericles.

The second tempest, which separates Pericles from Thaisa, forces her burial in the same sea which delivers her to Ephesus and to the one man who can bring her back to life. Like the Fishermen who restore Pericles from the sea's devastation, Cerimon's benevolent skill restores another tempest victim. The image of the sea as burial ground is superseded by its generative and creative function, the great womb of life which heralds the birth of Marina and the rebirth of her father.

The sea's benevolent tides and winds bring Pericles' ship to Miteline and reunion with his daughter; not in storm but on a tranquil sea, the recognition occurs on the day of Neptune's feast, the one day in the year when the god of the sea cannot be angry. Marina restores the sick king not as a victim of a sea-storm but as the victim of life's tempest, and so the language of the sea poignantly informs the language of recognition: birth and death in tempest are the keys which reveal name and identity. Surging waters which formerly gave rise to grief are now the tears of woe delivered weeping. Recognition produces ecstatic imagery of the 'great sea of joys' which does not destroy, but 'rushing upon' Pericles, overbears 'the shores of [his] mortality', joys that 'drown [him] with their sweetness' (5.1.187–9).[1]

The 'blown sails' now turned towards Ephesus continue the surge of the sea which finally brings Pericles back to Thaisa, and restores the mother to her child. Out of the chaos of life a new concord and harmony emerge like a calm achieved after a storm. As the unifying matrix of the play, the sea is the great backdrop or canvas whose dimensions determine the nature of the events and their significance for the characters. The 'watery element' was even in Shakespeare's time notorious for its generative as well as

---

[1] The approaching moment of recognition in *Temp.* contains similar imagery in which 'understanding' is spoken of as a sea:

> Their understanding
> Begins to swell, and the approaching tide
> Will shortly fill the reasonable shores
> That now lie foul and muddy.

(5.1.79–82)

destructive powers, an oxymoron whose dialectical oppositions, creation and destruction, are used in *Pericles* more fully and coherently than in any other play in the canon.

FAITH IN APPEARANCES

An undercurrent to the various trials and adventures throughout the play is the tension between what things appear to be and what they truly are. In *Pericles* the old dichotomy of appearances versus reality becomes an expression of the play's epistemology, the process by which the truth beneath the fictional veneer is discerned. Pericles' greatest act of faith is his choice to believe in the resurrected Marina despite what he thinks are the known facts, and despite the knowledge painfully earned from previous experience that shows trust in appearances to be dangerous. This attitude towards epistemology, carefully established and reinforced throughout the play, makes the final demand for belief all the more difficult for him to bear.

Pericles' love-quest in Antioch which began the play is the first of many illustrations of deceptive appearance: though 'clothèd like a bride', and 'apparelled like the spring' (1.1.7, 13) the Daughter's glorious beauty conceals a soul blackened with sin. Likewise, he is moved to fly from Antioch because of a better-founded mistrust of Antiochus' demeanour, which 'Seemed not to strike, but smooth' (1.2.77). Mistrust in demeanour produces a fear of 'seeming' in Pericles which follows him on his journeys, making him and his judgement vulnerable. For example, his experience in Antioch clouds his dealings with Simonides: the letter affirming Thaisa's love for him is not, as Pericles fears, Simonides' subtlety to find an excuse to execute him. Simonides obviously had no intention in his playful dissembling of making Pericles seriously anxious, but his previous experience has understandably taught him fear.

Unfortunately, he elects in his next disaster to trust the honour of Cleon and Dioniza. Perhaps in Act 2 their expressions of gratitude were genuine, but their inner envy soon enough overturns their protestations of loyalty; Dioniza becomes the murderous 'harpy' who betrays with 'angel's face' (4.3.46–7). Subsequently they conceal their guilt by a show of grief; Marina's tomb is an arranged stage-set under Dioniza's direction for the acting of 'borrowed passion' (4.4.24); and the monument and epitaph in glittering golden characters, no more than the props of 'foul show' (23). As Gower describes it, the 'vizor' for 'black villainy' is the 'soft and tender flattery' (44–5) of the epitaph: words which persuade Pericles to accept things the way they appear to be.

Not all appearances are malevolently deceptive. Cleon believes that he who 'makes the fairest show, means most deceit' (1.4.74), and while proved right about himself and his wife subsequently, he is wrong in interpreting the white flags of Pericles' fleet as a sign of duplicity. Likewise, the Lords of Pentapolis mistakenly take Pericles' shabby outward appearance as an indication of his true status. Both Simonides and Thaisa are wiser; each in his or her own way becomes enamoured of the inward man; Thaisa is rewarded with a loving husband, Simonides by the revelation of Pericles' royal identity. Pessimism, however natural, is often mistaken: Thaisa is not dead in childbirth as Lychorida announces and Pericles believes; Pericles is not lost in the storm at sea, as Thaisa concludes.

Act 4 contains a whole catalogue of misdirections. Dioniza's feigned concern for Marina hides murderous intention; Marina is mistaken in her view of Leonine; even the Pirates act in a way Leonine does not suspect. In the brothel, nothing is as it seems, or rather Marina's perceptions of it are incomprehensible to the bawds, and theirs to her. Lysimachus compromises his honourable birth and station by coming to the brothel at all; and since his disguise is apparently entirely transparent ('Here comes the Lord Lysimachus disguised' (4.5.22)), all it accomplishes is to emphasise his degradation – it reduces him to the bawds' level.

Guided by Gower through the play's epistemology, only the audience knows the difference between the way things seem to be and what they are in truth, that those who are believed dead are in fact alive.[1] By the end of the fourth act, the deceptions of appearance have been enough to make any of the characters dubious, most of all Pericles. For that very reason, the ultimate test of trusting an appearance is laid upon him: he must believe that Marina is indeed his buried daughter, and he must perform an act of faith by trusting what his eyes tell him and by believing in 'seeming':

> Falseness cannot come from thee, for thou
> Lookest modest as justice, and thou seemst
> A palace for the crownèd truth to dwell in.
> I will believe thee and make senses credit
> Thy relation to points that seem impossible . . .   (5.1.116–20)

An allusion to Christian theology seems inescapable – '*credo quia impossibile*': there is no merit in believing the obvious; to believe the impossible *because* it is impossible is the sign of grace.[2]

At the most vulnerable moment of his life, then, Pericles chooses to place his trust in appearances despite the wounding cruelty of his past experiences. The greatest faith is always required in one's weakest moments, which makes Pericles' leap all the more heroic for its effort and its inherent potential for disaster. His will to believe thus wills the miracle to happen. The play dares to *repeat* the miracle of truth defying seeming impossibility, when Pericles is led to the conviction that Thaisa, though thrown into the sea with his own arms, is the living woman who appears before him in the final scene.

Belief in the impossible is a tenet of romance and myth but also, as *Pericles* shows, a tenet of life itself, in which faith rather than knowledge leads to a higher realm of understanding. The audience, through its interaction with Gower in the Prologue, is

---

[1] Unlike the characters in the play who are misled by trusting their sight, Gower encourages the audience to rely on the judgement of their eyes to verify events: 'to the judgement of your eye / I give my cause, who best can justify.' (1.0.41–2); 'But tidings to the contrary / Are brought your eyes, what need speak I?' (2.0.15–16); 'Your ears unto your eyes I'll reconcile' (4.4.22). The audience's imaginative faith is also something determined by the sense of sight: 'In your supposing once more put your sight' (5.0.21).

[2] 'Tertullian's rule of faith', now a truism in Christian theology. What he actually wrote was 'Crucifixus est dei filius; non pudet, quia pudendum est. Et mortuus est dei filius; credibile est, quia ineptum est. Et sepultus resurrexit: certum est, quia impossibile' (i.e. 'God's son is crucified; one is not ashamed of it, because it is [so] shameful. And God's son is dead; it is believable, because it is absurd. And he rose from the grave: it is certain because it is impossible'), *De Carne Christi*, 5.4 (A. Kroymann (ed.), *Tertulliani Opera* Pars II: *Opera Montanastica*, 1954, II, 881).

made aware of this before the play proper begins: as everyone knew, Gower was dead and buried in the church just round the corner from the Globe, but his appearance in the theatre brings 'tidings to the contrary' (2.0.15) to everyone's eyes. Miracles indeed are real, they happen, at least when a Shakespeare wills them.

GOOD GOVERNMENT AND THE TRUE PRINCE

In *Pericles* the nature of good government and the role of a true prince are an important part of the play's conceptual and developmental structure. The political ideas which inform the play are not the stuff of legend taken from Gower but the commonplace notions of Renaissance political theory – the essential material of the history plays, and of varying importance in all Shakespeare's works. In the play's kings and governors – Antiochus, Pericles, Simonides, Cleon, Lysimachus – a comparative view of various governments and their relationships to the ideal is presented in terms of the way a true prince acts for the moral and material benefit of his subjects.

Antiochus' transgression is not only a matter of moral degradation but also a defilement of the nature of kingship. Antiochus betrays the divinity of the kingly office: it is tyranny when kings, who are 'earth's gods' (1.1.104), misuse their authority in vice and then attempt to conceal it. His sin not only betrays his office and corrupts his state, but also corrupts his Daughter's role as royal heir; their relationship is a perversion of primogeniture that deforms both order and degree. The play thus begins with the worst form of government, the worst kind of relationship between king, heir, and people, mired in sin and tyranny.

As well as being earth's gods, kings are also men who err and therefore need the advice of good counsellors who will neither themselves flatter nor permit flattery in others. Most of 1.2 reads like a page taken from Castiglione's *Courtier*, devoted as it is to the good relationship between prince and counsellor. Shakespeare's Hellicanus, so different from his minor counterpart in Gower and Twine, is the image of Castiglione's courtier whose responsibilities include

not to suffre [the prince] to be deceived, and to worke that evermore he may understande the truth of everye thinge, and bolster him against flatterers and raylers, and all suche as shoulde endevour to corrupt his minde with unhonest delites.[1]

The Lords of Tyre do nothing out of the ordinary beyond wishing their king 'Joy and all comfort' (1.2.34), but this evidently proves enough of a flattering indulgence to launch Hellicanus into his political lesson concerning the proper role of courtiers.[2] His freedom to give honest and open advice despite the 'dart in princes' frowns' (1.2.53) is a measure of the merits of Pericles' court, and a defining characteristic of Pericles' potential as a ruler. Pericles' recognition that it is devastating to the body

---

[1] Baldassare Castiglione, *The Book of the Courtier*, translated by Sir Thomas Hoby, 1561, *The Tudor Translations* vol. XXIII (1900), p. 337.
[2] Though not indicated in the text, there is no reason why appropriate stage action should not be used to motivate Hellicanus' protest; an extreme version of this was supplied at National 1994 where Pericles indulged himself in a long melancholy piano solo, and Hellicanus broke into the courtiers' fulsome applause.

15   Antiochus (Morgan Sheppard) orates over the enigmatical mask of the Daughter: Act 1, Scene 1, in Terry Hands's 1969 production at the Royal Shakespeare Theatre, Stratford-upon-Avon

politic when kings 'let their ears hear their faults hid' (1.2.61) makes his Tyre a direct antithesis of the cloak-and-dagger style of Antiochus' court, where a counsellor of the chamber can be additionally engaged as a hired assassin. Hellicanus' 'reproof, obedient and in order' (1.2.42) not only fits his role of wise counsellor but also provides healing balm for the king's melancholy, the true joy and comfort a prince requires from his court, not the other courtiers' empty flattery. Knowing Hellicanus' probity, Pericles can confidently bestow his authority and concern for his subjects on the 'wisdom's strength' (1.2.118) of the counsellor; and, though shaken by his misadventure in Antioch, he can leave Tyre assured of the ties binding faithful subject to loving king: 'time of both this truth shall ne'er convince: / Thou show'dst a subject's shine, I a true prince' (1.2.122–3).

Despite the warm feelings that end this scene, the image of stable, good government has not quite shown itself in the play. Yes, Pericles' 'princely charity' (1.2.99), and selfless fear for his subjects govern his decision to leave Tyre, and yes, he allows his wise courtier to guide his course, but there is something uncomfortable about a king running away from a danger which threatens his realm as well as himself. Though well meant, Hellicanus' advice is not right in the present circumstances, since it leaves Tyre without its ruler in time of peril. Although Pericles leaves his kingdom for different reasons than did Richard II, both make the same error of going abroad at a time when there is good reason not to do so. Though Antiochus' threat of war never materialises (assassination, not invasion, is his scheme), Tyre soon begins to manifest interior disorder in society's upper ranks.

The play proceeds from Tyre's insecurity to a state in crisis. The famine in Tarsus is a metonym for Cleon's impotent governance.[1] A prince's responsibilities include feeding and protecting his people: Cleon rhapsodises at considerable length about his people's starvation, without ever indicating that it should have been his business to attempt to do something about it; and as soon as Pericles' ships are sighted, Cleon instantly decides that it is an invasion fleet (despite the Messenger's attempts at reassurance), and disclaims any intention of resisting. The function of the scene, which otherwise has little point in the play (and is usually ruthlessly abridged in performance), is to show a different but, in its own way, equally disastrous condition of misgovernment: Antiochus is an incestuous tyrant; Cleon a self-indulgent idler, who unpacks his heart with words not deeds. Antioch is a police state; Tarsus is emblematically wasting away before our eyes. The relief of the famine is accomplished by Pericles, a public act of magnanimity.

By realistic criteria, this action may seem surprising, but it actually forms part of an evolving image of Pericles as a man with a public role. In Antioch, though on a semi-public mission, seeking a wife through whom he may assure the succession (1.2.69–72), he seems to have been absolutely on his own: the text gives no indication that he was attended as a prince would normally be. In isolation, then, he feared for his life and fled. In Tyre, his anxieties have left him isolated from his court and subjects (1.2.35–6); Hellicanus takes the risk of breaking into his self-imposed solitude. However, instead of leaving Tyre incognito and by stealth, which would seem a logical consequence of Hellicanus' advice, Pericles evidently travels in a fleet, on the neighbourly mission to relieve Tarsus. The beneficial actions which a prince should bestow upon his people, and which Pericles is prevented from doing for Tyre by his fear of Antiochus, he is seen to be accomplishing for Tarsus. This, actually, is the only entirely public action that Pericles undertakes in princely manner until the very end of the play; it is important in that it establishes that he is indeed capable of royal behaviour.

His magnanimity is contrasted with Cleon's ingratitude. It would be a mistake to see Dioniza's attempt to murder Marina as her iniquity, for which Cleon bears no respon-

---

[1] Cleon is not King of Tarsus, but Lord Governor, a distinction without a difference in the political world of the play.

sibility. He is equally guilty, despite his lamentations, since he has permitted a situation where Dioniza is unrestrained in her immoral purposes, and subsequently (as she scornfully predicts) he agrees to conceal the supposed murder. Like another henpecked leader, he is infirm of purpose, and despite his criticisms, concedes to Dioniza the decisions that are his alone to make. The significance of killing a royal heir is not lost on Cleon: Marina's death will terminate Pericles' lineage and thus create a barren rule (another parallel with Macbeth: see *Macbeth* 3.1.61). That this act should come at the hands of another prince, one who owes the salvation of his country to Pericles, makes the sin worse; as Cleon admits, 'of all the faults beneath the heavens / The gods do like this worst' (4.3.20–1). Yet actually it is Cleon whose generation becomes extinct. Like Antiochus' Daughter, Philoten is also denied proper inheritance of the royal right because of the parent's sin: a sin committed, ironically, in order to improve her fortunes.

The first act juxtaposes both tyrant (Antiochus) and wastrel (Cleon) with Pericles, a 'better prince and benign lord' (2.0.3), but also stresses the subjects' role in kingly rule; the king is only as strong as the loyalty and devotion of the people he governs. Believing that Tyre is a 'kingdom without a head' (2.4.35), the Lords of Tyre confront Hellicanus with their concerns for the vulnerability of the body politic without its ruler; but it is just as vulnerable when subjects fall into dissension as the Lords of Tyre do. To avert the crisis of mutiny, Hellicanus admirably succeeds in uniting the Lords in an honourable cause and draws the obvious political moral: 'When peers thus knit a kingdom ever stands' (2.4.58). Should the king return to Tyre with the Lords they will 'like diamonds sit about his crown' (2.4.53). In keeping with the play's use of jewels as an image of kingship, it is appropriate that the lustre of a king's crown is emblematised not by its precious stones but by the shining devotion of loyal subjects. Nonetheless, the Tyre to which Pericles tries to hurry home at the end of the twelve-month period is a country that 'stands / In a litigious peace' (3.3.2–3). It is, perhaps, not surprising that Pericles should have enjoyed an extended honeymoon in Pentapolis, but the plain fact is that a king's place is with his subjects, and Pericles' delay in returning creates a sense of unease.

It should be evident that the strengths and weaknesses of government, and the relationships between ruler and subject, are central to the first five scenes of the play. In 2.1, the three Fishermen of Pentapolis, not peers of the realm but humble subjects, still know what it means when order and degree are abused by social injustice (2.1.28–32). The Fishermen's political lesson concerns both the greed of the powerful and the sufferings of the weak and the poor, a portion of society of no less importance in a king's care.[1] Yet, according to the Third Fisherman, the 'good King Simonides' has not purged the land of 'these drones that rob the bee of her honey' (2.1.43–4). One of the consequences of this imbalance of wealth is that the poor have learned to 'get more with begging' than with working (2.1.59–60); as in Jacobean London, the beggars in

---

[1] Something which Lear learns in the course of the storm; as a king he has 'ta'en / Too little care' of the poor naked wretches (3.4.32–3), and on Dover Beach he condemns the powerful: 'Plate sin with gold, / And the strong lance of justice hurtless breaks' (4.6.165–6).

Pentapolis may be in real want, or may be rogues. What the Fishermen's discussion indicates is that even in a fairy-tale Elysium like Pentapolis there are things which even a good king cannot eradicate from human nature. Despite this apparent weakness in his rule, Simonides deserves his title of 'good king' for his 'peaceable reign and good government'; he is in Pericles' estimation, even before he meets Simonides, a 'happy king since he gains from his subjects the name of good by his government' (2.1.90–5). Yet the criticisms remain.

When we reach Simonides' court, however, the fairy-tale style of its jousting, feasting, dancing, and so on make it a different quantity from the other royal environments so far encountered. Because its keynotes are splendour, ritual, and good nature, it seems exempt from serious consideration as an exemplification of rule in society. Simonides' principles are apt for the fairy-tale role: he is a lover of honour who judges men by their inner worth; he delights in generous hospitality, the good will of fellowship, and the harmony of the civilised arts. No wonder Pericles finds in him an emblem of true kingliness, a 'model which heaven makes like to itself' (2.2.11), and who reminds Pericles of his own father:

> Yon king's to me like to my father's picture,
> Which tells in that glory once he was,
> Had princes sit like stars about his throne,
> And he the sun for them to reverence;
> None that beheld him, but like lesser lights
> Did vail their crowns to his supremacy . . .
>
> (2.3.36–41)

Yet even in these friendly surroundings, Pericles conceals his royal lineage and title. True royalty, however, can never be really hidden; Pericles' valour at arms, his conduct in Simonides' court, his proficiency in the arts, and his courage in the face of Simonides' dissembled threat all make it easy for Simonides to recognise the signs of inherent royalty (2.5.76–8).

This is one of the recurring motifs in the last plays: the king's heirs, whether or not they know their degree, nonetheless manifest their royalty: Cymbeline's sons, Imogen, Perdita, and Ferdinand all reveal 'how hard it is to hide the sparks of nature' (*Cym.* 3.3.79): the qualities of a true prince which are both inherited and learned. Like her father before her, Marina reveals the essence of who she is; and Gower tells us that she shares her father's gift in 'music's letters' (4.0.8), and that in her the 'grace' of princely education 'makes high both the art and place / Of general wonder' (4.0.10–11).

The fact that Lysimachus does not instantly perceive her princely nature is a danger-signal: in the early stages of corruption by vice, he is slower on the uptake than was Simonides of her father. Once deterred from his lustful designs on her, he recognises that her 'training hath been noble' (4.5.104); later he believes that 'her sweet harmony, / And other chosen attractions' (5.1.40–1) will be appropriate physic for the sick Pericles (he means her other artistic accomplishments, *not* her physical beauty). Yet even at that point he has not really recognised what she is: he tells Hellicanus that

She's such a one, that were I well assured
Came of a gentle kind, and noble stock,
I do wish no better choice and think me rarely to wed.   (5.1.63–5)

As we have noted (p. 64) Lysimachus degrades himself and his office by sharing the moral gutter of the brothel with his unwholesome subjects. Unlike Hal/Henry V, or the Duke of Vienna in *Measure for Measure*, who can walk unrecognised among their people, Lysimachus is instantly identified by the bawds; like Hal he compromises his princely dignity by encouraging the inhabitants of the stews; and like the Duke, he has allowed the brothels of Miteline to flourish. His moral failings as a ruler are not in the same class as those of Antiochus and Cleon. Lysimachus, his government, and his city are redeemable and will be redeemed by Marina's virtue and nobility; but he and his country are saved just in time.

Pericles himself has fallen far from royal responsibility, too. Although the 'realistic' objections to his behaviour since 3.4 are wide of the point, there is a criticism of Pericles implied in the way Gower's focus abandons him, as he himself abandons Marina. Just as Pericles neglected his kingdom, leaving it in the care of Hellicanus, the royal heir is now neglected, left in the care of much less reliable deputies. His reactions to the pageant of her burial put on by Cleon and Dioniza are understandable, but improper on the part of a king: his withdrawal into something like catatonia, as described by Hellicanus in 5.1, is an extreme version of the kind of dumbfounded inertia that overwhelms Henry VI and Richard II when events become beyond them. Even more sinister, it suggests a development of the kind of impotence revealed by Cleon in 1.4, the final failure of a king to do anything at all. Clearly, this is a disastrous state for all those who depend upon the maintenance of rule.

Marina, by obliging her father to recognise her identity, rescues Pericles from this state of inanition: more, the recognition is also that between king and royal heir, a restoration of time's continuance and stability in the bond of primogeniture. As the language of recognition slowly reveals the familial identities, so too the royal identities carefully emerge as an important part of the process. Marina's 'derivation was from ancestors / Who stood equivalent with mighty kings' (5.1.85–6); her name was given to her by 'one that had / Some power, [her] father, and a king' (145–6); her mother 'was the daughter of a king' (155). In a last effort to convince him of her story's truth, Marina speaks her father's name for the first and only time in the play: 'I am the daughter to King Pericles / If good King Pericles be' (175–6), a moving moment which asserts her title and right in the presence of her father. Not just the child restored to Pericles, Marina is the 'heir of kingdoms, and another like / To Pericles [her] father' (202–3), the 'very princess' (213). The harmony restored manifests the happy ending but its political implications are more serious than usual for a fairy-tale. Right of rule as passed on to the heir, the continuance of the kingly office and royal line, the security of a nation which rests 'upon the king' – these were very real preoccupations of Shakespeare's time that found expression repeatedly in his plays.

Like Leontes, who was made to learn what a kingdom is without an heir, Pericles also suffers the loss of self without Marina, without the heir which gives meaning to his role as king. Part of the harmony restored at the end of *The Winter's Tale* is a result of finding that which had been lost from Sicilia's political structure, and which is re-established with Perdita's restoration to her right: a revisitation of the endings of *Pericles* and *Cymbeline* in the recoveries of the royal heirs. It is only at the end of these plays that the image of true political order is, not so much restored (for that would imply it was there to begin with), as presented for the first time with a sense of wholeness. Nowhere in *Pericles* is that political wholeness achieved until the last few lines of the play in which Pericles paints a picture of the future in terms of good government: he and Thaisa will rule in her father's kingdom now that, since Simonides' death, Pentapolis is without a head; and their children will take their rightful place as sovereigns of Tyre. This final world picture of order includes within it the proper fulfilment of Pericles' kingly role, and the marriage of princes whose responsibility is to propagate more heirs – the cornerstones of the foundations of good government ruled by the true prince. It is also worth remarking that in the play, unlike the sources, there is no stress laid upon the punishment of offenders: in the Epilogue Gower mentions that their populace rose against Cleon and Dioniza, but the other assorted nasties are simply ignored; there is a splendid sense of magnanimity in this turning of a fresh leaf on which only good words will be written.

MUSIC

Music is of central significance in the romances in two ways. First, a great deal of music is actually performed; secondly, the emblematic function of music as symbol of the entire universe as a tuned instrument, rendered discordant by human sin, is frequently evoked to illustrate the plays' process from disorder to new harmony. Both uses are freely deployed in *Pericles*,[1] often yoked together for combined theatrical and dramatic effect. So, in the first scene, Antiochus calls for music to accompany his Daughter's entry; but having penetrated the meaning of the riddle, Pericles moralises the implications to her:

> You are a fair viol, and your sense the strings,
> Who, fingered to make man his lawful music,
> Would draw heaven down and all the gods to hearken;
> But being played upon before your time,
> Hell only danceth at so harsh a chime.   (1.1.82–6)

A more comfortable illustration of the relationship between music and social order occurs at the banquet in 2.3, where first there is a 'soldiers' dance' (90), a no doubt noisy affair but one which aurally might exemplify what Fluellen in *Henry V* calls 'the

---

[1] A list of the directions for music, taken from the text of the Riverside Shakespeare, is to be found in *A Shakespeare Music Catalogue* (Bryan N. S. Gooch and David Thatcher, 1991, II, 1283). There are many other places in the play where music would be appropriate, even though not specified in the text. It is perhaps a reflection upon the uncertainties concerning authorship that so little music inspired by *Per.* has been written: see *ibid.*, pp. 1289–91.

disciplines of the wars'; it is followed by the gentler harmonies to which Pericles and Thaisa dance their *pas de deux*, in which their mutual suitability and subsequent marriage is foretold.[1]

Pericles declares his education has been 'in arts and arms' (2.3.78), and the former is emphasised by the praises bestowed on him by Simonides for his excellence in dancing, and his 'delightful pleasing harmony' (2.5.25–7). As 'music's master' (29), Pericles is the hero who is also the artist.[2] Similarly, emphasis is given to Marina's musical accomplishments: her education in 'music's letters' (4.0.8) is chief among her virtues; her singing, Gower tells us, makes the 'night-bird mute' (26); she sings 'like one immortal', and her dancing is 'goddess-like to her admirèd lays' (5.0.3–4). The prince who performs music and dances emblematises in his or her person the universal harmonies to which human government aspires.

Music is also required for its thaumaturgic properties. In the resuscitation of Thaisa, Cerimon calls for 'rough and / Woeful music' (3.2.85–6) as part of his arsenal of medical knowledge whereby a patient in a coma can yet be restored to life. Although aided by the gods, Cerimon is not, as he himself stresses, a magician, but what would now be called a naturopath; and one of his chief aids, called upon twice, is the right kind of stimulating music.[3] Likewise, it is Marina's 'sweet harmony' (5.1.40) which Lysimachus believes may offer a remedy for the comatose Pericles. Her music is 'a goodly present', a 'prosperous and artificial feat' in the administration of 'sacred physic' (5.1.61–70).[4] Though the text indicates that Marina sings, the song lyric did not find its way into Q;[5] nonetheless the build-up it receives is sufficient to indicate that the song was expected to have a dramatic effect in the process of Pericles' revival.

---

[1] A dance shared between a man and a woman held a symbolic significance for the Elizabethans. See Thomas Elyot's *The Boke Named the Governour*, 1531: 'It is diligently to be noted that the company of man and woman in daunsing, they both observinge one nombre and tyme in their mevynges, was nat begonne without speciall consideration, as well for the necessarye conjunction of those two persones, as for the intimation of sondry vertues: whiche be by them represented. And for as moche as by the joynyng of a man [and] a woman in daunsinge may be signified matrimonie, I could in declarynge the dignitie and commoditie of that sacrament make intier volumes: if it were nat so communely knowen to all men', (ed. Donald W. Rude, 1992, pp. 92–3).

[2] Much is made by the Wilkinsisers of the oddness that Simonides declares himself 'beholding to you / For your sweet music this last night' (2.5.24–5), when so far as Q is concerned, no such music is performed; yet there is in *PA* a page describing such a musical episode. However, even Oxford admits that a dramatist might use a reference such as Simonides' 'as a *substitute* for the performance itself (in order to indicate Pericles' musical skills without having to display them)', *Companion*, p. 558.

[3] Shakespeare makes a significant departure from his sources at this point; in Gower and Twine, music does not play a role in Thaisa's revival. However, all recent directors seem determined to ignore the text and make Cerimon some sort of witch-doctor. See Molly Mahood's excellent discussion beginning 'Cerimon is no necromancer': *Bit Parts in Shakespeare's Plays*, 1992, p. 19.

[4] A biblical parallel with Marina's mission is David's cure of King Saul by the power of music in 1 Samuel 16.14–23. David alleviates the king's distempered spirits with the music of the harp; in Gower, Marina both sings and plays the harp.

[5] John Henderson Long notes that 'this scene provides one of the few instances where a song lyric is missing from a Shakespeare play', *Shakespeare's Use of Music: The Final Comedies*, 1961, p. 45. It is scarcely credible that the deplorable and wholly inappropriate lyric found in *PA* can have been that used in the performance at the Globe.

In the other late plays, moments of similarly great intensity are heightened by association with special music. 'Solemn music' accompanies Posthumus' vision of his dead family in *Cymbeline* (4.4); the final image of restoration and reunion in that play is defined as a universal concord: 'The fingers of the pow'rs above do tune / The harmony of this peace' (5.5.466–7). Paulina calls for music to 'awake' Hermione's statue. Just before he renounces his magic, Prospero's last extraordinary effort is to require 'some heavenly music' that will work upon the irrational senses of the courtiers' minds; when they awake it is into a world of clearer understanding and reconciliation.

The actual importance of music in the recognition scene in *Pericles* is somewhat different, and even more profound. Marina's singing does not revive Pericles because while music is efficacious in the revival of someone far gone in physical illness, Pericles is sick in his soul, not his body; he is not in the same condition as Thaisa was, who as a victim *in extremis* needed the musical stimulation to penetrate and reawaken her moribund senses. It is not Marina's music, but her words, that Pericles needs to heal him. Only when her resurrection has been achieved in language is Pericles led to the next stage of his spiritual journey by music that is heavenly, not mortal. Music accompanies resurrection as part of the other-worldly experience achieved in reunion and the harmony of recognition; the music of the spheres is an epiphany, an entry into the higher realm of the spiritual and invisible world. To be sure, the 'heavenly music' (5.1.226) is an aural spectacle, a divine audition which only Pericles and the audience are allowed to hear; that is as it should be. Pericles' reunion with his daughter wakens him to a higher consciousness in tune with the perfect harmony of the universe, what Knight called 'a reality beyond the reach of wisdom'.[1] The music of the spheres is different from earthly music, however beautiful. It does not awaken, or stir sensual reactions, but rather *entrances*: it conveys one into a holy state wherein the divine becomes perceptible, the supernal prelude to the theophany, Pericles' vision of Diana. Just as the condition upon which joy can exist is the experience of suffering, so the experience of the music of the spheres is a *Verklärung*, whose essential preparation has been the Wagnerian music of the storms that came before.

To say this makes it sound as if *Pericles* as a whole were an opera; and in one important sense this is close to the truth. In the first lines of the Prologue, Gower presents the forthcoming action in terms of song: its music a part of the antique tradition of storytelling sung on special occasions. It is thus not merely fanciful to perceive the play as a whole to be precisely that song.[2] Like a musical score, the play can be read in terms of sounds weaving the harmonies and dissonances of the story's various movements; its many musical stages and structures make the language and the scenography as analogues of *Sturm und Drang*, leading to a heavenly harmony that, in operatic terms, resembles the end of *Parsifal* more than any other work.

---

[1] *Crown*, p. 18. The music of the spheres is an example of what Frye described as the ecstasis of the poet's view of a spiritual world: 'Here . . . we have not a direct mimesis of life but a spectacular mimesis of it, able to look down on experience because of the simultaneous presence of another kind of vision. In drama this spectacular mimesis is attained by the help of music as well as spectacle', *Anatomy*, p. 301.

[2] Many productions take Gower literally, and set his choruses to music. See pp. 19–23.

16 Griffith Jones as Gower in Ron Daniels's 1979 production at The Other Place, Stratford-upon-Avon

RESURRECTION AND THE DOUBLE RECOGNITION

It has often been objected that the second recognition scene in *Pericles* can hardly be as moving as the first; an inherent criticism of Shakespeare's dramaturgy is implied. Indeed, the reunion of Thaisa with her family does not attain the same intensity as the recognition between Pericles and Marina.[1] In part, the structure and focus of the play contradict the notion that Shakespeare is trying to do the same thing twice and in the same way. The second recognition scene is less a dramatic let-down than a redefinition of death and resurrection on a different and more immediate theatrical level. For one thing, Pericles has less incredulity to overcome; he is predisposed both by the events of the previous scene and by his divine vision to balk less at Thaisa's reappearance. If 5.1 as a whole can be thought of as a movement of a great symphony, 5.3 is its recapitulation in simpler, shorter, sweeter major-key harmonies.

Of all the many real and presumed deaths that are referred to in the play only one occurs on stage: Thaisa's faint at the recognition of Pericles' voice and appearance. The alarmed Pericles interprets her sudden silence and swoon as death (5.3.14), making her recovery a direct mimesis of resurrection. In no other romance where resurrection plays a significant thematic role is the visual metaphor of dying and coming back to life so immediately juxtaposed and portrayed. To see Thaisa recovered, to hear the 'voice of dead Thaisa' (5.3.32), and to see her 'buried a second time' (5.3.41) within Pericles' arms, is a metonymy of the greatest Christian mystery, the 'Great miracle' (5.3.55) which Pericles speaks of. The ultimate meaning and value of this mystery is embodied in love; in the play it takes its definitive form in the restoration of Pericles' family – seen together on stage for the first time in the second recognition.

No two recognition scenes in Shakespeare are identical, though they share common characteristics. The comedies offer an image of the joy and harmony when people discover their mutual identities at the conclusion of forming new relationships. In the romances, the relationships, not new but already formed, undergo a spiritual metamorphosis through the emblem of resurrection and its saving grace[2] – a far richer and profounder experience that indeed seems to touch the very shores of immortality.[3]

---

[1] The problems of a double recognition are avoided in *WT* by having the reunion between Leontes and Perdita occur offstage, and described to the audience, thereby reserving all the dramatic intensity for the statue scene.

[2] In the last plays, characters come back to life at an alarming rate in the final scenes: Cymbeline's two sons, Imogen (*Cym.*), Perdita and Hermione (*WT*), Ferdinand (*Temp.*). The last scene in *Cym.*, for example, contains three resurrections, a great deal of the dialogue revolving around death and revival: 'Is not this boy reviv'd from death' (5.5.120), 'that sweet rosy lad / Who was Fidele' (121–2), 'But we saw him dead' (126), 'for I was dead' (259), 'which being dead many years, shall after revive' (438–9), 'For many years thought dead, are now reviv'd' (455).

[3] The profound effects of the recognition scenes in the last plays are partly due to the juxtaposition of *anagnorisis* and *peripeteia* involved in the discovery of identities; in the romances these scenes work more powerfully than similar scenes of recognition in the comedies. Inga-Stina Ewbank has made this point admirably: 'Aristotle saw the finest form of *anagnorisis* as one attended by *peripeteia*, and it is probably not fortuitous that when, in the seventeenth chapter of the *Poetics*, he came to discuss the various methods by which discoveries, or recognitions, may be brought about, nearly all his examples dealt with the discovery of the identity of persons. For in the discovery of a close relation, long thought dead or lost, recognition and reversal would seem to be particularly closely connected – dramatically virtually simultaneous, as

The difference between the comedies and the romances bears a little further examination. Perhaps the plays that most nearly anticipate the romances are *Twelfth Night* and *Measure for Measure*. In the former, both Viola and Sebastian believe the other to be drowned, and discover finally what the audience has long known. Their reunion is joyful, but the theatrical experience is tempered by the dramatist's sustaining the joke of the long delay in their recognition; we enjoy wondering how long it will take for the penny to drop. Clearly, this is not the dramatic situation in *Pericles*. Nearer to the condition is the end of *Measure for Measure*, in which Isabella really believes that her brother is dead until the Duke unveils his little surprise. The closest parallel to this, dramaturgically, is the end of *The Winter's Tale*, where Paulina likewise stage-manages the revivification of Hermione. That there is a similarity is unquestionable; that there is a difference likewise evident. In *Measure for Measure* the entire dramatic action problematises the Duke's behaviour in a way that the romances avoid; Paulina is not playing a peculiar cat-and-mouse game with Leontes, but is leading him through repentance to spiritual renewal in a way that no theologian could object to.

Metamorphosis or spiritual translation lies at the heart of the Christian concept of resurrection, and it is merely a commonplace to say that Shakespeare is using his romances as 'types' or 'figures' of that concept. A distinction might be helpful. Theologically, the only human being so far to have experienced resurrection is Jesus. The revivals of the dead that he performed, for instance the raising of Lazarus, are often described as 'resuscitations' to distinguish them from Jesus' resurrection. Resuscitation is something that happens almost daily in any major hospital, when someone who is technically dead is brought back to life by the application of medical technology and technique. But resuscitation can be also, of course, a type or figure of resurrection. Thaisa's resuscitation at Cerimon's hands is a profoundly moving event which powerfully figures resurrection, but she revives the same person that she had formerly been, and the world she awakens to is one of sadness and prolonged grief. When she 'dies' the second time she revives into a world redeemed by love, a new reality that has conquered the impossible; the 'dead queen re-lives' (5.3.60) as a person who recognises that life itself has been miraculously transformed.

The key element in Jesus' resurrection which signalled it as a different event from resuscitation was that while he was still himself, he was *changed*. Mary Magdalene does not recognise him, one of the most intensely moving passages in the Bible. At the tomb, she sees two angels:

And they say unto her, Woman, why weepest thou? She saith unto them, Because they have taken away my Lord, and I know not where they have laid him. And when she had thus said, she turned herself back, and saw Jesus standing, and knew not that it was Jesus. Jesus saith unto her, Woman, why weepest thou? whom seekest thou? She supposing him to be the gardener, saith

---

some of Shakespeare's Comedies and all of his Romances show. The emotional shift of the wonder as such is often conveyed by spectacle or music, or both; and the sense of emotion outstripping language is, as many commentators have pointed out, an essential part of the impact of Shakespearian reunion and recognition scenes. Sometimes this sense *is* the meaning', Ewbank, p. 113.

unto him, Sir, if thou have borne him hence, tell me where thou hast laid him, and I will take
him away. Jesus saith unto her, Mary.   (John 20.13–16)

Then she recognises him, but he will not allow her to touch him. There are other
stories in the Gospels that make it clear that the resurrected Jesus was somehow
different, himself but not the same: a very plausible condition for someone who has, as
St Paul says, 'put on immortality':

> And as we have borne the image of the earthy, we shall also bear the image of the heavenly. Now
> this I say, brethren, that flesh and blood cannot inherit the kingdom of God; neither doth
> corruption inherit incorruption. Behold, I shew you a mystery; We shall not all sleep, but we
> shall be changed, In a moment, in the twinkling of an eye, at the last trump: for the trumpet shall
> sound, and the dead shall be raised incorruptible, and we shall be changed. For this corruptible
> must put on incorruption, and this mortal must put on immortality.   (1 Cor. 15. 49–53)[1]

It is nothing less overwhelming than this that Shakespeare has attempted to realise
on stage, when both Pericles and Thaisa awake to new realities and are 'changed' from
their former selves.[2] The saving grace of what Pericles perceives as Marina's resurrection in turn resurrects the spiritually dead Pericles, to a new kind of life.[3] That
Marina is alive is not something new to the audience, but it is in her resurrection, as
seen through Pericles' eyes ('This cannot be my daughter, burièd', 5.1.160), that the
audience witnesses a process of spiritual transfiguration, no less an experience for
them than it is for Pericles: slow, painfully joyous, ecstatic;[4] like Pericles, we are 'wild
in our beholding' (5.1.218).

   Shakespeare's great dare indeed achieves, in these theatrical resurrections, something of the mystery and promise in Christ's own resurrection; through their secular
figuration of transformation and glory, eternal salvation is glimpsed.[5] At the same

---

[1] Both quoted from the 'Authorised', i.e. King James, version. 'It is clear from the NT that the Resurrection
was in no sense a restoration of Jesus to an earthly life as He had previously lived it; but neither was it
merely a series of visions which assured the disciples that Jesus was still alive and present with them in
spiritual power' (*Oxford Dictionary of the Christian Church*, 1974, p. 1178[a]).

[2] In describing the mythology of resurrection, we have naturally used the ideology which would have been
most familiar to Shakespeare and his audience, the Christian. While it is the most complete and rich
version of this mythology, it is not of course the only one, and those to whom it is foreign or unacceptable
can easily think of alternatives. For instance, in John Fowles's *The Magus* (1966/1977) there is a very
complete modern pagan interpretation of a myth of sin, misleading appearances, trial by suffering, and
redemption through the resurrection of a beloved which, set as it is in Greece, has a number of interesting
parallels with the play.

[3] Cyrus Hoy characterises the important roles daughters play in the last plays as 'redemptive graces' who
in one way or another 'redeem the father figure'; see 'Fathers and daughters in Shakespeare's
romances', in Carol McGinnis and Henry E. Jacobs (eds.), *Shakespeare's Romances Reconsidered*, 1978, pp.
77–88. *Per.* contrasts several parent–daughter relationships: Antiochus–Daughter, Simonides–Thaisa,
Pericles–Marina, Cleon and Dioniza–Philoten.

[4] Traversi describes the effect of the recognition as the 'vision of a new and transformed humanity which
is the true end of the whole play. Nowhere in Shakespeare's late plays, not even in *Temp.*, is the "brave
new world" of a human semblance transfigured by entry into the divinely sanctioned state of "grace" more
splendidly conveyed' (*Last Phase*, p. 38).

[5] The two recognition scenes occur under divine sanction, set as they are on Neptune's annual feast and at
the Temple of Diana, respectively. The world of *Per.*, as in the other late plays, may be dominated by
pagan gods (Neptune, Diana in *Per.*, Jupiter in *Cym.*, Apollo in *WT*) but the pagan point of reference is
a metonym for the Christian framework that can be seen operating in these plays.

time, in experiencing the restorative grace that resurrection has brought, the audience may recall the purpose of the story itself as declared in the Prologue; Gower's tale in the form of Shakespeare's play represents the 'restorative' power of art, the means of re-creation in both senses of the word.

NOTE ON THE TEXT

There is only one substantive edition of *Pericles*: the first quarto (Q1), printed by two printers, William White and Thomas Creede, for Henry Gosson in 1609. This text has what we believe to be an undeservedly bad reputation: most authorities join in condemning Q1 as a 'bad' (i.e. memorially reconstructed) text. It is certainly true that it shares many features with the other Shakespearean quartos such as the first quartos of *King Lear*, *Hamlet*, or *Romeo and Juliet*, traditionally regarded as 'bad' (though most scholars now believe *King Lear* Q1 (1608) at least to have been printed from the author's manuscript). These features include massive mislineation, the printing of verse as prose and vice versa, all sorts of verbal errors, inconsistencies, and mistakes in the stage directions, and very peculiar punctuation and spelling.

Unlike the other Shakespearean plays that appeared in 'bad' quartos, however, *Pericles* was not subsequently published in the First Folio of 1623, so if the text of *Pericles* Q1 is claimed to be corrupt, it is not because its readings can be shown to be corrupt by comparison with some allegedly better text, but rather by some absolute standard (e.g. 'this reading simply cannot be right'). Although Q1 was reprinted many times, no different version of the text was issued in quarto form – as was the case with both *Hamlet* and *Romeo and Juliet*, where a different, apparently superior, text was published by another stationer shortly after the first quartos appeared, and *King Lear*, which appears in considerably different form in the First Folio. The first quarto of *Pericles* has more in common with *King Lear* Q1 than with any other Shakespearean quarto, and in our view is most likely to derive from a similar source.

The reliability of Q1 has been further brought into question by the uncertainties generally felt concerning its authorship, and by the existence of George Wilkins's novella *The Painfull Aduentures of Pericles Prince of Tyre*, published the year before Q1, and apparently recalling the play as it was performed on the stage by the King's Men.

Pericles was not included in a Shakespeare collection until the Third Folio of 1663–4. In such circumstances of uncertainty, virtually all editors since the eighteenth century have yielded to the temptation to emend Q1 very freely, often, in recent years, by importing material from *Painfull Aduentures* (see Abbreviations and Conventions, above, p. *x* and Introduction, pp. 8–10). Such editions, which begin by presuming the Q1 text corrupt, in effect begin by campaigning against it, often unjustifiably emending what can actually be shown to make sense.

Our edition takes the opposite approach. We believe that the case for Q1's being memorially reconstructed is very much weaker than its proponents admit. There seems to be just as good a case for believing it to be based upon incompletely revised draft papers, written by the author or copied from authorial papers by a scribe or scribes. If *Lear* Q1 is indeed derived from 'foul papers', then, in our view, so is *Pericles* (see Textual Analysis, pp. 197–210 for discussion). Our edition is conservative: where

Q1's reading can be defended, we do so, emending only when forced to admit defeat. Very little indeed has been taken from *Painfull Aduentures*, which we regard as highly unreliable.

We do not claim that this edition presents *Pericles* as it was staged by the King's Men (i.e. in its fully realised theatrical form) because we consider this form unrecoverable; our text aims at presenting the pre-theatrical document which was used as printers' copy for Q1 in a cleaned-up form, together with such additions to the staging as would immediately have suggested themselves to the King's Men's bookholder.

In accordance with the principles of the series, spelling and punctuation have been modernised as far as possible in accordance with late twentieth-century practice.[1] Characters are identified in speech headings by name rather than rank (e.g. SIMONIDES rather than KING) and the spelling of names in speech headings is regularised.[2] Additions to stage directions in the text are placed in square brackets. The collations at the foot of the page record the substantive departures from Q1.

Each collational entry begins with the line number and the *lemma* (a word or phrase from the text, or a reference such as SD, meaning stage direction). The lemma is followed by a square bracket, and the source of the reading (i.e. the text or editor in which the reading was first printed). While it is not normal editorial practice to collate rejected readings where the edition follows the copy-text (Q in this case), we have done so quite frequently when other editors' emendations have been accepted in recent editions: in these instances, the rejected readings are listed chronologically. Sometimes the term *conj.* appears in the collation: this means an editor has *conjectured* that the reading is correct, a conjecture not actually printed until some later edition; both the editor who adopted it, and the author of the conjecture are given. Readings originating in this edition are collated as *This edn*. The term *subst.* in a collation entry means that our reading is *substantively* the same as our source, but may differ from it, for example, in spelling or punctuation.

Where prose was printed as verse, or verse as prose, we include this information in the collation, together with the name of the editor who first proposed the lineation we adopt. Where verse has been mislined in Q1, we include the original lineation in the collation. Where a single verse line is shared by two speakers, that is where the second speaker completes a line, the second speaker's line is indented or 'stepped'.

[1] Most of the edition's punctuation is based on the formal, grammatical, norm of the late twentieth century. In two scenes in the play in particular, however, these norms seemed inappropriate and contrary to the linguistic texture of the writing: the 'common', colloquial speech of the bawds in the Miteline brothel (4.2 and 4.5). In these scenes, the characteristic prose rhythms of Cockney speech were caught well by Q's punctuation, which we have consequently on the whole retained, since we felt unable to improve on it.

[2] Proper names are regularised, based on the commonest spelling in Q, unless there is a metrical reason for retaining a different form (e.g. 'Hellicane' at 2.0.17, instead of the usual 'Hellicanus').

Pericles, Prince of Tyre

LIST OF CHARACTERS
In order of appearance

GOWER, *as Chorus*
ANTIOCHUS, *King of Antioch*
PERICLES, *Prince of Tyre*
DAUGHTER *of Antioch*
THALIARD, *a lord of Antioch*
HELLICANUS, *a lord of Tyre*
3 LORDS *of Tyre*
ESCANES, *a lord of Tyre*
CLEON, *Governor of Tarsus*
DIONIZA, *wife to Cleon*
LORD, *of Tarsus*
3 FISHERMEN *of Pentapolis*
SIMONIDES, *King of Pentapolis*
THAISA, *daughter to Simonides*
3 LORDS *of Pentapolis*
FIRST KNIGHT, *of Sparta*
SECOND KNIGHT, *of Macedon*
THIRD KNIGHT, *of Antioch*
FOURTH KNIGHT
FIFTH KNIGHT
MARSHAL
LYCHORIDA, *nurse to Marina*
2 SAILORS
CERIMON, *a lord of Ephesus*
SERVANT *to Cerimon*
PHILEMON, *a servant to Cerimon*
2 GENTLEMEN *of Ephesus*
LEONINE, *a servant to Dioniza*
MARINA, *daughter to Pericles and Thaisa*
3 PIRATES
PANDER
BOULT, *a servant to the Pander*
BAWD, *wife to the Pander*
2 GENTLEMEN *of Miteline*
LYSIMACHUS, *Governor of Miteline*
LORD, *of Miteline*
The Goddess DIANA
[*Lords, Gentlemen, Sailors, Pirates, Poor Man, Attendants, Servants, Messengers, Companion Maid to Marina*]

Notes

A list of characters first appeared in F3, as 'The Actors names', with additional descriptive phrases: Antiochus is 'a *Tyrant* of Greece' followed by 'Hesperides, *Daughter* to Antiochus' (a pardonable misapprehension: see 1.1.28); 'Philoten, *Daughter* to Cleon' is also included, although in fact she is only mentioned, and does not appear in the play. Modifications and corrections were made by Rowe and Malone. Most of the names derive from Book VIII (lines 251–2036) of Gower's *Confessio Amantis*, the play's primary source. Pronunciation of the names and places is given in brackets, in both the International Phonetic Alphabet, and in a do-it-yourself form. The stressed syllable is *preceded* by the stress-mark '. For the different locations of the play's action see map facing p. 1.

GOWER ('gaʊə; 'Gow-er not Go-er) A resurrection of the fourteenth-century poet, John Gower (?1330–1408), whose version of the Apollonius of Tyre story is told in *CA* (1390s), which Shakespeare used as his main source for the play. See Introduction, pp. 27–36 for a discussion of the Chorus.

ANTIOCHUS (æn'taɪəʊkəs; An-'tye-oh-kuss) History records seven kings of Syria with the name of Antiochus between 324 and 129 BC. Antiochus the Great, referred to by Gower at Prologue 17, reigned 223–187 BC. It is highly unlikely that Shakespeare knew anything about the historical figure other than what little information he found in his sources, much less that he was attempting to depict him with historical accuracy. In *CA* he is 'the great Antiochus, / Of whom that Antioche toke / His firste name' (282–4); in *PPA* he is 'the most famous and mightie king Antiochus, which builded the goodly citie of Antiochia in Syria, and called it after his own name, as the chiefest seat of all his dominions' (cf. Prologue 18–19). As the story of his death indicates (see 2.4.7–12) he seems to be connected with Antiochus of Syria who is one of the Antichrist figures of the Bible (see 2 Maccabees 9).

ANTIOCH ('ænti:ɒk; 'An-tee-ock; usually three syllables but sometimes two: 'æntjɒk; 'Ant-yock (see 1.2.7)) 'Antiochia' (*PPA*); present-day Antakya on the River Orontes in Turkey, founded c. 300 BC by Seleucus I Nicator who named it after his father, Antiochus (presumed to be a Macedonian noble). In the first century AD Antioch was the third-largest city of the Roman empire and capital of the proconsular province of Syria.

PERICLES ('pɛrɪkli:z; 'Per-ik-leez) Called 'Apollinus' (*CA*), 'Apollonius' (*PPA*); the name of the hero in all previous versions of the story; Shakespeare is the first narrator of the story to change the name of the central character (see pp. 1–8). The name may have appealed to the dramatist for its Latin association with peril (*periculum*) or because it simply fitted a verse line better than Apollonius.

TYRE ('taɪə; 'Tye-r), also Tyrus ('taɪrəs; 'Tye-russ) 'Tyrus' (*PPA*); an ancient Phoenician trading city on the coast of Syria; present-day Tyr in Lebanon.

DAUGHTER *of Antiochus* Not named in either source; simply referred to as the 'daughter' (*CA*), 'the Ladie' (*PPA*).

THALIARD (probably 'tæli:ja:d; 'Tal-ee-yard) 'Taliart' (*CA*), Antiochus' privy counsellor; 'Taliarchus' (*PPA*).

HELLICANUS (hɛlɪ'keɪnəs; Hell-ick-'ay-nuss) 'Hellican' (*CA*).

ESCANES ('ɛskəni:z; 'Es-can-ees).

CLEON ('kli:ɒn; 'Klee-on) 'Stranguilio' in both sources; not the governor but a well-to-do citizen and merchant of Tarsus. Cleon is a name familiar in Greek drama.

TARSUS ('ta:səs; 'Tar-suss) Usually spelled in Q as 'Tharsus', and perhaps so pronounced, but probably not: compare 'Thaisa', 'Thaliard', where the 'Th' is pronounced 'T'. 'Tharse' (*CA*), 'Tharsus' (*PPA*). A city on the River Cyndus in Cilicia, present-day Turkey. St Paul came from Tarsus.

DIONIZA (daɪəʊ'naɪzə; Die-on-'eye-za) 'Dionyse' (*CA*), 'Dionisiades' (*PPA*).

3 FISHERMEN *of Pentapolis* One seems to be called 'Patch-breech' (see 2.1.14), but this may be merely a derogatory nickname.

SIMONIDES (sɪ'mɒnədi:z; Sim-'mon-id-eez) 'Artestrates' (*CA*), 'Altistrates' (*PPA*); a familiar Greek name in classical authors.

PENTAPOLIS (pɛn'tæpɒlɪs; Pen-'tap-oh-liss) 'Pentapolim' (*CA*). In the play it is declared to be, and clearly imagined as, a city in Greece (see 2.1.59–60); in actual fact, it is a collective name for the five cities of Cyrenaica on the North African coast in what is now Libya.

THAISA (usually taɪ'i:sə; Tye-'ee-sa, but sometimes 'taɪɪsə; 'Tye-iss-a) In *CA* Apollonius' wife is not given a name; 'Lucina' in *PPA*.

LYCHORIDA (laɪ'kɒrɪdə; Lye-'kor-rid-da) 'Lichorida' (*CA*), 'Ligozides' (*PPA*).

CERIMON ('sɛrɪmɒn; 'Serr-im-on) So in both sources. The name seems appropriate in its suggestion of ceremony, since he officiates in a ceremonial capacity in the scenes in which he is present.

EPHESUS ('ɛfɛsəs; 'Eff-ess-us) So in both sources. On the western coast of Asia Minor; famous for its great temple to Diana as well as a site for magic and thaumaturgy. Shakespeare makes it the setting in *Err.*

PHILEMON ('fɪləmɒn; 'Fill-im-on) Not in *CA*. In *PPA* one of Cerimon's assistants is called 'Machaon', but Dioniza's daughter is named 'Philomacia'. In a distant German analogue he bears the name of 'Filominus'.

LEONINE ('li:əʊnaɪn; 'Lee-oh-nine) In *CA* the name of the brothel-owner in Miteline; 'Theophilus' in both sources.

MARINA (originally probably mə'raɪnə; Ma-'rine-na; but now universally mə'ri:nə; Ma-'ree-na) Means child of the sea (see 3.3.12–13). In *CA* or *PPA* she is called 'Thaise' and 'Tharsia' respectively.

BOULT (bəʊlt; Bolt) In the sources he is simply referred to as the brothel-keeper's 'man' (*CA*), 'the villain' (*PPA*).

LYSIMACHUS (laɪ'sɪməkəs; Lie-'simm-a-kuss) 'Athenagoras', lord of Miteline (*CA*), 'Athanagoras', prince of Machilenta (*PPA*). The name does not occur anywhere in either source but appears often in classical authors like Plutarch (see n. to 1.3.3–5).

MITELINE ('mɪtəlaɪn; 'Mit-tel-lyne or 'mɪtəli:n; 'Mit-tel-een) 'Machilenta' (*PPA*). Chief city on the island of Lesbos, off the west coast of Asia Minor; present-day Mitilini in Greece.

DIANA (daɪ'ænə; Die-'anna) Rarely mentioned in either source, but serves as the regent goddess of the play.

THE PLAY OF PERICLES, PRINCE OF TYRE

[Prologue] *Enter* GOWER

GOWER To sing a song that old was sung,
From ashes, ancient Gower is come,
Assuming man's infirmities,
To glad your ear and please your eyes.
It hath been sung at festivals, 5
On ember-eves and holy days,
And lords and ladies in their lives
Have read it for restoratives.
~~The purchase is to make men glorious:~~
Et bonum quo antiquius eo melius. 10
If you, born in those latter times
When wit's more ripe, accept my rhymes,

Title page] See Textual Analysis, p. 197   **Head-title**] Q (Tyre.&c.)   **Prologue**] *This edn; not in* Q   **6 holy days**]
Holydayes Q; holy-ales *Theobald MS.; Malone; conj. Farmer*   **11 those**] Q; these Q2

Prologue

0 SD Enter Gower The entrance of Gower has the effect of resurrection from the dead, a seminal theme in the last plays.

1 sing a song that old was sung The first of many significant references to and use of musical terms in the play. That poetry was originally a sung form is a commonplace; the 'song' Gower comes to present is the ancient tale of Apollonius of Tyre in play form. See Introduction, pp. 29–31, for the deliberately archaic style used throughout the play and especially in Gower's choruses.

2 From ashes Gower, who died in 1408, was buried in the Church of St Saviour (now Southwark Cathedral), a short distance from the Globe.

3 Assuming man's infirmities Taking on the mortal conditions of a living man.

6 ember-eves The evenings before the ember-days (Wednesday, Friday, Saturday of the four ember weeks, one for each season of the year) observed in the Christian Church calendar as periods of fasting, prayer and abstinence.

6 holy days Feasts of religious obligation observed in the Church calendar; often emended to 'holy-ales' ('ales' were rural festivals) but, as

Hoeniger notes, no other reference to holy-ales, as distinct from e.g. 'church-ales', or 'Whitsun-ales', has been found. Because the modern spelling 'holidays' would give a false impression, we retain Q's two words.

8 for restoratives as a means for healing or renewal.

9 purchase (1) acquisition, (2) beneficial gain.

9 glorious A literal meaning does not seem to be implied here, rather the 'glory' is the healthy by-product of a tale taken as a restorative; *OED* sv 4 cites Chaucer's use of the word, with its similar sense related to the lustre of health: 'For as the crystal glorious ye shyne, / And lyke ruby ben your chekes rounde' (in the ballad 'To Rosemounde', lines 3–4). See 78 where Antiochus' daughter is said to be a 'glorious casket'.

10 Et . . . melius And the older a good thing is, the better. A commonplace axiom (Tilley O38).

11 those From Gower's point of view, his audience is in the future, hence the tense. Many editors emend to 'these'.

12 wit's more ripe knowledge or intelligence is more sophisticated (than in Gower's own time of writing i.e. the fourteenth century).

85

And that to hear an old man sing
May to your wishes pleasure bring,
I life would wish, and that I might 15
Waste it for you, like taper light.
This Antioch then, Antiochus the Great
Built up this city for his chiefest seat,
The fairest in all Syria.
I tell you what mine authors say: 20
This king unto him took a peer,
Who died, and left a female heir,
So buxom, blithe, and full of face,
As heaven had lent her all his grace;
With whom the father liking took, 25
And her to incest did provoke.
Bad child, worse father, to entice his own
To evil, should be done by none:
But custom what they did begin
Was with long use accounted no sin. 30
The beauty of this sinful dame
Made many princes thither frame
To seek her as a bedfellow,
In marriage pleasures, playfellow;

17 Antioch then,] Antioch, then Q   17 Great] great, Q   21 peer] Q; *fere Dyce*

12 accept my rhymes An appeal to the sophisticated Elizabethan auditor to listen to Gower's more archaic forms of poetic expression. A similar appeal to the audience to accept his story is made by Time in *WT* 4.1.9–15, 'Let me pass / The same I am, ere ancient'st order was, / Or what is now receiv'd. I witness to / The times that brought them in; so shall I do / To th' freshest things now reigning, and make stale / The glistering of this present, as my tale / Now seems to it.'

16 Waste . . . taper light The pleasure offered from Gower's life-affirming story is like a candle which consumes itself while giving light. A proverbial saying (Tilley C39, 'A candle (torch) lights others and consumes itself'). See 2.2.33–4.

18 chiefest seat centre of Antiochus' authority in Syria.

20 mine authors say Gower is part of the long tradition of storytellers who have related this particular tale. *CA* incorporates past versions of the story and references to other authorities in 'olde bokes'; see 279–81, 1160, 1334, 1554.

21 peer an equal in rank, but also a companion or mate (*OED* sv *sb* 3). The Oxford editors complain that the only *OED* meaning = 'wife' is dated *c.* 1330; but that was Gower's approximate birthdate.

22 Who . . . heir Like Antiochus' daughter, Marina becomes a motherless heir, a characteristic of Shakespeare's romance heroines (Imogen, Perdita, Miranda).

23 buxom bright, lively (*OED* sv *a* 3) or full of health, vigour (*OED* sv *a*4).

23 blithe cheerful, spirited.

23 full of face (1) beautiful, (2) with a round face.

26 provoke move to commit.

29–30 But custom . . . no sin Based on *CA* 353–4: 'And suche delite he toke therin, / Him thought that it was no sin.' A proverbial saying (Tilley C934, 'Custom makes sin no sin').

29 But custom By habit.

30 accounted considered.

32 frame direct their course.

Which to prevent he made a law *Antiochus created a decree* 35
To keep her still, and men in awe: *To keep her always & scare many away*
That whoso asked her for his wife, *That whomever asked for her hand in*
His riddle told not, lost his life. *If he couldn't answer the king of all marriage, meant*
So for her many of wight did die, *For her sake, a multitude of people lost their*
As yon grim looks do testify. *These ugly cut-off heads tell you* 40 *lives,*
What now ensues, to the judgement of your eye *what now follows,*
I give my cause, who best can justify. *give you the story, to make your own judgement.*   *Exit*

[1.1] *Enter* ANTIOCHUS, *Prince* PERICLES, *and followers*

ANTIOCHUS Young prince of Tyre, you have at large received *You fully comprehend the danger*
The danger of the task you undertake.
PERICLES I have, Antiochus, and with a soul *my heart made fearless by the*
Emboldened with the glory of her praise, *praise of her worth, I am*
Think death no hazard in this enterprise. *willing to risk death 5 for her hand.*
ANTIOCHUS ~~Music~~!

[*Music plays*]
Bring in our daughter, clothèd like a bride *designer clothes worthy*
For embracements even of Jove himself, *of God,*

---

38 told not,] Q2; tould, not Q   **Act 1, Scene 1   1.1]** *Malone; not in* Q   3 have, Antiochus,] have *(Antiochus)* Q   **3–5**
I . . . enterprise] *Malone's lineation; lined* I . . . emboldned / With . . . hazard / In . . . enterprise Q   **6–7** Music! /
Bring . . . bride] *Hoeniger's lineation; one line* Q   **6 SD]** *Malone; not in* Q

36 i.e. to keep her always with him and to prevent others from demanding her in marriage (Malone *subst.*). Compare *PPA* p. 427, 'which false resemblance of hateful marriage, to the intent he might alwaies enjoy, he invented a strange devise of wickednesse, to drive away all suters that should resort unto her'.

36 in awe control or constrain by fear.

38 His . . . not if he could not solve the riddle.

39 of a. One of the archaisms used in the Gower choruses.

39 wight (1) person, (2) poor creature. The word occurs eight times in Shakespeare.

40 yon grim looks The impaled heads of the unsuccessful suitors. They are visible throughout the Prologue and Scene 1, but there is no indication where and how they were displayed, nor how, when, and by whom removed. (In *PA* they are said to be 'placed upon his castle wall'; perhaps they were set along the balustrade of the upper stage, though this would seem to require that stage-

keepers removed them before 1.2 began.) See illustration 10, p. 39.

41–2 What now . . . can justify The first of several direct appeals Gower makes to the audience regarding the ensuing performance. The truth of the play (cause) can be judged and confirmed (justified) by what they see. Judgement is often a request that Choruses in the drama of the period make of their audiences; Shakespeare follows the convention, with variations, in several of the plays employing Choruses: see *H5*, *Rom.*, *WT*. See Introduction, p. 35, for a comparison between Gower and the Chorus of *H5*.

Act 1, Scene 1

Location Antioch: see map facing p. 1.

1 at large received learned fully and understood.

5 hazard danger, risk.

8 Jove The Romans' father-god, Jupiter; which makes this instance of its use by the incestuous Antiochus ironic.

At whose conception, till ~~Lucina reigned,~~
~~Nature this dowry gave: to glad her presence,~~
~~The senate house of planets all did sit~~
To knit in her their best perfections.

Enter Antiochus' DAUGHTER

PERICLES   See where she comes, apparelled like the spring,
Graces her subjects, and her thoughts the king
Of every virtue gives renown to men,
~~Her face the book of praises where is read~~
~~Nothing but curious pleasures, as from thence~~
~~Sorrow were ever razed, and testy wrath~~
~~Could never be her mild companion.~~
You gods that made me man and sway in love,
That have inflamed desire in my breast
To taste the fruit of yon celestial tree
Or die in the adventure, be my helps,
As I am son and servant to your will
To compass such a boundless happiness.

---

9 reigned] rained Q   18 razed] *Dyce subst.;* racte Q   23 the] Q3; th' Q   25 boundless] *Rowe;* bondless Q

---

9 From the time of her conception to her birth; Lucina (literally 'light-bringer', and pronounced Lu-sy-na, not as in Italian Lu-chee-na) was the Roman goddess of childbirth, who became assimilated into the goddess Juno. See 3.1.10.

10–12 Her dowry is that she was conceived and born during an astrologically auspicious time when the planets were sympathetically conjoined in the heavens; as a consequence, her life is under their positive influence; 'to glad her presence' may mean either to make her presence delightful to those about her (NS subst.), or that 'presence' could refer to 'Nature' who is improved ('gladdened') by the perfect woman who has been created. The importance given to the position of the planets at birth was a common literary conceit; see *Ado* 5.2.40: 'No, I was not born under a rhyming planet'; also Marlowe's *1 Tamburlaine* 1.1.12–15, 'a man, / At whose byrth-day *Cynthia* with *Saturne* joinde, / And *Jove*, the Sun, and *Mercurie* denied / To shed their influence in his fickle braine'; also Sidney's *Arcadia* (one of the play's sources: see Introduction, p. 3), ch. II. 6: 'The senate house of the planets was at no time [so] set, for the decreeing of perfection in man.'

14 Graces her subjects With Graces for her

subjects. In classical mythology, the goddesses who bestowed beauty and charm and were themselves the embodiment of both; they were the sisters Aglaia, Thalia, and Euphrosyne.

15 gives which gives.

16 Her face the book of praises The book is a metaphor frequently used in Elizabethan literature, not only for the face but also for the human form; see also 2.3.2–3; eighteen instances in Shakespeare.

17 curious excellent, fine (*OED* sv *a* 14).

17 as as if.

18 razed erased; compare *Mac.* 5.3.42: 'Raze out the written troubles of the brain', *Son.* 25.11: 'Is from the book of honour rasèd quite'.

22–30 To taste…hard The last labour of Hercules was to enter the garden of Hesperus (his daughters were called the Hesperides, 28) which was guarded by a dragon and pick the golden apples from the tree. The association with Hercules, the achievement of a dangerous task, characterises Pericles' first adventure in the play according to the conventions of mythic and folkloric heroism. 'To taste the fruit of yon celestial tree' also brings to mind the forbidden tree of knowledge from the Bible. Antiochus' grim rejoinder at 29 makes the whole enterprise of a love-quest seem unsavoury.

ANTIOCHUS Prince Pericles –
PERICLES That would be son to great Antiochus.
ANTIOCHUS Before thee stands this fair Hesperides,   *She stands before you with temptation, dangerous to seek.*
          With golden fruit, but dangerous to be touched;
          For death like dragons here affright thee hard.
          Her face like heaven enticeth thee to view   *Her beauty is so enticing to view her*
          Her countless glory which desert must gain;   30 *naked; beauty must be worthy of;*
          And which without desert, because thine eye   *And without worth, because you want to reach what you view, you'll be*
          Presumes to reach, all the whole heap must die.   *killed.*
          Yon sometimes famous princes, like thyself,   *The dead princes, like you, drawn*   35
          Drawn by report, adventurous by desire,   *by gossip, adventurous because of desire,*
          Tell thee with speechless tongues and semblance pale   *Tell you with their heads, without a proper burial, here*
          That, without covering save yon field of stars,   *Stand, killed for love.*
          Here they stand, martyrs slain in Cupid's wars,
          And with dead cheeks advise thee to desist   *Their death advise thee to*   40
          For going on death's net, whom none resist.   *Stop before you die, or you will.*
PERICLES Antiochus, I thank thee, who hath taught   *Thank you for teaching me about*
          My frail mortality to know itself,   *my mortality.*
          And by those fearful objects to prepare   *And by the heads, prepare me to what's*
          This body, like to them, to what I must: *coming.*   45
          For Death remembered should be like a mirror
          Who tells us life's but breath, to trust it, error.
          I'll make my will then, and as sick men do   *Living will, as sick people,*
          Who know the world, see heaven, but feeling woe   *are close to heaven*
          Grip not at earthly joys as erst they did;   *want not worldly things anymore*   50
          So I bequeath a happy peace to you   *and to, so I wish you happiness,*
          And all good men as every prince should do.   *and everyone else as well (because I'm a prince)*
          My riches to the earth from whence they came,
          [*To the Daughter*] But my unspotted fire of love to you.
          Thus ready for the way of life or death   *So I'm ready for you or death*   55
          I wait the sharpest blow.   *I await the challenge*

When A. snaps Peri down,

26 Pericles –] *Malone*; Pericles. Q   54 SD] *Malone subst.; not in* Q   56 blow. / ANTIOCHUS Scorning] *Malone*; blow (*Antiochus*) / Scorning Q

29 **dangerous . . . touched** See 88–90.
34 **heap** i.e. the entire body (*OED sb* 1c, citing this example).
35 **Yon . . . princes** See Prologue 40 and n.
38 **yon field of stars** A reference to the painted 'heavens' (the planets, stars, and signs of the zodiac) under the roof which extended over the Globe stage.
41 **For** From. Possibly another deliberate

archaism, since *OED* does not recognise this idiom; compare Prologue 39 n.
47 **life's but breath** A proverbial saying (Dent B641.1, 'Life is but a breath').
48–50 **and . . . did** Paraphrased: worldly men when 'sick', *in extremis*, no longer grasp at 'earthly' pleasures as they formerly did, since they now 'see heaven'.
56 **blow** Q's reading 'blow (*Antiochus*)' completes

ANTIOCHUS Scorning advice? Read the conclusion then,
            [*Gives Pericles the riddle*]
        Which read and not expounded 'tis decreed,
        As these before thee, thou thyself shalt bleed.
DAUGHTER Of all 'sayed yet, mayst thou prove prosperous,   60
        Of all 'sayed yet, I wish thee happiness.
PERICLES Like a bold champion I assume the lists
        Nor ask advice of any other thought
        But faithfulness and courage.
               [*He reads*] *the riddle*
I am no viper, yet I feed   65
On mother's flesh which did me breed.
I sought a husband, in which labour
I found that kindness in a father.
He's father, son, and husband mild;
I, mother, wife, and yet his child.   70
How they may be, and yet in two,
As you will live resolve it you.

---

57 advice?] aduice; Q   57 SD] *This edn; not in* Q   60, 61 'sayed] *Collier subst.;* sayd Q   64 SD] *Steevens; The Riddle.* Q

a pentameter, which recommended it to Alexander. However, it is the last line on the page, and the catchword is 'Scorning', which duly becomes the first word on the next page (set by the same compositor). Everyone realises that the speech beginning 'Scorning' is spoken by Antiochus, not Pericles, and the reasonable inference is that some feature of the MS. copy misled the compositor into thinking that 'Antiochus' was part of Pericles' line, rather than the speech heading it undoubtedly is.

57 the conclusion the riddle (*OED sb* 7b citing this line).

57, 64 SD Both in *CA* and in *PPA*, Apollonius hears the riddle spoken by Antiochus; the invitation to 'read' the riddle strongly suggests a written scroll which Pericles then receives, reads aloud for the benefit of the audience (who need to hear it) and ponders it in an aside (73 ff.) after having solved it.

60, 61 'sayed assayed = attempted ('of all that have attempted the riddle so far, may you . . .').

62 assume undertake, enter upon.

62 lists palisades enclosing the space used in tilting (*OED sv sb*³ 9a; hence 9b (*transf.*) place or scene of combat or contest).

65–72 Compare the riddle in the sources: *CA* 413–18, 'With felonie I am up bore, / I ete, and have it not forlore / My moders flesshe, whose husbonde / My fader for to seche I fonde, / Which

is the sonne eke of my wife / Herof I am inquisitife'; *PPA* (p. 428), '*I am carried with mischiefe, I eate my mothers fleshe: I seeke my brother my mothers husband and I can not finde him.*' For a discussion of the riddle see P. Goolden, 'Antiochus's riddle in Gower and Shakespeare', *RES* n.s. 6 (1955), 245–51. Riddles are a common feature of the last plays: see Jupiter's prophecy in *Cym.* 5.4.138–44; the oracle of Apollo in *WT* 3.2.132–6.

65–6 viper . . . breed Vipers' offspring were said to eat their way out of their mother's body at birth.

68 kindness (1) kinship, (2) favour, i.e. her father did her the favour of saving her the 'labour' of finding a husband.

69–70 He's father . . . child The incestuous relationships are clear insofar as Antiochus can be her father and husband, and she his wife and child; how he can be her son, and she his mother may seem perplexing. However, Antiochus usurps the position of a son by assuming the role of a son-in-law; the Daughter has taken on the role of her mother. It is also a paradox which prepares carefully for the spiritual rebirth Marina gives to Pericles at the end of the play: 'Thou that begetst him that did thee beget' (5.1.190).

71 How they . . . in two The relationships represent six people yet there are only two persons.

this is hard to take

Personae? to something encompasses the world

[*Aside*] Sharp physic is the last, but O you powers   *O Gods Why*
That gives heaven countless eyes to view men's acts,   *Are you allow these*
Why cloud they not their sights perpetually,   *acts to be seen by you.*
If this be true, which makes me pale to read it?
[*To Daughter*] Fair glass of light, I loved you, and could still
Were not this glorious casket stored with ill;
But I must tell you, now my thoughts revolt –
For he's no man on whom perfections wait,   80
That knowing sin within will touch the gate –
You are a fair viol, and your sense the strings,
Who, fingered to make man his lawful music,
Would draw heaven down and all the gods to hearken;
But being played upon before your time,   85
Hell only danceth at so harsh a chime.
Good sooth, I care not for you.
ANTIOCHUS Prince Pericles, touch not upon thy life,
For that's an article within our law
As dangerous as the rest. Your time's expired.   90
Either expound now or receive your sentence.
PERICLES Great king,
Few love to hear the sins they love to act;
'Twould braid yourself too near for me to tell it.
Who has a book of all that monarchs do,   95
He's more secure to keep it shut, than shown;
For vice repeated is like the wandering wind, –

73 SD] *NS; not in* Q   77 SD] *This edn; not in* Q

73 SD Many editors make the whole of Pericles' speech an aside, which is possible, but theatrically difficult (it leaves Antiochus and the Daughter standing inactive for too long).

73 **sharp . . . last** i.e. the final consequence of solving the riddle is death; a bad ('sharp') dose of medicine ('physic') to take.

74 **countless eyes** The stars.

77 **glass of light** The image of the daughter as a beautiful vessel, hence 'glorious casket' (78); her outward appearance is thus deceptive, a mere reflection of reality, because it is 'stored with ill' or contains 'sin within' (81). Outward appearance as opposed to inward reality is a theme which runs throughout the play; see 2.2.56–7, and Introduction, pp. 63–5.

82 **viol** Six-stringed instrument played with a bow, the precursor of the modern violin. Pericles

makes an elaborate conceit out of the parallel between playing the viol and sexual relations.

82 **sense** sensual nature, sexual desire (Onions, also *OED* sv *sb* 4b); compare 5.3.27.

87–8 At the end of his speech, Pericles must make some gesture which causes Antiochus to think that he is going to touch the Daughter; 88 does not suggest that the gesture is threatening, but it seems likely that it was one of repulsion. A parallel is thereby created with the moment when Pericles pushes Marina away (5.1.79).

94 **braid** upbraid.

97–101 **For vice . . . hurt them** An elaborate simile about the danger in divulging the sins of a perpetrator, whose meaning has, not surprisingly, confused editors: 'repeated' = talked about; 'blows' = which blows; 'others' eyes' = the eyes of the public; 'to spread' = in spreading. The implication

~~Blows dust in others' eyes to spread itself,~~
~~And yet the end of all is bought thus dear,~~
~~The breath is gone, and the sore eyes see clear;~~   100
~~To stop the air would hurt them. The blind mole casts~~
~~Coped hills towards heaven, to tell the earth is thronged~~
~~By man's oppression, and the poor worm doth die for't.~~
Kings are earth's gods: in vice their law's their will;
And if Jove stray, who dares say Jove doth ill?   105
It is enough you know, and it is fit
What being more known, grows worse to smother it.
All love the womb that their first being bred,
Then give my tongue like leave, to love my head.
ANTIOCHUS [*Aside*] Heaven, that I had thy head! He has found the
            meaning,   110
But I will gloze with him – young prince of Tyre,
Though by the tenor of our strict edict,
Your exposition misinterpreting,
We might proceed to cancel of your days;
Yet hope, succeeding from so fair a tree   115
As your fair self, doth tune us otherwise.
Forty days longer we do respite you;
If by which time our secret be undone,
This mercy shows we'll joy in such a son;
And until then your entertain shall be   120
As doth befit our honour and your worth.
                        [*Exeunt all but*] *Pericles*

110 SD] *Steevens; not in* Q   112 our] F3*; your* Q   114 cancel] F3 *subst.;* counsell Q   121 SD] *Malone subst.; Manet Pericles solus.* Q

of the passage is that an injury will follow from indiscreet revelations; the exact meaning remains obscure.

101–3 The blind . . . die for't The poetic superiority of these lines has often been remarked on as making them stand out texturally from the scene. The point of the previous lines is here expressed more happily: the mole ('poor worm') who represents Pericles and has good reason to proclaim the tyrant's oppression, may suffer death for his action: molehills lead to the finding and killing of moles. 'Coped' = peaked or domed; see 4.5.114 'under the cope'; 'thronged' = afflicted; 'worm' *OED* sv *sb* 2a 'any animal that creeps or crawls (applied figuratively to human beings); also *OED* sv *sb* 10 'an abject, miserable creature'; see *Temp.* 3.1.31, 'Poor worm, thou art infected.'

110 thy head i.e. your intelligence.
111 gloze talk speciously, use fair words (*OED* sv *v*¹ 3).
112 tenor Course of meaning which holds on or continues throughout something written; general sense or meaning of a document (*OED* sv *sb*¹ 1a).
114 cancel of the cancelling of.
115 Yet hope . . . tree The first of three references which associate Pericles with the image of a tree that gives hope; see 1.2.30–1, 2.2.43–7. The 'hope' that Antiochus expresses, i.e. that such a tree will bear fruitful success, is of course mendacious.
118 secret be undone i.e. the riddle be solved.
120 your entertain (1) your entertainment, (2) the hospitality you will receive.

PERICLES How courtesy would seem to cover sin
~~When what is done is like an hypocrite,~~
~~The which is good in nothing but in sight.~~ Only looks good.
If it be true that I interpret false,   125
Then were it certain you were not so bad
As with foul incest to abuse your soul,
Where now you're both a father and a son
By your untimely claspings with your child,
Which pleasures fits a husband, not a father;   130
And she an eater of her mother's flesh
By the defiling of her parents' bed;
And both like serpents are, who though they feed
On sweetest flowers yet they poison breed.
Antioch farewell: for wisdom sees, those men   135
Blush not in actions blacker than the night,
Will show no course to keep them from the light.
One sin, I know, another doth provoke:
Murder's as near to lust as flame to smoke;
~~Poison and treason are the hands of sin,~~   140
~~Ay, and the targets to put off the shame.~~
Then lest my life be cropped, to keep you clear,
By flight I'll shun the danger which I fear.   *Exit*

Enter ANTIOCHUS

ANTIOCHUS He hath found the meaning,

---

128 you're] F3 *subst.;* you Q   129 untimely] Q; uncomely *NS, conj. Delius*   135 sees, . . . men] sees . . . men, Q   137 show]
shew Q; 'schew *Theobald MS., conj. Malone;* shun *Malone*

122–4 **How . . . sight** Polite but hypocritical behaviour is good only in its outward appearance. A
proverbial saying (Tilley C732, 'Full of courtesy full
of craft').
128 **Where** Whereas.
129 **untimely** inopportune (*OED* sv *a* 3). The
word is also associated with abortions and monstrous births (*OED* 1b) which, in view of the importance of birth-imagery in the play (see Introduction,
pp. 47–9), probably has a significance here; and in
other such contexts as *OED* 1d, citing the Countess
of Pembroke's translation of Psalm 53.4: 'their
brood . . . of springing thornes Be by untimely
rooting over-thrown'.
130 **Which pleasures fits** The pleasures of
which are appropriate to.
131 **eater . . . flesh** See 65–6 n.

136 **Blush** Who blush.
137 i.e. will not reveal the measures they take to
be undiscovered. Compare 1.2.23: 'He'll stop the
course by which it might be known.'
138 **One sin . . . provoke** Compare *R3* 4.2.64,
'So far in blood that sin will pluck on sin'. A proverbial saying (Dent S467.1, 'Every sin brings in
another').
141 **targets** shields.
144 Hoeniger calls this 'Scene 1b' on the grounds
that following Pericles' exit the stage is bare, and
this was the conventional indication of a new scene
in Jacobean drama. It is possible, however, that the
intention was to have Antiochus enter from the
other door before Pericles had left, thus giving point
and energy to his subsequent musings and conspiracy; the two characters might even exchange

For which we mean to have his head.   145
He must not live to trumpet forth my infamy
Nor tell the world Antiochus doth sin
~~In such a loathèd manner;~~
And therefore instantly this prince must die,
For by his fall my honour must keep high.   150
Who attends us there?

Enter THALIARD

THALIARD   Doth your highness call?
ANTIOCHUS Thaliard, you are of our chamber, Thaliard,
And our mind partakes her private actions
To your secrecy; and for your faithfulness
We will advance you, Thaliard: 155
Behold, here's poison, and here's gold.
We hate the prince of Tyre, and thou must kill him.
It fits thee not to ask the reason why:
Because we bid it.
Say, is it done?
THALIARD   My lord, 'tis done.

Enter a MESSENGER

ANTIOCHUS   Enough.   160
Let your breath cool yourself, telling your haste.
MESSENGER My lord, Prince Pericles is fled.   [*Exit*]
ANTIOCHUS As thou wilt live fly after, and like an arrow
Shot from a well-experienced archer hits

---

158 why:] F3; why? Q   **159–61**] *This edn's lineation; lined* Because . . . done? / *Thali.* My . . . done. / SD / *Anti.*
Enough . . . haste Q   **162** SD] *Malone; not in* Q   **163–5**] *Malone's lineation; prose* Q

silent glances. It is true that *PA*'s description sounds like a new scene, but only to those still in thrall to scenic conventions: '*Antiochus* being now priuate in his lodging, and ruminating with himselfe . . .' (sig. B3ᵛ).

152 of our chamber i.e. one of his attendants; see *AYLI* 2.2.5, *Mac.* 2.3.101.

153 partakes imparts, communicates.

160 Say . . . enough Compare *John* 3.3.65–6: 'K. *John. A Grave. Hub.* He shall not live. K. *John.* Enough.'

160 SD In Q the direction precedes Antiochus' line beginning 'Enough' (160); most editors follow Dyce in moving the entry to after 'Enough'. We think our arrangement better, in which the Messen-

ger enters in the middle of the final phrases of the conspiracy, causing Antiochus to break off hastily.

161 Probably 'Let the breath you are panting also be used to tell me the reason for your haste.'

163–6 Q's punctuation, chiefly commas, has been mainly retained for this speech, since it neatly suggests Antiochus' anxious state of mind. The speech, and that of Thaliard following, is set as prose in Q, but this may be no more than a new compositor finding difficulty with his copy: the scene begins Compositor Y's stint at the top of sig. B1ʳ (160 SD), and Antiochus' language is quite similar to that at the foot of the previous page, which Compositor X set as fractured verse. For these reasons, it seems best to adopt Malone's lineation.

    The mark his eye doth level at, so thou   165
    Never return unless thou say 'Prince Pericles is dead.'
THALIARD My lord, if I can get him within my pistol's length,
    I'll make him sure enough,
    So farewell to your highness.
ANTIOCHUS Thaliard adieu, till Pericles be dead   170
    My heart can lend no succour to my head.

                                           [Exeunt]

[1.2] *Enter* PERICLES *[and an Attendant]*

PERICLES ~~Let none disturb us.~~ *[Exit Attendant]* Why should this change
    of thoughts,
    The sad companion, dull-eyed melancholy,
    Be my so-used a guest, as not an hour
    In the day's glorious walk or peaceful night,
    The tomb where grief should sleep, can breed me quiet?   5
    Here pleasures court mine eyes, and mine eyes shun them,
    And danger, which I feared, is at Antioch,
    Whose arm seems far too short to hit me here;
    Yet neither pleasure's art can joy my spirits,

166–9] *This edn's lineation; prose* Q   170 SH] Q4; *not in* Q   171 SD] *This edn; Exit* Q2; *not in* Q   Act 1, Scene 2 1.2] *Malone; not in* Q   0 SD] *This edn; Enter Pericles with his Lords.* Q   1 SD] *This edn; not in* Q   3 Be my] *Dyce;* By me Q   3 so-used] *hyphenated this edn; unhyphenated* Q   5 quiet?] *Malone;* quiet Q

165 level aim.

167 pistol's length range of a shot. Antiochus has already given Thaliard poison for his task; that Thaliard should think of a pistol in addition shows enthusiastic willing. The anachronistic pistol is typical of Shakespeare.

168 make sure (1) render harmless, (2) disable, destroy.

171 My ... head i.e. 'I will have no peace of mind.'

171 SD While most editors follow Rowe in giving Thaliard a separate exit at 170, there is no reason why he should not hear Antiochus' urgent final couplet, with its reaffirmation of the conspiracy.

Act 1, Scene 2

  Location Tyre: see map facing p. 1.

  1.2.0 SD Though the Oxford editors defend it, Q's direction is hard to believe: that Pericles should enter with his Lords, only to speak an instant dismissal to them and have them traipse out again. Our

'attendant' is borrowed from Stratford 1986's solution to the difficulty: two attendants set the throne; Pericles entered, and gave them his order. Some such simple theatrical adjustment makes the scene less awkward. It is true that *PA* does contain what many commentators consider a far more intelligible version of it: see Textual Analysis, pp. 209–10.

  1 change of thoughts i.e. from a positive to a negative or sombre frame of mind.

  3 Be my so-used Q's 'By me' leaves the sentence without a verb; it is surprising that Malone did not think an emendation necessary, but Dyce's neat transposition gives adequate sense; 'so-used' = frequent, customary.

  4 day's glorious walk Literally the day, the progress of the sun.

  5 breed give, bestow.

  8 Whose arm ... short A variation of a proverbial saying (Tilley K87, 'Kings have long arms').

  9 can joy make cheerful.

Nor yet the other's distance comfort me.   10
Then it is thus: the passions of the mind
That have their first conception by misdread
Have after-nourishment and life by care:
And what was first but fear what might be done,
Grows elder now and cares it be not done,   15
And so with me. The great Antiochus,
'Gainst whom I am too little to contend,
Since he's so great can make his will his act,
Will think me speaking though I swear to silence;
Nor boots it me to say, I honour him,   20
If he suspect I may dishonour him;
And what may make him blush in being known,
He'll stop the course by which it might be known.
With hostile forces he'll o'er-spread the land,
And with the stint of war will look so huge   25
Amazement shall drive courage from the state;
Our men be vanquished ere they do resist,
And subjects punished that ne'er thought offence –
Which care of them, not pity of myself,
Who once no more but as the tops of trees,   30
Which fence the roots they grow by and defend them,

---

13 after-nourishment] *hyphenated Tonson; unhyphenated* Q   **16** me. The] *Edwards; me the* Q   **20** him] *Rowe; not in* Q   **25** the stint] Q; th'ostent *Malone; conj. Tyrwhitt*   **30** once] Q; am *Malone, conj. Farmer*

12 have . . . misdread are born from fear.

13 i.e. are sustained and kept alive by anxiety.

15 cares it be not done takes anxious care to prevent what earlier seemed only a possibility; with a play on 'care' (13).

20 boots it me does it help me.

25 the stint 'limitation, restriction with respect to a mode of action' (*OED* Stint *sb*[1] 2a) offers the senses of restriction or limitation Pericles might anticipate war bringing; alternatively 'a unit of measure' (*OED* 4), in which case Pericles is talking about the period of action allotted in war.

26 Amazement Fear, terror.

28 ne'er thought offence never imagined they had done wrong.

30 Who once no more i.e. 'I who once was but am no more'. Most editors adopt Farmer's conjecture 'am' since the sentence otherwise lacks a verb; but suppression of the verb when an adverb could carry the verbal function was not uncommon.

30–1 Who once . . . them The tree as a symbol of royal greatness was a commonplace of the period and used frequently by Shakespeare; see *3H6* 5.2.14–15, 'Whose top-branch overpeer'd Jove's spreading tree, / And kept low shrubs from winter's pow'rful wind'; *R3* 3.7.167; *R2* 1.2.18; *H5* 2.2.26–8, 'There's not, I think, a subject / That sits in heart-grief and uneasiness / Under the sweet shade of your government'; *Cym.* 5.5.453–57; and *H8* 5.4.52–4, 'He shall flourish, / And like a mountain cedar reach his branches / To all the plains about him.' The image is ultimately derived from the Bible: see Ezek. 31.3, 'Beholde, Asshur was like a cedre in Lebanon with faire branches, and with thicke shadowing boughes, and shot up verie hie, and his top was among the thicke boughes.' Nature which is both protector and nourisher is repeated at 55–6 with reference to Pericles' role as monarch.

~~Makes both my body pine and soul to languish,~~
~~And punish that before that he would punish.~~

Enter [HELLICANUS *and*] *all the* LORDS *to Pericles*

1 LORD Joy and all comfort in your sacred breast.
2 LORD And keep your mind ~~till you return to us~~ *keep your wits about you*   35
        Peaceful and comfortable. *until you return to us in peace.*
HELLICANUS Peace, peace, and give experience tongue.
        They do abuse the king that flatter him,
        For flattery is the bellows blows up sin,
        ~~The thing the which is flattered, but a spark~~   40
        ~~To which that wind gives heat and stronger glowing;~~
        Whereas reproof, obedient and in order,
        Fits kings as they are men, for they may err.
        ~~When Signior Sooth here does proclaim peace~~
        ~~He flatters you, makes war upon your life.~~ / *Pericles reacts in some way to what Hel. said.*   45
        [*Kneels*] Prince, pardon me, or strike me if you please,
        I cannot be much lower than my knees.
PERICLES All leave us else: ~~but let your cares o'erlook~~

---

33 SD HELLICANUS *and*] *Dyce; not in* Q   35–6] *Malone's lineation; prose* Q   40 spark] *This edn;* sparke, Q   41 wind]
Edwards; sparke Q; breath *Malone;* blast *Collier;* spur *Sisson*   41 stronger glowing] Q4; *lined* stronger / Glowing Q   44
peace] Q; a peace *Malone*   46 SD] *Oxford; after line 47* Collier²; *at line 58* Malone   46 pardon] Q2; paadon Q

33 Punish in advance he whom Antiochus wishes to punish; because Pericles feels he can no longer be the protector of his people, his anxiety is a punishment he is receiving already.

35 **till you return to us** If taken literally, this remark is surprising, since at this point Pericles has just returned to them from Antioch, and so far has not made known his intention of leaving again. The Lord probably means 'return in spirit', since it is clear Pericles is suffering from a melancholy which deprives him of his former disposition.

37 **give experience tongue** allow one with more maturity to speak. Hellicanus has often been criticised for a needless tirade against flattery in this speech, which follows the kind wishes of the Lords; but from Hellicanus' point of view what Pericles needs now in his present state of melancholy is not kind thoughts (which flatter) but a stiff talking-to, hence 42–3: 'reproof, obedient and in order, / Fits kings as they are men, for they may err'. Hellicanus, if over-zealous, appropriately adopts the role re-quired of wise counsellors, hence Pericles' appreciative recognition (60–3).

38 **abuse . . . flatter him** Listening to flattery was considered one of the worst abuses of the king's office, resulting in actions detrimental to the state and to himself, hence 45 where the idea is reiterated.

39 **blows** which blows.

40–1 **spark . . . wind** The wind produced by the bellows blows upon, and inflames, the spark. Q's 'sparke . . . sparke' cannot be right; any synonym for 'wind' might be the right word. We presume this to be homœoteleuton by the compositor.

44 **Signior Sooth** Sir Flattery, Sir Sweet Words. See 'blandishment, flattery, a smooth or plausible word or speech' (*OED* Sooth *sb* 8).

46 SD What Hellicanus says in 46–7 makes it a near-inescapable inference that he kneels here, either at the beginning of his sentence (as in the Oxford edition) or afterwards, as Collier preferred.

~~What shipping and what ladings in our haven,~~
~~And then return to us.~~

                                     [*Exeunt Lords*]

                      Hellicanus, thou hast   50
Moved us. What seest thou in our looks?
HELLICANUS An angry brow, dread lord.
PERICLES If there be such a dart in princes' frowns,
How durst thy tongue move anger to our face?
HELLICANUS How dares the plants look up to heaven,   55
From whence they have their nourishment?
PERICLES Thou knowst I have power to take thy life from thee.
HELLICANUS I have ground the axe myself, do but you strike
   The blow.
PERICLES   Rise, prithee rise, ~~sit down,~~ thou art
No flatterer. [*Hellicanus sits*] I thank thee for't,
   and heaven forbid   60
That kings should let their ears hear their faults hid.
Fit counsellor and servant for a prince,
Who by thy wisdom makes a prince thy servant,
What wouldst thou have me do?
HELLICANUS   To bear with patience
Such griefs as you yourself do lay upon yourself.   65
PERICLES Thou speakst like a physician, Hellicanus,
That ministers a potion unto me,
That thou wouldst tremble to receive thyself.
Attend me then: I went to Antioch,
Whereas thou knowst against the face of death   70
I sought the purchase of a glorious beauty

---

49 ladings] Q; lading's *Rowe* 50 SD] *Malone²; not in* Q 58–60] *This edn's lineation; lined* selfe, / Doe . . . blowe. / *Per.* Rise . . . flatterer, / I . . . forbid Q 60 SD] *This edn; not in* Q 60 heaven] Q2; heauē Q 64–5] *Knight's lineation; prose* Q

49 ladings cargoes.
49 haven harbour.
51–4 What seest . . . face? The significance of a king's displeasure as witnessed in his countenance was a commonplace in the theories of kingship; compare *John* 4.2.212–13: 'to know the meaning / Of dangerous majesty, when perchance it frowns'.
55 dares . . . plants For singular inflection with plural subject, see Abbott 333.
61 let their . . . hid allow themselves to listen to flattery which conceals their faults.
64 To bear with patience A significant enjoinder Pericles receives at various times in his

spiritual journey throughout the play; see Introduction, pp. 53–8.
69 Attend Listen to. Pericles begins one of many narratives which are found throughout the play; like Gower, several characters engage in storytelling; for the significance of the play's narrative structures see Introduction, pp. 27–36.
70 Whereas Where.
71 purchase . . . glorious Compare Prologue 9 where 'purchase' and 'glorious' are also yoked. 'Purchase' here means something obtained, gained, or acquired (*OED* sv *sb* 8a); for a similar use of the word 'purchase' as applied to a love-quest, see

From whence an issue I might propagate,
~~Are arms to princes and bring joys to subjects.~~
Her face was to mine eye beyond all wonder — *whisper*
The rest, hark in thine ear: as black as incest,   75
Which by my knowledge found, the sinful father
Seemed not to strike, but smooth — ~~but~~ *and* thou knowst this,
'Tis time to fear when tyrants seem to kiss —
Which fear so grew in me I hither fled
~~Under the covering of a careful night,~~   80
~~Who seemed my good protector, and being here,~~
~~Bethought me what was past, what might succeed.~~
I knew him tyrannous, and tyrants' fears
Decrease not but grow faster than the years;
And should he doubt, as no doubt he doth,   85
That I should open to the listening air
How many worthy princes' bloods were shed
To keep his bed of blackness unlaid-ope,
To lop that doubt he'll fill this land with arms,
And make pretence of wrong that I have done him,   90
When all, for mine (if I may call't offence)
Must feel war's blow, who spares not innocence,
Which love to all, of which thyself art one,
Who now reprov'dst me for't —
HELLICANUS   Alas sir.
PERICLES Drew sleep out of mine eyes, blood from my cheeks,   95
         Musings into my mind, with thousand doubts
         How I might stop this tempest ere it came,
         And finding little comfort to relieve them
         I thought it princely charity to grieve for them.
HELLICANUS Well my lord, since you have given me leave to speak,   100
         Freely will I speak. Antiochus you fear,
         And justly too I think you fear the tyrant,

78 seem] Q2; seemes Q   82 Bethought me] *Rowe*; Bethought Q   83 fears] F4; feare Q   85 doubt] *Malone*; doo't Q
88 unlaid-ope] *hyphenated this edn; unhyphenated* Q   91 call't] *Malone*; call Q   94 for't –] *Malone subst.; fort.* Q

Temp. 4.1.13–14, 'as my gift, and thine own acquisition / Worthily purchas'd, take my daughter'.
  72 issue Understood as a plural, hence the verbs
in the next line.
  73 Are arms Which are arms; i.e. give strength
to kings.

77 Seemed Pretended.
77 smooth flatter.
80 careful (1) watchful, (2) full of care.
85 he doubt he suspect, anxiously fear.
88 unlaid-ope unrevealed, concealed.

Who either by public war or private treason
Will take away your life.
Therefore my lord, go travel for a while   105
Till that his rage and anger be forgot,
Or till the destinies do cut his thread of life.
Your rule direct to any; if to me,
Day serves not light more faithful than I'll be.
PERICLES I do not doubt thy faith.   110
But should he wrong my liberties in my absence?
HELLICANUS We'll mingle our bloods together in the earth,
From whence we had our being and our birth.
PERICLES Tyre, I now look from thee then, and to Tarsus
Intend my travel, where I'll hear from thee,   115
And by whose letters I'll dispose myself.
The care I had and have of subjects' good
On thee I lay, whose wisdom's strength can bear it.
I'll take thy word for faith, not ask thine oath;
Who shuns not to break one, will crack both.   120
But in our orbs we'll live so round and safe
That time of both this truth shall ne'er convince:
Thou show'dst a subject's shine, I a true prince.

Exeunt

104–9] *Rowe's lineation; prose* Q   117 subjects'] *Malone;* subiects Q   120 will crack both] Q; will sure crack F3; will crack them *NS*   123 SD] *Rowe; Exit* Q

107 **destinies** the three goddesses of fate (the Fates). To the Greeks and Romans they controlled the birth, life, and death of everyone: Clotho, the spinner who spun the 'thread of life'; Lachesis, the disposer of lots, who assigned to each man his destiny; and Atropos, who carried the shears that cut the thread at death. Compare 3.3.8, 'the strict fates'.

108 **direct** hand over, assign.

111 **liberties** privileges, rights (*OED* Liberty *sb* 7b; also 7c, domains or property); here, the territories over which his royal prerogative extends.

116 **dispose myself** make my decisions i.e. based on news from home.

119–20 **I'll take ... crack both** Pericles' trust (faith) in Hellicanus is so great that he will accept his 'word' of honour without, as a prince would normally require of a subject, asking him to swear an 'oath'; since a man who will break his word will certainly also break an oath. An axiomatic statement which foreshadows the oath-breaking of Cleon and Dioniza; see 1.4.99–103; 3.3.20–33.

121 **our orbs** i.e. our different worlds. Compare *Cym.* 5.5.371–2, 'after this strange starting from your orbs, / You may reign in them now'.

121 **round** (1) plainly, (2) straightforwardly; used also as a play on 'orbs' in which Pericles and Hellicanus move in different spheres of action, hence 'round'.

122 **of both ... convince** 'shall never refute this truth concerning both of us' (the truth contained in the next line). 'Convince' is here used in the etymological sense of 'overcome', from the Latin *convincere* (Hoeniger).

123 **subject's shine** i.e. the light of a subject's loyalty.

[**1.3**] *Enter* THALIARD

THALIARD So this is Tyre, and this the court. Here must I kill King
Pericles, and if I do it not I am sure to be hanged at home. 'Tis
dangerous. Well, I perceive he was a wise fellow and had good
discretion that, being bid to ask what he would of the king, desired
he might know none of his secrets. ~~Now do I see he had some reason~~   5
~~for't, for if a king bid a man be a villain, he's bound by the indenture~~
~~of his oath to be one.~~ Husht, here comes the lords of Tyre.

Enter HELLICANUS, ESCANES, *with other lords*

HELLICANUS You shall not need, my fellow-peers of Tyre,
      Further to question me of your king's departure.
      His sealed commission left in trust with me   10
      Does speak sufficiently he's gone to travel.
THALIARD [*Aside*] How? The king gone?
HELLICANUS If further yet you will be satisfied
      Why as it were unlicensed of your loves
      He would depart, I'll give some light unto you.   15
      Being at Antioch –
THALIARD [*Aside*] What from Antioch?
HELLICANUS Royal Antiochus, on what cause I know not,
      Took some displeasure at him, at least he judged so;
      And doubting lest he had erred or sinned,   20
      To show his sorrow he'd correct himself,
      So puts himself unto the shipman's toil,
      With whom each minute threatens life or death.
THALIARD [*Aside*] Well, I perceive
      I shall not be hanged now, although I would;   25

Act 1, Scene 3 1.3] *Malone; not in Q* 0 SD] Q *(Enter Thaliard solus)* 8–23] *Rowe's lineation; prose Q* 10 sealed] sea- /
led Q 12 SD] *Malone; not in Q* 16 Antioch –] *Rowe; Antioch.* Q 17 SD] *Malone; not in Q* 24–5] *This edn's lineation;
prose Q* 24 SD] *Malone; not in Q*

Act 1, Scene 3
  Location Tyre.
  3–5 a wise fellow ... secrets In North's
Plutarch (1612 edn, p. 890) in the *Life of Demetrius*,
the story is told of the poet Philippides who, when
the ruler Lysimachus asked what he might give
him, said 'Euen what it shall please thee, ô king, so
it be none of thy secrets'.
  6 indenture contract of service between servant
and master.
  14 unlicensed of your loves without receiving

your approval and good wishes. As in *CA* 499–502,
'Our prince . . . Without comune assent, / That
sodeinly is fro us went'.
  20 doubting fearing.
  21 correct expiate.
  25 although I would Thaliard has already stated
(1–2) that if he fails to kill Pericles in Tyre he will be
hanged when he returns home; by being in Tyre
'now', i.e. in Pericles' absence, he has received a
temporary respite.

But since he's gone, the king's seas must please:
He 'scaped the land to perish at the sea.
I'll present myself.
[*Aloud*] Peace to the lords of Tyre.
HELLICANUS   Lord Thaliard
From Antiochus is welcome.
THALIARD   From him I come   30
With message unto princely Pericles;
But since my landing I have understood
Your lord has betake himself to unknown travels.
Now message must return from whence it came.
HELLICANUS We have no reason to desire it,   35
Commended to our master not to us.
Yet ere you shall depart this we desire:
As friends to Antioch we may feast in Tyre.

Exeunt

[1.4] *Enter* CLEON *the Governor of Tarsus, with* [DIONIZA] *his wife and others*

CLEON My Dioniza, shall we rest us here,
And by relating tales of others' griefs
See if 'twill teach us to forget our own?
DIONIZA That were to blow at fire in hope to quench it,
For who digs hills because they do aspire   5
Throws down one mountain to cast up a higher.
O my distressèd lord, even such our griefs are:

26–7] *Malone's lineation; prose* Q   26 king's seas] Q; king it sure *Steevens, conj. Percy;* king's ears it *Dyce*   28–30] *This edn's lineation; prose* Q   29 SD] *This edn; not in* Q   29 SH] Q4; *not in* Q   31–8] *Rowe's lineation; prose* Q   33 betake] Q; betooke Q2; betaken *Edwards;* betoke *Oxford*   38 SD] Q2; *Exit* Q   Act 1, Scene 4   1.4] *Malone; not in* Q   0 SD DIONIZA] *Steevens; not in* Q   5 aspire] *NS;* aspire? Q

26 the king's seas must please it must now be up to the king's (Antiochus') seas to do his pleasure (bidding) and kill Pericles, hence 'perish' in the next line. *OED* Sea *sb* 1e gives the sense of naval operations: in this line 'seas' is therefore used in synecdoche for 'navy.' Twine tells how Antiochus 'commanded a great Navie of ships to be prepared to scoure the seas abroad, if haply they might meet with him [Apollonius]' (*PPA*, p. 430).

33 betake An irregular participial formation,

see Abbott 343–4 and see *H8* 2.4.153–4 'have . . . spake'.

36 Commended Since it was commended.

Act 1, Scene 4
Location Tarsus: see map facing p. 1.
4 blow . . . quench it Proverbial (Tilley F251, 'Do not blow the fire thou wouldst quench').
5–6 digs . . . higher A wonderful image of futility.

[handwritten: Dioniza med S]

Here they are but felt and seen with mischief's eyes,
But like to groves, being topped, they higher rise.

CLEON O Dioniza,   10
    Who wanteth food and will not say he wants it,
    Or can conceal his hunger till he famish?
    Our tongues and sorrows to sound deep
    Our woes into the air, our eyes to weep,
    Till tongues fetch breath that may proclaim   15
    Them louder, that if heaven slumber while
    Their creatures want, they may awake
    Their helpers to comfort them.
    I'll then discourse our woes felt several years,
    And wanting breath to speak, help me with tears.   20

[handwritten left margin: Sit on DS side of bench]

DIONIZA I'll do my best, sir.   *[handwritten: To pacify]*
CLEON This Tarsus o'er which I have the government,
    A city on whom plenty held full hand –
    For riches strewed herself even in her streets –
    Whose towers bore heads so high they kissed the clouds,   25
    And strangers ne'er beheld but wondered at,
    Whose men and dames so jetted and adorned,
    Like one another's glass to trim them by;
    [handwritten: Whose] Their tables were stored full to glad the sight,
    And not so much to feed on as delight;   30
    All poverty was scorned, and pride so great,
    The name of help grew odious to repeat.

---

15 fetch] feteh Q

8 with mischief's eyes with the eyes of misfortune or calamity.

9 groves . . . rise The action of pruning (being 'topped') only makes things grow higher, so the suggestion offered in 2–3 is here likened to a source of more misery.

13–16 tongues . . . louder Freely paraphrased: 'we give voice to our lamentations, and we cry till we catch our breath to proclaim them louder'.

16–17 heaven . . . Their For 'heaven' with plural pronoun see *Mac.* 2.1.4–5, 'There's husbandry in heaven, / Their candles are all out'.

17 they the tongues of the creatures in want.

18 helpers those in heaven.

19 then therefore, i.e. for the reasons explained in the lines above.

20 wanting breath . . . tears As in 14–15: while Cleon catches breath to lament their woes, Dioniza assists by weeping.

21 I'll do my best, sir The Oxford editors complain that Q has Dioniza 'ludicrously respond to Cleon's rhetoric as though it were a literal request'. However, literal reaction to hyperbole is one of the signs of irony, which we take Dioniza to be employing. For the relationship between Cleon and Dioniza, see Introduction, pp. 67–8.

22 This Tarsus 'This is Tarsus'; an obvious aid to the audience to let them know what place Cleon (who is not named in the scene, nor indeed until 3.1.77) is governor of.

23 plenty held full hand The image is that of the cornucopia. See 53, 'plenty's cup'.

27 jetted dressed in a fashionable or stylish manner.

32 repeat mention.

to recall

DIONIZA O 'tis too true.

CLEON But see what heaven can do by this our change.
These mouths who but of late, earth, sea, and air,   35
Were all too little to content and please,
Although they gave their creatures in abundance,
As houses are defiled for want of use,
They are now starved for want of exercise;
Those palates who not yet two savours younger   40
Must have inventions to delight the taste,
Would now be glad of bread and beg for it;
Those mothers who to nuzzle up their babes
Thought nought too curious, are ready now
To eat those little darlings whom they loved.   45
So sharp are hunger's teeth that man and wife
Draw lots who first shall die to lengthen life.
Here stands a lord, and there a lady weeping,
Here many sink, yet those which see them fall
Have scarce strength left to give them burial.   50
Is not this true?

Stay turned away to mumble.   *to hide*

DIONIZA Our cheeks and hollow eyes do witness it.

CLEON O let those cities, that of plenty's cup
And her prosperities so largely taste,
With their superfluous riots hear these tears,   55
The misery of Tarsus may be theirs.

Enter a LORD

LORD Where's the Lord Governor?

CLEON   Here: speak out thy sorrows

37 they] Q2; thy Q   **40** two savours] *This edn;* too sauers Q; two summers *Theobald MS.; Steevens, conj. Mason*   **57–61** *This edn's lineation; lined* Where's . . . Gouernor? / *Cle.* Here, . . . bringst / in . . . expect / *Lord.* Wee . . . neighbouring / shore . . . hitherward / *Cleon.* I . . . much. / Q

35 earth, sea, and air Three of the four elements from which all other substances are composed; the fourth element is fire. See 3.1.34.

40–2 The usual emendation 'summers' for Q 'sauers' (40) is unnecessary and misses the point: the lines are about eating, one of the key images of the play (see Introduction, pp. 49–51). Paraphrased, the lines mean 'Those gourmets ("palates") who only a couple of meals, or gastronomic experiences ("savours"), earlier were craving variety and novelty ("inventions") in their food, are now begging bread gladly.' The entire clause is hyperbole, but so is most of Cleon's lament.

43 nuzzle (1) nurture and (2) nurse (*OED* sv *v*² 2 and 4).

44 nought too curious i.e. did not have to give it a second thought, or give their choice careful consideration.

55 superfluous (1) indulgent, (2) having more than enough.

55 riots revels.

55 these tears this lamentation, this cry for help.

56 May they share our grief, i.e. understand it.

Which thee bringst in haste, for comfort is
Too far for us to expect.

LORD   We have descried
Upon our neighbouring shore a portly sail   60
Of ships make hitherward.

CLEON   I thought as much.
One sorrow never comes but brings an heir.
That may succeed as his inheritor,
And so in ours. Some neighbouring nation,
Taking advantage of our misery,   65
Hath stuffed the hollow vessels with their power
To beat us down (the which are down already)
And make a conquest of unhappy me,
Whereas no glory's got to overcome.

LORD That's the least fear. For by the semblance   70
Of their white flags displayed they bring us peace,
And come to us as favourers, not as foes.

CLEON Thou speakst like him's untutored; to repeat,
Who makes the fairest show, means most deceit.
But bring they what they will and what they can,   75
What need we leave? Our ground's the lowest
And we are half-way there. Go tell their general
We attend him here, to know for what he comes,
And whence he comes, and what he craves.

LORD I go, my lord.   [*Exit*]

---

58 thee] Q; thou Q4   64 ours. Some] *Edwards*; ours, some Q   66 Hath] *Rowe³*; That Q   68 me] Q; men *Malone*   70–3]
Malone's lineation; prose Q   73 him's] *Malone*; himnes Q   76 leave] Q; feare Q4   76 Our] Q *(our)*; the Q4; On *NS*   77–
9] *Rowe's lineation; prose* Q   80 SD] *Malone²*; *not in* Q

60 portly sail stately or majestic fleet; compare
MV 1.1.9.
   62–3 One . . . inheritor Proverbial (Tilley
M1012); compare *Ham.* 4.5.78–9, 'When sorrows
come, they come not single spies, / But in battal-
ions.'
   68 me Malone emended Q's 'mee' to 'men'; the
Oxford edition revived the idea, printing 'mē' without explanation. Q's word seems right; Cleon's self-
indulgent despair is well caught by the wimpish
style of this line.
   69 Where no glory is obtained in such a conquest.
   71 white flags displayed A white flag showed
that a ship had no hostile intention, but had come to
trade or bring succour or that it sought the shelter of

an anchorage (as Pericles requests, 98). It was a
regular signal even in pirate voyages, hence Cleon's
distrust expressed (74). See Falconer, p. 26.
   73 him's untutored he who is unschooled.
   73 to repeat let me tell you again, let me put it to
you another way.
   76 leave? Q's word only needs a question-mark to
make sense: as their 'ground's the lowest', there's no
point in attempting to shift to a different ground of
defence.
   76–7 Our ground's . . . there A military usage
is also implied: the higher ground in battle was the
most advantageous. See *R3* 5.3.15, 'Let us survey
the vantage of the ground.'

CLEON Welcome is peace, if he on peace consist;   81
       If wars, we are unable to resist.

                  Enter PERICLES *with attendants*

PERICLES Lord Governor, for so we hear you are,
          Let not our ships and number of our men
          Be like a beacon fired t'amaze your eyes.   85
          We have heard your miseries as far as Tyre
          And seen the desolation of your streets;
          ~~Nor come we to add sorrow to your tears,~~
          ~~But to relieve them of their heavy load;~~
          And these our ships ~~you happily may think~~   90
          ~~Are like the Trojan horse was stuffed within~~
          ~~With bloody veins expecting overthrow,~~
          Are stored with corn to make your needy bread,
          And give them life whom hunger starved half dead.
ALL [*Kneeling*] The gods of Greece protect you,   95
     And we'll pray for you.
CLEON   Arise I pray you, rise. [*They rise*]
          We do not look for reverence, but for love,
          And harbourage for ourself, our ships, and men.
CLEON The which when any shall not gratify
       Or pay you with unthankfulness in thought,   100
       Be it our wives, our children, or ourselves,
       The curse of heaven and men succeed their evils,
       Till when the which, I hope, shall ne'er be seen.

---

92 veins] Q; *views Malone; banes Collier*   95 SD] *This edn; not in* Q   96–8] *Rowe's lineation; lined* And . . . you. / *Per.*
Arise . . . reuerence, / But . . . men. Q   96 SD] *This edn; not in* Q

85 beacon fired t'amaze Beacons of fire were set along the coast of England to warn of the impending invasion of the Spanish Armada; the beacon is thus a symbol of alarm ('amaze'). Falconer notes (p. 79) that later in Elizabeth's reign, the beacon was used as a luminous mark to aid ships by night.

90 happily haply, perhaps.

91 Trojan horse Pericles is reassuring Cleon that, unlike the Trojan horse with its concealed soldiers, Pericles' ships are completely peaceful.

91 was which was.

92 bloody veins A metaphor for the Greek warriors; compare 'vessels' (66).

92 expecting overthrow awaiting the overthrow (of Troy).

93 needy (1) those subjects in need, (2) much needed.

99–102 The first of Cleon's two self-fulfilling curses; see also 3.3.20–4. The speech also looks forward to Dioniza's criminal ingratitude in the planning of Marina's murder in Act 4.

99 gratify show gratitude for (*OED* sv *v* 1).

100 in thought i.e. even in thought.

102 succeed follow or come after in the course of events (*OED* sv *v* 6a).

Your grace is welcome to our town and us.
PERICLES Which welcome we'll accept, feast here awhile,   105
    Until our stars that frown lend us a smile.

Exeunt

[**2.0**] *Enter* GOWER

GOWER Here have you seen a mighty king
    His child, iwis, to incest bring,
    A better prince and benign lord
    That will prove awful both in deed and word.
    Be quiet then, as men should be   5
    Till he hath past necessity.
    I'll show you those in troubles reign,
    Losing a mite, a mountain gain.
    The good in conversation,
    To whom I give my benison,   10
    Is still at Tarsus, where each man
    Thinks all is writ he spoken can;
    And to remember what he does
    Build his statue to make him glorious;
    But tidings to the contrary   15
    Are brought your eyes, what need speak I?

Act 2, Scene 0   2.0] F3 *(Actus Secundus); not in* Q   2 iwis] Q *(I'wis);* I wis *Hoeniger*   11 Tarsus] Q4 *(Tharsus);*
Tharstill Q

106 Until . . . smile The stars were thought to
have an omnipotent influence on the lives and destinies of men; a frowning star (or planet) was un-
lucky or unfortunate. Pericles has not forgotten he
is still a refugee from Antiochus' threat.

Act 2, Scene 0
2 iwis Although often spelled at the time as in Q
('I'wis') or as 'I wis', this is perplexing to the modern reader, who would naturally think it a verb. It is
not; it is an adverb (the nearest linguistic equivalent
is German '*gewiss*') meaning 'certainly' (*OED* sv B).
4 awful awe-inspiring.
6 past necessity gone through trial or hardship.
7 those in troubles reign those who, reigning in
troubles.

8 mite a minute particle or portion; *OED* sv *sb²*
3a cites this example.
10 benison blessing.
12 writ Holy Writ, i.e. the gospel truth.
12 he spoken can An archaism from Early (pre-
sixteenth century) English for the present infinitive:
'he is able to speak'; see Abbott 349.
13 remember commemorate.
14 i.e. build him a statue to glorify him. See *CA*
571–77, 'That thei for ever in remembrance / Made
a figure in resemblance / Of hym and in a commen
place / Thei set it up: so that his face / Might every
maner man beholde, / So as the citee was beholde, /
It was of laton overgylt'.
15 tidings to the contrary bad news.

Dumb show

Enter at one door Pericles talking with Cleon, all the train with them.
Enter at another door, a gentleman with a letter to Pericles; Pericles shows
the letter to Cleon; Pericles gives the messenger a reward, and knights him.
Exit Pericles at one door, and Cleon [and his followers] at another

Good Hellicane that stayed at home
(Not to eat honey like a drone
From others' labours), for though he strive
To killen bad, keep good alive,
And to fulfil his prince' desire   20
Send word of all that haps in Tyre,
How Thaliard came full bent with sin,
And had intent to murder him;
And that in Tarsus was not best
Longer for him to make his rest.   25
He doing so put forth to seas,
Where when men been there's seldom ease.
For now the wind begins to blow,
Thunder above, and deeps below
Makes such unquiet that the ship,   30
Should house him safe, is wracked and split,
And he, good prince, having all lost,
By waves from coast to coast is tossed.
All perishen of man, of pelf,   35

16 SD.1 *show*] *shew.* Q   16 SD.5 *and his followers*] *This edn; not in* Q   17 Hellicane] Q3 *subst.; Helicon* Q   17 that] Q; hath
Steevens   21 prince'] *Malone;* prince Q   22 Sent word] *This edn;* Sau'd one Q; Sends word *Theobald MS., Steevens*   24
had intent to murder] Q *(corr.);* hid in Tent to murdred Q *(uncorr.);* hid intent to murder Q2–3   25 Tarsus] F3 *subst.;*
Tharsis Q

18–20 'Hellicanus acts not like a drone but like a
good bee, which kills drones and helps to preserve
the King (i.e. Queen bee)' (Hoeniger, citing Harold
F. Brooks). A proverbial image (Dent D612.1, 'To
eat honey like a drone').
20 **killen** Archaism for the infinitive 'to kill'.
23 **full bent with** Extent to which a bow may be
bent, degree of tension; hence degree of capacity
(Onions); but also 'intent upon.'
24 **had intent** The reading of uncorrected Q is
amusing; the correction does not imply consultation
of copy, merely common sense, but the tendency of
later editors to sophisticate by retaining Q uncorr.
'hid' is unjustifiable.
27 **doing** The Oxford edition reads 'dēing' (i.e.
'deeming') without explaining why an abbreviation
should be found in a short line. Gower is rather

mysterious about who is who in this chorus. He has
just finished recapitulating Thaliard's visit to Tyre,
and now tells us that Hellicanus passed on to
Pericles at Tarsus both the information and the
advice not to linger there. 'He doing so', then, is
Pericles acting on Hellicanus' advice.
28 See 1.3.23.
28 **been** be, are; plural form in Early Modern
English; see Abbott 332.
32 **Should** Which should.
32 **wracked** destroyed, ruined.
35 **perishen** perish; either (1) third person plural
in Early Modern English (see Abbott 332), or (2)
present tense in Early Modern English (see Abbott
349).
35 **pelf** possessions, wealth.

Ne aught escapend but himself;
Till fortune, tired with doing bad,
Threw him ashore to give him glad.
And here he comes; what shall be next
Pardon old Gower, this longs the text.   [*Exit*]

[**2.1**] *Enter* PERICLES *wet*

PERICLES Yet cease your ire, you angry stars of heaven!
Wind, rain, and thunder, remember earthly man
Is but a substance that must yield to you,
And I, as fits my nature, do obey you.
Alas, the seas hath cast me on the rocks,   5
Washed me from shore to shore, and left my breath
Nothing to think on but ensuing death.
Let it suffice the greatness of your powers
To have bereft a prince of all his fortunes,
And having thrown him from your watery grave,   10
Here to have death in peace is all he'll crave.

Enter three FISHERMEN

I FISHERMAN What to, pelch?

40 SD] *Malone; not in* Q   **Act 2, Scene I**   2.1] *Malone subst.; not in* Q   5 seas] Q; sea *Rowe³*   6 my breath] Q; me breath
Malone   12 What to, pelch?] Q *(What, to pelch?)*; What ho, Pilch! *Malone, conj. Tyrwhitt*

36 Ne aught escapend And no one escaped/
escaping; both present or past are available, since
the context mixes the two tenses freely.
  40 longs the text 'longs' = lengthens or pro-
longs (*OED* Long *v¹* 1.2, not after 1500); 'text' =
script of the speech (*OED* sv *sb¹* 1a); hence 'The
very text to it has proved of too considerable length
already' (Steevens subst.) i.e. 'I have been talking
long enough.' An alternative interpretation, favoured by many editors, is to emend to "longs" =
belongs to (*OED* Long *v²* 2); 'the text' = the action
of the following performance; see 3.0.53–7, 'what
ensues . . . / Shall for itself, itself perform, / I nill
relate. Action may / Conveniently the rest convey,
/ Which might not, what by me is told.'

Act 2, Scene I
  Location Pentapolis: see map facing p. 1.
  1–4 An interesting contrasting parallel with *Lear*
3.2.14–19 is suggested in these lines. Where Lear

rages defiantly at the storm and stands as the 'slave'
or helpless victim of the elements, Pericles submits
to their power as befits his character ('nature'). In
this respect he has more in common with Duke
Senior in *AYLI* for whom the elements 'feelingly
persuade me what I am' (2.1.11).
  6–7 'Breath' as used twice in the play so far to
denote a speaking ability (see 1.4.15, 20); there is
nothing left for Pericles to speak about except
thoughts of death.
  11 SD In both *CA* and *PPA* it is a single fisherman
who helps Apollonius. By adding the other
fishermen Shakespeare created an effective comic
opportunity.
  12 What to, pelch? An ancient piece of argot
seems to be concealed in this line. 'To pilch' meant
to pilfer or steal, and 'pilcher' was a common term
of abuse in the early seventeenth century, either
meaning a thief (from the verb) or a 'fishy' fellow (a
pun from the fish, the pilchard). Either or both

2 FISHERMAN Ha, come and bring away the nets.

1 FISHERMAN What Patch-breech, I say.

3 FISHERMAN What say you, maister?   15

1 FISHERMAN Look how thou stirr'st now, come away, or I'll fetch
th'with a wanion.

3 FISHERMAN Faith maister, I am thinking of the poor men that were
cast away before us even now.

1 FISHERMAN Alas poor souls, it grieved my heart to hear what pitiful   20
cries they made to us to help them, when, welladay, we could scarce
help ourselves.

3 FISHERMAN Nay maister, said not I as much when I saw the porpoise
how he bounced and tumbled? They say they're half fish, half flesh,
a plague on them, they ne'er come but I look to be washed. Maister,   25
I marvel how the fishes live in the sea?

1 FISHERMAN Why, as men do a-land, the great ones eat up the little
ones. I can compare our rich misers to nothing so fitly as to a whale:
'a plays and tumbles, driving the poor fry before him, and at last
devours them all at a mouthful. Such whales have I heard on   30
a'th'land, who never leave gaping till they swallowed the whole
parish, church, steeple, bells, and all.

PERICLES [*Aside*] A pretty moral.

16–44] *as prose, Malone; lined as verse* Q   **16–17** fetch th'] *This edn;* fetch'th Q; fetch thee Q4   **33** SD] *Dyce; not in* Q

could be a hearty abusive greeting ('What's up,
filth?' might be a modern equivalent). The *English
Dialect Dictionary* (ed. Joseph Wright, 8 vols.,
1896–1905) reveals that 'pelch' was a Warwickshire
word for a fat person, and the Second Fisherman
must have been substantially built if his gown
would make Pericles a pair of bases (see 146–49) –
but the *Dictionary* gives no date for this meaning.
Any of these meanings would do and are better than
the various emendations that have been proposed.

14 Patch-breech The Third Fisherman's name
or nickname; a derogatory reference to his appearance; compare *Temp.* 3.2.63, 'What a pied ninny's
this! Thou scurvy patch!'

15 maister Q's spelling is retained, to suggest the
dialect sound of the Fishermen's speeches.

16 how thou stirr'st now Ironical: the First
Fisherman is criticising the Third for his *failure* to
stir (hurry up); compare 3.2.87.

16–17 fetch th'with a wanion The First Fisherman is threatening to beat the Third ('fetch th'')
with a vengeance ('wanion').

20–1 Alas . . . them Compare *WT* 3.3.90 ff., 'O,
the most piteous cry of the poor souls!' and *Temp.*

1.2.8–9, 'O, the cry did knock / Against my very
heart. Poor souls, they perish'd.'

21 welladay alas, woe!

23–4 when . . . tumbled In traditional weather
lore this was considered as a sign of an oncoming
storm. See the manuscript *The booke of the Sea
Carte called the Rutter* (British Library Additional
Manuscript (Add. MS.) 37024 fol. 70ʳ): 'The
delphyne fysh swemmyng and leapyng often tymes
above the water, sygnyfyeth great wynd for that
quartar' (probably meaning quarter of a lunar, i.e.
seven days, *OED* Quarter *sb* 8b), and *The Naval
Tracts of Sir William Monson*, ed. M. Oppenheim,
1913, V, 286: 'there cannot be a truer sign of a storm
than whales and porpoises playing upon the water'.

27–8 the great ones . . . ones Proverbial (Tilley
F311, 'The great fish eat the small').

28 fitly aptly, suitably.

29 'a he.

29 fry small fish.

30–1 on a'th' of on the.

33 pretty moral A neat or ingenious symbolic
argument or saying. Simonides repeats the phrase at
2.2.45 in response to Pericles' motto, thus creating a

3 FISHERMAN But maister, if I had been the sexton I would have been
    that day in the belfry.   35

2 FISHERMAN Why, man?

3 FISHERMAN Because he should have swallowed me too, and when I
    had been in his belly, I would have kept such a jangling of the bells
    that he should never have left till he cast bells, steeple, church, and
    parish up again. But if the good King Simonides were of my   40
    mind –

PERICLES [*Aside*] Simonides?

3 FISHERMAN We would purge the land of these drones that rob the
    bee of her honey.

PERICLES [*Aside*] How from the fenny subject of the sea   45
    These fishers tell the infirmities of men,
    And from their watery empire recollect
    All that may men approve or men detect.
    [*Aloud*] Peace be at your labour, honest fishermen.

2 FISHERMAN Honest, good fellow, what's that? If it be a day fits you,   50
    search out of the calendar, and no body look after it.

PERICLES May see the sea hath cast upon your coast –

2 FISHERMAN What a drunken knave was the sea to cast thee in our
    way?

PERICLES A man, whom both the waters and the wind   55
    In that vast tennis-court hath made the ball

---

37 SH] *Malone;* 1. Q 42 SD] *Dyce; not in* Q 45 SD] *Dyce; not in* Q 45 fenny] Q; finny *Tonson* 49 SD] *This edn; not in*
Q 50–1] *as prose, Malone; lined as verse* Q 53–4] *as prose, Malone; lined as verse* Q

link between these two wise princes even before
they meet.

  34 sexton officer charged with care of the church
and its contents and with bell-ringing.

  35 belfry bell tower of a church.

  37–40 Because . . . again The Fisherman's
story recalls the biblical tale of Jonah, who was swallowed by a whale and cast up again (Jonah 1.17–
2.10). Compare *Temp.* 2.1.251, 'We all were sea-
swallow'd, though some cast again.' The images of
eating and regurgitation or vomiting recur throughout the play; see Introduction, pp. 49–51.

  43–4 drones . . . honey 'our rich misers' from
line 28; compare 2.0.18–20n.

  45 fenny subject 'fenny' means 'boggy,
swampy' (*OED* sv a^1 1) or 'muddy, dirty' (*OED* sv
a^1 3). Both meanings are more readily associated
with marshland than with the sea, but are not at all
impossible in a metaphorical sense: Shakespeare
frequently refers to the ooze and slime of the sea-
bottom; for him the sea is not simply water. Most

editors emend to 'finny' but then have to make 'subject' plural, since at this date 'finny' just means
'having fins'. 'Subject' means 'theme'.

  46 infirmities faults.

  47 recollect gather up.

  48 detect reveal in guilt or wrongdoing.

  50–1 If . . . it Freely paraphrased: 'If the day resembles anything like the creature that you appear
to be, then remove it ("search out") from the calendar and no one will miss it.'

  52 May You may (ellipsis of pronoun as subject:
see Abbott 399).

  56–7 vast . . . upon The metaphor of life as a
tennis game is a commonplace in Elizabethan drama
and literature, which often portrayed man as a tennis ball subject to the will of the gods, fortune or
some great force (such as the sea). One of the best-
known uses of the image is that by John Webster in
The Duchess of Malfi: 'We are meerly the Starres
tennys-balls (strooke, and banded / Which way
please them)' (in *The Works of John Webster*, ed.

For them to play upon, entreats you pity him.
He asks of you, that never used to beg.

1 FISHERMAN No friend, cannot you beg? Here's them in our country
    of Greece gets more with begging than we can do with working.   60
2 FISHERMAN Canst thou catch any fishes then?
PERICLES I never practised it.
2 FISHERMAN Nay then thou wilt starve sure, for here's nothing to be
    got nowadays unless thou canst fish for't.

PERICLES What I have been, I have forgot to know;   65
    But what I am, want teaches me to think on:
    A man thronged up with cold, my veins are chill,
    And have no more of life than may suffice
    To give my tongue that heat to ask your help,
    Which if you shall refuse, when I am dead,   70
    For that I am a man, pray you see me burièd.

1 FISHERMAN Die, ke-tha? Now gods forbid't; and I have a gown here,
    come put it on, keep thee warm: now afore me a handsome fellow.
    Come, thou shalt go home, and we'll have flesh for all day, fish for
    fasting-days and more, or puddings and flap-jacks, and thou shalt   75
    be welcome.

59–64] *as prose, Malone; lined as verse* Q   72 ke-tha] Q; ko-tha *Rowe;* quoth'a *Malone*   74 all day] Q; holidays *Malone*   75
more, or] Q; moreo'er *Malone, conj. Farmer*

David Gunby, David Carnegie, Antony Hammond, Doreen DelVecchio, 1995, vol. I, 5.4.54–5). For the force of the sea, see Sir Francis Drake's *The World Encompassed By Sir Francis Drake*: 'the distressed ship and helplesse men to the vncertaine and rowling seas, which tossed them, like a ball in a racket' (1628, p. 42 (sig. F3ᵛ); the author was Drake's nephew).
58 used to beg Pericles means he was not accustomed ('used') to ask alms continually (*OED* Beg v 1b (*intr.*)); i.e. that he is not, despite appearances, a professional beggar. In 78 the Second Fisherman takes him up on this: 'you said you could not beg', to which Pericles replies 'I did but crave.' A fine distinction is being drawn here: to crave (*OED* sv v 2) means 'to ask for something especially as a gift or favour', indistinguishable from 'beg' (*OED* sv v 2): 'to ask as a favour or an act of grace'. The Second Fisherman gets the point, in the next line differentiating a 'craver' from a professional beggar. In 124 Pericles returns the serve by 'begging' the armour from the Fishermen. Compare *R2* 5.3.78, 'A beggar begs that never begg'd before.'

62 practised engaged in.
67 thronged up overwhelmed.
69 tongue . . . help See 1.4.13–16 for a similar use of tongues needing breath to ask for help.
72 ke-tha Not in *OED*; very likely a dialect version of 'quoth'a'; i.e. 'Die, did he say?'
72 and if, with the implied meaning 'so long as'.
73 afore me A form of a mild oath i.e. 'upon my word'. Alternatively, the Fisherman's phrase may mean 'now there stands before me'.
74–5 flesh . . . fasting days We retain Q's reading since so much of the Fishermen's speeches is colloquial; the Fisherman's 'all day' implies 'for all of the day' or 'every day'; in either case Pericles' welcome is cause for a special celebration. Malone's emendation 'holidays' for Q's 'all day' is quite attractive since holidays (flesh-days: days on which butcher's meat was eaten) are frequently juxtaposed in Elizabethan literature with fasting-days (days of self-denial when fish was eaten).
75 puddings stuffing.
75 flap-jacks pancakes.

PERICLES I thank you sir.

2 FISHERMAN Hark you my friend: you said you could not beg?

PERICLES I did but crave.

2 FISHERMAN But crave? Then I'll turn craver too, and so I shall   80
'scape whipping.

PERICLES Why, are your beggars whipped then?

2 FISHERMAN Oh not all, my friend, not all; for if all your beggars were
whipped I would wish no better office than to be beadle. But
maister, I'll go draw up the net.   85

        [*Exeunt 2 and 3 Fishermen*]

PERICLES [*Aside*] How well this honest mirth becomes their labour!

1 FISHERMAN Hark you sir, do you know where ye are?

PERICLES Not well.

1 FISHERMAN Why I'll tell you, this is called Pentapolis, and our king,
the good Simonides.   90

PERICLES The good Simonides do you call him?

1 FISHERMAN Ay sir, and he deserves so to be called for his peaceable
reign and good government.

PERICLES He is a happy king since he gains from his subjects the name
of good by his government. How far is his court distant from this   95
shore?

1 FISHERMAN Marry sir, half a day's journey; and I'll tell you, he hath
a fair daughter, and tomorrow is her birthday, and there are princes
and knights come from all parts of the world to joust and tourney
for her love.   100

PERICLES Were my fortunes equal to my desires I could wish to make
one there.

1 FISHERMAN Oh sir, things must be as they may, and what a man
cannot get, he may lawfully deal for his wife's soul.

80–1] *as prose, Malone; lined as verse* Q   82 your] *Yale;* you Q   85 SD] *Dyce subst.; not in* Q   86 SD] *Dyce; not in* Q   89–
90] *as prose, Malone; lined as verse* Q   89 is] Q2; I Q   89 Pentapolis] *Rowe; Pantapoles* Q   92–102] *as prose, Malone; lined
as verse* Q

79 **crave** ask earnestly (*OED sv v* 2).

81 **'scape whipping** In Elizabethan times the
regular punishment for begging was whipping; the
Second Fisherman jokingly suggests he can escape
whipping simply by using the more unusual word
'craver' for the activity of begging. For the phrase,
'shall scape whipping', see *Ham.* 2.2.530.

84 **beadle** Parish officer appointed to punish
petty offenders.

99 **joust** Engage in sporting combat in which
two knights on horseback encountered each other
with lances (*OED sv v* 3 and *sb* 1).

99 **tourney** compete in a tournament; also 132.

101–2 **make one** be one of those participating in
the joust.

103 **things . . . may** Proverbial for 'he that cannot do as he would must do as he may'; see Tilley
T202 and *H5* 2.2.20.

103–4 **what . . . soul** This obscure joke has bewildered editors; Hoeniger's explanation makes the
most sense: 'what the fisherman means is that if a
man cannot get rich any other way, he may decide to
deal for wealth with his wife's soul, i.e. rent her out
to another man'. Hoeniger cites Marston's *The*

Enter SECOND *and* THIRD FISHERMEN, *drawing up a net*

2 FISHERMAN Help maister help, here's a fish hangs in the net like a   105
poor man's right in the law, 'twill hardly come out. Ha, bots on't,
'tis come at last, and 'tis turned to a rusty armour.

PERICLES An armour, friends? I pray you let me see it.
Thanks fortune yet, that after all thy crosses
Thou givest me somewhat to repair myself,   110
And though it was mine own, part of my heritage,
Which my dead father did bequeath to me
With this strict charge even as he left his life:
'Keep it my Pericles, it hath been a shield
'Twixt me and death', and pointed to this brace,   115
'For that it saved me, keep it; in like necessity,
The which the gods protect thee, fame may defend thee.'
It kept where I kept, I so dearly loved it,
Till the rough seas that spares not any man
Took it in rage; though calmed, have given't again.   120
I thank thee for't; my shipwreck now's no ill
Since I have here my father gave in his will.

1 FISHERMAN What mean you sir?

PERICLES To beg of you, kind friends, this coat of worth,
For it was sometime target to a king: 125
I know it by this mark. He loved me dearly,

---

104 SD SECOND *and* THIRD FISHERMEN] *Steevens subst.; the two Fisher-men* Q   108 pray] Q *(corr.)*; pary Q *(uncorr.)*   109
yet] Q *(corr.)*; yeat Q *(uncorr.)*   109 all thy crosses] *Theobald MS, Delius*; all crosses Q   114–15 'Keep . . . death']
Keepe . . . death Q   116–17 'For . . . thee.'] For . . . thee: Q   117 thee, fame] Q; thee from, *Malone*   120 have] Q; hath Q2

Dutch Courtesan as an instance of this common wit-
ticism: 'A poore decayed mechanicall mans wife,
her husband is layd up, may not she lawfully be layd
downe, when her husbands onely rising, is by his
wifes falling . . . They sell their bodies: doe not better persons sell their soules?' (ed. Peter Davison,
1968, 1.1.102–24).

105 hangs With a play on the law's delays (*OED*
v 17b, citing Starkey's *England* 1.iv.118: 'I see many
mennys materys heng in suite ii, iii, or iiij yere'); an
appropriate image for the simile that follows.

106 bots on't A curse, i.e. 'a plague on it!' (or
'rot it!'); 'bots' is a disease in horses caused by para-
sitic worms or maggots.

110 repair restore.

111 And though Even though; Pericles has just
thanked fortune for giving him something (even
though it is his own).

115 brace armour. See Supplementary Note.

116 like necessity similar danger or trial.

117 The which . . . thee This phrase needs ex-
plication, or emendation. It could be freely paraphrased as: 'from which danger may the gods protect you, and your fame (i.e. reputation, honour in
battle; see 133) defend you'. The Oxford editors
suggest a complex emendation: 'The which the
gods forfend, the same may defend thee.' This requires (a) a misreading by the compositor of
'forfend' as 'protect' (difficult to envisage) and (b)
misreading long *s* as f (less common than one would
expect).

119–20 seas . . . spares . . . have For ellipsis of
the nominative see Abbott 399–400; this use of ellipsis is quite common in the play.

122 my father gave what my father gave.

124 beg See 58 n.

124 coat of worth the armour.

125 target shield.

And for his sake I wish the having of it,
And that you'd guide me to your sovereign's court,
Where with it I may appear a gentleman,
And if that ever my low fortune's better   130
I'll pay your bounties; till then, rest your debtor.

3 FISHERMAN Why, wilt thou tourney for the lady?

PERICLES I'll show the virtue I have borne in arms.

1 FISHERMAN Why, do'ee take it, and the gods give thee good an't.

2 FISHERMAN Ay, but hark you my friend, 'twas we that made up this   135
garment through the rough seams of the waters. There are certain
condolements, certain vails. I hope sir, if you thrive, you'll remember from whence you had them.

PERICLES Believe't I will.

By your furtherance I am clothed in steel,   140
And spite of all the rupture of the sea
This jewel holds his building on my arms.
Unto thy value I will mount myself
Upon a courser, whose delight steps
Shall make the gazer joy to see him tread.   145
Only, my friend, I yet am unprovided
Of a pair of bases.

---

130 fortune's] Q; fortunes *Steevens* 134 do'ee] Q *(corr.)* (do'e); di'e Q *(uncorr.)* 141 rupture] Q; rapture *Rowe³*
144 delight] Q; delightful F3; delightsome *Oxford* 146–7] *Malone's lineation; prose in* Q

129 **appear** present myself as.
131 **pay your bounties** repay your acts of generosity.
133 **virtue** (1) courage (*OED* sv *sb* 7), (2) superiority, excellence, unusual ability (*OED* sv *sb* 5a).
134 **do'ee** do thee.
134 **an't** of it.
135 **made up** fitted together; a tailor's term, hence 'seams' (136); a further indication that a complete suit of armour has been washed ashore.
137 **condolements** A malapropism; possibly a blunder for 'emoluments' or a confusion with 'dole' = portion or share. Such malapropisms are common in Shakespeare's comic characters; see Dogberry in *Ado* and Costard in *LLL*.
137 **vails** (1) tips or gratuities: (*OED* Vail *sb¹* 4a, 5); (2) as a verb: to do homage (as in 4.0.29) (*OED* Vail *v²* 11); (3) remnants of cloth after a suit was made up (which continues the tailoring image) (*OED* Vail *sb¹* 6). The Second Fisherman, who is obviously asking for recompense for the armour from Pericles, may have confused or combined all three meanings.

138 **them** Probably refers to the pieces that make up Pericles' armour.
141 **rupture** the breaking of waves (Onions); 'a break in a surface or substance' (*OED* sv *sb* 3a).
142 **jewel . . . building . . . arm** The jewel is metaphorical for Pericles' armour, or 'brace', whose function when applied in a different sense of the word is a beam or prop used to strengthen a building (*OED* sv *sb²* 17); the 'building' = Pericles' body; compare *Cym.* 4.2.354–5, 'The ruin [i.e. Cloten's body] speaks that sometime / It was a worthy building.'
143 **Unto thy value** As high as the value (worthiness) of the 'jewel'.
144 **courser** horse.
144 **delight steps** delightful steps; 'delight' as an adjective is not recorded in *OED*, but for nouns used as adjectives, see Abbott 5; for the licence of converting one part of speech into another see Abbott 22, and compare *Ham.* 3.1.156, 'the honey of his music vows'.
147 **pair of bases** See Supplementary Note to 115.

2 FISHERMAN We'll sure provide, thou shalt have my best gown to
    make thee a pair, and I'll bring thee to the court myself.
PERICLES Then honour be but a goal to my will,   150
    This day I'll rise or else add ill to ill.

                                                      [*Exeunt*]

Enter MR

[**2.2**] *Sound a sennet. Enter* [*King*] SIMONIDES *and* THAISA [*above. Enter*
LORDS], *attendants.* [*Simonides and Thaisa sit*]

Servant

Caution the
King

SIMONIDES Are the knights ready to begin the triumph?
~~I LORD~~ They are my liege, and stay your coming
    To present themselves.
SIMONIDES Return them, we are ready, and our daughter here,
    In honour of whose birth these triumphs are,   5
    Sits here like beauty's child, whom nature gat
    For men to see, and seeing wonder at.
THAISA It pleaseth you, my royal father, to express   *to encourage*
    My commendations great, whose merit's less.
SIMONIDES It's fit it should be so, for princes are   10
    A model which heaven makes like to itself.
    As jewels lose their glory if neglected,
    So princes their renowns if not respected.
    'Tis now your honour, daughter, to entertain
    The labour of each knight in his device.   *to accept*   15
THAISA Which to preserve mine honour I'll perform.
               The FIRST KNIGHT *passes by*
SIMONIDES Who is the first that doth prefer himself?

148–49] *as prose, Malone; lined as verse* Q   150 a goal] Q; *equal* NS, *conj. Staunton*   151 SD] *Rowe; not in* Q   **Act 2, Scene**
2   2.2] *Malone; not in* Q   0 SD.1 *Sound a sennet*] *Oxford subst.; not in* Q   0 SD.1 *King*] *This edn; not in* Q   0 SD.1 *above.*
Enter] *This edn; not in* Q   0 SD.2 LORDS] *Malone; not in* Q   0 SD.2 *attendants*] Q2; attendaunce Q   0 SD.2 *Simonides and*
Thaisa sit] *This edn; not in* Q; *and sit on* 2. *thrones / Oxford*

Act 2, Scene 2
  Location Pentapolis. The material for the scene
is not found in *CA* or in *PPA*.
  2.2.0 SD.1 *above* See Supplementary Note.
  1 triumph Here = 'tournament'; a public entertainment or festivity. Tournaments of this kind
were often staged in the reigns of Elizabeth I and
James I.
  2 stay await.
  4 Return Answer.
  5 In honour of whose birth The same occasion

which marks a suitor's victory occurs in *TNK*
2.5.36, 'You have honor'd her fair birthday with
your virtues.'
  6 gat begat (begot, fathered).
  6–7 Like Antiochus, Simonides describes his
daughter's conception; see 1.1.9–10.
  14 entertain receive.
  15 The Knight's emblematic design and motto
on his shield. See Supplementary Note.
  17 prefer present.

THAISA A knight of Sparta, my renownèd father,
And the device he bears upon his shield
Is a black Ethiop reaching at the sun,   20
The word: *Lux tua vita mihi.*

SIMONIDES He loves you well that holds his life of you.

The SECOND KNIGHT [*passes by*]

Who is the second that presents himself?

THAISA A prince of Macedon, my royal father,
And the device he bears upon his shield   25
Is an armed knight that's conquered by a lady,
The motto thus in Spanish:
Pue per doleera kee per forsa.

The THIRD KNIGHT [*passes by*]

SIMONIDES And with the third?

THAISA   The third, of Antioch,
And his device a wreath of chivalry, the word: 30
Me pompæ provexit apex.

The FOURTH KNIGHT [*passes by*]

SIMONIDES What is the fourth?

THAISA A burning torch that's turnèd upside down,
The word: *Qui me alit me extinguit.*

SIMONIDES Which shows that beauty hath his power and will, 35

---

22 SD *passes by*] Malone *(passes); The second Knight.* Q 27 Spanish:] Spanish Q 28 *Pue per doleera kee per forsa*] Q; *Piu per dulçura que per forza* / Malone 28 SD *The* THIRD] Q4; *3.* Q 28 SD *passes by*] Malone *(passes); not in* Q 29–30] *This edn's lineation; And . . . third? / Thai. The . . . deuice / A . . . apex.* Q 29 with] Q; *what's* Q4 30 chivalry] Q2; *Chiually* Q 31 *pompæ*] *Theobald MS., Steevens; Pompey* Q 31 SD *The* FOURTH] Q4; *4.* Q 31 SD *passes by*] Malone *(passes); not in* Q

20 **Ethiop** Technically, an Ethiopian, inhabitant of modern Ethiopia; but generically used in Shakespeare to mean a black-skinned African.
21 **word** motto.
21 *Lux . . . mihi* Your light is life to me. Young (p. 455) records that hanging in the Shield Gallery at Whitehall was one with this precise motto. The Knight's device of life dependent on the sun is an emblem of necessity.
22 **holds his life of you** believes his life is dependent on you.
24 **Macedon** i.e. Macedonia.
26 **armed . . . lady** The Second Knight's device represents armed force ironically overcome by feminine gentleness.
28 *Pue per doleera kee per forsa* More by gentleness rather than by force. See Supplementary Note.
30 **wreath of chivalry** 'a chaplet or garland of flowers, leaves, or the like, esp. worn or awarded as

a mark of distinction' (*OED* Wreath *sb* 11), worn as a crown. See 2.3.9–10, where Pericles receives the wreath of victory. The device represents love as honour.
31 *Me . . . apex* Literally: the peak of the triumph leads me forth.
34 *Qui . . . extinguit* Who feeds me extinguishes me. The torch is extinguished by the wax that fed it; compare Prologue 16 n., and *Son.* 73: 'Consum'd with that which it was nourish'd by'. Proverbial (Tilley T443, 'A torch turned downward is extinguished by its own wax'). See A. R. Braunmuller, 'The natural course of light inverted: an *Impresa* in Chapman's *Bussy D'Ambois*' (*Journal of the Warburg and Courtauld Institutes*, 34 (1971), 356–60); Braunmuller traces the device back to 1540 and discusses its alternative interpretations. Here, the implication of the device is love as a self-consuming passion.

Which can as well inflame as it can kill.
                    The FIFTH KNIGHT [*passes by*]
THAISA The fifth, an hand environèd with clouds
              Holding out gold that's by the touchstone tried,
              The motto thus: *Sic spectanda fides.*
                    The SIXTH KNIGHT [*passes by*]
SIMONIDES And what's the sixth and last, the which   40
              The knight himself with such a graceful courtesy delivered?
THAISA He seems to be a stranger, but his present is
              A withered branch that's only green at top,
              The motto: *In hac spe vivo.*
SIMONIDES A pretty moral: 45
              From the dejected state wherein he is,
              He hopes by you his fortunes yet may flourish.
I LORD He had need mean better than his outward show
              Can any way speak in his just commend,
              For by his rusty outside he appears   50
              To have practised more the whipstock than the lance.
2 LORD He well may be a stranger, for he comes
              To an honoured triumph strangely furnishèd.
3 LORD And on set purpose let his armour rust
              Until this day, to scour it in the dust.   55
SIMONIDES Opinion's but a fool that makes us scan

---

36 SD *The* FIFTH] F3; 5. Q   36 SD *passes by*] Malone *(passes); not in* Q   39 SD *The* SIXTH] F3; 6. Q   39 SD *passes by*] Malone *(passes); not in* Q   45–6] *Rowe's lineation; one line* Q

38 gold . . . tried Referring to the method of testing the genuineness of gold by the colour it left when rubbed on black quartz ('the touchstone'); proverbial as a symbol of fidelity: see Tilley T448, 'As the touchstone tries gold, so gold tries the man.' The device shows love as faith.

39 Sic . . . fides Thus is faithfulness to be tried. Both device and motto belonged to King Francis II of France (Scott-Giles, p. 20).

41 knight himself Pericles is the only knight without a page and therefore has to present his device himself; see Supplementary Note to 2.1.115.

41 delivered presented.

42 present the object he has presented.

43 withered . . . top Earlier (1.2.30–1), Pericles referred to his kingly position: 'but as the tops of trees, / Which fence the roots they grow by and defend them'; as a shipwrecked man in rusty armour he is far removed or 'withered' ('the dejected state' in 46) from his former state but by the 'green

at top' he shows he still can hope. See also Supplementary Note to 2.1.115.

44 In . . . vivo In this hope I live; device and motto appear to be Shakespeare's invention.

49 commend commendation.

51 whipstock the handle of a whip, i.e. like the one used for driving horses.

53 furnishèd (1) equipped, (2) dressed.

56–7 Opinion . . . inward man Freely paraphrased: 'Anyone who believes (has "opinion") that it is reasonable to judge ("scan") the person within by outward appearance ("habit") is a fool.' See *R3* 3.1.9–11, 'Nor more can you distinguish of a man / Than of his outward show, which, God he knows, / Seldom or never jumpeth with the heart'; *MV* 3.2.73, 'So may the outward shows be least themselves.' For a similar situation in which a suitor comes meanly attired to a tournament, see *TNK* 2.5.23–4, 'Mark how his virtue, like a hidden sun, / Breaks through his baser garments.'

The outward habit by the inward man.
But stay, the knights are coming;
We will withdraw into the gallery.

                                      [*Exeunt*]
[*Flourish.*] *Great shouts* [*within*], *and all cry,* '*the mean knight*'

[**2.3**] [*A banquet brought in.*] *Enter King* [SIMONIDES, THAISA, MARSHAL, *lords, attendants*], *and* KNIGHTS *from tilting*[*, with torches*]

SIMONIDES Knights, to say you're welcome were superfluous;
   ~~To place upon the volume of your deeds,~~
   ~~As in a title page, your worth in arms~~
   ~~Were more than you~~ expect or more than's fit,
   ~~Since every worth in show commends itself.~~   5
   Prepare for mirth, for mirth becomes a feast;
   You are princes, and my guests.
THAISA But you, my knight and guest,   *to crown*
   To whom this wreath of victory I give
   And crown you king of this day's happiness.   10
               [*Thaisa crowns Pericles*]

59 SD.1 *Rowe; not in* Q 59 SD.2 *Flourish*] *This edn; not in* Q 59 SD.2 *within*] *Dyce; not in* Q **Act 2, Scene 3** 2.3] *Malone subst.; not in* Q 0 SD.1 *A banquet brought in*] *Malone (a Banquet prepared); not in* Q 0 SD.1–2 SIMONIDES, THAISA, MARSHAL, *lords, attendants*] *Malone subst. (omits* MARSHAL*); not in* Q 0 SD.1 MARSHAL] *Hoeniger; not in* Q 0 SD.2 *with torches*] *This edn; not in* Q 2 To] F4; I Q 10 SD] *This edn; not in* Q

57 by about, concerning. See Abbott 145 and compare *LLL* 4.3.148, 'I would not have him know so much by me', also *Ado* 5.1.303–4, 'virtuous / In any thing that I do know by her'.

59 withdraw … gallery If Simonides and Thaisa are already on the upper stage (see Supplementary Note to 2.2.0 SD.1), 'withdraw' here must mean 'go within'. The presumption is that Simonides and the others watch the Knights' contest offstage, as the next direction implies (though we add the word 'within' to eliminate ambiguity). The 'gallery' perhaps suggests the royal gallery: 'From early in Elizabeth's reign and on into that of King James I, [the presentation of the impresas] was facilitated by a special wooden stage constructed by the Office of the Works below the royal gallery' (Young, p. 453). The scene ends with the offstage cheering; Scene 3 is imagined as being a little later, and in a different environment.

59 SD.2 *mean* of low degree, base.

Act 2, Scene 3
  Location Pentapolis. Clearly, this is a scene of a royal feast. The minimum directions necessary for the scene to be actable have been added; directors will doubtless want to add more. There must be a table or tables with chairs, since the Marshal (whose presence, despite the speech heading for him at 22, Hoeniger was the first editor to perceive) directs the Knights to their places; there's eating from about 27 on, drinking healths at 51, and dancing (which undoubtedly implies music) at 90 or so. Simonides at 103 commands pages and lights to escort the Knights to their lodgings. The torches are presumably present throughout, for the night-time imagery used throughout the scene makes clear that it takes place in the evening.

3 title page Title pages in early printed books were often descriptively elaborated (as was that of *Pericles* Q) to advertise the excellence of the contents.

5 in show i.e. by action, in deeds.

9–10 For a similar situation of the disguised victor receiving the garland of victory see' *TNK* 2.5.1 ff.

PERICLES 'Tis more by fortune, lady, than my merit.
SIMONIDES Call it by what you will the day is yours,
    And here, I hope, is none that envies it.
    ~~In framing an artist, art hath thus decreed~~
    ~~To make some good, but others to exceed;~~   15
    ~~And you are her laboured scholar.~~ Come, queen a'th'feast,
    For, daughter, so you are, here take your place.
    Marshal: the rest as they deserve their grace.
KNIGHTS We are honoured much by good Simonides.
SIMONIDES Your presence glads our days, honour we love;   20
    For who hates honour hates the gods above.
~~MARSHAL~~ *servant* Sir, yonder is your place.
PERICLES   Some other is more fit.
1 KNIGHT Contend not sir, for we are gentlemen
    Have neither in our hearts nor outward eyes
    Envies the great, nor shall the low despise.   25
PERICLES You are right courteous, knights.
SIMONIDES   Sit sir, sit.
    [*Aside*] By Jove I wonder, that is king of thoughts,
    These cates resist me, he ~~not~~ *but* thought upon.   *to lust!!*
THAISA [*Aside*] By Juno that is queen of marriage,
    All viands that I eat do seem unsavoury,   30
    Wishing him my meat. [*To Simonides*] Sure he's a gallant *to admire*
        gentleman.
SIMONIDES He's but a country gentleman:
    H'as done no more than other knights have done,

---

12 yours] Q4; your Q 18 Marshal: the] *This edn;* Martiall the Q 24 Have] Q; That Q4 25 Envies] Q; Envie Q4; Envied *Sisson* 25 shall] Q; do Q4 27 SD, 29 SD, 36 SD] *Cam.; not in* Q 31 SD] *Hoeniger; not in* Q 32–4] *Boswell's lineation; lined more / Then . . . Staffe, / Or . . . passe.* Q 33 H'as] *This edn;* ha's Q

14 **framing** shaping, creating.
16 **laboured scholar** i.e. over whom art took special effort (*OED ppl. a* 3, citing this line).
16 **queen a'th'feast** queen of the feast. In this context, it means grand hostess, cynosure: compare *WT* 4.4.67–8, 'present yourself / That which you are, mistress o'th'feast'.
18 **Marshal: the rest** Q's 'Martiall the rest' is bound to be misread either as a command to Thaisa, or as a comment upon the Knights' bearing; actually the phrase is addressed to the Marshal, ordering him to 'place' the guests according to their degree.
20 **glads** gladdens.
23–5 **we are gentlemen . . . despise** Para-

phrased: 'we are gentlemen [who] have neither [that] in our hearts nor outward eyes [which] envies the great, nor shall the low despise'. No emendation is required.
28 **cates** delicacies, i.e. the food.
28 **resist me** repel me (Onions), i.e. 'I have lost my appetite.'
28 **he not thought upon** when he is not thought upon; i.e. 'when I don't think about him (Pericles) my appetite is gone'.
31 **meat** food.
33, 34 **H'as** He has. The contraction is retained for the sake of metre, and Q's unusual placement of the apostrophe is modernised.

H'as broken a staff or so, so let it pass.
THAISA To me he seems like diamond to glass. · *to compare*   35
PERICLES [*Aside*] Yon king's to me like to my father's picture,
       Which tells in that glory once he was,
       Had princes sit like stars about his throne,
       And he the sun for them to reverence;
       None that beheld him, but like lesser lights   40
       Did vail their crowns to his supremacy;
       Where now his son's like a glow-worm in the night,
       The which hath fire in darkness, none in light;
       Whereby I see that time's the king of men:
       He's both their parent, and he is their grave,   45
       And gives them what he will, not what they crave. *recalling from scene. Fisherman Scene*
SIMONIDES What, are you merry, knights?
KNIGHTS Who can be other in this royal presence?
SIMONIDES Here, with a cup that's stirred unto the brim,
       As do you love, fill to your mistress' lips,   50
       We drink this health to you.
KNIGHTS   We thank your grace.
            [*The Knights drink to Thaisa*]
SIMONIDES Yet pause awhile, yon knight doth sit too melancholy,
       As if the entertainment in our court
       Had not a show might countervail his worth.
       Note it not you, Thaisa?   *to deny (vehemently)*   55
THAISA What is't to me, my father?
SIMONIDES   O attend, my daughter,
       Princes in this should live like gods above,

34 H'as] *This edn;* ha's Q   36 Yon] Q2; You Q   42 son's] *Malone;* sonne Q   49 stirred] Q *(stur'd);* stor'd *Malone*   51 SD *This edn; not in* Q

34 a staff i.e. the lances knights used in tilting.
35 diamond to glass Proverbial (Dent D323.1, 'Diamonds cut glass', 'As hard as a diamond').
37 tells speaks of, i.e. resembles.
37–40 glory . . . lights The image of the king as a resplendent sun was a commonplace idea in the theories of kingship. Shakespeare makes much use of it in *R*2 and throughout the other history plays to convey the radiant splendour of the kingly office. See 2.4.53, 'You shall like diamonds sit about his crown.'
41 vail lower (*OED v*² 2).
42–3 glow-worm in the night . . . none in light A proverbial image (Dent G142.1, 'To be like a glow-worm'; Meres's *Palladis Tamia* (1598), 'As

the glow-worme shineth brightest when the night is darkest', p. 174ʳ).
49 stirred unto the brim See *OED* Stir *v* 8a and 8b 'to excite to passion' or 'to move strongly a person's spirit'; in this sense the cup is 'stirred' (a transferred epithet) by the Knights' ardour, full ('unto the brim'). Most editors adopt Malone's emendation 'stor'd' = full, although none of the senses in *OED* exactly matches.
50 to in honour of.
50 mistress' Hoeniger rightly notes that this refers to Thaisa, the queen of the feast, and object of the Knights' quest: hence, the singular. The added SD makes the point unambiguous.
54 countervail be equal to (*OED v* 2).

Who freely give to every one that come to honour them,
And princes not doing so are like to gnats,
Which make a sound, but killed are wondered at.   60
Therefore to make his entrance more sweet,
Here, say we drink this standing bowl of wine to him.

THAISA Alas my father, it befits not me
　　　Unto a stranger knight to be so bold,
　　　He may my proffer take for an offence,   65
　　　Since men take women's gifts for impudence.

SIMONIDES How? do as I bid you or you'll move me else.

THAISA [*Aside*] Now by the gods, he could not please me better.

SIMONIDES And furthermore tell him, we desire to know of him
　　　Of whence he is, his name and parentage.   70

　　　　　　　[*Thaisa goes to Pericles*]

THAISA The king my father, sir, has drunk to you –

PERICLES I thank him.

THAISA Wishing it so much blood unto your life –

PERICLES I thank both him and you, and pledge him freely.

THAISA And further, he desires to know of you   75
　　　Of whence you are, your name and parentage.

PERICLES A gentleman of Tyre, my name Pericles,
　　　My education been in arts and arms,
　　　Who, looking for adventures in the world,
　　　Was by the rough seas reft of ships and men,   80
　　　And after shipwreck driven upon this shore.

　　　　　　　[*Thaisa returns to her place*]

THAISA He thanks your grace, names himself Pericles,
　　　A gentleman of Tyre, who only by misfortune of the seas,
　　　Bereft of ships and men, cast on this shore.

SIMONIDES Now by the gods, I pity his misfortune   85
　　　And will awake him from his melancholy.

68 SD] *Rowe; not in* Q 70 SD] *This edn; not in* Q 81 SD] *This edn; not in* Q

60 **killed . . . at** Freely paraphrased: 'when they are killed you are amazed how such small insects could have made such a loud noise'.
　61 **entrance** i.e. his arrival here.
　62 **standing bowl** a bowl with feet on which it rests.
　65 **proffer** offering (*OED sb* 1).
　70 Simonides' request concerning derivation, name, and lineage foreshadows the same questions that Pericles asks of Marina in 5.1.

74 **pledge him** drink to his health.
　78 **been** has been.
　78 **arts and arms** A standard collocation for a well-rounded gentleman; compare *LLL* 2.1.45, 'Well fitted in arts, glorious in arms'.
　80 **reft** bereft, deprived.
　83–4 **who . . . cast** 'who only because of misfortune . . . was cast'.

Come gentlemen, we sit too long on trifles,
And waste the time which looks for other revels:
Even in your armours, as you are addressed,
Will well become a soldiers' dance;   90
I will not have excuse with saying 'this
Loud music is too harsh for ladies' heads',
Since they love men in arms as well as beds.

                          They dance

So, this was well asked 'twas so well performed.
[*To Pericles*] Come sir, here's a lady that wants breathing too,   95
And I have heard you knights of Tyre
Are excellent in making ladies trip,
And that their measures are as excellent.

PERICLES In those that practise them they are, my lord.
SIMONIDES O that's as much as you would be denied   100
Of your fair courtesy: unclasp, unclasp.

                 [*Pericles and Thaisa*] *dance*

Thanks gentlemen to all, all have done well,
But you the best. Pages and lights, to conduct

---

95 SD] *This edn; not in* Q   101 SD *Pericles and Thaisa dance*] *This edn; They daunce* Q

87 on trifles concerning things of little purpose.
89 addressed dressed.
90 a soldiers' dance There is no reason to suppose, as most editors do, that supernumerary ladies join in the dance; on the contrary, the Knights dance among themselves according to the traditional ceremonies surrounding the tournament. See Long, pp. 40–1: 'their dance was part of the tourney in which only the Knights engaged . . . Clearly the dance is a military one, probably the same type as that described in Peele's *Arraignment of Paris*, wherein a stage direction (2.2) states, *Hereupon enter Nine Knights treading a warlike almain, by drum and fife* . . . In T. Morley's *First Book of Consort Lessons* (1599) is an almain for this occasion, 'Mounsieurs Almaine' No. 15.' Compare *PPA* which has 'daunsing in armour' at the wedding feast, p. 444.
91 I will not have excuse 'I will not accept any reasons you offer not to dance.'
91–3 this . . . arms 'this' is an adjective which modifies 'loud music' (the noise made by the Knights' armour while dancing); 'men in arms' = men in armour, with an obvious pun intended.
93 SD-103 What is happening here is not really hard to fathom, but a summary may be useful. Simonides has initiated the dancing, in which 'they' (the six Knights) dance. At 95 Simonides addresses

Pericles directly, and leads him to Thaisa to dance with her. The two of them dance a duet. A small problem occurs in 101: many editors make this two half-lines, divided by the stage direction. But this is nonsense; a pentameter cannot be kept waiting during a dance! At the end of the second dance, Simonides calls the festivities to a halt with another particular word of praise to Pericles.
94 So . . . well asked This was well worth the asking, i.e. I did well to suggest it.
95 breathing exercising.
97 trip dance, with a possible *double entendre* (fall down for sexual intercourse).
98 measures dancing steps, especially those of a grave or stately gait.
100–1 that's . . . courtesy Simonides offers a translation of Pericles' expression of modesty: 'That's as much as to say you would be denied [the honour of dancing with the princess] as a consequence of your good manners.'
101 unclasp, unclasp Pericles, having participated in the 'soldiers' dance' in which he wears his armour, would now have to 'unclasp' (i.e. unbuckle) it in order to dance with a lady. A more graceful dance than the soldiers' dance is implied here. For a similar direction for the removal of a garment see *WT* 4.4.647, 'Unbuckle, unbuckle.'

> These knights unto their several lodgings,
> ~~Yours sir, we have given order be next our own.~~   105

PERICLES ~~I am at your grace's pleasure.~~

SIMONIDES Princes, it is too late to talk of love,
> And that's the mark I know you level at,
> Therefore each one betake him to his rest,
> Tomorrow all for speeding do their best.   110

> [*Exeunt*]

[2.4] *Enter* HELLICANUS *and* ESCANES

The whole story is in this initial thought (handwritten)

HELLICANUS No, Escanes, know this of me:
> Antiochus from incest lived not free,
> For which the most high gods not minding longer
> To withhold the vengeance that they had in store,
> Due to this heinous capital offence,   5
> Even in the height and pride of all his glory,
> When he was seated in a chariot
> Of an inestimable value, and his daughter with him,
> A fire from heaven came and shrivelled up
> Those bodies even to loathing, ~~for they so stank~~   10
> ~~That all those eyes adored them ere their fall,~~
> ~~Scorn now their hand should give them burial.~~

ESCANES 'Twas very strange.

HELLICANUS   And yet but justice; for though
> This king were great, his greatness was no guard
> To bar heaven's shaft, but sin had his reward.   15

---

107 SH] Q4 (*King.*); *not in* Q   110 SD] *Malone; not in* Q   **Act 2, Scene 4   2.4**] *Malone subst.; not in* Q   **3–6**] *Malone's lineation;* minding, / Longer . . . that / They . . . heynous / Capitall . . . pride / Of Q   **7–9**] *Dyce's lineation;* in / A . . . daughter / With . . . shriueld / Vp Q   **13–15**] *Malone's lineation;* strange. / Hell. And . . . great, / His . . . shaft, / But . . . reward. Q

105 be to be.
108 mark target; a term in archery.
108 level aim.
110 speeding success.

Act 2, Scene 4
  Location Tyre.
3–9 Malone's and Dyce's lineation, retained here, does not make good pentameters of these lines, but no one has come up with better.
3 minding having a mind; intending (*OED* Mind *v* 6b).

7–10 The retributive punishment suffered by Antiochus and his Daughter echoes occasions in the Bible when fire is said to come down from heaven to destroy the wicked; classical literature offers examples of similar punishments sent from the gods.
11 eyes adored eyes that adored.
12 should that should.
15 shaft bolt, arrow.
15 sin . . . reward The biblical source is Rom. 6.23, 'the wages of sin is death'; see also Marlowe's *Doctor Faustus* 1.1.40, 'The reward of sin is death.'

In the beginning there was the Word, and the Word was given flesh + dwells among us. (handwritten)

ESCANES 'Tis very true.

Enter [three] LORDS

1 LORD ~~See, not a man in private conference~~
         ~~Or council has respect with him but he.~~
2 LORD It shall no longer grieve without reproof.
~~3 LORD~~ And cursed be he that will not second it.   20
1 LORD Follow me then. Lord Hellicane, a word.
HELLICANUS With me? and welcome happy day, my lords.
1 LORD Know that our griefs are risen to the top,
         And now at length they overflow their banks.
HELLICANUS Your griefs, for what? Wrong not your prince you love.   25
1 LORD Wrong not yourself then, noble Hellicane.
         But if the prince do live, let us salute him,
         Or know what ground's made happy by his breath.
         If in the world he live we'll seek him out,
         If in his grave he rest we'll find him there   30
         And be resolved: he lives to govern us,
         Or dead, give's cause to mourn his funeral,
         ~~And leave us to our free election~~.
2 LORD ~~Whose~~ death indeed, the strongest in our censure,
         And knowing this kingdom is without a head –   35
         ~~Like goodly buildings left without a roof,~~
         ~~Soon fall to ruin~~ – your noble self,
         That best know how to rule, and how to reign,
         We thus submit unto, our sovereign.
ALL Live noble Hellicane.   40

---

16 SD *three*] *Malone; two or three* Q   18 has] ha's Q   25] *Rowe's lineation;* what / Wrong Q   40 SH] Q *(Omnes)*

16 SD Q's 'two or three' is one of the ambiguous
directions in the play which used to be thought
characteristic of 'foul-papers' copy: see Textual
Analysis, p. 207. Since three Lords are specified in
the SHs, the direction has been emended; compare
3.2.44 SD.
  19 grieve provoke to anger, offend (*OED v* 6).
  23 griefs grievances.
  27 salute greet.
  27–33 As Hoeniger says, a much-debated passage. The Lord's speech, paraphrased, means something like this: 'If the prince is alive, and here, let us
know it so we may salute him; if he is alive, and

somewhere else, tell us where so we can seek him
out; if he's dead, we'll find his grave and thereby
reach a resolution of our doubts: either he lives to
govern us, or, if he is dead, that gives us cause to
mourn him and leaves us to our choice of his succes-
sor.' The grammar is slightly shaky, but not unusually so for *Per*.
  28 what ground . . . breath i.e. 'what country is
made happy with his presence'.
  34 death indeed . . . censure [Pericles'] death
[is] indeed the more likely ('strongest') in our
judgement ('censure').

Best way to communicate so people understand.

HELLICANUS Try honour's cause; forbear your suffrages:
              If that you love Prince Pericles, forbear.
              ~~Take I your wish, I leap into the seas,~~
              ~~Where's hourly trouble for a minute's ease.~~ '
              A twelvemonth longer let me entreat you   45
              To forbear the absence of your king;
              If in which time expired he not return,
              I shall with agèd patience bear your yoke;
              ~~But if I cannot win you to this love,~~
              Go search like nobles, like noble subjects,   50
              And in your search spend your adventurous worth,
              Whom if you find and win unto return,
              You shall like diamonds sit about his crown.
1 LORD   To wisdom he's a fool that will not yield;
              And since Lord Hellicane enjoineth us,   55
              We with our travels will endeavour.
HELLICANUS Then you love us, we you, and we'll clasp hands;
              When peers thus knit a kingdom ever stands.

                                                            [*Exeunt*]

[2.5] *Enter King* [SIMONIDES] *reading of a letter at one door, the* [*three*]
KNIGHTS *meet him*

1 KNIGHT Good morrow to the good Simonides.
SIMONIDES Knights, from my daughter this I let you know,

---

58 SD] *Rowe; not in* Q   Act 2, Scene 5   2.5] *Malone subst.; not in* Q   0 SD *King* SIMONIDES] *Malone subst.; the King* Q

41 Hellicanus rejects the Lords' offer, implying it is dishonourable, by recommending them to 'try' the effect (*OED* sv *v* 11a) of honour instead in the course of the crusade-like action described in 45 ff. See 2.5.59, 'I came unto your court for honour's cause.'

41 forbear your suffrages refrain (*OED* Forbear *v* 5) from offering me your votes (*OED* Suffrage *sb* 3); compare *Tit.* 1.1.217–18, 'People of Rome, and people's tribunes here, / I ask your voices and your suffrages.'

43 Take I i.e 'If I should accept'.

44 Where's . . . ease Hellicanus earlier expressed a similar awareness of the perils of the sea (1.3.23).

46 To forbear To bear or endure with patience; compare *TGV* 5.4.27, 'Love, lend me patience to forbear a while.'

50 like nobles like members of the nobility that you are; also with a play on 'noble' (the gold coin worth a third or half a pound), hence 'spend' and 'worth' in the next line. See *R3* 1.3.80–1, 'to ennoble those / That scarce some two days since were worth a noble'.

53 You . . . crown See 2.3.38, where Pericles says his father 'Had princes sit like stars about his throne'; these images of kingly splendour create a nexus of the three kings: Pericles and his father and Simonides.

56 The Lords, like Pericles, are sent to travel; for the use of the overriding symbol of journey see Introduction, pp. 58–61.

Act 2, Scene 5
   Location Pentapolis.

That for this twelvemonth she'll not undertake
A married life. Her reason to herself is only known,
Which from her by no means can I get.   5
2 KNIGHT May we not get access to her, my lord?
SIMONIDES Faith, by no means, she hath so strictly
Tied her to her chamber that 'tis impossible.
One twelve moons more she'll wear Diana's livery;
This by the eye of Cynthia hath she vowed,   10
And on her virgin honour will not break it.
3 KNIGHT Loath to bid farewell, we take our leaves.

                                        [*Exeunt Knights*]

SIMONIDES So, they are well dispatched.
Now to my daughter's letter: she tells me here
She'll wed the stranger knight   15
Or never more to view nor day nor light.
'Tis well, mistress, your choice agrees with mine,
I like that well. Nay how absolute she's in't,
Not minding whether I dislike or no.
Well, I do commend her choice and will no longer   20
Have it be delayed. Soft, here he comes,
I must dissemble it.

                    Enter PERICLES

PERICLES All fortune to the good Simonides.
SIMONIDES To you as much. Sir, I am beholding to you
For your sweet music this last night.   25

---

12 SD] *Dyce; not in* Q

8 Tied Confined.

9–11 Not to be taken literally; Simonides has invented an excuse to get rid of the Knights; see 13.

9 One twelve moons i.e. one year; appropriately used in connection with Diana, goddess of the moon.

9 Diana's livery i.e. remain a virgin; a livery is the distinctive clothing worn by someone in service (here used figuratively).

10 eye of Cynthia i.e. the moon; Diana was also called Cynthia, from her birthplace, Mount Cynthus in Delos.

14–16 Thaisa's resolve as relayed in a letter to her father agrees with the sources; *CA* 906–11, 'But if I have Appolinus, / Of all this worlde what so betide, / I will none other man abide. / And certes if I of him faile, / I wot right welle withoute faile, / Ye

shall for me be doughterles'; *PPA* (p. 441), 'these are to let you understand, that I would marry with the Sea-wrecked man, and with none other'.

18 absolute resolved, certain.

22 dissemble it pretend. Simonides is characterised in the scene as a fun-loving practical joker.

25–7 music . . . harmony In both sources Apollonius plays the harp at the banquet of the previous night; see *CA* 785–91, 'He tak'th the harpe, and in his wise / He tempreth, and of suche assise / Synginge he harpeth forth with all, / That as a voyce celestiall / Hem thought it sowned in her ere, / As though that it an angell were. / They gladen of his melodie'; also *PPA* p. 438, 'When Apollonius had received the harp, he went forth . . . playing before the king, and the residue with such cunning and sweetnes, that he seemed

I do protest my ears were never better fed
With such delightful pleasing harmony.
PERICLES It is your grace's pleasure to commend,
    Not my desert.
SIMONIDES   Sir, you are music's master.
PERICLES The worst of all her scholars, my good lord.   30
SIMONIDES Let me ask you one thing:
    What do you think of my daughter, sir?
PERICLES A most virtuous princess.
SIMONIDES And she is fair too, is she not?
PERICLES As a fair day in summer, wondrous fair.   35
SIMONIDES Sir, my daughter thinks very well of you,
    Ay, so well that you must be her master,
    And she will be your scholar, therefore look to it.
PERICLES I am unworthy for her schoolmaster.
SIMONIDES She thinks not so; peruse this writing else. *Read this*   40
PERICLES [*Aside*] What's here?
    A letter that she loves the knight of Tyre?
    'Tis the king's subtlety to have my life –
    [*Aloud*] O seek not to entrap me, gracious lord,
    A stranger, and distressèd gentleman,   45
    That never aimed so high to love your daughter,
    But bent all offices to honour her.
SIMONIDES Thou hast bewitched my daughter, and thou art
    A villain.
PERICLES   By the gods I have not.
    Never did thought of mine levy offence,   50

41–2] *Malone's lineation; one line* Q 41 SD] *Malone; not in* Q 44 SD] *This edn; not in* Q 48–9] *Malone's lineation;*
daughter, / And . . . villaine Q 49–52] *Rowe's lineation; Per.* By . . . thought / Of . . . actions / Yet . . . loue, /
Or . . . displeasure. Q

rather to be Apollo then Apollonius, and the kings guests confessed that in all their lives they never heard the like before.' The harping leads next day to Apollonius' being employed to instruct the princess 'in the Art of Musicke, and other good qualities, wherein hee is skilfull' (*PPA* p. 439); hence 'music's master' in 29, and also 37–9 where Simonides ironically encourages Pericles to be Thaisa's schoolmaster. The play elects not to dramatise this episode, though it is described in *PA*.
    28–9 commend . . . desert See the similar expressions of modesty: 2.2.8–9 (Thaisa) and 2.3.11 (Pericles).
    35 As a fair . . . fair A proverbial image (Dent s966.1, 'As fair as the summer's day'); compare *Son.* 18 ('Shall I compare thee to a summer's day?').

38 she . . . scholar As in *PPA*, 'my daughter much desireth to be your scholler' (p. 439).
    40 else i.e. if you do not believe me.
    43 subtlety cunning, craftiness.
    46 to as to.
    47 bent all offices directed all my duty; see 2.1.150, 'honour be but a goal to my will'.
    48 Thou hast bewitched my daughter A favourite paternal accusation in Shakespeare; see *MND* 1.1.27, *Oth.* 1.2.63, 1.3.61–4, *WT* 4.4.423, 434.
    50 levy probably wrongly used for 'level' = 'aim at'; see *OED* sv *v* 7 which cites other misuses of 'levy' for 'level', though the earliest example is 1618; alternatively, *OED* sv *v* 5 'to undertake, commence, make (war)'.

Nor never did my actions yet commence
A deed might gain her love or your displeasure.
SIMONIDES Traitor, thou liest.
PERICLES   Traitor?
SIMONIDES   Ay, traitor.
PERICLES Even in his throat – unless it be the king –
That calls me traitor I return the lie.   55
SIMONIDES [*Aside*] Now by the gods I do applaud his courage.
PERICLES My actions are as noble as my thoughts,
That never relished of a base descent.
~~I came unto your court for honour's cause,~~
~~And not to be a rebel to her state;~~   60
~~And he that otherwise accounts of me,~~
~~This sword shall prove he's honour's enemy.~~
SIMONIDES No?

Enter THAISA

Here comes my daughter, she can witness it.
PERICLES Then, as you are as virtuous as fair,   65
Resolve your angry father if my tongue
Did e'er solicit or my hand subscribe
To any syllable that made love to you?
THAISA Why sir, say if you had, who takes offence
At that would make me glad?   70
SIMONIDES Yea mistress, are you so peremptory?
[*Aside*] I am glad on't with all my heart.
[*Aloud*] I'll tame you, I'll bring you in subjection.
Will you, not having my consent,
Bestow your love and your affections   75
Upon a stranger? – [*Aside*] who for aught I know,

---

56 SD] *Malone; not in* Q   63–4] *Malone's lineation; one line* Q   72 SD] *To right of line 73* Q   73 SD] *This edn; not in* Q   74 you, not]* Q4; *you not,* Q   76 SD] *To right of line 77* Q

52 might that might.
54–5 Even . . . lie Paraphrased: 'To anyone (except the king) who calls me a traitor I respond that he lies in his throat.' A proverbial saying (Tilley T268, 'To lie in one's throat').
56 courage i.e. in talking to me this way.
58 relished had a trace or tinge.
59–62 Pericles' extended defence of his honour should please Simonides; see 2.3.20–1, 'honour we love; / For who hates honour hates the gods above'.

60 her i.e. honour's; usually personified as feminine.
64 witness verify. See *Oth.* 1.3.170, 'Here comes the lady; let her witness it.'
66 Resolve Assure, inform.
68 made love spoke amorously (*not* had sex).
70 that would that which would.
71 peremptory determined, self-willed.
76–8 who . . . myself According to the theories of kingship, one of the conditions of essential royalty is that it cannot be hidden even in disguise.

> May be, ~~nor can I think the contrary,~~
> As great in blood as I myself.
> [*Aloud*] Therefore, hear you mistress, either frame
> Your will to mine, and you sir, hear you, 80
> Either be ruled by me, or I'll make you –
> Man and wife.
> Nay come, your hands, and lips must seal it too; *Kiss*
> And being joined, I'll thus your hopes destroy,
> And for further grief, God give you joy! 85
> What are you both pleased?

THAISA   Yes, if you love me sir. *to touch*

PERICLES Even as my life my blood that fosters it.

SIMONIDES What are you both agreed?

BOTH Yes, if't please your majesty. *to enjoy*

SIMONIDES It pleaseth me so well that I will see you wed, 90
> And then with what haste you can, get you to bed.

Exeunt

[3.0] *Enter* GOWER

GOWER Now sleep y-slackèd hath the rouse,
> No din but snores about the house,
> Made louder by the o'er-fed breast,
> Of this most pompous marriage feast.
> ~~The cat with eyne of burning coal~~ 5
> ~~Now couches from the mouse's hole;~~

---

79 SD] *This edn; not in* Q 81 you –] Q4; you, Q 82–6] *Malone's lineation;* Man . . . hands, / And . . . ioynd, / Ile . . . griefe: / God . . . pleased? / *Tha.* Yes . . . sir? Q 87 life my] Q2; life, my Q 89 SH] Q *(Ambo)* Act 3, Scene 0 3.0] *Malone (Act III); not in* Q 1 rouse] *This edn;* rout Q 2 about the house] Q; the house about *Malone* 6 from] Q; 'fore *Steevens, conj. Malone*

Shakespeare makes various uses of this concept in ironical situations; compare the hidden royalty of Guiderius and Arviragus in *Cym.* 4.2, and Perdita and Florizel in *WT* 4.4.

79 **frame** shape.

87 'Even as my life loves the blood which fosters it'.

Act 3, Scene 0

1–2 It is a truth universally acknowledged that it would be nice if Gower's opening couplet were to rhyme. Malone's emendation entails rearrangement; that adopted here a mere spelling change.

'Rouse' means 'party with drink' (*OED* sv *sb*³ 2); see *Oth.* 2.3.64, *Ham.* 1.4.8.

1 **y-slackèd** reduced to quiet inactivity. The archaic 'y-' prefix of the past participle, common in Spenser, is used two or three times in Shakespeare, see Abbott 345.

4 **pompous** grand, splendid.

5 **eyne** eyes. Archaic noun plural, cultivated by Spenser.

6 **couches** lies to sleep (*OED* Couch *v*¹ 16b), which cites the earliest use of the word in Gower's *CA*; *OED* *v*¹ 1c 'said of animals'. The cat who is usually alert and on the prowl (has eyes of burning

Gower has it's own style from the rest of the play heightened gestures.

And crickets sing at the oven's mouth,
Are the blither for their drouth.
Hymen hath brought the bride to bed,
Where by the loss of maidenhead
A babe is moulded. Be attent,
And time that is so briefly spent
With your fine fancies quaintly eche;
What's dumb in show I'll plain with speech.

10

[*Dumb show*]

Enter Pericles and Simonides at one door with [*lords and*] *attendants, a
messenger meets them, kneels and gives Pericles a letter, Pericles shows it
Simonides, the lords kneel to him; then enter Thaisa with child, with
Lychorida a nurse, the king shows her the letter, she rejoices: she and
Pericles take leave of her father, and* [*all*] *depart*

By many a dearne and painful perch
Of Pericles the careful search,
By the four opposing coigns

15

7–8 crickets sing at the oven's mouth / Are Q *subst.;* crickets at . . . / Sing *NS*   7 crickets] *Rowe³;* cricket Q   10 Where by] Q2; Whereby Q   13 eche] *Malone;* each Q   14 SD.1 *Dumb show*] Q5; *not in* Q   14 SD.2 *lords and*] *This edn; not in* Q   14 SD.6 *all depart*] *This edn;* / *depart* Q; / *depart with Lychorida and their Attendants. Then exeunt Simonides and the rest.* / *Dyce*   17 coigns] *Rowe³ subst.;* Crignes Q

---

coal) does not lie in wait for the mouse but 'now' sleeps like everybody else. For the entire conceit, see *MND* Epilogue, especially 387–90 and 401–5.

6 from away from, i.e. from catching mice because the cat is asleep; see Abbott 158.

7–8 The lines make slightly awkward sense, with Rowe's emendation 'crickets'. Because it is based on the presumption of memorial error, NS's elegant emendation ('And crickets at the oven's mouth / Sing the blither for their drouth') has, regretfully, been declined.

7 crickets The common house-cricket, 'an insect that squeaks or chirps about ovens and fireplaces', so called because it makes a dry sound; see *OED* Cricket *sb¹* 1.

8 blither happier.

8 drouth A variant spelling of 'drought'; dryness.

9 Hymen God of marriage.

11 moulded formed, shaped from something (*OED* Mould *v²* 5 (*transf.* and *fig.*): 'To create, produce, or form out of certain elements or material'). Compare *H8* 5.4.25–6 where the word is used in reference to a baby: 'All princely graces / That mould up such a mighty piece as this'.

11 attent attentive.

13 fancies imagination.

13 quaintly skilfully, cleverly.

13 eche supplement, augment; a variant spelling of 'eke'; compare *H5* 3.0.35, 'And eche out our performance with your mind'.

14 plain explain, make plain, i.e. the dumb show that immediately follows.

15 dearne Either 'kept unrevealed' (*OED* Dern *a* 2) or 'secret, not generally known' (*OED a* 3), or 'serving to conceal, lying out of the way' (*OED a* 4, citing this line). The word is now obsolete, and since it was uncommon in Shakespeare's day, it was probably meant to be one of Gower's archaisms. To help convey this to the modern reader, we have kept Q's spelling.

15 painful painstaking. In other words, the courtiers have taken care to look for Pericles in all the obscure as well as all the obvious places.

15 perch Measure of land, 16½ feet (approx. 5 metres) in length (*OED* sv *sb²* 5a).

17 coigns corners, i.e. of the earth.

Which the world together joins,
Is made with all due diligence
That horse and sail and high expense   20
Can stead the quest. At last from Tyre,
Fame answering the most strange enquire,
To th'court of King Simonides
Are letters brought, the tenor these:
Antiochus and his daughter dead,   25
The men of Tyrus on the head
Of Hellicanus would set on
The crown of Tyre, but he will none;
The mutiny, he there hastes t'oppress;
Says to 'em, if King Pericles   30
Come not home in twice six moons,
He, obedient to their dooms,
Will take the crown. The sum of this,
Brought hither to Pentapolis,
Y-ravishèd the regions round,   35
And every one with claps can sound:
Our heir-apparent is a king!
Who dreamt? Who thought of such a thing?
Brief, he must hence depart to Tyre;
His queen, with child, makes her desire –   40
Which who shall cross along to go;
Omit we all their dole and woe.

---

21 quest. At] *Malone;* quest at Q   29 t'oppress] Q; t'appease *Steevens*   34 Pentapolis] Q6; *Penlapolis* Q   35 Y-ravishèd] *Theobald MS.; Steevens;* Iranyshed Q

21 **stead** assist, contribute to.
22 'Fame' = rumour (*OED* Fame *sb*[1] 1b), 'strange' = of a foreign or distant place (*OED* sv *sb*[1] 1b), 'enquire' = act of enquiry, search (*OED* sv *sb*); freely paraphrased: 'rumour responding to this wide-spread search of distant lands'.
24 **tenor** Course of meaning which holds on or continues throughout something written; the general sense or meaning of a document (*OED* sv *sb*[1] 1a)
24 **these** as follows, the substance of the news in 25–33. Because 'letters' is plural, so is 'these', even though their 'tenor' is the same.
29 **oppress** put down, suppress (*OED* sv *v* 3).
31 **twice six moons** i.e. a year; compare 2.5.9, 'One twelve moons more'.

32 **dooms** judgements.
35 **Y-ravishèd** Enraptured (another archaism). The *n* in Q's 'Iranyshed' is probably a turned letter. *OED* spellings include 'yrauisshid', 'rauysshed'. For the whole passage see *CA* 1019–27, 'This tale after the kynge it had / Pentapolin all oversprad. / There was no joye for to seche, / For every man it had in speche, / And saiden all of one accorde: / A worthy kynge shall ben our lorde, / That thought us first an hevines, / Is shape us nowe to great gladnes. / Thus goth the tydynge over all.'
36 **can** began to; an archaic form of ''gan'.
36 **sound** declare, proclaim.
39 **Brief** Briefly, in short.
42 **dole** grief; i.e. of their leave-taking.

Lychorida her nurse she takes,
And so to sea. Their vessel shakes
On Neptune's billow; half the flood   45
Hath their keel cut, but fortune, moved,
Varies again; the grizzled north
Disgorges such a tempest forth,
That, as a duck for life that dives,
So up and down the poor ship drives.   50
The lady shrieks, and well-a-near
Does fall in travail with her fear;
And what ensues in this fell storm
Shall for itself, itself perform.
I nill relate. Action may   55
Conveniently the rest convey,
Which might not, what by me is told.
In your imagination hold
This stage the ship, upon whose deck   59
The sea-tossed Pericles appears to speak.   [*Exit*]

56–7 convey, / Which . . . not, what . . . told.] *This edn;* conuay; / Which . . . not? what . . . told, Q   60 sea-tossed] *Rowe³ subst.;* seas tost Q   60 SD] Q5 *subst.; not in* Q

---

45 Neptune's billow The waves; Neptune was the god of the sea who had both storm and calm under his control.

45 half the flood i.e. half their voyage; 'flood' = figurative synonym for 'sea'.

46 keel The first timber of a ship to be laid down, and the backbone which unites the whole structure.

46–7 fortune, moved, / Varies 'moved' means 'angered' (as at 1.2.51); 'Varies' means 'Changes': angry fortune has decided to deal Pericles yet another blow, by sending a tempest from the north. Theobald's emendation (fortune's mood) is unnecessary.

47 grizzled horrible, grisly, frightening.

47 north 'A mariner names the winds of all the corners by the thirty-two points of the compass, but only those blowing from north, east, south and west and a few others are described in this way by Shakespeare. The rest take their names from a season or month of the year. All are given their proper characteristics' (Falconer, p. 142). The *booke of the Sea Carte* (see 2.1.23–4 n.) says 'The north wynd rysing immedyatly after eny south wynde, causith great tempest on the sea' (fol. 69ʳ); also 'Yf [lightnings] shyne from th northe, it shallbe great wynd. And yf they come from the northest, it shall rayne xviiij houres therafter' (fol. 69ᵛ). For the sharp effects of the north wind, see *R2* 5.1.76–7 and 1.4.6–8, *Ham.* 5.2.95, *Cym.* 1.3.36.

48 tempest Defined nautically as a degree above a storm (Falconer, p. 36).

50 drives A ship that 'drives' is one which is being carried before the wind (Falconer, p. 45).

51 well-a-near alas; an old north-country word and variant of 'well-a-day' (Onions).

52 travail labour (birth).

52 with because of; i.e. her fear of the tempest brought on labour.

53 fell fierce, cruel.

55 nill will not.

55 Action i.e. theatrical performance.

56 Conveniently Fittingly, properly.

58 hold entertain the thought, believe.

[**3.1**] *Enter* PERICLES *on shipboard*[*; storm*]

PERICLES The god of this great vast, rebuke these surges
          Which wash both heaven and hell, and thou that hast
          Upon the winds command, bind them in brass,
          Having called them from the deep, ~~O still~~   *scream not*
          ~~Thy deafening dreadful thunders, gently quench~~   *piercingly,*   5
          ~~Thy nimble, sulphurous flashes!~~ [*Calling*] O how, Lychorida,
          How does my queen? Then, storm, venomously
          Wilt thou spite all thyself? The seaman's whistle
          Is as a whisper in the ears of death,
          Unheard. [*Calling*] Lychorida! Lucina, O   10
          Divinest patroness, and midwife gentle
          To those that cry by night, ~~convey thy deity~~
          ~~Aboard our dancing boat,~~ make swift the pangs
          Of my queen's travails! Now Lychorida.

                    Enter LYCHORIDA [*with a baby*]

LYCHORIDA Here is a thing too young for such a place,   15
           Who, if it had conceit would die, as I am like to do.

I'm the QUEEN!

Act 3, Scene 1   3.1] *Malone; not in* Q   0 SD *on*] Q4; *a* Q   0 SD*; storm*] *This edn; not in* Q   6 flashes!] flashes: Q   6 SD] *This edn; not in* Q   7 Then, storm, venomously] *This edn;* then storme venomously, Q   8 spite] Q (*speat*); spit F4   10 Unheard.] *Malone;* Vnheard Q   10 SD] *This edn; not in* Q   10 Lychorida!] *Malone; Lychorida?* Q   11 midwife] *Steevens;* my wife Q   14 SD *with a baby*] *This edn; not in* Q; *with an infant / Steevens*

Act 3, Scene 1

Location At sea.

1 The god Neptune; an indirect plea, hence the use of 'the' rather than the vocative 'thou'.

1 vast Synonym for the sea as a boundless, desolate expanse. See 2.1.56 (as an adjective), 'In that vast tennis-court'; and *Tim.* 4.3.437, 'Robs the vast sea', and *Tim.* 5.4.78, 'Taught thee to make vast Neptune weep'.

2 thou Aeolus, the god of the four winds.

3 bind them in brass See *2H6* 3.2.89–90, 'And he that loos'd them forth their brazen caves, / And made them blow'; compare also Nashe, *Summer's Last Will* lines 1793–4: 'imprison him . . . with the windes in bellowing caues of brass' (Nashe, *Works*, ed. R. B. McKerrow, (1910) 1958, III, 289).

6 nimble, sulphurous Adjectives used frequently in Shakespeare to describe lightning; compare *Lear* 2.4.165, 'nimble lightnings', 4.7.33–4, 'nimble stroke / Of quick cross lightning', 3.2.4, 'You sulph'rous and thought-executing fires', *Temp.* 1.2.203–4, 'the fire and cracks / Of sulphur-

ous roaring'; also *Cor.* 5.3.152–3, *Cym.* 5.5.240, *Temp.* 1.2.204, *MM* 2.2.115.

8 spite Q's 'speat' is recognised by *OED* as a variant spelling of 'spite': in this context, 'in order to vent spite or spleen upon another' (*OED v* 2b); Pericles is saying to the storm that it is so vicious it will spite itself, i.e with the poison ('venomously') it is spitting.

8 seaman's whistle Silver whistle (or 'pipe') used by master and boatswain, most helpfully during a storm, to issue orders to the sailors. 'Upon the winding of the master's whistle, the boatswain takes it with his, and sets the sailors with courage to do their work, every one of them knowing by their whistle what they are to do' (Falconer, p. 59). See 4.1.62, 'the boatswain whistles', also *Temp.* 1.1.6–7, 'Tend to th' master's whistle.'

10 Lucina Goddess of childbirth; see 1.1.9 and n.

15 thing being, creature; the word can be applied to human beings.

16 conceit capacity to understand.

Every little thing I do is magic Every thing I do just turns you on.

Take in your arms this piece of your dead queen.
PERICLES How? How Lychorida?
LYCHORIDA Patience, good sir, do not assist the storm.
Here's all that is left living of your queen,   20
A little daughter. For the sake of it
Be manly and take comfort.

[He takes the baby]

PERICLES   O you gods!
Why do you make us love your goodly gifts
And snatch them straight away? We here below
Recall not what we give, and therein may   25
Use honour with you.
LYCHORIDA Patience, good sir, even for this charge.   *[Exit]*
PERICLES Now mild may be thy life,
For a more blusterous birth had never babe;
Quiet and gentle thy conditions, for   30
Thou art the rudeliest welcome to this world
That ever was prince's child; happy what follows.
Thou hast as chiding a nativity
As fire, air, water, earth, and heaven can make
To herald thee from the womb.   35
Even at the first thy loss is more than can
Thy portage quit with all thou canst find here;
Now the good gods throw their best eyes upon't.

Men Curry Milk

22 SD] *This edn; not in* Q; *She gives him the infant* / Oxford, *after line* 27   27 SD] *This edn; not in* Q   35 womb:] Q; womb.
Poor inch of nature! *Hoeniger, conj. Collier*

17 **piece** (1) masterpiece, (2) part. A highly evocative word which is used frequently for the heroines of the last plays; compare 4.2.34, 113, 4.5.103, *Cym.* 5.4.140 and 5.5.446, *WT* 4.4.32, 422, 5.1.94, 5.3.38, *Temp.* 1.2.56, *H8* 5.4.26.

19 **do . . . storm** Lychorida enjoins Pericles to patience because his rages only exacerbate the storm. Compare *Temp.* 1.1.13–14, 'You mar our labor . . . you do assist the storm.'

22 **Be manly** i.e. take courage; compare *Temp.* 1.1.10, 'Play the men.'

24–6 **We . . . you** Paraphrased, Pericles is saying that because we do not deal dishonourably with the gods (by withdrawing worship) we have a right to expect the gods to deal justly with us; 'with' (26) = in relation to (Abbott 193).

26 **Use** Enforce or put into practice (*OED v* 2).

27 **even for this charge** i.e. particularly for the sake of this baby who is now in your care.

28–38 Pericles blesses the newborn child.

30 **thy** be thy.

30 **conditions** mode or state of life.

31 **rudeliest** most roughly, most harshly.

33 **chiding** brawling, noisy.

36–7 **Even . . . here** Even at the very beginning of your life you have lost more than can ever be compensated ('quit' = requite) to you.

37 **portage** Two possible meanings: (1) *OED sv sb*¹ 1b, 'that which is carried or transported; cargo; freight', or (2) *OED sv sb*¹ 4, 'a mariner's venture, in the form of freight or cargo, which he was entitled to put on board, if he took part in the common adventure and did not receive wages, or which formed part of his wages'. Even with 'all thou canst find here' serving as Marina's 'portage', it will not be enough to requite her for her loss, i.e. of her mother.

Enter two SAILORS

1 SAILOR What courage sir? God save you.

PERICLES Courage enough, I do not fear the flaw;   40
             It hath done to me the worst. Yet for the love
             Of this poor infant, this fresh new seafarer,
             I would it would be quiet.

1 SAILOR Slack the bowlines there! Thou wilt not wilt thou?
             Blow and split thyself.   45

2 SAILOR But sea-room, and the brine and cloudy billow
             Kiss the moon, I care not.   *Sailor 2*

1 SAILOR Sir, your queen must overboard. The sea works high,
             The wind is loud and will not lie till the ship
             Be cleared of the dead.

PERICLES   That's your superstition?   50

1 SAILOR Pardon us, sir; with us at sea it hath been still observed,

---

44 Slack] Q *(corr.)* *(Slacke);* Slake Q *(uncorr.)* **44** there! Thou . . . thou?] *Dyce subst.;* there; thou . . . thou: Q
50 superstition?] *This edn;* superstition. Q

---

40 flaw violent gust of wind; here used figuratively for the storm.

44 Slack the bowlines there An order to the sailors. In rough weather, the bowline (pronounced, and sometimes spelled 'bolin'), a rope fastened to the middle part of a sail to make it stand sharp or close by a wind, is eased ('slacked') in preparation for taking in sail (Falconer, p. 115).

44–5 Thou . . . thyself In the tradition of the mariner, the First Sailor (like the Second Sailor in 47) rails at the storm; compare *Temp.* 1.1.7, 'Blow till thou burst thy wind', also *Cym.* 4.2.56, 'With winds that sailors rail at', and 5.5.293–5, 'For he did provoke me / With language that would make me spurn the sea / If it could so roar to me.' 'In mishap and disaster, they [seamen] can jest at a doom that may be theirs any moment. From a fellow seaman who may share the same fate even while he speaks, it shows fatalism that is not unheroic, but it would not come well from anyone else' (Falconer, p. 64). Compare 4.1.60.

46 But sea-room 'Just give us room to manoeuvre' i.e. in order to keep clear of the lee-shore; addressed to the storm. If only they have that, the storm can do its worst, hence the rest of the line and the next. Compare *Temp.* 1.1.7, 'Blow till thou burst thy wind, if room enough!'

46 and . . . brine . . . cloudy billow if . . . sea water . . . sea spray which flies like vapour or rises in clouds. Compare *Oth.* 2.1.12, 'The chidden billow seems to pelt the clouds.'

48 sea works high waves are extraordinarily big, rough, and turbulent.

49 lie abate, subside.

50 'The belief that a corpse will bring pollution and disaster to a ship in which it is carried is widespread among sailors' (*N&Q*, 9 ser. vol. 7 (1901), 75–6; see also the preceding discussion in vol. 6 (1900), 246–7, 313, 374, 437). There is an earlier entry in *N&Q* 5 ser. vol. 1 (1874), 166 which cites Thomas Fuller's *Holy Warre* (1639), 'His [Saint Louis'] body was carried into France, there to be buried, and was most miserably tossed; it being observed, that the sea cannot digest the crudity of a dead corpse, being a due debt to be interrèd where it dieth; and a ship cannot abide to be made a bier of.' The Sailors' superstition recalls the fear of mariners in Jonah 1.11–15: 'Then said thei unto him, What shal we do unto thee, that the sea maie be calme unto us? (for the sea wroght and was troublous) And he said unto them, Take me, and cast me into the sea: so shal the sea be calme unto you: for I knowe that for my sake this great tempest is upon you . . . So thei toke up Jonah, and cast him into the sea, & the sea ceased from her raging.'

50 superstition? Pericles seems taken aback, rather than hostile.

51–3 with us at sea . . . overboard straight The most difficult crux in the play. Editors almost universally do two things, we think mistakenly (their usual reading is 'with us at sea it hath been still observ'd; and we are strong in custom. There-

And we are strong. In ease turn therefore, briefly yield 'er
PERICLES As you think meet, for she must overboard straight:
  Most wretched queen.

  [*Enter* LYCHORIDA *and* SAILORS *carrying Thaisa*]

LYCHORIDA Here she lies sir.   55
PERICLES A terrible child-bed hast thou had, my dear:
  No light, no fire, th'unfriendly elements
  Forgot thee utterly, nor have I time
  To give thee hallowed to thy grave, but straight
  Must cast thee, scarcely coffined in care,   60
  Where for a monument upon thy bones,
  The air-remaining lamps, the belching whale,
  And humming water must o'erwhelm thy corpse,
  Lying with simple shells. O Lychorida,
  Bid Nestor bring me spices, ink, and taper,   65

52 strong. In ease turn therefore,] *This edn;* strong in easterne, therefore Q; strong in custom. Therefore *Singer, conj. Boswell;* strong in earnest. Therefore *Steevens, conj. Mason;* strong astern. Therefore *Knight*   **52–4** yield 'er. / PERICLES As you think meet; for she must over board straight: / Most wretched queen] Q; yield 'er, for she must over board straight. / *Per.* As you think meet; most wretched Queen *Malone*   **54** SD] *This edn; not in* Q   **60** coffined in çare] *This edn;* Coffind, in oare Q; coffin'd, in the ooze *Steevens*   **62** The air-remaining] *This edn;* The ayre remayning Q; And aye-remaining *Steevens, conj. Malone;* And e'er-remaining *Globe*   **65** taper] Q; paper Q2

fore briefly yield 'er, for she must overboard straight.') First, since no one has found it possible to make any sense out of Q's 'easterne', Boswell's conjecture 'custom' has found general favour, despite its graphic dissimilarity (however spelled) from 'easterne'. We keep as many of Q's letters as possible, based on graphic considerations, assuming the original reading to have been something like 'ease turne'. Our reading may be paraphrased: 'and we are resolute, determined ("strong") about it. Accept our decision calmly ("In ease"), don't make us force you; change your mind ("turn"), and quickly ("briefly") give her up.' Secondly, editors reassign 'for she must overboard straight' to the Sailor. On the contrary, it is part of Pericles' enforced 'yielding' of Thaisa that he should have this phrase of wry acceptance of the Sailor's superstition.

  51 still observed always (or continually) adhered to (or complied with).
  52 strong resolute, determined.
  52 briefly quickly, promptly: *OED adv* 2.
  53 meet best, appropriate, proper.
  53 straight immediately, straight away.
  54 SD It is unlikely that Thaisa's body is revealed lying in the discovery space since that would require the action to move away from the front and centre of the stage to its rear. The quiet intensity of Pericles' 'priestly farewell', and his statement that he will

'bring the body presently' surely imply that her body is carried on and laid downstage.
  59 hallowed to thy grave in holy burial.
  60 Pericles apparently means that he has scarcely time to lay Thaisa with due care and observance in her coffin. Steevens's emendation is adopted by most editors, but the simpler emendation proposed here seems adequate.
  61 for instead of.
  62 air-remaining lamps The stars that always hang in the firmament (the stars which have air as opposed to Thaisa who does not). Pericles says that Thaisa, 'scarcely coffined in care', will have only the stars, the whale, and the water for her monument, all of which will 'o'erwhelm' her corpse (62–3). Steevens emended to 'aye-remaining lamps', which means something quite different: that *instead* of a proper burial, and the funerary lamps that were in Roman times placed in sepulchres, Thaisa's body will be overwhelmed by whale and water. It seems a far-fetched reading, since Pericles was no Roman.
  62 belching spouting. Compare *Tro.* 5.5.23: 'Before the belching whale'.
  63 humming Compare *R3* 1.4.22, 'What dreadful noise of waters in my ears'.
  65 taper candle. Q2's alteration has the dubious advantage of being a stock phrase: 'ink and paper'. On the principle *difficilior lectio potior*, Q's word is

My casket, and my jewels; ~~and bid Nicander~~
~~Bring me the satin coffin.~~ Lay the babe
Upon the pillow. Hie thee whiles I say
A priestly farewell to her. Suddenly, woman.

> [*Exit Lychorida with the baby*]

2 SAILOR Sir, we have a chest beneath the hatches,   70
     Caulked and bitumed ready.
PERICLES I thank thee. Mariner, say, what coast is this?
1 SAILOR We are near Tarsus.
PERICLES   Thither, gentle mariner,
     Alter thy course for Tyre. When canst thou reach it?
1 SAILOR By break of day if the wind cease.   75
PERICLES O make for Tarsus.
     There will I visit Cleon, for the babe
     Cannot hold out to Tyrus; there I'll leave it
     At careful nursing. Go thy ways, good mariner,
     I'll bring the body presently.   80

> *Exeunt*[*, Pericles carrying Thaisa*]

---

69 SD] *Malone subst.; not in* Q   73 SH] *Edwards;* 2. Q   74 for] Q; *from NS, conj. Collier*   80 SD *Exeunt*] *Rowe;* / *Exit* Q
80 SD *Pericles, carrying Thaisa*] *This edn; not in* Q

preferable: Pericles wants various things brought to him, and a taper to write by is not unreasonable, if it is night-time (suggested by 75 and by the general colour of the imagery, which conveys this as a night-scene).

67 coffin Synonymous with 'coffer', a box for valuables lined with satin; compare 3.4.1–2, '. . . and some certain jewels / Lay with you in your coffer'.

69 priestly farewell Like the blessing (28–38) Pericles gives the newly born Marina, this 'priestly farewell' refers to the prayer given at the burial of the dead at sea; see BCP for the forms of prayer to be used at sea.

69 Suddenly Immediately.

70 hatches trapdoors or grated frameworks covering the openings in the deck of a ship (*OED* sv *sb*¹ 3b).

71 Caulked . . . bitumed Stopped up (i.e. the seams); made watertight with bitumen, or pitch (*OED* Bitume *v*).

73 Tarsus If Pentapolis is in Greece, as the play declares, a glance at the map (facing p. 1) would suggest that any reasonable course from thence to Tyre would not go anywhere near Tarsus. However, Shakespeare probably had in mind the naviga-

tional customs of English seamen of the sixteenth century, whose practice was to steer from headland to headland, within sight of land; this coastal navigation was known at the time as 'pilotage'. It is therefore quite possible that Shakespeare imagined Pericles' ship sailing to the north of Cyprus, rather than the south. For English navigation at the time, see David W. Waters, *The Art of Navigation in England in Elizabethan and Early Stuart Times*, 1958, chapter 1.

74 Alter thy course for The mariner is maintaining a course for Tyre; Pericles asks him to alter it.

78 Tyrus Latinised form of Tyre.

80 SD *carrying Thaisa* Thaisa's 'body' must be brought on stage for Pericles' eulogy (Hoeniger's vague idea that Lychorida took Pericles to the inner stage for this speech is dramatically absurd as well as outdated in terms of knowledge about the Elizabethan stage). Pericles makes arrangements for the jettisoning of the coffin, but it must be made clear that this does not happen in the scene: so Thaisa must be carried off, most appropriately by Pericles (see 5.3.17 and n.) to where the funeral arrangements can be concluded.

[3.2] *Enter Lord* CERIMON *with a* SERVANT [*and a poor man*]

CERIMON Philemon, ho!

Enter PHILEMON

PHILEMON Doth my lord call?
CERIMON Get fire and meat for these poor ~~men~~. *folk*
                                          [*Exit Philemon*]
        'T'as been a turbulent and stormy night.
~~SERVANT~~ *Philemon* I have been in many, but such a night as this,   5
        Till now I ne'er endured.
CERIMON ~~Your master will be dead ere you return,~~
        ~~There's nothing can be ministered to nature~~
        ~~That can recover him.~~
        [*To poor man*] Give this to the pothecary
        And tell me how it works.   10
                            [*Exeunt Servant and poor man*]

                    Enter two GENTLEMEN   *stir*

1 GENTLEMAN Good morrow.
2 GENTLEMAN   Good morrow to your lordship,
CERIMON ~~Gentlemen~~ *Friends*, why do you stir so early?
1 GENTLEMAN   ~~Sir,~~
        Our lodgings standing bleak upon the sea
        Shook as the earth did quake.
        The very principals did seem to rend and all to topple;   15

Act 3, Scene 2   3.2] *Malone; not in* Q   0 SD *and a poor man*] *Hoeniger (and another Poor Man, both storm-beaten); not in* Q; *and some Persons who have been shipwrecked / Malone*   3 SD] *This edn; after line 4 Hoeniger; not in* Q   9 SD] *Hoeniger; not in* Q   10 SD.1] *Hoeniger; not in* Q   12–13] *This edn's lineation; early? / 1. Gent. Sir . . . sea* Q

Act 3, Scene 2

Location Ephesus: see map facing p. 1.
3.2.0 SD, 9 SD, 10 SD.1 poor man Hoeniger correctly rejects Malone's direction: the Servant is not in Cerimon's employ; rather, he has come to Cerimon for assistance for his ailing master (7); indeed they (the 'poor men' that Cerimon refers to in 3, the Servant and the other) may be poor only in the sense that they have had a fruitless or taxing errand on a rough night. Philemon, obviously, is Cerimon's steward or equivalent. Neither is there any justification for Malone's assumption that the poor men are victims of shipwreck; on the contrary, they both have come seeking Cerimon's medical assistance.
5–6 but . . . endured See also 4.1.58. Unpre-

cedented storms are similarly described in *JC* 1.3.5–10, *Lear* 3.2.45–8, and *Mac.* 2.4.1–4.
8 ministered to nature administered to the vital or physical powers of man, to his physical strength or constitution (*OED* Nature *sb* 6a) to restore him to health.
9 pothecary aphetic form of 'apothecary': one who prepared and sold drugs for medicinal purposes.
13 bleak upon exposed to.
14 as as if.
15 principals main rafters of a house (*OED* Principal *sb* 7).
15 all to topple i.e. everything seemed to topple.

Pure surprise and fear made me to quit the house.

2 GENTLEMAN   That is the cause we trouble you so early,
        'Tis not our husbandry.

CERIMON   O you say well.

1 GENTLEMAN   But I much marvel that your lordship,
        Having rich tire about you, should at these early hours   20
        Shake off the golden slumber of repose.
        'Tis most strange nature should be so conversant
        With pain, being thereto not compelled.

CERIMON   I hold it ever virtue and cunning
        Were endowments greater than nobleness and riches;   25
        Careless heirs may the two latter darken and expend;
        But immortality attends the former,
        Making a man a god.
        'Tis known I ever have studied physic,
        Through which secret art, by turning o'er authorities,   30
        I have, together with my practice, made familiar
        To me and to my aid the blest infusions that dwells
        In vegetives, in metals, stones; and can speak of the
        Disturbances that nature works and of her cures,
        Which doth give me a more content in course of true delight   35
        Than to be thirsty after tottering honour, or
        Tie my pleasure up in silken bags

21–3] *This edn's lineation;* Shake . . . strange / Nature . . . Paine, / Being . . . compelled Q

18 husbandry eagerness to work.

19–106 Almost all editors reline this passage, attempting to make it as 'regular' as possible. However, the results vary from the unconvincing to the unbelievable. The dramatic situation calls for a very relaxed, naturalistic kind of delivery, arising from Cerimon's self-confidence, and it seems least intrusive to leave the lineation mainly as in Q.

20 tire accoutrement, outfit (*OED* sv *sb*[1] 1); an aphetic form of 'attire' understood here in the broader sense of 'luxury'.

22 conversant used to, familiar with.

23 pain toil, trouble.

24 hold it ever have always believed or thought it. For the use of the present tense for a past action which is continuous see Abbott 346.

24 virtue that virtue.

24 cunning (1) knowledge, (2) skill.

26 darken (1) sully or stain, (2) overshadow.

26 expend waste i.e. by excess.

29 physic medical science.

30 secret art So called because the exploration of medical science tried to reveal the 'secrets' of nature; see *OED* Secret *a* 1.

30 turning o'er reading and researching carefully.

31 practice practical investigations, experiments.

32 infusions liquid extracts.

33 vegetives plants. Compare *Rom.* 2.3.15–16, 'O, mickle is the powerful grace that lies / In plants, herbs, stones, and their true qualities.'

35 a more content . . . delight a greater satisfaction in pursuit of real happiness; 'course' = the action of running or racing (*OED* sv *sb* 1).

36 tottering insecure, fluctuating; compare *R3* 3.2.37, 'what news, in this our tott'ring state?', and *TNK* 5.4.20, 'And with our patience anger tott'ring Fortune'.

37 Tie . . . bags Confine my pleasure to the acquisition of wealth.

Always much as much sense as possible.

To please the fool and death.

2 GENTLEMAN Your honour has through Ephesus
     Poured forth your charity, and hundreds call themselves   40
     Your creatures, who by you have been restored;
     And not your knowledge, your personal pain,
     But even your purse still open, hath built Lord Cerimon
     Such strong renown as time shall never –

          Enter two or three [SERVANTS] *with a chest*

SERVANT So, lift there.   45
CERIMON What's that?
SERVANT Sir, even now did the sea toss up upon our shore
     This chest; 'tis of some wreck.
CERIMON Set't down, let's look upon't.
Philemon 2 GENTLEMAN 'Tis like a coffin, sir.   50
CERIMON Whate'er it be, 'tis wondrous heavy.
     Wrench it open straight.
     If the sea's stomach be o'ercharged with gold,
Philemon   'Tis a good constraint of fortune it belches upon us.
2 GENTLEMAN 'Tis so, my lord.   55
CERIMON How close 'tis caulked and bitumed. Did the sea cast it up?
SERVANT I never saw so huge a billow, sir, as tossed it upon shore.
CERIMON Wrench it open.
Philemon   Soft; it smells most sweetly in my sense.
2 GENTLEMAN A delicate odour.
CERIMON   As ever hit my nostril.   60

44 never –] *Malone;* neuer. Q; never raze *Dyce;* ne'er decay *Staunton*   44 SD SERVANTS] *Malone; not in* Q   56 bitumed]
Theobald MS., Malone; bottomed Q   58–9] *This edn's lineation; one line* Q   60–1] *This edn's lineation;* Odour. / *Cer.*
As . . . it. Q

38 To . . . death i.e. only a fool can take pleasure
in worldly wealth, and only death can enjoy it in the
end. A probable allusion to the *Danse Macabre* or
the Dances of Death in which the figures of the Fool
and Death are portrayed, seen especially in *memento
mori* woodcuts.
   41 creatures i.e. dependants who acknowledge
a debt of life.
   42 not not only.
   42 pain labour.
   43 still always.
   44 never – The Gentleman's line ends in a
period in Q, the sentence incomplete. It seems more
likely, and more appropriate, that he is interrupted
by the servants with the coffin than that the compositor omitted a word. The dialogue has been

about death; the sudden appearance of the apparent
coffin makes a better period than any of the suggested emendations.
   54 constraint 'the exercise of force to determine
action' (*OED* sv *sb* 1); paraphrased: 'if the sea's
stomach is overbloated ("o'ercharged") with gold it
is a good exertion of fortune's force that it has
caused the sea to vomit on us [this chest]'. Cerimon
appropriately applies physician's language to both
'sea' and 'fortune'. For similar images applied to the
sea, see *Temp.* 3.3.55–6, 'the never-surfeited sea /
Hath caus'd to belch up you'.
   54 it that it, i.e. the sea.
   56 close tightly.
   59 Soft Pause a moment.

So, up with it.

O you most potent gods! what's here, a corpse?

2 GENTLEMAN Most strange.

CERIMON Shrouded in cloth of state, balmed and entreasured

With full bags of spices! A passport too!   65

Apollo, perfect me in the characters.

[*Reads*] ~~Here I give to understand~~

~~If ere this coffin drives a-land,~~

I, King Pericles, have lost

This queen, worth all our mundane cost.   70

Who finds her, give her burying:

She was the daughter of a king.

Besides this treasure for a fee,

The gods requite his charity.

If thou livest Pericles, thou hast a heart   75

That ever cracks for woe. This chanced tonight.

2 GENTLEMAN Most likely sir.

CERIMON   Nay certainly tonight,

For look how fresh she looks.

They were too rough that threw her in the sea.

Make a fire within; fetch hither all my boxes in my closet.   80

[*Exit a Servant*]

Death may usurp on nature many hours, and yet

The fire of life kindle again the o'er-pressed spirits.

~~I heard of an Egyptian that had nine hours lain dead,~~

~~Who was by good appliance recovered.~~

Enter one with napkins and fire

64–6] *This edn's lineation; prose* Q   65–6 too! / Apollo] *Malone; to Apollo* Q   67 SD] *This edn; not in* Q; *He reads out of a scrowl / Malone*   73 Besides] Q4; Besides, Q   76 ever] Q; euen Q4   76 woe. This] *Malone; woe, this* Q   77–8] *This edn's lineation; sir. / Cer. Nay . . . looks* Q   80 SD] *Dyce; not in* Q   83 lain] Q *(lien)*

61 it i.e. the lid of the chest.

64 cloth of state fabric worn by royalty; more precisely a 'cloth of state' was the canopy which hangs above the chair of state or is held by four corners over the monarch; see *H8* 2.4.0 SD, 'The KING *takes place under the cloth of state*', and 4.1.47–8, 'They that bear / The cloth of honour over her'.

64 balmed anointed.

65 passport Any document which gave foreigners in a strange country right of passage.

66 Apollo It is appropriate that Cerimon invokes the god of medicine (also the god of learning), who first taught men the healing art.

66 perfect . . . characters instruct me in understanding the letters.

70 mundane cost earthly value.

76 ever cracks for forever breaks because of. Compare *Lear* 2.1.90, 'my old heart is crack'd', *Cor.* 5.3.9, *WT* 3.2.173–4.

76 chanced happened.

76 tonight last night.

79 rough careless, hasty (*OED* sv *adv* 1).

82 o'er-pressed afflicted beyond endurance.

82 spirits The technical/medical use of the term: the *tertium quid* that mediates between the soul and body: see C. S. Lewis, *The Discarded Image*, 1964, pp. 166–9.

83 heard have heard.

84 appliance i.e. with the application of medicine.

Well said, well said: the fire and clothes. The rough and   85
Woeful music that we have, cause it to sound beseech you.
                    [*Music plays*]
The viol once more – how thou stirr'st thou block!
The music there. [*Music*] I pray you give her air:
Gentlemen, this queen will live:
Nature awakes, a warmth breathes out of her.   90
She hath not been entranced above five hours:
See how she 'gins to blow into life's flower again.
I GENTLEMAN The heavens through you increase our wonder,
        And sets up your fame for ever.
CERIMON She is alive! Behold her eyelids,   95
        Cases to those heavenly jewels which Pericles hath lost,
        Begin to part their fringes of bright gold;
        The diamonds of a most praised water doth appear,
        To make the world twice rich. Live, and make us weep
        To hear your fate, fair creature, rare as you seem to be.   100
                    She moves
THAISA O dear Diana, where am I? where's my lord?
        What world is this?
2 GENTLEMAN   Is not this strange?
I GENTLEMAN   Most rare.
CERIMON Hush, my gentle neighbours, lend me your hands:
        To the next chamber bear her. Get linen.

---

85 rough] Q; still *NS, conj. Delius*   86 SD] *Hoeniger subst.; not in* Q   88 SD] *Hoeniger; not in* Q   90 awakes, a warmth
breathes] *Steevens;* awakes a warmth breath Q; awakes a warm breath Q2   99 rich. Live] *Malone;* rich, liue Q   102 2
Gentleman . . . rare] *one line* Q (*2.Gent. . . . rare)*

85 **Well said** Well done. The phrase is common
in Shakespeare's plays: compare *Rom.* 1.5.86.
85–6 **the rough . . . music** See Supplementary
Note.
87 **viol** See 1.1.82n. Many editors adopt Q4's
'viall' (modern 'vial' or 'phial' = container), citing
in support *CA,* 1199, 'And putte a liquour in hire
mouth'. As 'violl' and 'viall' were alternative spellings for each other, no linguistic certainty exists.
However, Hoeniger notes 'the whole context of
lines 85–88 is devoted to music'; and Cerimon calls
for a variety of things, mainly to restore Thaisa's
bodily heat, but there is no mention of anything to
be taken internally. Q's reading makes better dramatic sense in the context.
87 **once more** i.e. once again.
87 **how thou stirr'st** Compare 2.1.16 'Look how
thou stirr'st now': like the First Fisherman,
Cerimon is sarcastically drawing attention to how

little the other is stirring. The intended effect in
both cases is 'hurry up'.
87 **block** blockhead, dolt.
91 **entranced** in a trance, in a swoon.
96 **Cases** The eyelids are metaphorically compared to jewel cases for the gems that are the eyes:
compare *WT* 5.2.12–13, 'to tear the cases of their
eyes'.
97 **fringes** eyelashes; as in *Temp.* 1.2.409, 'The
fringed curtains of thine eye advance'.
98 **water** A technical term relating to the quality
of a diamond (*OED* sv *sb* 20a); compare *Tim.*
1.1.17–18, ''Tis a good form. / And rich. Here is a
water, look ye.'
100 **rare** extraordinary.
101–2 **where . . . this** Taken directly from *CA,*
1214–15, 'She spake, and said: Where am I? /
Where is my lorde, what worlde is this?'

Now this matter must be looked to, for her relapse   105
Is mortal. Come, come, and ~~Æsculapius~~ guide us.
(margin: May the Gods in Nature)
            They carry her away. Exeunt

[**3.3**] *Enter* PERICLES *at Tarsus, with* CLEON *and* DIONIZA
[*and* LYCHORIDA *with the infant Marina*]

(margin: Enter UL after Pericles)

PERICLES Most honoured Cleon, I must needs be gone:
~~My twelve months are expired,~~ and Tyrus stands
In a litigious peace. You and your lady
Take from my heart all thankfulness; ~~the gods~~
~~Make up the rest upon you.~~
CLEON Your shakes of fortune, though they haunt you mortally,   5
Yet glance full wonderingly on us.
DIONIZA O your sweet queen! That the strict fates had pleased *(margin: to comfort)*
You had brought her hither to have blest mine eyes with her.
PERICLES We cannot but obey the powers above us;   10
Could I rage and roar as doth the sea she lies in,
Yet the end must be as 'tis. My gentle babe Marina,
Whom, for she was born at sea I have named so,
Here I charge your charity withal, leaving her
The infant of your care, ~~beseeching you to give her~~   15
~~Princely training that she may be mannered as she is born.~~

(margin left: Carried off UR; Deeper Pause; bottom: Dioniza her hood)

---

106 SD *Exeunt*] Q (*Exeunt omnes.*)   **Act 3, Scene 3   3.3**] *Malone subst.; not in* Q   0 SD.1 *at Tarsus*] *Atharsus* Q   0 SD.2 *and* LYCHORIDA] *Dyce subst.; not in* Q   0 SD.2 *with the infant Marina*] *This edn; not in* Q   1–4] *Malone's lineation; Per. Most . . . twelue / months . . . peace. / You . . . thankfulnesse, / The . . . you* Q   6 shakes] Q; *shafts Steevens; strokes Round*   6 haunt] Q (*hant*)*; hate* F3*; hurt Steevens*   7 wonderingly] Q; *wand'ringly Steevens; woundingly Deighton*

106 Is mortal Would be fatal.
106 Æsculapius Apollo's mortal son by Coronis, known for his healing powers; he devised a means of reviving corpses, thus making Cerimon's invocation highly appropriate.

Act 3, Scene 3
Location Tarsus.
2 twelve months Compare 3.0.31, 'twice six moons'.
3 litigious contentious, therefore precarious.
5 Make . . . you i.e. supply you with the gratitude for which my heart is insufficient in giving.
6 shakes damaging blows, violent shocks (*OED* Shake *sb*¹ 6a).
6–7 Paraphrased: 'the blows of fortune, though they pursue you with deadly effect, have the conse-

quence of touching and amazing us fully'. There seems no reason to emend the lines with 'shafts' or 'strokes' for 'shakes', 'hurt' for 'haunt', 'woundingly' for 'wonderingly' as most editors have done.
7 glance ricochet (*OED* sv *v*¹ 1a, of a weapon).
8 strict cruel. The fates are so called because they paid no regard to the wishes of anyone. Compare 1.2.107 n.
12–13 Marina . . . named so The heroines in the romances have similar metaphorical names: Imogen/Fidele = faithful (*Cym.*), Perdita = loss (*WT*), Miranda = wonder (*Temp.*).
13 for because.
16 mannered as she is born i.e. brought up with the moral character, and in a good way of life, in the custom which befits her princely rank. Compare *Ham.* 1.4.15, 'And to the manner born'.

CLEON   Fear not, my lord, but think your grace
          That fed my country with your corn, for which
          The people's prayers still fall upon you, must in your child
          Be thought on. If neglection should therein make me vile,   20
          The common body by you relieved
          Would force me to my duty; but if to that
          My nature need a spur, the gods revenge it
          Upon me and mine to the end of generation.
PERICLES   I believe you; your honour and your goodness   25
          Teach me to't without your vows. Till she be married,
          Madam, by bright Diana whom we honour,
          All unsistered shall this heir of mine remain,
          Though I show will in't. So I take my leave;
          Good madam, make me blessèd in your care   30
          In bringing up my child.
DIONIZA   I have one myself
          Who shall not be more dear to my respect
          Than yours, my lord.
PERICLES   Madam, my thanks and prayers.
CLEON   We'll bring your grace e'en to the edge a'th'shore,
          Then give you up to the masked Neptune and   35

---

28 unsistered] Q *(vnsisterd);* unscissor'd *Steevens*   28 heir] Q *(heyre);* hair *Steevens*   29 show will] Q; show ill *Theobald MS, Dyce*   31–6] *Malone's lineation; prose* Q

20 **neglection** neglect.
21 **common body** the people, i.e. the common weal.
23 **need a spur** require incentive. Compare *JC* 2.1.123, 'What need we any spur but our own cause', *Mac.* 1.7.25–6, 'I have no spur / To prick the sides of my intent', *WT* 4.2.9, 'which is another spur to my departure'.
24 **to . . . generation** (1) to the end of my posterity, (2) to the end of human kind.
26 **Teach me to't** Convince me.
28 **unsistered . . . heir** Steevens's emendation, 'unscissored . . . hair' has so far been universally adopted, because it seems to relate to Pericles' subsequent vow, reported by Gower in 4.4.27–8, that 'He swears / Never to wash his face nor cut his hairs.' An auditory error is presumed by editors. But the reaction Gower reports is to Marina's alleged death, and so is not necessarily applicable to the present scene. To be sure, *CA*'s version of this scene (1309–14) reads 'And this avowe to god I make, / That I shall never for hir sake / My berde for no likynge shave, / Till it befalle, that I have / In covenable tyme of age / Besette hir unto

mariage.' It seems, however, that Shakespeare decided to develop two separate versions of Pericles' vow: the first, here, is a statement registering a resolution not to marry again, so that Marina will have no sibling (but 'unsistered' may be used in deliberate preference to 'unbrothered' in view of the stress on daughters in the last plays). Later, when the news of her death is given him, Gower gives us a second vow which ironically recalls the first. Our presumption is that Shakespeare realised the dramatic opportunity for a richer complex of concepts than that in the source.
29 **will** a piece of wilfulness, a whim (*OED* sv *sb*' 9b). Pericles' resolution not to marry again and thereby to provide another heir (as required by a king's obligation) is an extreme, intuitive, reaction which, however, the action of the whole play justifies. For a similar sentiment regarding a king's obligation to marry again see *WT* 5.1.23–34.
32 **respect** heed, care, attention (*OED* sv *n* 13c).
35 **masked** Neptune, masked, conceals his hostile (stormy) visage; Cleon is expressing his hope that Neptune will mask his hostility.

The gentlest winds of heaven.

PERICLES   I will embrace your offer, come dearest madam.
O no tears Lychorida, no tears,
Look to your little mistress on whose grace
You may depend hereafter; come my lord.   40

[*Exeunt*]

[**3.4**]   *Enter* CERIMON, *and* THAISA

CERIMON   Madam, this letter and some certain jewels
Lay with you in your coffer, which are
At your command; know you the character?
THAISA   It is my lord's.
That I was shipped at sea I well remember,   5
Even on my bearing time, but whether there
Delivered, by the holy gods I cannot
Rightly say; but since King Pericles,
My wedded lord, I ne'er shall see again,
A vestal livery will I take me to   10
And never more have joy.
CERIMON   Madam, if this you purpose as ye speak,
Diana's temple is not distant far,
Where you may abide till your date expire;
Moreover if you please a niece of mine   15
Shall there attend you.

37–40] *This edn's lineation; prose* Q   40 SD] *Rowe; not in* Q   **Act 3, Scene 4**   3.4] *Malone subst.; not in* Q   0 SD THAISA]
Q4; *Tharsa* Q   2–3] *Malone's lineation;* command: / . . . Charecter? Q   4 SH] *Thar.* Q   4–11] *This edn's lineation, after*
Steevens; prose Q   6 bearing] *Edwards, conj. Ridley;* learning Q; eaning F3; yielding *conj. Mason*   10 vestal] Q *(vastall)*
12 SH] *Cler.* Q

---

39 grace favour.

Act 3, Scene 4
Location Ephesus.
2 coffer synonymous with coffin; compare
3.1.67 n.
3 character handwriting.
6 Even on Just at.
6 bearing time time of child-bearing. Q's 'learning' is usually unconvincingly emended to 'eaning',
a term to do with the breeding of sheep. We prefer
Ridley's conjecture, 'bearing', which has a consider-

able graphic similarity to 'learning' in Secretary
hand.
10 vestal livery The clothes (and therefore the
life) of a vestal virgin; the vestal virgins were Roman
priestesses dedicated to chastity (Vesta was a virgin
goddess), and responsible for the preservation of the
sacred fire in Vesta's temple.
13 Diana's temple Ephesus was renowned for
its great temple to Diana.
14 date term of life (legal terminology; compare
Rom. 1.5.108–9 where 'date' and 'expire' are
linked).

THAISA My recompense is thanks, that's all,
Yet my good will is great though the gift small.

to thank

[*Exeunt*]

go to follow / turn back pr / circle / look back Intermission

[**4.0**] *Enter* GOWER

GOWER Imagine Pericles arrived at Tyre,
    Welcomed and settled to his own desire.
    His woeful queen we leave at Ephesus,
    Unto Diana there's a votaress.
    Now to Marina bend your mind,   5
    Whom our fast-growing scene must find
    At Tarsus, and by Cleon trained
    In music's letters; who hath gained
    Of education all the grace
    Which makes high both the art and place   10
    Of general wonder. But alack
    That monster envy, oft the wrack
    Of earnèd praise, Marina's life
    Seeks to take off by treason's knife;
    And in this kind, our Cleon hath   15
    One daughter and a full-grown wench,

(handwritten annotations in margin: Rev / Enter Off / on blackout PS / Facing PS / Ty / T+R / Rev / Ty / Kev / Both / X UR Exit)

---

17 SH] *Thin.* Q 18 *Exeunt*] *Rowe; Exit* Q **Act 4, Scene 0** 4.0] *Malone* (Act IV); *not in* Q 10 high] Q *(hie);* her *Steevens* 10 art] Q; heart *Steevens* 14 Seeks] *Rowe; Seeke* Q 15–16 our Cleon hath / . . . a full-grown wench,] Q; hath our Cleon / . . . a wench full-grown, *Steevens*

17 **My . . . all** See *TN* 3.3.14, 'I can no other answer make but thanks.'

Act 4, Scene 0

2 **to** according to.

4 **there's a votaress** there as a woman vowed or devoted (to the service or worship of a god). See 2.5.9–10, where Simonides had made reference to Thaisa's devotion to Diana.

5–11 **Now to Marina . . . grace . . . wonder** Compare *WT* 4.1.24–5, 'To speak of Perdita, now grown in grace / Equal with wond'ring'.

5 **bend** turn.

6 **fast-growing scene** Compare *WT* 4.1.5–6, 16–17, 'that I slide / O'er sixteen years and leave the growth untried', 'I turn my glass, and give my scene such growing / As you had slept between.'

8 **music's letters** the study of music.

9 **grace** attractive quality (*OED* sv *sb* 2a); something that imparts beauty (2b); with a possible pun on the musical usage (ornament and embellishment, 3).

10–11 **makes high . . . wonder** her graceful accomplishments have elevated or distinguished both the art (of music) and the level of wonder at it. For a similar use of 'high' in this sense, see *Temp.* 3.3.88, 'My high charms work', and 5.1.25 and 177, 'with their high wrongs', 'A most high miracle'.

10 **place** placement, level.

12 **envy** (1) ill-will, malice, (2) jealous mortification at another's excellence or advantages.

12 **wrack** ruin, wreck.

14 **treason** treachery.

15 **kind** manner, way; i.e. in the same category as Marina.

15–16 **hath . . . wench** This makes a poor rhyme, but editorial attempts to improve it by emendation have not proved either graceful or convincing.

Even right for marriage-sight. This maid
Hight Philoten, and it is said
For certain in our story she
Would ever with Marina be: 20
Be't when they weaved the sleded silk
With fingers long, small, white as milk,
Or when she would with sharp neele wound
The cambric, which she made more sound
By hurting it, or when to th'lute   25
She sung, and made the night-bird mute
That still records with moan, or when
She would with rich and constant pen
Vail to her mistress Dian still.
This Philoten contends in skill   30
With absolute Marina, so
The dove of Paphos might with the crow
Vie feathers white. Marina gets

17 right] Q; ripe Q2   17 marriage-sight] Q (marriage sight); marriage-rite *Collier*   23 neele] *N.S.;* needle Q; neeld *Malone*   26 -bird] *Theobald MS., Malone;* bed Q   31–3 so . . . white] Q; so / With the dove of Paphos might the crow / Vie feathers white *Steevens conj. Mason*

17 Even . . . marriage-sight Now ready to be seen at her wedding, i.e. now of marriageable age.

18 Hight Called, named.

18 Philoten pronounced Fíl-loh-tin.

21 sleded fine-drawn; a variant spelling of 'sleaved' = to divide silk by separation into fine filaments to be used in the weaver's sley or slay, for use in embroidery; *OED* spellings include 'sleyd'; see also *Tro.* 5.1.31 (F1 version), 'sleyd silke'.

22 small slender.

23 neele A variant spelling of 'needle'; compare 5.0.5.

24 cambric fine linen.

24 sound whole.

25 hurting it i.e. wounding it with the sharp needle.

25 lute stringed instrument, played like a guitar, in vogue in the fourteenth to seventeenth centuries.

26 night-bird nightingale.

27 records with moan recollects, or remembers with grief. The nightingale's music has been bettered by Marina's singing and therefore is reduced to continually bemoaning the fact. There is also a complex of images in these three lines, since the nightingale proverbially sang in pain because of the thorn embedded in its breast. Marina 'wounds' the cambric (23–4) which causes it to 'make more sound/By hurting it' (24–5), an image

which leads inevitably to the idea of the anguished nightingale that 'still records with moan' (27).

28 rich . . . pen Compare 'with rough and all-unable pen' (*H5* Epilogue 1).

29 Vail Do homage.

29 still always.

31 absolute perfect.

31–3 so . . . with . . . Vie . . . white 'Vie' means 'increase in number by addition', 'add on' (*OED* sv *v* 6a and b); 'with' = by, signifying juxtaposition (see Abbott 193). Thus Marina, just by the juxtaposition with the crow (Philoten), can add to or increase her white feathers, i.e. Philoten by contending with Marina only makes the latter look the whiter. The image is proverbial (Tilley B435, 'Black best sets forth white'); see also *Rom.* 1.5.48, 'So shows a snowy dove trooping with crows'. The collocation of the dove or the colour white with the crow's blackness was favoured by Shakespeare: see *MND* 3.2.141–3, 'That pure congealed white, high Taurus' snow, / Fann'd with the eastern wind, turns to a crow / When thou hold'st up thy hand.'

32 dove of Paphos white dove sacred to Venus; Paphos was her favourite city in Cyprus. See *Temp.* 4.1.92–4, 'I met her Deity / Cutting the clouds towards Paphos; and her son / Dove-drawn with her', and *Lucr.* 57–8, 'But beauty, in that white entituled / From Venus' doves'.

All praises, ~~which are paid as debts~~
~~And not as given,~~ this so darks   35
In Philoten all graceful marks
That Cleon's wife with envy rare
A present murder does prepare
For good Marina, that her daughter
Might stand peerless by this slaughter.   40
The sooner her vile thoughts to stead,
Lychorida our nurse is dead,
And cursèd Dioniza hath
The pregnant instrument of wrath
Pressed for this blow. The unborn event   45
I do commend to your content;
~~Only I carried wingèd time~~
~~Post on the lame feet of my rhyme,~~
~~Which never could I so convey~~
~~Unless your thoughts went on my way.~~   50
Dioniza does appear
With Leonine, a murderer.   *Exit*

[4.1] *Enter* DIONIZA, *with* LEONINE

DIONIZA Thy oath remember, thou hast sworn to do't;
'Tis but a blow which never shall be known.
Thou canst not do a thing in the world so soon

38 murder] *Oxford; conj. Walker;* murderer Q   44 wrath] F3; wrath. Q   48 on] Q2; one Q   Act 4, Scene 1   4.1] *Malone subst.; not in* Q   1–4] *Rowe's lineation; prose* Q

34 **praises . . . debts** Compare *WT* 1.2.94, 'Our praises are our wages.'
35 **darks** darkens, overshadows.
37 **envy** see 12 n.
39–40 **that . . . peerless** The threat Dioniza perceives in the rivalry of the two girls recalls Duke Frederick in *AYLI* 1.3.80–2, 'she robs thee of thy name, / And thou wilt show more bright and seem more virtuous / When she is gone'.
41 **stead** aid, assist.
42 **dead** The Oxford editors want to have Lychorida's tomb revealed at this point, on the grounds that it is 'clearly required later'; but it is not: Marina is gathering flowers to strew on Lychorida's grave, but there is nothing in the text to indicate that the scene takes place *at* the

graveside; and 'tomb' is Oxford's own invention for 4.1.16.
44 **pregnant** receptive, disposed, inclined, ready (*OED* sv *a²* 3d).
45 **Pressed** Seized and forced into service (*OED* sv *v²* 2d); as 4.1.1–12 make clear, Leonine is an unwilling tool.
46 **content** pleasure, i.e. in viewing it performed.
47 **carried** have carried.
47 **wingèd time** A common metaphor for time's passage in the Renaissance; see *WT* 4.1.3–4, 'in the name of Time, / To use my wings'.
48 **Post** In haste, speed.

Act 4, Scene 1
Location Tarsus.

stop him from leaving

Convince him to manipulate

To yield thee so much profit. Let not conscience,
Which is but cold in flaming, thy love-bosom
Inflame too nicely; nor let pity, which
Even women have cast off, melt thee, but be
kiss ___ A soldier to thy purpose.

LEONINE I will do't, but yet she is a goodly creature.

DIONIZA The fitter then the gods should have her. *Enjoy*   *to enjoy*   10
Here she comes weeping for her ~~only mistress'~~ death. *you can't, you killed the nurse. nurse killed.*
Thou art resolved? — *risk a little pat.*

LEONINE   I am resolved.

to relish
to remind

Enter MARINA *with a basket of flowers*

MARINA No: I will rob Tellus of her weed
To strew thy green with flowers; the yellows, blues,
The purple violets, and marigolds,   15

5–8] *Deighton's lineation; prose* Q **5** cold in flaming, thy love-bosom / Inflame] *This edn;* cold, in flaming, thy loue bosome, enflame Q; cold, or flaming love thy bosom / Enslave *Deighton* **12** resolved?] Q2; resolude. Q **13–20]** *Rowe's lineation; prose* Q

4–6 Let not conscience . . . nicely Dioniza is warning Leonine not to allow conscience, which is slow or 'cold' in starting (the process of reasoning between right and wrong), to grow into a flame which would warm his heart or sense of compassion ('love-bosom') in an over-subtle or scrupulous way ('too nicely') and thus weaken his resolve to murder; the sense is carried on in the next lines.

8 soldier to enlisted in, committed to.

10 fitter . . . gods . . . her Here, 'gods' is intended as an ironical pun on 'goodly' in the previous line; see *R3* 1.2.104–8, 'he was gentle, mild, and virtuous! / The better for the King of Heaven that hath him . . . Let him thank me that holp to send him thither; / For he was fitter for that place than earth.'

11 only unique in quality, character, or rank (*OED sv a* 5).

11 mistress i.e. Lychorida; mistress in this sense means a woman who has a protecting or guiding influence (Onions and Schmidt). The Oxford editors' elaborate conjectures of misreadings ('miſtres' for 'nurſes') or mishearings ('mistress' for 'fostress') are both far-fetched and unnecessary. Compare *Cym.* 3.3.103–5, 'Euriphile, / Thou wast their nurse . . . And every day do honor to her grave', a similar situation in which a nurse is mourned.

13–17 For a similar scene in which flowers are intended for a grave see *Cym.* 4.2.218–29, especially the phrase 'Whilst summer lasts'. Like Marina, Arviragus describes flowers that are associated with

death. See also *WT* 4.4 in which Perdita is associated more extensively with flowers.

13 No Editors have been curiously reluctant to comment on Marina's entry: with whom is she disagreeing, since no one has spoken to her? Presumably with herself, since lines 13–20 are a soliloquy. If so, the implication is that the third word in the line, 'will', should be stressed (i.e. 'whatever the reasons for not doing so, I *will* pluck flowers for your grave').

13 Tellus The goddess of the earth, hence the earth personified.

13 weed garment i.e. of flowers.

14 thy green The grass covering Lychorida's grave: a neologism, not in *OED*.

14 yellows, blues i.e. yellow (probably the marigold mentioned in the next line) and blue (the bluebell or wild hyacinth) flowers.

15 purple violets Of the five species of English violet, Shakespeare most frequently alludes to the purple violet. The violet was a symbol of meekness and humility; it is always associated with death, since it is a spring flower which withers before full summer arrives. See Ellacombe, p. 311. Compare *Ham.* 4.5.184–5, 'I would give you some violets, but they wither'd all when my father died', and 5.1.238–40, 'Lay her i'th'earth, / And from her fair and unpolluted flesh / May violets spring!'

15 marigolds The two distinguishing properties of the marigold – that it is always in flower, and that it turns its flowers to the sun and follows its guid-

Shall as a carpet hang upon thy grave
While summer days doth last. Ay me, poor maid,
Born in a tempest when my mother died,
This world to me is as a lasting storm
Whirring me from my friends.   20

DIONIZA How now Marina, why do you keep alone? *(X to Marina)*
Slow down How chance my daughter is not with you? *to inquire*
figure it Do not consume your blood with sorrowing; *to comfort*
out Have you a nurse of me? Lord, how your favour's *to set*
Changed with this unprofitable woe.   25 *to volley*
Come give me your flowers ere the sea mar it. *Take flowers*
Walk with Leonine, the air is quick there *Push firmly but gently on*
And it pierces and sharpens the stomach. *Marina's back* *to explain*
Come Leonine, take her by the arm, walk with her. *to enact*

MARINA No I pray you, I'll not bereave you of your servant.   30

DIONIZA Come, come, I love the king your father and yourself *to explain*
Explain With more than foreign heart. We every day *to guilt*
convince Expect him here; when he shall come and find
Our paragon to all reports thus blasted
He will repent the breadth of his great voyage,   35
Blame both my lord and me that we have taken
No care to your best courses. Go I pray you, *Push again slightly to encourage*

---

19 is as a] *NS, conj. Cam.*; is a Q; is like a Q4 24 me] me? Q 26 flowers ere the sea mar it;] Q *(flowers ere the sea marre it,)*; flowers. On the sea-margent *Hudson*; flowers. O'er the sea-margin *Theobald MS.* 31–42] *Rowe's lineation subst.*; *prose* Q

ance in their opening and shutting – made it a favourite flower of writers. It was an emblem of constancy in affection, and sympathy in joy and sorrow. See Ellacombe, p. 157 and *TNK* 1.1.11, 'Marigolds on death-beds blowing'.
20 Whirring Whirling.
20 friends Not used in the modern sense but as 'one's relatives, kinsfolk, people' (*OED* sv *sb* 3). See *TGV* 3.1.106–7, 'But she I mean is promis'd by her friends / Unto a youthful gentleman of worth.' The word is used twice by Pericles as part of the important information which he seeks from his daughter, 5.1.122 and 136.
21 keep remain. Compare *Mac.* 3.2.8, 'How now, my lord, why do you keep alone.'
22 How chance How is it.
23 Do . . . sorrowing An allusion to the belief that every sigh drew a drop of blood from the heart. See *MND* 3.2.97, 'With sighs of love, that costs the fresh blood dear', *2H6* 3.2.61, 'blood–consuming sighs', *3H6* 4.4.22, 'And stop the rising of blood-

sucking sighs', *Rom.* 3.5.59, 'Dry sorrow drinks our blood.'
24 Have you . . . me i.e. make me your nurse.
24 favour appearance, facial expression (*OED* sv *sb* 9a).
26 ere the sea mar it i.e. before the salt air wilts it (the flowers collectively, since they are gathered together in the basket).
27 quick refreshing, enlivening (*OED* sv *a* 18c, citing this example).
28 pierces . . . stomach affects and increases the appetite.
32 With . . . heart i.e. as if I were related to your family.
34 paragon . . . reports the model of excellence according to all reports. Compare 4.2.113–14, 'say what a paragon she is', and *Cym.* 3.7.43 and 5.5.147, 'That paragon, thy daughter'.
34 blasted withered.
37 to . . . courses of what was best for you.

Walk and be cheerful once again, reserve
That excellent complexion, which did steal
The eyes of young and old. Care not for me,
I can go home alone.

MARINA   Well, I will go,
But yet I have no desire to it.

DIONIZA Come, come, I know 'tis good for you.
Walk half an hour, Leonine, at the least,
Remember what I have said?   45

LEONINE I warrant you, madam.

DIONIZA I'll leave you, my sweet lady, for a while;
Pray walk softly, do not heat your blood.
What, I must have care of you.

MARINA   My thanks sweet madam.

                                        [*Exit Dioniza*]

Is this wind westerly that blows?

LEONINE   South-west.   50

MARINA When I was born the wind was north.

LEONINE   Was't so?

MARINA My father, as nurse says, did never fear,
But cried 'Good seamen!' to the sailors,
Galling his kingly hands haling ropes,
And clasping to the mast, endured a sea   55
That almost burst the deck.

LEONINE When was this?

MARINA   When I was born;

38 reserve] Q; *resume NS*   43–5] Q4*'s lineation; prose* Q   47–9] *Rowe's lineation; prose* Q   49 SD] *Malone; not in* Q   52–6]
Malone's lineation subst.; prose Q   52 nurse] Q2; nutse Q

38 reserve preserve, guard, maintain.
48 softly slowly.
50 South-west Rather surprisingly, the south and south-west winds had negative associations for Shakespeare. See *2H4* 2.4.363–4, 'like the south / Borne with black vapor', *Tro.* 5.1.18, 'the rotten diseases of the south', *Cor.* 1.4.30, 'the contagion of the south', *Cym.* 2.3.131, 'The south-fog rot him', and 4.2.349, 'the spungy south', *Temp.* 1.2.323–4, 'A south-west blow on ye, / And blister you all o'er.' Here Leonine's grim response is intended as an ill omen of his treacherous intentions.
51 north See 3.0.47 n.
52 says The historic present (also in 60).
54 Galling Chafing, wounding.
54 haling ropes *OED* recognises 'haling' as a verbal noun distinct from, though meaning the

same as, 'hauling', the familiar nautical term (Falconer, p. 110): 'That which others commonly call pulling a rope the seafaring men call ever hauling.' Pericles is following the tradition of Drake in 'galling his kingly hands haling ropes': 'For I must have the gentleman to haul and draw with the mariner . . . let us show ourselves all to be of a company . . . I would know him, that would refuse to set his hand to a rope, but I know there is not any such here' (cited in Julian Corbett, *Drake and the Tudor Navy*, 1898, II, 262, who does not give the source).
56 burst the deck 'burst' is the correct nautical term used in conjunction with 'deck', the planked floors of a ship extending from side to side (Falconer, p. 105).

Never was waves nor wind more violent,
And from the ladder-tackle washes off
A canvas-climber; 'Ha!' says one, 'wolt out?'   60
And with a dropping industry they skip
From stem to stern, the boatswain whistles, and
The master calls and trebles their confusion.

LEONINE Come say your prayers.

MARINA   What mean you?

LEONINE   If you require
A little space for prayer, I grant it: 65
Pray, but be not tedious, for the gods
Are quick of ear, and I am sworn
To do my work with haste.

MARINA Why will you kill me?

LEONINE   To satisfy my lady.

MARINA Why would she have me killed now?   70
As I can remember by my troth,
I never did her hurt in all my life,
I never spake bad word, nor did ill turn
To any living creature. ~~Believe me, law,~~
~~I never killed a mouse, nor hurt a fly;~~   75
~~I trod upon a worm against my will,~~
~~But I wept for't.~~ How have I offended, wherein
My death might yield her any profit, or
My life imply her any danger?

LEONINE   My commission
Is not to reason of the deed but do't.   80

MARINA You will not do't for all the world I hope.

58–61] *Rowe's lineation; prose* Q   62–3] *Malone's lineation; prose* Q   62 stem] *Malone;* sterne Q   64–8] *This edn's lineation; prose* Q   70–9] *Malone's lineation subst.; prose* Q   79–87] *Rowe's lineation; prose* Q

58 **was** For third person plural in *-s*, see Abbott 333.

59 **ladder-tackle** rope ladder in the rigging.

60 **canvas-climber** sailor who climbs the ladder-tackle in order to trim the sails.

60 **wolt out** 'Wolt' is an obsolete version of the second person singular of 'will' (*OED* sv *v*¹ A3aγ). For sailors railing at a storm see 3.1.44–5 n.; the various sea-folk in the play tend to be identified by their distinctive language, so it is preferable to keep Q's form rather than regularise.

61 **dropping** dripping-wet.

62 **stem to stern** i.e. from the front of the ship to the back.

66 **be not tedious** i.e. don't take too long.

70 **now** Not intended with a temporal significance but as an emphatic addition.

71 **As** As far as.

74 **law** An exclamation or interjection which intensifies a statement; see Onions, who cites *LLL* 5.2.414, 'so God help law!'

77 **wherein** in what way; compare *R3* 1.4.177, 'Wherein, my friends, have I offended you?'

79 **imply** import, cause.

> You are well favoured, and your looks foreshow
> You have a gentle heart; I saw you lately
> When you caught hurt in parting two that fought:
> Good sooth it showed well in you; do so now.   85
> Your lady seeks my life, come you between,
> And save poor me the weaker.

LEONINE I am sworn and will dispatch.

Enter PIRATES

1 PIRATE Hold, villain!

[Leonine flees]

2 PIRATE A prize, a prize!   90

3 PIRATE Half part mates, half part. Come let's have her aboard
    suddenly.

I Pirate

[Exeunt Pirates with Marina]

Enter LEONINE

Val'dez

LEONINE These roguing thieves serve the great pirate Valdes,
    And they have seized Marina – ~~let her go,~~

---

86 life, come you] lifeCome, you Q 89 SD] *This edn; not in* Q; *Leonine runs away / Malone* 92 SD.1] *Malone; Exit* Q
93–9] *Rowe's lineation; prose* Q 94 Marina –] *Marina,* Q

82–3 **your looks...heart** Compare *John* 4.1.87, 'He hath a stern look, but a gentle heart', and *R3* 1.4.263 (Clarence to the Second Murderer), 'I spy some pity in thy looks.'
82 **well favoured** of a good countenance.
82 **foreshow** show forth, reveal.
88 **dispatch** get rid of or dispose of (anyone) by putting to death; to make away with, kill (*OED* sv *sb* 4).
88 SD, 92 SD Like the stage direction in *WT* 3.3.58, *Exit pursued by a bear*, the Pirates' sudden entrance and exit with the abducted Marina is not clumsy dramaturgy, but rather in keeping with the romance tradition of surprising and improbable events. In RSC 1989, the Pirates slid at great speed down ropes from 'aloft', a great *coup de théâtre*.
90 **prize** ship or property captured at sea (*OED* sv *sb³* 2b); here used figuratively of Marina. Compare *WT* (Autolycus speaking of his next victim) 4.3.31, 'A prize, a prize!'
91 **Half part** Go shares. The Third Pirate claims his part of the booty.
93 **roguing thieves** Pirates were often thus described in the frequent proclamations and edicts against them throughout the reigns of Elizabeth and

James. From 1605 onwards the threat of Mediterranean pirates caused especial uneasiness in London. 'One corsair made his way as far up the Thames as Leigh in Essex before being taken. Petitions which reached the King through Henry Wriothesley, Earl of Southampton, at last led him to consider sending out a fleet to suppress the pirate stronghold at Algiers whose "inhabitants consist principally of desperate rogues and renegadoes, that live by rapine, theft, and spoil"' (Falconer, p. 49). See *2H6* 1.1.222–8, 'Pirates may make cheap pennyworths of their pillage / And purchase friends and give to courtezans [which is what happens to Marina] . . . all is shar'd and all is borne away.' Also *TN* 5.1.69, 'Notable pirate, thou salt-water thief'. For 'roguing', compare *WT* 4.3.98–100, 'having flown over many knavish professions, he settled only in rogue'.
93 **Valdes** There is no particular reason to suppose (as did Malone and Hoeniger after him) that the name is taken from the Spanish admiral Pedro de Valdes, captured by Drake in 1588; though, as Malone suggests, the name would have had a certain relish for the audience of the time.

There's no hope she will return: I'll swear she's dead,   95
And thrown into the sea. But I'll see further;
Perhaps they will but please themselves upon her,
Not carry her aboard. If she remain,
Whom they have ravished must by me be slain.   *Exit*

[**4.2**] *Enter the three Bawds* [PANDER, BAWD, BOULT]

Enul   as Slut

PANDER Boult.

BOULT Sir.

PANDER Search the market narrowly, Miteline is full of gallants, we lost
   too much money this mart *month* by being too wenchless.

BAWD We were never so much out of creatures, we have but poor three,   5
   and they can do no more than they can do, and they with continual
   action are even as good as rotten.

PANDER Therefore let's have fresh ones whate'er we pay for them. If
   there be not a conscience to be used in every trade we shall never
   prosper.   10

BAWD Thou sayst true, 'tis not our bringing up of poor bastards, as I
   think, I have brought up some eleven —

BOULT Ay, to eleven, and brought them down again, but shall I search
   the market?

Act 4, Scene 2   4.2] *Malone subst.; not in* Q   0 SD] *This edn; Enter the three Bawdes* Q; Enter Pandar, Bawd, and Boult
F3   **4** much] Q2; much much Q   **4**] too wenchless] wenchless *NS*   **12** eleven –] *Malone;* eleuen. Q

95 no hope . . . return i.e. there is no chance of
her return. Compare 1.3.27.
95–6 dead . . . sea An ironic echo of her mother's own fate.

Act 4, Scene 2
  Location Miteline: see map facing p. 1.
  0 SD *Bawds* A bawd is someone who works in the
trade of prostitution, whose main responsibility is
to procure customers and prostitutes. The three
bawds each have names associated with their profession: a pander is also a procurer as well as a go-
between in illicit affairs; to 'boult' (or bolt) in its
figurative sense (*OED* sv *v*¹ 2) is 'to examine by
sifting; to search and try'; Williams, p. 136, suggests
that he is 'perceived as the sifting-cloth between
container and that which is to be contained'.
The phallic significance of his name is also implied
(*OED* sv *sb*¹ 1, an arrow, and 5, a door-bolt). Here,
Pander and Bawd are man and wife and run the
brothel; Boult is their servant. For the punctuation

in this scene, and in 4.5, see Note on the Text,
p. 80.
  3 narrowly closely, with scrutiny.
  4 mart market time.
  5 creatures prostitutes.
  6–7 continual action constant sexual servicing
of clients.
  7 rotten infected and consequently sick.
  8–10 If . . . prosper The Pander's twisted concept of conscience or good conduct in business
includes sparing no expense in purchasing new
merchandise. This kind of illogical expression is
indicative of the bawds' 'professional idiom' in general and a source of much of the humour in their
scenes.
  11–12 'tis not . . . eleven The Bawd's contribu-
tion to their prosperity is to have brought up eleven
children; ' 'tis not' = not only.
  13 to eleven i.e. to eleven years of age.
  13 brought them down i.e. reduced them to
working in a brothel.

Pander

~~BAWD~~ ~~What else man?~~ The stuff we have, a strong wind will blow it to   15
   pieces, they are so pitifully sodden.

Bawd ~~PANDER~~ Thou sayst true, there's two unwholesome a' conscience, the
   poor Transylvanian is dead that lay with the little baggage.

BOULT Ay, she quickly pooped him, she made him roast-meat for
   worms, but I'll go search the market.   *Exit*   20

PANDER Three or four thousand chequins were as pretty a proportion
   to live quietly and so give over.

BAWD Why to give over I pray you? Is it a shame to get when we are old?

PANDER Oh, our credit comes not in like the commodity, nor the
   commodity wages not with the danger: therefore if in our youths we   25
   could pick up some pretty estate, 'twere not amiss to keep our door
   hatched, besides the sore terms we stand upon with the gods will be
   strong with us for giving o'er.

BAWD Come, other sorts offend as well as we.

PANDER As well as we, ay, and better too, we offend worse, neither is   30
   our profession any trade, it's no calling, but here comes Boult.

Enter BOULT *with the* PIRATES *and* MARINA

BOULT Come your ways my masters, you say she's a virgin.

PIRATE Oh sir, we doubt it not.

---

17 there's two] Q; they're too *Malone*   33 SH] *Rowe subst.; Sayler* Q

---

16 sodden made rotten by venereal disease; the literal meaning is 'boiled' (*OED* sv *ppl. a* 1); the sweating treatment for venereal disease is appropriately implied here for one who has become diseased in the 'stews', as brothels were commonly called. Compare *Tro.* 3.1.41, 'Sodden business! There's a stew'd phrase indeed!'

17 there's . . . conscience Paraphrased: 'there's two of them diseased, even I must admit'.

18 baggage a worthless, good-for-nothing woman; a strumpet (*OED* sv *sb* 6; the playful sense is not recorded until 1672).

19 pooped infected him with venereal disease. 'Poop', originally a nautical term for the stern of a ship (*OED* sv *n¹*) became a vulgar term for the female genitals. See Williams, p. 1071. The implication here is clear that the 'Transylvanian' died from venereal disease caught from the 'baggage'; this extended meaning of 'pooped' is not recorded elsewhere.

21 chequins Italian gold coins.

21 proportion i.e. fortune.

22 give over retire, give up the trade.

23 get earn money.

24 credit reputation.

24 commodity profit (*OED* sv *sb* 2c).

25 wages not is not commensurate with; 'the commodity . . . danger' might be paraphrased: 'our reputation does not come in like the profit nor is the profit equal to the risk'.

27 hatched shut. The hatch was the smaller door inset within a larger full-sized door commonly found in brothels. Riverside, p. 1516, reproduces the woodcut frontispiece of the anonymous *Holland's Leaguer* (1632), which purports to show a London brothel with a hatch in the door.

28 strong with us a good reason or argument for us.

29 sorts classes of people.

31 trade a recognised trade.

31 calling occupation (*OED* sv *vbl. sb.* 11a); with an ironic reference to the Christian doctrine of vocation (*OED vbl. sb.* 9a). Compare 1 Cor. 7.20, 'Let every man abide in the same vocation wherein he was called.' Compare also *1H4* 1.2.104–5, ''tis no sin for a man to labor in his vocation'.

BOULT Master, I have gone through for this piece you see, if you like
    her, so, if not I have lost my earnest.   35
BAWD Boult, has she any qualities?
BOULT She has a good face, speaks well, and has excellent good clothes:
    ~~there's no farther necessity of qualities can make her be refused.~~
BAWD What's her price, Boult?
BOULT I cannot be bated one doit of a thousand pieces.   40
PANDER Well, follow me my masters, you shall have your money pres-
    ently. Wife take her in, instruct her what she has to do that she may
    not be raw in her entertainment.

Exit MR   *[Exeunt Pander and Pirates]*

BAWD Boult, take you the marks of her, the colour of her hair, complex-
    ion, height, her age, with warrant of her virginity, and cry, 'He that   45
    will give most shall have her first, such a maidenhead were no cheap
    thing if men were as they have been.' Get this done as I command
    you.
BOULT Performance shall follow.   *Exit*

MARINA Alack that Leonine was so slack, so slow,   50
        He should have struck, not spoke, or that these pirates,
        Not enough barbarous, had not o'er-board thrown me
        For to seek my mother.
BAWD Why lament you pretty one?
MARINA That I am pretty.   55
BAWD Come, the gods have done their part in you.
MARINA I accuse them not.
BAWD You are light into my hands where you are like to live.

---

43 SD] *Malone; not in* Q   50–3] *Malone's lineation; prose* Q

34 gone through done my utmost (i.e. in bar-
gaining for her).
34 piece item of trade goods (*OED* sv *sb* 6a): to
the bawds, Marina is dehumanised into an object;
the word was coming into use contemptuously or
with a sexual connotation for a woman (*OED* sv *sb*
9b). See also Williams, p. 1025.
35 earnest deposit paid to secure an item of
merchandise.
40 'I cannot get them to go half a farthing ("doit")
below a thousand pieces'; i.e. they won't accept less
than a thousand pounds. 'Piece' was used absolutely
at the time for an English gold coin (originally the
unite of James I) worth about twenty shillings (*OED*
Piece *sb* 13b).
40 bated abated, i.e. reduced. Compare *TNK*
1.1.220, 'Keep the feast full, bate not an hour on't.'

40 doit Dutch coin, worth half a farthing; used
generically as the smallest amount of money.
43 raw . . . entertainment inexperienced . . .
sexual practice.
45 warrant confirmation.
50–3 Alack . . . mother There are two clauses
here dependent upon 'Alack'; (paraphrased) 'Alack
that Leonine did not kill me' and 'Alack [under-
stood] that the pirates had not thrown me overboard'. Malone emended 'had not' to 'had but'
which makes more elegant grammar, but Q is not
unusually irregular.
56 done . . . you i.e. done well by you. A proverbial saying (Tilley G188, 'God has done his part';
Dent cites Udall's *Respublica* 1.276: 'Indeed, God
and nature in me have done their part').
58 light fallen.

MARINA The more my fault to 'scape his hands where I was to die.

BAWD Ay, and you shall live in pleasure.   60

MARINA No.

BAWD Yes indeed shall you and taste gentlemen of all fashions, you shall fare well, you shall have the difference of all complexions. What, do you stop your ears?

MARINA Are you a woman?   65

BAWD What would you have me be, and I be not a woman?

MARINA An honest woman, or not a woman.

BAWD Marry whip the gosling, I think I shall have something to do with you, come you're a young foolish sapling and must be bowed as I would have you.   70

MARINA The gods defend me.

BAWD If it please the gods to defend you by men, then men must comfort you, men must feed you, men stir you up.

[*Enter* BOULT]

Boult's returned. Now sir, hast thou cried her through the market?

BOULT I have cried her almost to the number of her hairs, I have drawn her picture with my voice.   75

BAWD And I prithee tell me, how dost thou find the inclination of the people, especially of the younger sort?

BOULT Faith they listened to me as they would have harkened to their father's testament, there was a Spaniard's mouth watered and he went to bed to her very description.   80

BAWD We shall have him here tomorrow with his best ruff on.

BOULT Tonight, tonight, but mistress do you know the French knight that cowers i'th'hams?

---

59 was to] Q; was like to Q4   60 pleasure] Q2; peasure Q   68 whip the] Q; whip thee, Q4   73 men stir] Q; men must stir Q4   73 SD] Q4; *not in* Q   84 i'th'] Q *(ethe)*

59 **fault** misfortune.

63 **difference ... complexions** variety of men of every race and disposition.

67 **honest** honourable, decent, chaste. Compare *WT* 2.1.68, ''Tis pity she's not honest–honorable.'

68 **gosling** young prostitute; prostitutes in Southwark were commonly referred to as 'Winchester geese', because the brothels there were located on land belonging to the Bishop of Winchester, whose London palace was in Southwark.

68–9 **have ... you** have trouble with you.

69 **sapling ... bowed** A proverbial image (Tilley T632, 'Best to bend while it is a twig').

72 **by men** by way of men.

73 **stir** (must) stir; (must) rouse or enliven.

75 **almost ... hairs** Two meanings suggest themselves: (1) Boult has cried (= advertised) her as many times as the number of hairs on her head, or (2) Boult has cried her as far as numbering the hairs on her head. In either sense he has been thorough.

82 **ruff** neck ornament made of plaited linen.

84 **cowers i'th' hams** walks in a crooked or bending manner, probably as a result of his venereal disease (see 88); 'hams' = backs of thighs.

BAWD Who, Monsieur Verollus? 85

BOULT Ay, he; he offered to cut a caper at the proclamation, but he
made a groan at it and swore he would see her tomorrow.

BAWD Well, well, as for him, he brought his disease hither, here he does
but repair it, I know he will come in our shadow to scatter his
crowns in the sun. 90

BOULT Well, if we had of every nation a traveller, we should lodge them
with this sign.

BAWD [*To Marina*] Pray you come hither awhile, you have fortunes
coming upon you, mark me, you must seem to do that fearfully
which you commit willingly, despise profit, where you have most 95
gain. To weep that you live as ye do makes pity in your lovers:
seldom but that pity begets you a good opinion, and that opinion a
mere profit.

MARINA I understand you not.

BOULT O take her home mistress, take her home, these blushes of hers 100
must be quenched with some present practice.

BAWD Thou sayst true i'faith, so they must, for your bride goes to that
with shame, which is her way to go with warrant.

BOULT Faith, some do and some do not, but mistress if I have bargained
for the joint – 105

BAWD Thou mayst cut a morsel off the spit.

BOULT I may so.

BAWD Who should deny it? Come young one, I like the manner of your
garments well.

BOULT Ay by my faith, they shall not be changed yet. 110

BAWD [*Giving money*] Boult, spend thou that in the town, report what a
sojourner we have, you'll lose nothing by custom. When nature

86 Ay, he; he] *Globe;* I, he, he Q   93 SD] *Dyce; not in* Q   96–7 lovers: seldom] *Malone;* louers seldome, Q   102 SH] F3;
Mari. Q   105 joint –] *Malone;* ioynt. Q   111 SD] *This edn.; not in* Q

85 Verollus derived from the French *vérole* = pox.

86 offered attempted.

86 cut a caper A dancing movement in which one leaps into the air and kicks the feet together.

89 repair renew, revive.

89 our shadow i.e. under our roof, the shelter of our house.

90 crowns . . . sun 'Crowns of the sun' were French gold coins; 'in the sun' is in metaphorical apposition to the 'shadow' of the previous line. A secondary bawdy meaning is implied because 'French crown' was a euphemism for the visible

signs on the head caused by syphilis (see Williams, pp. 546–7).

92 this sign i.e. Marina's beauty, charms. Brothels often carried a distinctive sign by which to recognise them, but the Oxford editors' notion that such a sign was hung out at the beginning of the scene is unlikely and unnecessary.

98 mere sheer, absolute.

103 shame modesty, shyness.

103 warrant entitlement.

112 by custom i.e. by way of getting customers; Boult can expect to receive his share of the earnings.

framed this piece, she meant thee a good turn, therefore say what a
paragon she is, and thou hast the harvest out of thine own report.

BOULT I warrant you mistress, thunder shall not so awake the beds of   115
eels, as my giving out her beauty stirs up the lewdly inclined. I'll
bring home some tonight.

BAWD Come your ways, follow me.

MARINA If fires be hot, knives sharp, or waters deep,
            Untied I still my virgin knot will keep.   120
            Diana aid my purpose.

BAWD What have we to do with Diana, pray you will you go with us?

                                                                Exeunt

[**4.3**] *Enter* CLEON, *and* DIONIZA

DIONIZA Why are you foolish, can it be undone?

CLEON O Dioniza, such a piece of slaughter
            The sun and moon ne'er looked upon.

DIONIZA   I think
            You'll turn a child again.

CLEON Were I chief lord of all this spacious world   5
            I'd give it to undo the deed. O lady
            Much less in blood than virtue, yet a princess
            To equal any single crown a'th'earth
            I'th'justice of compare! O villain, Leonine!
            Whom thou hast poisoned too: 10

---

122 SD] F3; *Exit* Q   Act 4, Scene 3   4.3] *Malone subst.; not in* Q   1 are] Q4; ere Q   3–4] *This edn's lineation; . . .* vpon. / *Dion.* I thinke . . . Q   4 child] Q4; chidle Q   5–13] *Malone's lineation; prose* Q   6 O] Q; A NS

115–16 thunder . . . eels It was commonly believed that eels were roused from the mud by thunder.

120–1 virgin knot . . . purpose The threat to the heroine's chastity is a common characteristic of the last plays. Compare in *Temp.* Caliban's attempt to rape Miranda (1.2.347–8), and Prospero's warning to Ferdinand not to 'break her virgin-knot before / All sanctimonious ceremonies' are accomplished (4.1.15–16).

Act 4, Scene 3
Location Tarsus.
The exchange between Dioniza and Cleon parallels that of Macbeth and Lady Macbeth after the murder of Duncan, as well as the interview between Albany and Goneril in *Lear* 4.2. The cruel treachery of a misdeed, the arrogant defiance of a female, and the guilt of the crime in all three examples form the basis of the dialogue.

1 can . . . undone Compare *Mac.* 5.1.68, 'What's done cannot be undone.' Proverbial saying (Tilley T200).

4 turn . . . again Compare *Mac.* 2.2.51–2, ''tis the eye of childhood / That fears a painted devil'.

6 O lady Spoken as an apostrophe to Marina.

7 Much . . . virtue i.e. more so in virtue than by way of lineage.

9 I'th'justice of compare In a just comparison.

If thou hadst drunk to him't had been a kindness
Becoming well thy face. What canst thou say
When noble Pericles shall demand his child?

DIONIZA That she is dead.
Nurses are not the fates to foster it,   15
Not ever to preserve. She died at night,
I'll say so: who can cross it unless you play
The impious innocent, and for an honest attribute,
Cry out 'she died by foul play'.

CLEON   O, go to.
Well, well, of all the faults beneath the heavens   20
The gods do like this worst.

DIONIZA   Be one of those
That thinks the petty wrens of Tarsus will
Fly hence and open this to Pericles.
I do shame to think of what a noble strain you are,
And of how coward a spirit.

CLEON   To such proceeding   25
Who ever but his approbation added,
Though not his prime consent, he did not flow

---

12 face] Q; fact *Dyce*   14–24] *This edn's lineation; prose* Q   18 impious] Q; *pious Collier conj. Mason*   25–39] *Malone's lineation; prose* Q   27 prime] *Dyce;* prince Q

11 drunk to him pledged him, i.e. while giving him the poison.

12 Becoming . . . face i.e. becoming your hypocrisy. Most editors since Dyce emend 'face' to 'fact' = 'deed', but the emendation seems unnecessary if Q's 'face' is taken to mean a false or feigning appearance (*OED* sv *sb* 10). See 46–7 where Dioniza is described as the angel-faced harpy, and *Mac.* 1.7.82, 'False face must hide.'

15–16 Nurses . . . preserve Most editors find 'foster it' a difficult problem because there is no obvious antecedent for 'it', but the pronoun here is the object of the verb used indefinitely (Abbott 226); compare 2.5.22, 'I must dissemble it', *Lear* 4.1.52, 'I cannot daub it further', or *3H6* 3.3.225, 'To revel it with him'. Dioniza's meaning is that nurses are not like the Fates who decide the length of life nor are they capable of preserving life for ever.

17 cross contradict.

18 impious innocent To Dioniza's distorted values, any attempt on Cleon's part to tell the truth, to play the innocent, would be impious. Her indignation and contempt create a rich double irony and

syntactical balance. Collier adopted *PA*'s 'pious', a typical memorial simplification.

18 attribute reputation.

22–3 wrens . . . Pericles Dioniza is referring to the folk-tale belief that birds revealed hidden murders: see *Mac.* 3.4.124–5, 'By maggot-pies and choughs and rooks brought forth / The secret'st man of blood'.

24–5 shame . . . coward Lady Macbeth offers similar rebukes to her husband in regard to shame and cowardice, *Mac.* 1.7.43, 'And live a coward in thy own esteem', and 2.2.61–2, 'but I shame / To wear a heart so white'. Editors freqently adopt Steevens's emendation 'cow'd', but its only real merit is metrical.

25–8 Paraphrased, these lines mean something like 'anyone who ever merely went along with ("his approbation added") such an act without first really believing it to be good ("without his prime consent") is not acting honourably'.

27 prime Dyce's emendation seems necessary; it is hard to find a meaning for Q's 'prince'.

27–8 flow . . . courses i.e. did not descend from honourable origins; 'courses' = water courses, the

From honourable courses.

DIONIZA   Be it so then.

Yet none does know but you how she came dead,
Nor none can know, Leonine being gone.   30
She did distain my child and stood between
Her and her fortunes: none would look on her,
But cast their gazes on Marina's face,
Whilst ours was blurted at and held a mawkin
Not worth the time of day. It pierced me through,   35
And though you call my course unnatural,
You not your child well loving, yet I find
It greets me as an enterprise of kindness
Performed to your sole daughter.

CLEON   Heavens forgive it.

DIONIZA   And as for Pericles, what should he say?   40
We wept after her hearse, and yet we mourn;
Her monument is almost finished, and
Her epitaphs in glittering golden characters
Express a general praise to her, and care
In us at whose expense 'tis done.

CLEON   Thou art like   45
The harpy, which to betray, dost with
Thine angel's face seize with thine eagle's talons.

DIONIZA   Ye're like one that superstitiously

28 courses] Q; sources *Dyce*   31 distain] *Dyce*; disdaine Q   33 Marina's] Q2; *Marianas* Q   40–7] *This edn's lineation; prose*
Q   43 golden] F3; goldē Q   47 talons] Q *(talents)*

current followed by a river, maintaining the image
started with 'flow'.

31 distain Dyce's emendation is necessary.
Dioniza is not complaining that Marina treated
Philoten slightly: 'distain' means 'to deprive of its
colour, brightness, or splendour, to dim, to cause to
look pale or dim, to outshine' (*OED* sv *v* 3), and was
never spelled 'disdain'. Other uses of 'distain' in
Shakespeare mean to cast a stain on, overshadow
(Schmidt).

32–5 Compare *1H4* 3.2 for a similar description
of two rivals; Henry IV rebukes his son for the
public's praises given to Hotspur.

34 blurted at held contemptuously, treated with
derision.

34 mawkin an untidy female, especially a servant or country wench, a slut: *OED* Malkin *sb* 2.
Compare *Cor.* 2.1.208.

38 greets me i.e. presents itself to me.
41 yet still.
43 characters letters.
46 harpy The rapacious monster of ancient
fable, with the face and trunk of a woman and the
wings and claws of a bird of prey. In heraldry the
harpy was assigned to one who had committed
manslaughter.
46–7 harpy . . . talons The harpy deludes its
victim 'with' (= by, see Abbott 193) its angelic face
but seizes it with its claws. A proverbial saying
(Dent H176.1, 'Harpies have virgin's faces and vul-
ture's talons').
48 Ye're You are. Dioniza uses the second person
plural in sarcastic recognition of Cleon's status.
48–9 like one . . . flies Paraphrased: 'you would
appeal to heaven because winter's harshness kills
the flies'. Various interpretations of these lines have

Do swear to th'gods that winter kills the flies;
But yet I know, you'll do as I advise.   *[Exeunt]*   50

[4.4] [*Enter* GOWER]

GOWER Thus time we waste, and long leagues make short,
Sail seas in cockles, have and wish but for't,
Making to take your imagination
From bourn to bourn, region to region.
By you being pardoned we commit no crime   5
To use one language in each several clime
Where our scenes seems to live. I do beseech you
To learn of me, who stand in th'gaps, to teach you
The stages of our story. Pericles
Is now again thwarting the wayward seas,   10
Attended on by many a lord and knight,
To see his daughter, all his life's delight.
Old Hellicanus goes along; behind
Is left to govern it, you bear in mind,
Old Escanes, whom Hellicanus late   15

49–50] Q4*'s lineation; . . .* kills / . . . youle / . . . aduise. Q   50 SD] *Rowe; not in* Q   Act 4, Scene 4   4.4] *Malone subst.; not in* Q   0 SD] Q4*; not in* Q   3 your] *Malone;* our Q   7–8] F3*;* liue, / . . . you / . . . gappes / . . . you. Q   8 in th'gaps] *This edn;* with gappes Q; i'th'gaps *NS, conj. Bullen*   8 you] F4*;* you, Q   9 story.] *Tonson;* storie Q   10 the] Q2*;* thy Q

been offered, but the meaning clearly is Dioniza's criticism of Cleon's over-scrupulous sense of what constitutes cruelty.

Act 4, Scene 4
1 **waste** consume; compare Prologue 16, 'Waste it for you, like taper light'.
1 **leagues** A league is approximately three miles.
2 **Sail . . . cockles** The appeal is to the imagination that can sail the sea in cockle-shells; compare *TNK* 3.4.13–15, 'Then would I make / A carreck of a cockleshell, and sail / By east and north-east to the King of Pigmies.'
2 **and . . . for't** just by wishing for it.
3 **Making** Proceeding in a certain direction (*OED* Make v¹ 35), usually applied to ships. A nautical application is in keeping with the concept of voyage which Gower is establishing in relation to the audience's imagination.
3 **your** Although Hoeniger defends Q, Malone's emendation is sound: the stress Gower lays

throughout on the need to arouse the participation of the audience's imagination is surely conclusive.
4 **bourn** frontier.
5 **we . . . crime** Time, the Chorus in *WT*, makes a near-identical disclaimer (4.1.4–9).
6 **clime** country.
7 **scenes seems** For singular inflection with plural subject see Abbott 333. The plural 'scenes' follows logically from those that have taken place in 'each several clime'.
8 **in th'gaps** i.e. the gaps of time between the performed actions, which Gower fills with his narrative. Compare *WT* 4.1.5–7, 'I slide / O'er sixteen years and leave the growth untried / Of that wide gap', and 5.3.154, 'Perform'd in this wide gap of time'.
8 **teach** (1) tell, (2) show.
9 **stages** The notion of the different theatrical 'stages' of the narrative is also implied here.
10 **thwarting** crossing.
10 **wayward** obstinate, perverse.

Of late. time
Advanced in Tyre to great and high estate.
S+ Well-sailing ships, and bounteous winds have brought
This king to Tarsus — think this pilot thought — Ty
So, with his steerage, shall your thoughts groan
Rich To fetch his daughter home, who first is gone. S+ .   20
Like motes and shadows see them move awhile;
Your ears unto your eyes I'll reconcile.

[*Dumb show*]

*Enter Pericles at one door, with all his train, Cleon and Dioniza at
the other. Cleon shows Pericles the tomb, whereat Pericles makes
lamentation, puts on sackcloth, and in a mighty passion
departs[, followed by the others]*

Enter UR in great mourning   *Rich*
GOWER See how belief may suffer by foul show:
This borrowed passion stands for true old woe,
S+ And Pericles in sorrow all devoured,   25
With sighs shot through, and biggest tears o'er-showered,
Leaves Tarsus and again embarks. He swears *Rich*

16 Tyre] *Schanzer, conj. Walker;* time Q   17 winds have brought] F3; winds / Haue brought Q   18 this pilot thought –]
this Pilat thought Q; his pilot thought; *Steevens;* this pilot – thought *conj. Mason*   19 groan] Q *(grone);* grow on *Malone;*
go on *NS, conj. Malone*   21 motes] moats Q   21 them move awhile] them / Moue a while Q   22 SD.1 *Dumb show*] *Malone;*
not in Q   22 SD.5 *followed by the others*] *This edn; not in* Q   23 SH] *Gowr.* Q   24 true old] Q; true-ow'd *NS*

18 **think this pilot thought** In its broadest
scope, 'thought' is anything which is formed in the
mind; it is the imagination which steers the play's
course. Here Gower continues to link nautical language with that of the imagination. Naval pilots
'are properly those who . . . are employed for the
conduction of ships into roads and harbours . . .
And this they perform by their being acquainted
with the depths, heights, and the flowings of the
tides . . . and likewise by their knowledge of those
kinds of sands as are moveable by the blowing of the
winds' (Falconer, p. 79). As pilots came to be of
increasing importance different categories grew up,
so that there were also pilots who could be borne for
a whole voyage (Gower's pilot); by 1603, it was
thought 'no unthrifty providence, especially in
ships of charge, to have of them continually aboard
for the prevention of all hazards' (Falconer, p. 80).
19 **with his steerage** steered by him, i.e.
thought personified.
19 **groan** i.e. long for; but also, in keeping with
the nautical imagery Gower has established, the
creaking of a ship's timbers is often described as a
'groan'.

20 **first is gone** who left before.
21 **motes** floating particles of dust in a ray of
light.
22 SD.3 *tomb* Probably the tomb was in the discovery space, and Cleon 'shows' it by drawing the
traverse. Tombs or monuments were common large
properties in the companies' inventories. The RSC
1947 version may very well resemble the original
(see illustration 3, p. 19).
22 SD.4 *sackcloth* coarse textile fabric used
chiefly for making sacks (*OED* sv *sb* 1a). Celebrated
because of its biblical role as the garment of penance
and mourning (e.g. Dan. 9.3, Matt. 11.21).
23 **suffer . . . show** be abused by deceitful
pretence.
24 **borrowed** put on, pretended.
24 **old** great, abundant (Onions).
27–9 **swears . . . sackcloth** Pericles' vow is a
retreat from the world and its customs of life; from
now on he withdraws into a world of living death
from which his daughter will at last revive him. The
vow is dramatically appropriate at this point in the
action; and if Gower is right here, it contradicts
3.3.28 (see n.).

Never to wash his face nor cut his hairs;
He puts on sackcloth, and to sea. He bears
A tempest which his mortal vessel tears,   30
And yet he rides it out. Now please you wit
The epitaph is for Marina writ
By wicked Dioniza.

 The fairest, sweetest, and best lies here,
 Who withered in her spring of year.   35
 She was of Tyrus the king's daughter,
 On whom foul death hath made this slaughter.
 Marina was she called; and at her birth,
 Thetis, being proud, swallowed some part a'th' earth.
 Therefore the earth, fearing to be o'er-flowed,   40
 Hath Thetis' birth-child on the heavens bestowed.
 Wherefore she does, and swears she'll never stint,
 Make raging battery upon shores of flint.

No vizor does become black villainy
So well as soft and tender flattery.   45
Let Pericles believe his daughter's dead,
And bear his courses to be ordered
By Lady Fortune, while our stir must play
His daughter's woe and heavy well-a-day
In her unholy service. Patience then,   50
And think you now are all in Miteline.   *Exit*

---

29 puts] *Malone;* put Q   29 sea. He] *Malone;* Sea he Q   32–3 writ, / By] *Malone's lineation; one line* Q   48 stir] Q *(Steare);* scene *Malone*²

29–31 bears . . . out See Introduction, pp. 53–8, for the importance of the hero's endurance under trial.

30 vessel Two meanings: ship (*OED sb*¹ 4a), but also body (*OED sb*¹ 3b). Gower is punning.

31 wit know (*OED sv v*¹ 1).

34–43 Marina's epitaph has attracted much abuse from editors ('shocking piece of fustian' (NS); 'sheer poetic drivel' (Hoeniger)). Epitaphs are not noted for their elegance (see, for instance, Shakespeare's, on the floor of Holy Trinity Church in Stratford-upon-Avon, or Claudio's doggerel to Hero in *Ado* 5.1.3–8); and it is dramatically suitable for Dioniza's verses to be bathetic, far-fetched, and basically inappropriate; Pericles is not in a critical frame of mind. Q's italics are retained for the epi-

taph because it is a different *kind* of text from Gower's narrative.

39 Thetis Sea-nymph and mother of Achilles.

39 swallowed . . . earth The swelling of the sea is a result of Thetis' pride at the birth of Marina ('*Thetis' birth-child*', 41) in her domain.

42 she i.e. Thetis.

42 stint cease.

44 vizor mask. See Tilley v92, 'A well-favoured visor will hide an ill-favoured face.'

48 stir *OED* gives 'stear' (Q: Steare) as a spelling of 'stir' (*sb* 2: 'bustle, activity of many'): it is Marina's adventures that are about to be performed actively on stage, and the common emendation, 'scene', is thus unnecessary.

49 well-a-day grief.

[**4.5**] *Enter two* GENTLEMEN

1 GENTLEMAN Did you ever hear the like?

2 GENTLEMAN No, nor never shall do in such a place as this, she being
once gone.

1 GENTLEMAN But to have divinity preached there, did you ever
dream of such a thing?   5

2 GENTLEMAN No, no. Come, I am for no more bawdy houses, shall's
go hear the vestals sing?

1 GENTLEMAN I'll do any thing now that is virtuous, but I am out of
the road of rutting for ever.

[*Exeunt*]

Enter [PANDER, BAWD, *and* BOULT]

PANDER Well, I had rather than twice the worth of her she had ne'er   10
come here.

BAWD Fie, fie upon her, ~~she's able to freeze the god Priapus and undo
a whole generation.~~ We must either get her ravished or be rid of her.
When she should do for clients her fitment, and do me the kindness
of our profession, she has me her quirks, her reasons, her master-   15
reasons, her prayers, her knees, that she would make a puritan of
the devil if he should cheapen a kiss of her.

BOULT Faith I must ravish her, or she'll disfurnish us of all our
cavalleria and make our swearers priests.

Act 4, Scene 5   4.5] *Malone subst.; not in* Q   9 SD.1] F3; *Exit* Q   9 SD.2] *Malone; Enter Bawdes 3.* Q   19 cavalleria] Q
(Caualereea)

Act 4, Scene 5
  Location Miteline.
  6 shall's A combination of 'let us' and 'shall we'
(Abbott 215).
  7 vestals vestal virgins, see 3.4.10 n.
  9 rutting copulation.
  9 SD.2 *Enter . . .* BOULT Most editors mark a
new scene here, but as the Oxford editors remark,
there is no reason that the Gentlemen could not be
exiting at one door while the bawds enter at another
(the imaginary location, the brothel, is the same).
  12 Priapus A god of fertility, son to Dionysus; a
figure of lechery, a Greek personification of the
erect penis.
  13 generation Because of Marina's frigidity, a
'whole generation' of offspring will not be begotten.
  14 fitment duty, i.e. what befits her responsibility as a prostitute.

  14–15 do me . . . has me For the suppression of
the preposition before the pronoun in these phrases,
see Abbott 220. In modern speech one would say
'and do *to* me the kindness of our profession, she has
for me'; the 'old dative', as Abbott calls it, survives
in a few modern expressions such as 'Will you do
me the honour'.
  15 quirks verbal subtleties, quibbles.
  17 cheapen bargain for.
  19 cavalleria chivalry, a body of knights (Italian); here used ironically to describe the brothel's
customers.
  19 swearers users of profane language; but more
specifically pertaining here to a group in society
known as 'swearers' or 'swaggerers', who fre-
quented taverns and bawdy houses. Pistol is Shakespeare's best-known example; see *2H4* 2.4.

PANDER Now the pox upon her green sickness for me. 20

BAWD Faith there's no way to be rid on't but by the way to the pox.

Enter LYSIMACHUS

Here comes the Lord Lysimachus disguised.

~~BOULT We should have both lord and lown if the peevish baggage would but give way to customers.~~

LYSIMACHUS How now, how a dozen of virginities? 25

BAWD Now the gods to bless your honour.

BOULT I am glad to see your honour in good health.

LYSIMACHUS You may so, 'tis the better for you that your resorters stand upon sound legs. How now, wholesome Iniquity, have you that a man may deal withal and defy the surgeon? 30

BAWD We have here one sir, if she would, but there never came her like in Miteline.

LYSIMACHUS If she'd do the deeds of darkness thou wouldst say.

BAWD Your honour knows what 'tis to say well enough.

LYSIMACHUS Well, call forth, call forth. 35

[Exit Bawd]

BOULT For flesh and blood sir, white and red, you shall see a rose, and she were a rose indeed, if she had but –

21 SD] *Oxford; after line 24* Q 29 legs. How now, wholesome Iniquity, have you] *Malone subst.;* legges, how now? wholsome iniquity haue you, Q 35 SD] *This edn; not in* Q 37 but –] *Malone;* but. Q

20 **green sickness** Literally, anaemia suffered by young women, here derogatively referring to her sexual inexperience, which the Pander regards as a disease.

21 **pox** syphilis; the word was also used as a mild curse as in 20, hence the connection made by the Bawd.

23 **lown** low-bred fellow.

25 **how** i.e. at what price, how much.

29 **wholesome Iniquity** This phrase seems to be addressed either to the Bawd or Boult, in allusion to the Vice of the Tudor interludes; Iniquity is the Vice's name in *Nice Wanton* (1550) and *Darius* (1565).

30 **deal withal . . . surgeon** have safe sexual intercourse with, not subsequently requiring the doctor.

33 **deeds of darkness** acts of copulation. Compare *Lear* 3.4.87–8, 'did the act of darkness with her'; usually singular, but in a brothel many such deeds may be imagined.

35 SD, 41 SD The SD at 9 brought the three brothel-keepers (the Pander, the Bawd, and Boult)

on stage. The Pander's last speech is at 20. Someone must leave the stage to bring Marina forth, as commanded by Lysimachus at 35. The Oxford editors propose the Pander who, however, seems not to have any other immediate connection with Marina. Most editors follow Dyce in sending Boult to fetch her at 41, bringing him and Marina back after the Bawd's encomium in 43. It seems simpler to give the Bawd the exit that Lysimachus' command implies at 35, and to move the entry (as Oxford does) to follow 41. Though this leaves the Pander with nothing overt to do, it seems a more natural theatrical sequence in view of the Bawd's ensuing anxious dialogue with Marina.

36 **white and red** A mixture of white and red found in the mottled or variegated roses; see Ellacombe, p. 253. The image of the rose is continued in 42.

37 **but** – 'A thorn' or 'a prickle' is understood, according to the proverb 'no rose without a thorn', with the bawdy innuendo that a 'rose' (vagina) implies a 'thorn' (penis). Compare *AYLI* 3.2.111–12, 'He that sweetest rose will find / Must find love's

LYSIMACHUS What prithee?

BOULT O sir, I can be modest.

LYSIMACHUS That dignifies the renown of a bawd no less than it gives   40
a good report to a number to be chaste.

[*Enter* BAWD *with* MARINA]

BAWD Here comes that which grows to the stalk, never plucked yet I
can assure you. Is she not a fair creature?

LYSIMACHUS Faith, she would serve after a long voyage at sea. [*Paying*
the Bawd] Well there's for you, leave us.   45

BAWD I beseech your honour give me leave, a word and I'll have done
presently.

LYSIMACHUS I beseech you do.

BAWD [*To Marina*] First, I would have you note, this is an honourable
man.   50

MARINA I desire to find him so, that I may worthily note him.

BAWD Next he's the governor of this country, and a man whom I am
bound to.

MARINA If he govern the country you are bound to him indeed, but how
honourable he is in that I know not.   55

BAWD Pray you, without any more virginal fencing, will you use him
kindly? He will line your apron with gold.

MARINA What he will do graciously I will thankfully receive.

LYSIMACHUS Ha' you done?

BAWD My lord she's not paced yet, you must take some pains to work   60

---

40 dignifies] Q4; dignities Q   41 chaste.] Q; chaste. [*Exit Boult*] *Dyce*   41 SD] *This edn; not in* Q; *Enter Boult with Marina*
/ *Dyce (in line 43)*   44–5 SD] *Edwards subst.; not in* Q   46 leave, a word and] *Malone subst.*; leaue a word, and Q   49 *To*
Marina] *Malone; not in* Q

---

prick', *Ven.* 574, 'What though the rose have
prickles, yet 'tis pluck'd.'

40–1 That ... chaste 'That' = modesty, 'to be'
= for being; paraphrased: 'Modesty dignifies a
bawd's reputation no less than it dignifies the reputation of many for being chaste'. Lysimachus is
commenting on the specious nature of Boult's claim
to modesty.

44 Faith ... sea i.e. she would satisfy a sex-
starved (and therefore undiscriminating) sailor.
This seems to depreciate the Bawd's praise; no
doubt Lysimachus pretends not to be impressed.

51 worthily note respect.

56 virginal fencing verbal quibbling about honourable (and therefore, to the Bawd, incomprehen-

sible) concerns. Marina has just engaged in what the
Bawd describes as 'virginal fencing' by challenging
the Bawd's meaning of 'note' and 'bound' in the
previous lines; and she continues in this style of
linguistic fencing in her interview with Lysimachus
from 65 ff.

58 graciously (1) like a gentleman, (2) (religious
sense): in a state of grace.

60–1 paced ... manage Images taken from the
training of horses; 'paced' = broken in, trained in
its paces; 'manage' = handling. Compare *TNK*
5.4.68–9, 'Forgets school-doing, being therein
train'd, / And of kind manage', or *AYLI* 1.1.11–13,
and see Williams pp. 985–6.

her to your manage. Come we will leave his honour and her together, go thy ways.

[*Exeunt Bawd, Pander, Boult*]

LYSIMACHUS Now pretty one, how long have you been at this trade?

MARINA What trade, sir?

LYSIMACHUS Why, I cannot name it but I shall offend.   65

MARINA I cannot be offended with my trade, please you to name it.

LYSIMACHUS How long have you been of this profession?

MARINA E'er since I can remember.

LYSIMACHUS Did you go to't so young, were you a gamester at five, or
at seven?   70

MARINA Earlier too sir, if now I be one.

LYSIMACHUS Why, the house you dwell in proclaims you to be a
creature of sale.

MARINA Do you know this house to be a place of such resort and will
come into't? I hear say you're of honourable parts and are the   75
governor of this place.

LYSIMACHUS Why, hath your principal made known unto you who I
am?

MARINA Who is my principal?

LYSIMACHUS Why, your herb-woman, she that sets seeds and roots of   80
shame and iniquity. Oh you have heard something of my power,
and so stand aloft for more serious wooing, but I protest to thee
pretty one, my authority shall not see thee, or else look friendly
upon thee. Come, bring me to some private place: come, come.

MARINA If you were born to honour show it now;   85

---

62 SD] *Malone; not in* Q   65 name it] F3 *(*name't*); name* Q   85-7 *Marina* If . . . it.] *Rowe's lineation; prose* Q

---

69 gamester sexual player, prostitute. Although
it could refer to amateurs, the term here is obviously
used of the professional, with the implication of
gambling, taking the risks of the profession. See
Williams, pp. 575–6.

73 creature of sale prostitute, one who sells her
body.

75 parts qualities.

77 principal employer.

80 herb-woman Neither *OED* nor Williams
recognises a cant meaning for this; it means what it
says, a woman who deals in herbs. Lysimachus explains his figurative meaning in the next lines.

82 aloft up high; i.e. to take a high moral ground.

83 authority . . . thee In the previous lines
Lysimachus has supposed that Marina is playing
hard to get in order 'for more serious wooing' (82)

which he now assures her is impossible for one of
his noble status and rank, the conditions of which
she cannot share or hope to attain through him
because of what he takes to be her profession.

85–6 born . . . put upon The distinction is one
where honour is attained by virtue of being born
into it (i.e. noble origins) and one which is attained
by virtue of an office which is bestowed. Although
some of the preceding dialogue, especially Marina's
lines, can be structured into pentameters, other
lines resist. It is dramatically preferable to delay
Marina's adoption of verse to this point, when
her naturally eloquent and elevated style, befitting
her moral nature, produces corresponding verse
from Lysimachus, the first sign that he is not
irredeemable.

          If put upon you, make the judgement good
          That thought you worthy of it.
LYSIMACHUS   How's this? How's this?
          Some more, be sage.
MARINA   For me that am a maid,
          Though most ungentle fortune have placed me in
          This sty, where since I came diseases have   90
          Been sold dearer than physic – that the gods
          Would set me free from this unhallowed place,
          Though they did change me to the meanest bird
          That flies i'th'purer air!
LYSIMACHUS   I did not think
          Thou couldst have spoke so well, ne'er dreamed thou couldst.   95
          Had I brought hither a corrupted mind,
          Thy speech had altered it, hold, here's gold
          For thee, persever in that clear way thou goest
          And the gods strengthen thee.
MARINA   The good gods preserve you.
LYSIMACHUS For me, be you thoughten that I came with   100
          No ill intent, for to me the very doors
          And windows savour vilely, fare thee well,
          Thou art a piece of virtue, and I doubt not
          But thy training hath been noble, hold,
          Here's more gold for thee, a curse upon him,   105

87–91] *This edn's lineation; prose* Q   92–6] *Rowe's lineation; prose* Q   97–107] *This edn's lineation; prose* Q

---

90 sty filthy dwelling; here figuratively meant as a place of bestial debauchery (Schmidt); compare *Ham.* 3.4.93–4, 'Stew'd in corruption, honeying and making love / Over the nasty sty'.

90–1 diseases . . . physic Paraphrased: 'the brothel's sicknesses cost more than doctors' cures'.

93 meanest smallest, most humble.

95 spoke spoken; see Abbott 343.

96–107 Q's punctuation of commas has been largely retained here for dramatic effect. Like Antiochus in his conversation with Thaliard in 1.1, Lysimachus is embarrassed: he is trying to make a graceful exit with his foot in his mouth, and his discomfort is better conveyed by running on his phrases than by grammatical correctness. Despite the efforts of well-meaning and moral editors, there is nothing to suggest that Lysimachus brought anything but a 'corrupted mind' to the brothel (he is known there and obviously frequents the place as a customer), and in these lines is trying to redeem some semblance of honour in front of the virtuous maid who has shamed him. His words, then, suggest someone who is trying to make the best of a humiliating situation. Obviously, this does not as yet redeem his moral character, nor by any means make him yet a suitable husband for Marina: the emphasis is rather on the dramatic effect of the heroine's moral conversion of the libertine, a theme Shakespeare also treats in *MM* and *AWW*.

98 persever continue (the accent is on the second syllable).

98 clear unspotted, unstained, pure; compare *TNK* 1.1.30–1, 'The honor of your bed, and for the sake / Of clear virginity'.

100 be you thoughten think.

103 piece of virtue i.e. a perfect specimen, a masterpiece of chastity; compare *Temp.* 1.2.56, 'Thy mother was a piece of virtue', and *Ant.* 3.2.28.

Die he like a thief that robs thee of thy goodness,
If thou dost hear from me it shall be for thy good.

[Enter BOULT*]*

BOULT I beseech your honour one piece for me.
LYSIMACHUS Avaunt, thou damnèd door-keeper.
      Your house, but for this virgin that doth prop it,   110
      Would sink and overwhelm you. Away.   *[Exit]*
BOULT How's this? we must take another course with you. If your
    peevish chastity, which is not worth a breakfast in the cheapest
    country under the cope, shall undo a whole household, let me be
    gelded like a spaniel, come your ways.   115
MARINA Whither would you have me?
BOULT I must have your maidenhead taken off, or the common hangman
    shall execute it. Come your ways, we'll have no more gentlemen
    driven away, come your ways I say.

Enter BAWD

BAWD How now, what's the matter?   120
BOULT Worse and worse mistress, she has here spoken holy words to
    the Lord Lysimachus.
BAWD Oh abominable.
BOULT He makes our profession as it were to stink afore the face of the
    gods.   125
Pandar
~~BAWD~~ Marry hang her up for ever.
BOULT The nobleman would have dealt with her like a noble man, and
    she sent him away as cold as a snowball, saying his prayers too.
BAWD Boult take her away, use her at thy pleasure, crack the glass of her
    virginity, and make the rest malleable.   130

---

107 SD] *Malone; not in* Q   109–11] *This edn's lineation; prose* Q   111 SD] *Rowe; not in* Q   118 ways] *Dyce;* way Q   119 SD
BAWD] *Rowe;* Bawdes Q   126 Marry] Q4; Marie Q

108 **piece** See 4.2.34 n.
109 **Avaunt** Begone.
109 **door-keeper** A word commonly used for
panders and bawds who stationed themselves at the
door of the brothel either to prevent untimely intrusion (see *Oth.* 4.2.27–30 and 93–4), or perhaps to
invite custom.
   113 **peevish** perverse, obstinate, coy (*OED* sv
a 4).
114 **cope** sky; see 1.1.101–3 n.
114 **undo** beggar, ruin financially.
117–18 **hangman . . . execute** With a play on

'head' of 'maidenhead'. Compare *Rom.* 1.1.23–6, 'I
will cut off their heads. / The heads of maids? / Ay,
the heads of maids, or their maidenheads.'
   118 **ways** Q's line is set so very tightly (two abbreviations, and no spacing around commas) that it
is possible that the terminal 's' was omitted
deliberately.
129–30 **crack . . . virginity** The comparison of
virginity to glass was proverbial (Tilley w646, 'A
woman and a glass are ever in danger'); compare
MM 2.4.124–6.
130 **malleable** capable of being fashioned or

BOULT   And if she were a thornier piece of ground than she is, she shall
    be ploughed.

MARINA   Hark, hark you gods.

BAWD   She conjures! Away with her, would she had never come within
    my doors. Marry hang you. She's born to undo us. ~~Will you not go~~   135
    ~~the way of womenkind? Marry come up my dish of chastity with~~
    ~~rosemary and bays.~~   [*Exit*]

BOULT   Come mistress, come your way with me.

MARINA   Whither wilt thou have me?

BOULT   To take from you the jewel you hold so dear.   140

MARINA   Prithee tell me one thing first.

BOULT   Come now your one thing.

MARINA   What canst thou wish thine enemy to be?

BOULT   Why, I could wish him to be my master, or rather my mistress.

MARINA   Neither of these are so bad as thou art, since they do better   145
    thee in their command. Thou holdst a place for which the painedst
    fiend of hell would not in reputation change. Thou art the damned
    door-keeper to every coistrel that comes enquiring for his Tib, to
    the choleric fisting of every rogue thy ear is liable, thy food is such
    as hath been belched on by infected lungs.   150

BOULT   What would you have me do? Go to the wars, would you? where
    a man may serve seven years for the loss of a leg and have not money
    enough in the end to buy him a wooden one?

---

134 conjures! Away] *This edn;* coniures, away Q   137 SD] Q4; not in Q

adapted (*OED* sv *a* 2). Once Marina has lost her
virginity she will be adaptable to the trade of prostitution, the Bawd thinks.

132 ploughed penetrated sexually. See Williams
pp. 1058–9, and compare *Ant.* 2.2.227–8: 'She
made great Caesar lay his sword to bed; / He
ploughed her, and she cropp'd.'

134 conjures invokes supernatural aid by the use
of magic. This inverted sense of morality is typical
of the three bawds.

136 Marry come up A proverbial phrase of reproof (Dent M699.2), meaning something like modern English 'Get along with you.'

136–7 dish . . . bays The Bawd sees Marina as a
roasted dinner, garnished with herbs ('bays'), for
Boult's pleasure.

138 your way i.e. the 'way of womenkind' as in
136; there is no need to emend to 'ways'.

140 jewel virginity.

143 What . . . enemy . . . be A riddle which ini-

tiates Marina's attempt to outmanoeuvre Boult; 'enemy' is the devil. Boult's reply (144) suggests he is
at a loss.

145–65 Most editors, following Rowe and
Malone, attempt to force Marina's speeches here
into verse. But the verse that results is so appalling
that it is preferable to leave the speeches prose.

145–6 since . . . command i.e. 'they are superior to you since they have you in their command'.

146 painedst most tormented.

148 coistrel knave, base fellow (*OED* sv *sb* 2).

148 Tib As a proper name, typifying women of
the lower class; whore (see Williams, p. 1388).

149 fisting The action of the verb 'to fist', see
OED v[1] 4, hence 'fisting' *vbl. n*; citing this example:
'making to accept'.

151–3 Boult's argument against going to war
echoes Falstaff's 'honour' monologue in *1H4* 5.1.

Sorry - I get fuckin giddy on 4 hours of sleep. I'll work on letting exhaustion make me softer.

MARINA Do anything but this thou dost, empty old receptacles, or
common shores of filth, serve by indenture to the common hang- 155
man. Any of these ways are yet better than this, for what thou
professest, a baboon, could he speak, would own a name too dear.
That the gods would safely deliver me from this place! Here, here's
gold for thee: if that thy master would gain by me, proclaim that I
can sing, weave, sew, and dance, with other virtues which I'll keep 160
from boast, and will undertake all these to teach. I doubt not but
this populous city will yield many scholars.

BOULT But can you teach all this you speak of?

MARINA Prove that I cannot, take me home again and prostitute me to
the basest groom that doth frequent your house. 165

BOULT Well I will see what I can do for thee, if I can place thee I will.

MARINA But amongst honest women.

BOULT Faith my acquaintance lies little amongst them, but since my
master and mistress hath bought you, there's no going but by their
consent: therefore I will make them acquainted with your purpose, 170
and I doubt not but I shall find them tractable enough. Come, I'll do
for thee what I can, come your ways.

Exeunt

[**5.0**] *Enter* GOWER

Marina thus the brothel 'scapes and chances
Into an honest house our story says.
She sings like one immortal, and she dances
As goddess-like to her admired lays:

167 women] F3; woman Q   Act 5, Scene 0   5.0] *Malone subst.; not in* Q

154 receptacles containers for garbage or sewage.

155 common shores The water's edge, used for dumping garbage for the tide to wash away, or open sewers like the infamous Fleet Ditch in London.

155 by indenture i.e. contractually, as an apprentice. Compare *MM* 4.2.8–59 for the notion of the bawd turned hangman.

157 baboon . . . dear i.e. the proverbially lecherous and violent baboon would claim to possess a reputation above such a profession as Boult's.

159 if . . . me See *CA* 1457–8, 'If so be, that thy maister wolde, / That I his good encrees sholde'.

161 these to teach So in *CA* 1472, 'I shall hir teche of thynges newe.'

165 groom stable boy, i.e. menial servant.

167 honest women So in *CA* 1465, 'Where that honeste women dwelle'.

Act 5, Scene 0

1–24 The only chorus in the play in which the lines rhyme alternately. For the unusual departure in the chorus's style, see Introduction, p. 30.

4 goddess-like A description attributed to other romance heroines: Imogen in *Cym.* 3.2.8, Perdita in *WT* 4.4.10, and Miranda in *Temp.* 5.1.187.

4 lays songs.

Deep clerks she dumbs, and with her neele composes   5
  Nature's own shape, of bud, bird, branch, or berry,
That even her art sisters the natural roses;
  Her inckle, silk, twin with the rubied cherry;
That pupils lacks she none of noble race
  Who pour their bounty on her, and her gain   10
She gives the cursèd bawd. Here we her place,
  And to her father turn our thoughts again
Where we left him on the sea. We there him lost,
  Where, driven before the winds, he is arrived
Here where his daughter dwells; and on this coast   15
  Suppose him now at anchor. The city strived
God Neptune's annual feast to keep, from whence
  Lysimachus our Tyrian ship espies
His banners sable, trimmed with rich expense,
  And to him in his barge with fervour hies.   20
In your supposing once more put your sight:
  Of heavy Pericles, think this his bark,
Where what is done in action – more, if might –
  Shall be discovered; please you sit and hark.   *Exit*

---

6 berry,] Q4; berry. Q   7 roses;] *Malone*; Roses Q   8 silk, twin] Q2 *subst.*; Silke Twine, Q   13 lost] *Malone*; left Q   14
Where] Q; Whence *Steevens*   20 fervour] Q *(corr.)*, (feruer); former Q *(uncorr.)*

---

5 **Deep clerks ... dumbs** She silences ('dumbs') profound scholars ('deep clerks') with her learning.
  5 **neele** needle.
  7 **sisters** makes her work as good as.
  8 **inkle** linen thread or yarn.
  8 **twin ... cherry** i.e Marina's embroidery is a perfect imitation of the object it represents. Compare the collocation of 'twin' with 'cherry' in *TNK* 1.1.178, 'Her twinning cherries shall their sweetness fall', and *MND* 3.2.207–8, 'So we grew together / Like to a double cherry.'
  9 **race** class, family.
  14 **Where** In the relative or conjunctive use (*OED* sv II.5) as a correlative to 'there': 'in or at the place in which'.
  17 **Neptune's annual feast** A festival in honour of the god held on 23 July. As so much of the play is

dominated by the sea it is appropriate that Neptune's feast should mark the occasion of Pericles' reunion with his daughter. *PPA* makes the occasion Apollonius' own birthday.
  19–20 **His ... him** Its ... it.
  19 **sable** black. Pericles is in mourning for Marina.
  19 **trimmed ... expense** Colours and ensigns in great ships, and especially such as belonged to a king, were often used by way of trim and hung out at every yard-arm.
  20 **hies** hurries.
  21 Again, Gower's constant appeal is to the imagination: i.e. see with or in your imagination.
  22 **heavy** sorrowful.
  22 **this** i.e. the stage.
  23 **if might** if it were possible.
  24 **discovered** shown, displayed.

[**5.1**] *Enter* HELLICANUS, *to him two* SAILORS[, *the First of Tyre,*
the Second of Miteline]

1 SAILOR Where is Lord Hellicanus? He can resolve you,
~~O here he is~~. Sir,
There is a barge put off from Miteline,
And in it is Lysimachus the governor,
Who craves to come aboard, what is your will?   5
HELLICANUS That he have his, ~~call up some gentlemen.~~
~~1 SAILOR Ho gentlemen, my lord calls.~~

Enter two or three GENTLEMEN

~~1 GENTLEMAN Doth your lordship call?~~
HELLICANUS ~~Gentlemen, there is some of worth would come aboard,~~
~~I pray greet him fairly.~~   10

Enter LYSIMACHUS[, LORD, *attendants*]

1 SAILOR [*To Lysimachus*] Sir,
This is the man that can in aught you would resolve you.
LYSIMACHUS Hail reverend sir, the gods preserve you.
HELLICANUS And you, to outlive the age I am,
And die as I would do.
LYSIMACHUS   You wish me well.   15

Act 5, Scene 1   5.1] *Malone subst.; not in* Q   0 SD.1–2 *the First of Tyre, the Second of Miteline*] *This edn, after Malone ('one*
belonging to the Tyrian vessel, the other to the barge'); not in Q   1–5] *Steevens's lineation subst.; prose* Q   7 SH] *Malone subst.;*
2. Say. Q   9–10] *Steevens's lineation; prose* Q   10 SD LORD, attendants] *This edn; not in* Q   11 SD] *This edn; not in* Q   11–
12] *This edn's lineation; prose* Q   13] reverend] Q *(reuerent)*   14–15] *Malone's lineation; prose* Q   15–18] *Rowe's lineation;*
prose Q

Act 5, Scene 1

Location Miteline. The main platform of the
stage may be taken as the deck of Pericles' ship, with
a curtained discovery space for Pericles' appearance
at 31; the doors, in this staging, lead to the waiting
barge from Miteline.

1–22 There is much coming and going in this
opening scene which, as many editors have rightly
remarked, is confusing to read. Shakespeare is
dramatising formal naval protocol: Falconer
observes, 'Shakespeare chooses to lead up to the
meeting [between Lysimachus and Pericles] with
the ceremony that belongs to an official visit [on
board a ship]. In this, he draws on his knowledge
of the uses of flags and ensigns and of the laws on
the right of entry into harbours by foreign

vessels . . . Hellicanus sees that no point of
ceremony is omitted [6–10] . . . the gentlemen escort the Governor on board their own ship. Formal
compliments are exchanged and the reason for the
visit stated [17–18]. This, again, is according to rule
and custom . . . Before answering, Hellicanus
makes sure who the visitor is . . . and on being told,
with formal precision, "I am the Governor of this
place you lie before", he in turn states, "Sir, our
vessel is of Tyre, in it the king", and conducts the
Governor to the king' (pp. 20–1).

1 resolve you satisfy you, clarify your enquiries.
5 craves earnestly requests. See 2.1.58 n.
9 some someone.
12 aught . . . resolve you explain everything to
you.

Being on shore, honouring of Neptune's triumphs,
Seeing this goodly vessel ride before us,
I made to it to know of whence you are.

HELLICANUS First what is your place?

LYSIMACHUS I am the governor of this place you lie before.   20

HELLICANUS Sir, our vessel is of Tyre, in it the king,
A man who for this three months hath not spoken
To anyone, nor taken sustenance,
But to prorogue his grief.

LYSIMACHUS Upon what ground is his distemperature?   25

HELLICANUS 'Twould be too tedious to repeat,
But the main grief springs from the loss
Of a belovèd daughter and a wife.

LYSIMACHUS May we not see him?

HELLICANUS   You may, but bootless.
In your sight, he will not speak to any.   30

LYSIMACHUS Yet let me obtain my wish.

HELLICANUS   Behold him.

[*Discovers* PERICLES]

This was a goodly person till the disaster
That one mortal night drove him to this.

LYSIMACHUS Sir, King, all hail, the gods preserve you;
Hail, royal sir.   35

HELLICANUS It is in vain; he will not speak to you.

LORD [*To Hellicanus*] Sir, we have a maid in Miteline

19–25] *Steevens's lineation subst.; prose* Q   26–9] *Malone's lineation; prose* Q   29–31] *This edn's lineation; prose* Q   29–30
bootless. In your sight, he] *This edn;* bootlesse. Is your sight see, Q (*uncorr.*); bootlesse. Is your sight, hee Q (*corr.*); bootless
is your sight, he Q4   30–2 [*Hellicanus*] . . . any. / *Lysimachus* Yet . . . wish. / *Hellicanus.* Behold . . . This.] Q4 *subst.;*
[*Hell.*] . . . wish. / *Lys.* Behold . . . person. / *Hell.* Till . . . this Q   31 SD] *Malone subst.; not in* Q   33 night] *Malone;* wight
Q   34–5] *Dyce's lineation; prose* Q   34 Sir, King,] *Oxford;* Sir King Q   37–8] *This edn's lineation; prose* Q   37 SD] *This edn;
not in* Q

---

16 Neptune's triumphs public festivities in
honour of Neptune; see 5.0.17 n.

19 place official position. The word is used in a
different sense in 20.

21 in it the king For the image of the melancholy king who has taken to ship, compare *WT*
4.4.762–5, 'The King is not at the palace. He is
gone aboard a new ship to purge melancholy
. . . for . . . thou must know the King is full of
grief.'

24 prorogue prolong (*OED* sv *v* 1).

29–30 See Supplementary Note.

29 bootless unavailing.

31 SD *PA* has Pericles lying on a couch, which

seems reasonable if the couch can be thrust forward:
Pericles invites Marina to sit beside him at 138. The
curtained discovery space would be the natural
place for Pericles' first appearance, but since the
scene is the lengthy climax of the play it would
surely take place on the main part of the stage. A
'discovery' could simply mean drawing a curtain, or
the more complex event we hypothesize here, involving the use of stage-keepers or supernumeraries
to move the couch forward.

33 one mortal night i.e. the night of Thaisa's
death; though Pericles' actual present condition is
owing to the death of his daughter, the two deaths
are closely connected.

I durst wager would win some words of him.
LYSIMACHUS 'Tis well bethought.
why are She, questionless, with her sweet harmony, 40
the rhythm And other chosen attractions, would allure
so odd And make a battery through his defend parts,
~~Which now are midway stopped.~~
~~She is all happy as the fairest of all,~~
~~And her fellow maids, now upon~~ 45
~~The leafy shelter that abuts against~~
~~The island's side.~~
HELLICANUS Sure all effectless, yet nothing we'll omit
That bears recovery's name.

[*Exit Lord*]

But since your kindness
We have stretched thus far, let us beseech you 50
That for our gold we may provision have,
~~Wherein we are not destitute for want,~~
~~But weary for the staleness.~~
LYSIMACHUS ~~O sir, a courtesy,~~
Which if we should deny, the most just God
For every graff would send a caterpillar, 55

39–58] *Malone's lineation; prose* Q   42 defend parts] Q; defended parts Q2; deafen'd ports *NS, conj. Steevens*   45 And her
fellow maids, now] Q; And with her fellow maids, is now *Malone*   49 SD] *Malone; not in* Q

38 **durst** dare.
41 **chosen** choice, excellent.
41 **allure** draw forth (*OED* sv *v* 4; earliest citation 1616). As the word need not have a sexual implication, the Oxford editors' absurd comment ('*Allure* seems singularly inappropriate, as though Marina . . . were expected to arouse Pericles sexually') and unnecessary emendation ('allarum') can be rejected.
42–3 **battery . . . stopped** Marina's qualities are expressed in military terms: the force of the battery will break down Pericles' defended ('defend'; see Abbott 22 for the licence of converting one part of speech into another) body ('parts' = that which pertains to the body, either a member or the whole) that are now halfway ('midway') to being suppressed ('stopped'). Q's 'defend' might well = deafened.
45 **And . . . maids** This, taken with the preceding and subsequent lines, makes an awkward construction, leading most editors to print 'And with her fellow maids'. But the phrase does not pertain to a group of women who are now on shore with

Marina, but rather to a generic group, here used as a comparison with Marina's virtues: she is all happy as the fairest of all and the fairest of her contemporaries.
45 **now** is now.
48 **all** entirely, completely.
48 **effectless** without result, useless.
52 **for** because of.
54 **God** A shift from the use of the plural pagan gods found throughout the play to the singular deity which, in the context, sounds right in view of the charity that Lysimachus offers. The singular 'God' also occurs at 2.5.85 in the context of a marriage blessing. It is not unusual to find the pagan and Christian deities combined in Shakespeare. See C. S. Lewis, writing of the philosophical iconography of the Renaissance Platonists: 'They believed not only that all myths and hieroglyphics hide a profound meaning, but also that this ancient pagan meaning is really in accordance with Christianity' (*Spenser's Images of Life*, ed. A. Fowler, 1967, p. 9).
55 **graff** grafted plant (*OED* sv *sb*¹).

And so inflict our province; yet once more
Let me entreat to know at large the cause
Of your king's sorrow.

HELLICANUS   Sit, sir, I will recount it to you –

[*Enter* MARINA *and another Maid*]

But see I am prevented.

LYSIMACHUS O, here's the lady that I sent for.   60
Welcome fair one. Is't not a goodly present?

HELLICANUS She's a gallant lady.

LYSIMACHUS She's such a one, that were I well assured
Came of a gentle kind, and noble stock,
I do wish no better choice and think me rarely to wed.   65
[*To Marina*] Fair one, all goodness that consists in beauty,
Expect even here, where is a kingly patient.
If that thy prosperous and artificial feat
Can draw him but to answer thee in aught,
Thy sacred physic shall receive such pay   70
As thy desires can wish.

MARINA   Sir, I will use
My utmost skill in his recovery, provided
That none but I ~~and my companion maid~~
Be suffered to come near him.

[*Marina sings*]

58–9] Collier's lineation; prose Q   58 SD Enter MARINA] Q4; not in Q   58 SD and another Maid] Malone subst.; not in Q   61 present] Q; presence Malone   64–5] Q4's lineation; lined Came . . . wish / No . . . wed Q   65 I do] Q; I'd Q4   65 to wed] Q; wed Q4   66 SD] This edn; not in Q   66 one,] Malone; on Q   68 feat] Collier; fate Q   71–4] Malone's lineation; prose Q   74 SD] Malone; The Song Q (after this edn's line 77; see Commentary)

56 inflict afflict, assail, with something painful or disagreeable (*OED* sv v 2, citing this line).

57 at large in full.

58 Sit Hellicanus' invitation indicates that there are chairs or stools on stage in addition to Pericles' couch.

58 SD The other Maid is required (73), but she is a great nuisance. Perhaps she accompanies Marina's song, but it is theatrically unthinkable that she should be present during the great recognition scene. Most directors sensibly cut the line and the character.

59 prevented anticipated in action (*OED* Prevent v 2).

61 goodly present Most editors, following Malone, emend to 'presence' referring to Marina's comely personage or bearing; but Q's 'present'

makes good sense in that her therapeutic qualities are being offered as a gift to the ailing king.

64 Came . . . kind Decended from a gentle, i.e. well-born, family.

66 consists resides.

67–70 The situation of a heroine administering to a royal patient is mirrored in *AWW* 2.1.110 ff.

67 Expect The object of the verb is 'kingly patient'.

68 prosperous successful.

68 artificial skilful (*OED* a 6), i.e. in the art of medicine, the 'sacred physic' in 70.

68 feat Q's 'fate' is a variant spelling of 'feat' (*OED* sv sb).

74 suffered allowed.

74 SD What does Marina sing? Like many songs sung in Elizabethan drama, this one is lost. There is

Roses bear thorns and are not hurt thereby;
to the heavens cast up a cheerful eye
God remains who created earth & sky
God remains who created earth & sky

LYSIMACHUS Marked he your music?

MARINA   No, nor looked on us.   75

LYSIMACHUS See, she will speak to him. Come, let us leave her,
    And the gods make her prosperous.

                 [*Exeunt all except Pericles and Marina*]

MARINA Hail sir, my lord lend ear.

PERICLES [~~Pushing her away~~] Hum, ha.

MARINA I am a maid, my lord, that ne'er before   80
    Invited eyes, but have been gazed on like a comet.
    She speaks, my lord, that may be hath endured
    A grief might equal yours, if both were justly weighed. [*Pushing her away*]
    Though wayward fortune did malign my state,
    My derivation was from ancestors   85
    Who stood equivalent with mighty kings;
    But time hath rooted out my parentage,
    And to the world, and awkward casualties,
    Bound me in servitude. [*Aside*] I will desist,
    But there is something glows upon my cheek   90
    And whispers in mine ear 'go not till he speak'.

[Handwritten margin note: *not clear / how to say / how make / to make sense*]

---

75 Marked] Q4; Marke Q   76–7 Come . . . prosperous] *lined as Steevens; prose* Q; *located here this edn; after line 74* Q   77 SD] *This edn; not in* Q   79 SD] *Hoeniger subst.; not in* Q   79–83] *This edn's lineation; prose* Q   84–95] *Malone's lineation; prose* Q   89 SD] *Malone; not in* Q

the text of a wretchedly bad song in *PA* which is copied from *PPA*; in *CA* she is described 'with hir harpe in honde' (line 1667), 'Where that she harpeth many a laie, / And like an angell songe with alle' (lines 1678–9). An intelligent solution was found at Stratford 1973, where Marina sang a pretty wordless melody.

76–7 Come . . . prosperous What looks like a major alteration of text is hardly that. We presume that the direction ('*The song*') is placed in Q a line late, and some relocation of Lysimachus' lines took place in consequence. While it is possible that Lysimachus and the others 'withdraw' before Marina sings, and then troop back again to ask if Pericles had marked her music, only to withdraw again, the effect might be dangerously reminiscent of amateur comic opera. We propose that Marina sings in front of everyone, following which Lysimachus makes the proposal that they withdraw. If the direction for the song was inserted ambiguously in the MS., it might have caused the compositor's misprision.

79 SD Q has no direction, but 'You would not do me violence' (95) and 'when I did push thee back'

(123) require some sort of physical action here. The sources specify violent action: in *CA* Pericles is 'wroth, / And after hir with his honde / He smote' (lines 1700–2); in *PPA* Apollonius 'rose up sodainly, and stroke the maiden on the face with his foote, so that shee fell to the ground, and the bloud gushed plentifully out of her cheekes' (pp. 466–7). It is not surprising that Shakespeare elected a less brutal action, but one which nonetheless incorporates the romance convention in which the heroine is struck or wounded: compare *Cym.* 5.5.229 when Posthumus strikes the disguised Imogen, and *WT* 4.4.425 ff. when Polixenes threatens to mutilate the beauty of Perdita and to devise her cruel death.

80 I . . . maid So in *CA*, line 1704, 'I am a mayde.'

81 like a comet Compare *1H4* 3.2.47, 'But like a comet I was wond'red at'.

84 wayward capricious, contrary.

88 awkward casualties adverse accidents; 'casualties' is from the Latin *casus* = event.

90 something . . . cheek i.e. she feels an inward prompting, the excitement of which causes her cheek to flush and prevents her from leaving.

PERICLES 'My fortunes – parentage – good parentage –
　　　　　To equal mine –' Was it not thus? What say you?
MARINA I said, my lord, if you did know my parentage
　　　　　You would not do me violence.
PERICLES   I do think so.   95
　　　　　Pray you turn your eyes upon me.
　　　　　You're like something that – What country-woman?
　　　　　Here of these shores?
MARINA   No, nor of any shores,
　　　　　Yet I was mortally brought forth and am
　　　　　No other than I appear.   100
PERICLES I am great with woe, and shall deliver weeping.
　　　　　My dearest wife was like this maid,
　　　　　And such a one my daughter might have been:
　　　　　My queen's square brows, her stature to an inch,
　　　　　As wand-like straight, as silver-voiced, her eyes   105
　　　　　As jewel-like and cased as richly, in pace
　　　　　Another Juno, who starves the ears she feeds

95–6] *This edn's lineation; prose* Q   97–8] *Dyce's lineation; prose* Q   97–8 that – What country-woman? Here] *Malone subst.;* that, what Countrey women heare Q   98 shores? . . . shores,] *Malone;* shewes? . . . shewes, Q   98–100] *Malone's lineation; prose* Q   101–9] *This edn's lineation; prose* Q

92 parentage . . . parentage A phrase of great resonance, sounding the central concept of lineage and family, so central to the recognition scenes of the last plays.

93 thus? . . . you? The recognition- scene is developed through the protracted use of questions and answers which tell a story; in *CA* this is condensed into a few lines; in *PPA* the whole of the story is told continuously, and not in reply to questions, immediately after Apollonius has struck his daughter. For the dramatic use Shakespeare makes of this narrative technique see Introduction, pp. 45–6.

97 What country-woman? 'A woman of what country?' Compare *TN* 5.1.231 'What countryman? What name? What parentage?'

98–100 No . . . appear Marina's answer is ironically presented in the form of a riddle, heard here with perplexity by a man who began the play solving a riddle with ease.

99 mortally humanly, i.e. not by spirits, since she was not born on land, yet she is none other than she appears, i.e. a human.

101 great . . . deliver weeping See *TNK* 5.3.137–8 for a similar association of weeping with birth, 'I see one eye of yours conceives a tear, / The

which it will deliver.' This is a pregnant conceit in more than one sense, since it is central to the play's themes of birth, life, death, and rebirth. The conceit continues to manifest itself throughout the recognition scene with increasing intensity: see 190 and n. and Introduction, pp. 47–8. For a similarly elaborated image which collocates woe and birth, compare *R2* 2.2.62–6, 'thou art the midwife to my woe, / And Bullingbrook my sorrow's dismal heir. / Now hath my soul brought forth her prodigy, / And I, a gasping new-deliver'd mother, / Have woe to woe, sorrow to sorrow join'd.'

102–3 Like Pericles, Leontes sees a resemblance of his wife in his daughter; see *WT* 5.1.227–8, 'I thought of her, / Even in these looks I made', and 5.2.35–6, 'the majesty of the creature in resemblance of the mother'.

104 square brows A forehead as high as it is broad, consequently a high forehead (Schmidt).

106 jewel-like and cased as richly Compare 3.2.95–6, 'behold her eyelids, / Cases to those heavenly jewels'.

106–7 in pace . . . Juno The goddess was often recognised by her walk; see *Temp.* 4.1.102, 'Great Juno comes, I know her by her gait', an echo of Virgil's *Aeneid*, 'vera incessu patuit dea' (1.405).

And makes them hungry the more she gives them speech.
Where do you live?

MARINA Where I am but a stranger. From the deck   110
You may discern the place.

PERICLES   Where were you bred?
And how achieved you these endowments which
You make more rich to owe?

MARINA If I should tell my history, it would seem
Like lies disdained in the reporting.

PERICLES   Prithee speak.   115
~~Falseness cannot come from thee, for thou~~
~~Lookest modest as justice, and thou seemst~~
~~A palace for the crownèd truth to dwell in.~~
~~I will believe thee~~ and make senses credit
Thy relation to points that seem impossible,   120
For thou lookst like one I loved indeed.
What were thy friends?
Didst thou not say when I did push thee back,
Which was when I perceived thee, that thou camst
From good descending?

MARINA   So indeed I did.   125

PERICLES Report thy parentage. I think thou saidst
Thou hadst been tossed from wrong to injury,
And that thou thought'st thy griefs might equal mine
If both were opened.

MARINA   Some such thing I said,
And said no more but what my thoughts   130
Did warrant me was likely.

PERICLES   Tell thy story.
If thine, considered, prove the thousandth part

110–15] *Malone's lineation; prose* Q   116–22] *This edn's lineation; prose* Q   118 palace] Q *(Pallas)*   123–9] *Malone's lineation; prose* Q   123 say] *Malone;* stay Q   128 thought'st] *Malone;* thoughts Q   129–31] *Collier's lineation; prose* Q   132–9] *Malone's lineation; prose* Q   132 thousandth] *Sewell;* thousand Q

107–8 who . . . speech Compare *Ham.* 1.2.144–5, 'As if increase of appetite had grown / By what it fed on', *Ant.* 2.2.236–7, 'she makes hungry / Where most she satisfies'.

113 to owe i.e. by owning them.

115 disdained in the reporting rejected in the very act of speaking.

119 credit account as true.

120 Thy relation What you recount.

122 friends relations; see 4.1.20 and n., 'Whir-ring me from my friends'. The question is repeated at 136.

123 push thee back See 79 SD and n.

125 descending lineage, descent.

126–7 I . . . tossed . . . injury Marina has not in fact said any of this, but 'thou saidst' is not to be taken literally; the use of the word 'tossed', associated as it usually is with the sea, is ironically poignant.

129 opened disclosed, made clear.

Of my endurance, thou art a man, and I
Have suffered like a girl. ~~Yet thou dost look~~
~~Like Patience, gazing on kings' graves, and smiling~~   135
~~Extremity out of act.~~ What were thy friends?
How lost thou thy name, my most kind virgin?
Recount, I do beseech thee, come sit by me.
                         [*Marina sits*]

MARINA My name is Marina.

PERICLES O I am mocked, and thou by some incensèd god   140
Sent hither to make the world to laugh at me.

MARINA Patience good sir, or here I'll cease.

PERICLES Nay I'll be patient; thou little knowest how thou
Dost startle me to call thyself Marina.

MARINA The name was given me by one that had   145
Some power, my father, and a king.

PERICLES How, a king's daughter, and called Marina?

MARINA You said you would believe me, but not to be
A troubler of your peace I will end here.

PERICLES But are you flesh and blood?   150
Have you a working pulse, and are no fairy
Motion? Well, speak on, where were you born?
And wherefore called Marina?

MARINA   Called Marina,
For I was born at sea.

PERICLES   At sea, what mother?

MARINA My mother was the daughter of a king, who died   155

---

137 thou thy] Q; thou them? Thy *Malone*   138 SD] *Oxford; not in* Q   140–50] *This edn's lineation; prose* Q   151–3] *Rowe's lineation; prose* Q   151–2 no fairy / Motion? Well] *Malone², conj. Mason;* no fairy? / Motion well Q; fairy? / No motion? – well *Steevens;* no fairy? / Motion! – Well *Dyce;* no fairy? / Motion as well *NS*   155–7] *This edn's lineation; prose* Q

---

133 **my endurance** what I have endured; my hardship.

135–6 **Like . . . act** Compare *TN* 2.4.114–15, 'She sat like Patience on a monument / Smiling at grief.' Pericles compares Marina to a statue of Patience who by her very nature can smile calamity ('extremity') out of the worst it can do. The inspiration for the image comes from the funeral monuments whose statuary adorned tombs, the most elaborate being those of kings. 'Extremity' most certainly does not have to be interpreted as the extreme act of despair (i.e. suicide) though some editors have done so.

137 **How lost thou thy name** Malone's emendation 'How lost thou them [i.e. her friends]? Thy

name' is very plausible, but in a scene in which name and identity are so clearly the central issue, it is preferable to retain Q. The concepts of 'name' and identity are bound up with family (the 'friends' Marina has lost); they are the focus of repetition at 144, 145, 147, 153, 195, 200, 205.

139–41 **Marina . . . laugh at me** Compare the recognition scene in *Lear* 4.7.58, 'Pray do not mock me', and 67–9, 'Do not laugh at me, / For (as I am a man) I think this lady / To be my child Cordelia.'

150–2 **But . . . no fairy / Motion?** See Supplementary Note.

153–4 **wherefore . . . sea** Compare 3.3.12–13, 'My gentle babe Marina, / Whom, for she was born at sea I have named so'.

            The minute I was born, as my good nurse
            Lychorida hath oft delivered weeping.
PERICLES O stop there a little, this is the rarest dream
            That e'er dulled sleep did mock sad fools withal;
            This cannot be my daughter, burièd.   160
            Well, where were you bred? I'll hear you more
            To th'bottom of your story, ~~and never interrupt you~~.
MARINA You scorn, believe me 'twere best I did give o'er.
PERICLES I will believe you by the syllable
            Of what you shall deliver, yet give me leave.   165
            How came you in these parts? Where were you bred?
MARINA The king my father did in Tarsus leave me,
            Till cruel Cleon with his wicked wife
            Did seek to murder me; and having wooed a villain
            To attempt it, who having drawn to do't,   170
            A crew of pirates came and rescued me,
            Brought me to Miteline.
            But good sir, whither will you have me? Why do you weep?
            It may be you think me an imposture; no, good faith:
            I am the daughter to King Pericles,   175
            If good King Pericles be.
PERICLES   Ho, Hellicanus?

            [*Enter* HELLICANUS, *followed by* LYSIMACHUS]

HELLICANUS Calls my lord?
PERICLES Thou art a grave and noble counsellor,
            Most wise in general; tell me if thou canst
            What this maid is, or what is like to be,   180

160–5] *This edn's lineation; prose* Q **160** be my daughter, burièd.] Q *(buried;)*; be my daughter; buried! F3; be. My daughter's buried, *Steevens;* be my daughter – buried! – *Sisson* **166–8**] *Malone's lineation; prose* Q **169–76**] *This edn's lineation; prose* Q **176** SH] Q4; *Hell.* Q **176** SD] *This edn; not in* Q **177–83**] *Malone's lineation; prose* Q

157 delivered weeping related in tears. A deliberate echo of 101 which does not have to be seen as an error by the so-called 'blundering reporter' (Edwards). The interview between father and daughter is deliberately resonant in growing intensity which is achieved, in part, through dramatic irony: the repetition of key qestions, words, images, and thoughts. See Introduction, pp. 45–6.

159 dulled See Abbott 374 for 'passive participles used as epithets to describe the state which would be the result of the active verb'.

160 be my daughter, burièd It is not clear why

editors have wanted to emend this perfectly clear phrase.

162 bottom end (as in 'bottom of the page').

170 drawn i.e. drawn his weapon.

173 whither . . . me? to what point are you bringing me with your questions?

174 imposture thing (or person) which is pretended to be what it is not (*OED* sv *sb* 2b).

176 be i.e. is alive.

178 grave serious.

179 in general i.e. in all things.

180 like likely.

That thus hath made me weep.

HELLICANUS   I know not,
But here's the regent, sir, of Miteline
Speaks nobly of her.

LYSIMACHUS   She never would tell her parentage;
Being demanded that, she would sit still and weep.

PERICLES O Hellicanus, strike me honoured sir,   185
Give me a gash, put me to present pain,
Lest this great sea of joys rushing upon me
O'erbear the shores of my mortality,
And drown me with their sweetness: O come hither,
Thou that begetst him that did thee beget,   190
Thou that wast born at sea, buried at Tarsus,
And found at sea again; O Hellicanus,
Down on thy knees, thank the holy gods as loud
As thunder threatens us, this is Marina.
                    [*Hellicanus kneels*]
What was thy mother's name? Tell me but that,   195
For truth can never be confirmed enough,
Though doubts did ever sleep.

MARINA First sir, I pray what is your title?

PERICLES I am Pericles of Tyre.
                    [*Marina kneels*]
But tell me now my drowned queen's name, as in   200
The rest you said thou hast been god-like perfect,
The heir of kingdoms, and another like

183–4] *This edn's lineation; prose* Q   185–9] *Malone's lineation; prose* Q   194 SD] *This edn; not in* Q   199–203] *This edn's lineation; lined* / *Per.* I . . . my / Drownd . . . sayd, / Thou . . . kingdomes, / And . . . father. Q   199 SD] *This edn; not in* Q   202 another like] Q *(an other);* another life *Steevens, conj. Mason;* a mother like *Malone*[2]

184 sit still always sit.

187–9 Lest . . . sweetness The image of the sea, which has so dominated the play, here culminates in its most powerful expression.

188 O'erbear Overwhelm.

190 begetst gives life to. The images of birth and rebirth as emblems of the restoration of the love bond between family members are central to the last plays. See *Cym.* 5.5.368–70, 'O, what, am I / A mother to the birth of three? Ne'er mother / Rejoic'd deliverance more.' The 'begetting' in question is wholly spiritual: there is *no* connotation of sexuality or incest implied. See Introduction, pp. 19–22.

194 SD, 199 SD, 208 SD Directions to kneel are imperative ('O Hellicanus, / Down on thy knees' and 'rise, thou art my child'), and so is a direction to rise. These seem the most likely locations.

197 i.e. even though doubts have been laid to rest.

201 you . . . thou According to Abbott 234 (citing this example), the close collocation of 'you' and 'thou' can be used in requests where there is a conditional phrase attached. Compare *R3* 3.3.52–3 'and if you plead as well for them / As I can say nay to thee for myself'.

201 god-like perfect as perfectly accurate as a god would be in relating the facts of her story.

202 another like Marina's history has been like Pericles': shipwreck, loss, danger, grief. There is no call to emend.

      To Pericles thy father.

MARINA Is it no more to be your daughter than
To say my mother's name was Thaisa? 205
Thaisa was my mother, who did end
The minute I began.

PERICLES Now blessing on thee, rise, thou art my child.

[They rise]

Give me fresh garments, mine own, Hellicanus;
She is not dead at Tarsus as she should have been 210
By savage Cleon, she shall tell thee all,
When thou shalt kneel, and justify in knowledge
She is thy very princess.
Who is this?

HELLICANUS   Sir, 'tis the governor of Miteline
Who hearing of your melancholy state 215
Did come to see you.

PERICLES I embrace you. Give me my robes.

[He is attired]

I am wild in my beholding, O heavens bless my girl.

[Music plays]

But hark what music? Tell Hellicanus, my Marina,
Tell him o'er point by point, for yet he seems to dote, 220

204–7] *Malone's lineation; prose* Q **208** thou art] Q4; th'art Q **208** SD] *This edn; not in* Q **209–13**] *Malone's lineation; prose* Q **209** garments, mine own, Hellicanus] *Steevens subst.*; garments, mine own *Hellicanus* Q **214–16**] *This edn's lineation; prose* Q **217** SD] *Oxford subst.; not in* Q **218** SD] *This edn; not in* Q; *after line 226 / Dyce* **219** music? Tell Hellicanus, my] *Steevens*; Musicke tell, *Hellicanus* my Q **220** dote] Q *(doat); doubt Malone*

206–7 end . . . began Compare *WT* 5.3.45, 'Dear Queen, that ended when I but began'; also *WT* 4.1.113–14 for the immediate juxtaposition of death with life: 'thou met'st with things dying, I with things new-born'.

209 fresh garments, mine own i.e. as a replacement of the sackcloth he has been wearing. The 'fresh garments' are symbolic of Pericles' restoration to the world from which he had withdrawn, as well as a symbol of a new spiritual health. The garments as he insists are, therefore, 'mine own' (i.e. his former clothing); in *CA* line 1747, Apollonius assumes his royal garments: 'And was arraied realy'. For a similar evocation of the symbol of fresh garments see *Lear* 4.7.21, where Lear awakes to a new spiritual awareness, and Prospero's resumption of his ducal garments, *Temp* 5.1.83–7. Some editors have imagined that 'mine own' modifies Hellicanus, or implies that Pericles is talking to Marina.

210 should have been was said to be.

212 justify in knowledge acknowledge, confirm as true; compare Prologue 42 and n., 'I give my cause, who best can justify.'

218 wild . . . beholding elated to the point of distraction at what I see; for 'wild', see *OED* sv *a* 10–12.

218 SD Music must be played here, although some commentators have misguidedly declared that since only Pericles hears it, it must be imaginary. But no one else sees Diana or hears her song either, and they are self-evidently present: the music is part of the theophany, and is as 'real' as the vision. See Supplementary Note.

220 point by point so *CA* line 1733, 'Fro poynt to poynt all she hym tolde.'

220 to dote to be deranged, out of one's wits (*OED* sv *v*[1] 1), with the sense that Hellicanus is bewildered.

How sure you are my daughter – but what music?
HELLICANUS My lord, I hear none.
PERICLES None? The music of the spheres! List, my Marina.
LYSIMACHUS It is not good to cross him, give him way.
PERICLES Rarest sounds, do ye not hear?   225
LYSIMACHUS Music my lord? I hear.
PERICLES   Most heavenly music,
    It nips me unto listening, and thick slumber
    Hangs upon mine eyes; let me rest. [*Sleeps*]
LYSIMACHUS A pillow for his head, so leave him all.
    ~~Well my companion friends, if this but answer~~   230
    ~~To my just belief, I'll well remember you.~~
                                    [*Exeunt all but Pericles*]
                    DIANA [*descends from the heavens*]
DIANA My temple stands in Ephesus, hie thee thither,
    And do upon mine altar sacrifice:
    There when my maiden priests are met together
    Before the people all   235
    Reveal how thou at sea didst lose thy wife,
    To mourn thy crosses with thy daughter's, call,
    And give them repetition to the life.
    Perform my bidding, or thou livest in woe:
    Do't, and happy, by my silver bow.   240
    Awake and tell thy dream.   [*She ascends*]
PERICLES Celestial Dian, goddess argentine,

228 SD] *Malone; not in* Q   230–1] *This edn's lineation; prose* Q   231 SD.1 *Exeunt . . . Pericles*] *Malone subst.; not in* Q   231 SD.2 *descends . . . heavens*] *Oxford; not in* Q   232–41] *Rowe's lineation; Ephesus; / then prose* Q   238 life] *Malone; like* Q   239 Perform] *Malone;* Or perform Q   241 SD] *Oxford; not in* Q

223 music of the spheres See Supplementary Note.

226 Music . . . I hear Lysimachus is humouring Pericles, in keeping with his advice in 224.

227 nips overpowers or overcomes (a person); reduces to a state of helplessness (*OED* sv *v*[1] 3a).

230–1 if . . . you 'belief' = opinion, or credit given; i.e. 'if all this that has happened confirms what my eyes have seen then I will remember it well'.

231 SD.2 DIANA *descends from the heavens* See Supplementary Note.

233–5 sacrifice . . . all Editors agree that there's something amiss with the poem here: 'sacrifice' has

no rhyme, and the short fourth line is odd in what might well be a song. Unfortunately, none of the proposed repairs is convincing.

237 crosses misfortunes, tribulations. Compare 2.1.109.

237 call proclaim loudly.

238 repetition to the life recount them in accurate detail.

240 silver bow Diana was also the huntress goddess whose bow and arrows were made of silver.

242 argentine silver, i.e. Diana's colour and the colour of chastity. Compare 5.3.6, 'Who, O goddess, wears yet thy silver livery'.

I will obey thee. Hellicanus!

[*Enter* HELLICANUS, LYSIMACHUS, *and* MARINA]

HELLICANUS   Sir.
PERICLES My purpose was for Tarsus, there to strike
    Th'inhospitable Cleon, but I am   245
    For other service first. Toward Ephesus
    Turn our blown sails, eftsoons I'll tell thee why.
    [*To Lysimachus*] Shall we refresh us, sir, upon your shore,
    And give you gold for such provision
    As our intents will need?
LYSIMACHUS   Sir, with all my heart,   250
    And when you come ashore I have another ~~sleight~~. suit
PERICLES You shall prevail were it to woo my daughter,
    For it seems you have been noble towards her.
LYSIMACHUS Sir, lend me your arm.
PERICLES   Come my Marina.

                            Exeunt

[5.2] [*Enter* GOWER]

GOWER Now our sands are almost run,
    More a little, and then dumb.
    This my last boon give me,
    For such kindness must relieve me:

---

243 SD] *Malone subst.; not in* Q   245–7] *Malone's lineation; lined* The . . . first, / . . . sayles Q   245 Th'inhospitable]
Oxford; The inhospitable Q   247–53] *Malone's lineation; prose* Q   248 SD] *This edn; not in* Q   251 sleight] Q; suit
Malone   Act 5, Scene 2   5.2] *Malone subst.; not in* Q   0 SD] Q4; *not in* Q   2 dumb] Q *(dum); done* Rowe

245 **inhospitable** To the Elizabethans a viola-
tion of hospitality (either by guest or host) was a
much more serious transgression than it would be
today. See *Lear* 3.7.39–41 where Gloucester accuses
Regan and Cornwall for abusing his hospitality, 'I
am your host, / With robber's hands my hospitable
favors / You should not ruffle thus'; and *Mac.*
1.7.14–16.
247 **blown** full sail (the correct naval term for
sails inflated by the wind).
247 **eftsoons** later, afterwards.
250 **intents** purpose.
251 **sleight** artful device or design; stratagem
(*OED* sv *sb*¹ 6). Lysimachus has already performed
such a sleight by bringing Marina to Pericles; he

now proposes 'another' one which will involve asking for her hand in marriage.

Act 5, Scene 2
1 **sands . . . run** i.e. the sand running through
the hourglass.
2 **More . . . dumb** Either: 'I have just a little
more to say and then I will be quiet', or 'There is
only a little more to our story and then it is finished.'
3–4 **This . . . boon . . . relieve me** 'boon' = a
favour begged; 'relieve' = to release. Gower is re-
questing one final act of the imagination from the
audience to conclude the play. Compare *Temp.* Epilogue 16, 20, 'Unless I be reliev'd by prayer', 'Let
your indulgence set me free.'

> That you aptly will suppose   5
> What pageantry, what feats, what shows,
> What minstrelsy, and pretty din,
> The regent made in Miteline
> To greet the king. So he thrived
> That he is promised to be wived   10
> To fair Marina, but in no wise
> Till he had done his sacrifice,
> As Dian bade; whereto being bound,
> The interim, pray you, all confound.
> In feathered briefness sails are filled,   15
> And wishes fall out as they're willed;
> At Ephesus the temple see,
> Our king and all his company.
> That he can hither come so soon,   19
> Is by your fancies' thankful doom.   [*Exit*]

[5.3] [*Enter* PERICLES, MARINA, HELLICANUS, LYSIMACHUS *at one door*; THAISA, CERIMON *at another, meeting*]

PERICLES   Hail Dian: to perform thy just command
             I here confess myself the king of Tyre,

20 SD] Q4; not in Q   Act 5, Scene 3   5.3] *Malone subst.; not in Q*   0 SD] *This edn; not in Q*

5 aptly willingly, readily.
6 feats acts of wonder.
9–10 thrived . . . wived A common collocation (Tilley T264, 'First thrive and then wive'); compare *Shr.* 1.2.56, 'Happily to wive and thrive as best I may'.
12 he i.e. Pericles; 'he' in 9–10 refers to Lysimachus.
14 confound bring to nought (*OED* sv *v* 1b) or waste, consume (*OED v* 1e), i.e. the time in the 'interim'.
15 In . . . briefness with the speed of a bird in flight, or with winged speed.
15 sails are filled Compare *Temp.* Epilogue 11–12, 'my sails / must fill'.
19–20 That . . . doom 'doom' = judgement, decision; that he can arrive there so soon is achieved by the will and gratifying ('thankful') decision of the audience's imagination.

Act 5, Scene 3
   Location Ephesus. Various directions, often very elaborate, have been supplied by editors (sometimes at the beginning of the preceding scene), but the bare minimum is offered here. The dramatic situation envisaged is that Pericles and those in his company have just arrived in Ephesus, where they encounter Thaisa and Cerimon. While there is no reason to deny the possibility that some spectacular staging was involved, representing Diana's temple on stage (with Thaisa and other acolytes in attendance), there is no need for it either. Both Gower's remark at 5.2.17 ('At Ephesus the temple see') and Diana's injunction ('There when my maiden priests are met together / Before the people all' 5.1.234–5) may well be read in the light of Gower's repeated appeals to the audience's imagination throughout the play. No supernumeraries are specifically required for the action. It seems, then, that while the scene offers opportunities for lavish staging, it can very well be represented much more economically.

Who frighted from my country, did wed at Pentapolis
The fair Thaisa. At sea in childbed died she,
But brought forth a maid-child called Marina,   5
Who, O goddess, wears yet thy silver livery.
She at Tarsus was nursed with Cleon, who
At fourteen years he sought to murder, but
Her better stars brought her to Miteline,
'Gainst whose shore riding, her fortunes brought the maid   10
Aboard us, where by her own most clear remembrance,
She made known herself my daughter.
THAISA   Voice and favour,
You are, you are, O royal Pericles!
PERICLES   What means the mum? [*Thaisa faints*]
                                     She dies, help gentlemen.
CERIMON Noble sir, if you have told Diana's altar true,   15
This is your wife.
PERICLES   Reverend appearer no,
I threw her overboard with these very arms.
CERIMON Upon this coast, I warrant you.
PERICLES   'Tis most certain.
CERIMON Look to the lady – O she's but overjoyed.
Early in blustering morn this lady was thrown   20
Upon this shore: I oped the coffin, found there
Rich jewels, recovered her, and placed her here
In Diana's temple.
PERICLES   May we see them?
CERIMON   Great sir,

3–12] *This edn's lineation; prose* Q   6 Who] F4; whom Q   12–13] *Malone's lineation; prose* Q   14 mum] Q; *nun Collier*   14
SD] *This edn; not in* Q; *Faints / Rowe (after line 13)*   15–17] *Malone's lineation; prose* Q   16] Reverend] Q (Reuerent)   19–
33] *This edn's lineation; prose* Q   20 in] Q; *one Malone*

6 wears . . . livery i.e. is still a virgin. Compare
MV 2.7.22, 'the silver with her virgin hue'.
8 At fourteen years So in *PPA*, 'when from that
time fourteene yeeres were expired, and I returned
thither to fetch my daughter', p. 472.
10 riding anchored; a ship rides when its anchors
prevent it from driving away with the tide or wind.
Compare *Son.* 137.6, 'Be anchor'd in the bay where
all men ride'.
12 favour appearance, face.
14 mum silence (*OED* sv *sb*[1] 2), or, even more
theatrically appropriate, 'an inarticulate sound
made with closed lips esp. as an indication of inability to speak' (*sb*[1] 1). Thaisa is struck dumb in her
emotion.

16 Reverend appearer One who appears de-
serving of reverence. Compare 5.1.13, 'Hail reverend sir.'
17 A confirmation that Pericles carries Thaisa's
body at the end of 3.1. See 3.1.80 SD n.
22–3 placed . . . temple Compare *Err.* 5.1.331–
56 where Egeon, who having lost his wife and child
at sea and having been separated from them for
many years, is reunited with his wife at the priory in
Ephesus, where she had become the abbess in the
intervening years. In both examples the reunion
takes place in front of the holy building in the last
scene.

They shall be brought you to my house, whither
I invite you. Look, Thaisa is recovered. 25
THAISA O let me look: if he be none of mine,
My sanctity will to my sense bend no
Licentious ear, but curb it spite of seeing.
O my lord, are you not Pericles?
Like him you spake, like him you are: 30
Did you not name a tempest, a birth, and death?
PERICLES The voice of dead Thaisa.
THAISA That Thaisa am I, supposed dead and drowned.
PERICLES Immortal Dian!
THAISA Now I know you better.
When we with tears parted Pentapolis 35
The king my father gave you such a ring.
PERICLES This, this! No more, you gods, your present kindness
Makes my past miseries sports; you shall do well
That on the touching of her lips I may melt,
And no more be seen. [*A kiss*] 40
O come, be buried a second time within these arms.
MARINA [*Kneels*] My heart leaps to be gone into my mother's bosom.
PERICLES Look who kneels here: flesh of thy flesh, Thaisa,
Thy burden at the sea, and called Marina,
For she was yielded there.
THAISA [*Raises and embraces her*] Blest, and mine own. 45
HELLICANUS [*Kneels*] Hail madam, and my queen.
THAISA I know you not.
PERICLES You have heard me say when I did fly from Tyre,
I left behind an ancient substitute;

34–8] *Malone's lineation; prose* Q 34 Immortal] Q4*;* I,mortal Q 39–42] *This edn's lineation; prose* Q 42 SD] *Malone subst.; not in* Q 43–50] *Rowe's lineation; prose* Q 45 SD] *This edn; not in* Q 46 SD] *This edn; not in* Q 47 SH] Q4*;* Hell. Q

26–8 if . . . seeing 'if he is not my husband my holy chastity will prevent me from yielding to desire despite what my eyes tell me'; 'sense' = sensual desire, as at 1.1.82.

32 voice of dead Thaisa Compare *Cym.* 5.5. 123, 126, 238, 'The same dead thing alive', 'we see him dead', 'The tune of Imogen'.

35 parted departed from.

36 father . . . ring Thaisa sees the ring on Pericles' finger.

37 No more, you gods His emotion has grown so great that enduring further joy would destroy him; the extreme ecstasy of the moment is carried into the following lines. Compare *Cym.* 5.5.234–5,

'If this be so, the gods do mean to strike me / To death with mortal joy.'

38 sports amusements, trifles.

38–40 you . . . seen Pericles would consider it a good death if the gods decided to dissolve his life upon his wife's kiss. The juxtaposition of extreme ecstasy with death is similarly articulated in Pericles' reunion with Marina (5.1.185–9). Compare *Oth.* 2.1.189–90 'If it were now to die, / 'Twere now to be most happy.'

41 buried . . . arms Compare *WT* 4.4.131–2, 'Not like a corse; or if – not to be buried, / But quick and in mine arms'.

45 yielded brought forth.

Can you remember what I called the man?
I have named him oft.

THAISA   'Twas Hellicanus then.   50

PERICLES ~~Still confirmation; embrace him dear Thaisa,~~
This is he.

            [*Thaisa raises and embraces Hellicanus*]
                    Now do I long to hear
How you were found? How possibly preserved?
And who to thank, besides the gods, for this
Great miracle?

THAISA   Lord Cerimon, my lord,   55
This man, through whom the gods have shown their power,
That can from first to last resolve you.

PERICLES   Reverend sir,
The gods can have no mortal officer
More like a god than you. Will you deliver
How this dead queen re-lives?

CERIMON   I will my lord.   60
Beseech you first go with me to my house,
Where shall be shown you all was found with her,
How she came placed here in the temple,
No needful thing omitted.

PERICLES   Pure Dian,   X to ll(·
Bless thee for thy vision, and we'll offer   65
Night oblations to thee. Thaisa,
This prince, the fair betrothèd of your daughter,
Shall marry her at Pentapolis;
~~And now this ornament makes me look dismal~~
~~Will I clip to form,~~   70

51–7] *This edn's lineation; prose* Q   52 SD] *This edn; not in* Q   58–60] *Steevens's lineation; prose* Q   60–4] *Malone's lineation; prose* Q   64–7] *Steevens's lineation; prose* Q   64–5 Dian, / Bless]* F3 *subst.; Dian* blesse Q*; Diana, I bless *Malone*   65 we'll] *This edn;* will Q; I will F3   66 thee.] Q4*; thee* Q   68–74] *This edn's lineation; prose* Q

57 resolve you clear everything up for you.
62 shown . . . her Pericles has already asked (23) to see the jewels buried with Thaisa, now Cerimon reiterates his offer to show the contents of Thaisa's coffin. Articles of identification are a common feature of the romance tradition by which the identity of the lost person is confirmed. See *WT* 5.2.32–4, 'there is such unity in the proofs. The mantle of Queen Hermione's; her jewel about the neck of it; the letters of Antigonus found with it', and *Cym.* 5.5.360–3, 'He, sir, was lapp'd / In a most curious

mantle, wrought by th' hand / Of his queen mother, which for more probation / I can with ease produce.'
66 Night oblations Evening prayers, offerings of devotion.
69 ornament Pericles probably refers ironically to his unkempt hair, which after fourteen years would be the reverse of ornamental.
69 makes which makes.
70 clip to form The (jocular) image is from topiary.

And what this fourteen years no razor touched,
To grace thy marriage-day, I'll beautify.
THAISA Lord Cerimon hath letters of good credit,
Sir, my father's dead.
PERICLES Heavens make a star of him. Yet there my queen,   75
We'll celebrate their nuptials, and ourselves
Will in that kingdom spend our following days;
Our son and daughter shall in Tyrus reign.
Lord Cerimon, we do our longing stay
To hear the rest untold; sir, lead's the way.   80

[*Exeunt*]

[**Epilogue**] [*Enter*] GOWER

GOWER In Antiochus and his daughter you have heard
Of monstrous lust, the due and just reward;
In Pericles, his queen and daughter seen,
Although assailed with fortune fierce and keen,
Virtue preserved from fell destruction's blast,   5
Led on by heaven, and crowned with joy at last.
In Hellicanus may you well descry
A figure of truth, of faith, of loyalty;
In reverend Cerimon there well appears
The worth that learnèd charity aye wears.   10
For wicked Cleon and his wife, when fame

73 credit,] Q4; credit. Q   75–80] *Rowe's lineation; prose* Q   80 SD] Q4; *FINIS.* Q   **Epilogue**   Epilogue] *Hoeniger; not in* Q
0 SD *Enter*] Q4; *not in* Q   5 preserved] *Tonson; preferd* Q

71 fourteen years If, as we maintain, Pericles makes his vow never to 'cut his hairs' during his visit to Marina's tomb (4.4.28) rather than when he leaves her in Cleon's care shortly after her birth (see 3.3.28 n.) then 'this fourteen years' cannot be right. But Shakespeare is often indifferent to matters of accurate or probable chronology, the most frequently cited case being that of *Othello*.
75 Heavens . . . him 'Translate him from mortal existence to the sphere of the stars'. Compare *Rom.* 3.2.22–3, 'cut him out in little stars, / And he will make the face of heaven so fine'.
75 there Pentapolis.
76 their Marina's and Lysimachus'.
79–80 we . . . rest untold i.e. 'we are delaying our desire to hear what is yet untold', the loose ends

of which can be conveniently related offstage. This is a typical Shakespearean ending where details of the play's events are left for later; compare *MM* 5.1.538–9; *MV* 5.1.297–9; *WT* 5.3.152–4; *Temp.* 5.1.312–14.
80 lead's the way i.e. 'lead us the way', a common formula for a general exeunt: compare *WT* 5.3.155, 'Hastily lead away'.

Epilogue
The use of the Epilogue to point to the moral of Gower's story is similar to *CA* 2001–16.
5 fell cruel, fierce.
10 aye ever.
11 fame report.

Rich   Had spread his cursèd deed, the honoured name
            Of Pericles to rage the city turn,
            That him and his they in his palace burn;
S+   The gods for murder seemed so content   15
            To punish, although not done, but meant.
ALL   So on your patience evermore attending,
            New joy wait on you: here our play has ending.   [*Exit*]

FINIS

13 Pericles] *Ridley;* Pericles, Q   18 SD] *Malone subst.; not in* Q

12 **his** Most editors adopt Q4's 'their' for Q's 'his' since Dioniza was the main culprit of the deed. The emendation is unnecessary since (1) Cleon is implicated in the murder by an act of omission, (2) he is the head of his household and therefore responsible for its crimes, (3) he assumes the punishment according to his own words at 3.3.23–4, 'the gods revenge it / Upon me and mine'.

12–14 **honoured . . . turn. . . burn** The plural use of 'turn' for the singular 'turns' is not irregular if 'city' is understood as the citizens or its people (compare *Cor.* 3.1.199, 'The people are the city'). Pericles' honoured name turns the city (i.e. the citizens) to rage, so that they burn Cleon and Dioniza. The play agrees with *CA*, where Cleon and Dioniza are burned; in *PPA* they are stoned to death.

14 **his** i.e. Cleon's family; see 12 n.

16 **meant** intended.

SUPPLEMENTARY NOTES

2.1.115 Q's 'brayse' is not recognised by *OED*. Of the various words that might be intended, most editors spell, as we do, 'brace', which means armour covering the arm, or arms (*OED* sv *sb²* 1a); *OED* also offers 'a coat of armour', but the only citation is this line (*OED* sv *sb²* 1b). Later Pericles says that (whatever it is) this 'coat of worth' (124) was 'target to a king' (125); 'target' usually means a shield, but here may be used metaphorically (as 'shield' is used metaphorically for armour in 114). To sum up: 'a rusty armour' is caught in the Fishermen's net; it seems to be a complete suit of armour since all that is lacking is 'a pair of bases' (147), the skirt that mounted knights wore over their mailed leggings (see *TNK* 3.6.54 ff. where Palamon puts on an 'armor' piece by piece). We presume, then, that 'shield', 'brace,' and 'target' are used in synecdoche for the whole suit. Or is 'target' literal? Each Knight in 2.2 has his squire 'present' (that is, display for attention) a shield with a painted or wrought device, and a motto: this was known as an 'impresa'. Pericles, lacking a page, makes his presentation himself: 'his present is / A withered branch that's only green at top, / The motto: *In hac spe vivo*' (2.2.42–4). Many editors imagine that Pericles, lacking a shield, is actually carrying this withered branch, but the only reason to think that he has no shield is *PA*, which we discount. How on earth do you paint a motto on a branch of wood? (Stratford 1986, which adopted this staging, had the motto written on a piece of paper; Pericles held the branch up to the upper stage so Thaisa could take the paper. It was a clever solution to a nonexistent problem.) So where did the shield come from? The simplest explanation is the best, that the fished-up armour included the target or shield. Why not? It's fairy-tale anyway. Subsequently, Pericles will paint the impresa with the withered branch on the shield, just as the other Knights will invent their impresas for the occasion.

2.2.0 SD.1 *above* The staging of this scene is uncertain: most editors draw heavily on *PA*, but we believe it is not to be relied on. Hoeniger, for instance, accepts the amazingly tedious staging described in *PA*: that each Knight enters with his page bearing the shield; the page presents the shield to Thaisa, who then passes it to Simonides, who returns it to Thaisa who returns it to the page! But at the same time, Hoeniger rejects *PA*'s clear statement that the king and his daughter place themselves 'in a Gallery', commenting that they cannot be 'on the upper stage, for how in that case would the squires present their shields to them?' Instead he invents a 'pavilion' erected on the main stage for the royal party. All this simply shows how an unreliable report such as *PA* can be a source of muddle. First, to 'present' an impresa does not mean physically to hand it over, let alone pass it from one person to another like a soup-bowl. The simple and obvious staging would be for each Knight to enter with his page, pass over the stage, and pause while the page knelt and raised the shield so its device and motto would be visible to Thaisa. Simonides doesn't need to see the impresa; he simply translates what Thaisa says (see also 28 n.). The page would then rise, and follow his Knight across the stage to the other exit. The effect of this easy, but visually effective, ceremonial would be heightened by having Thaisa and Simonides on the upper stage, out of the way of the parading Knights. So Stratford 1986 staged it, and we feel its theatrical logic is strong enough to justify the inserted direction.

2.2.15 See Andrew Welsh, 'Heritage in *Pericles*', in *Shakespeare's Late Plays* (Richard Tobias and Paul Zolbrod, (eds.) 1974, p. 110): 'These are not heraldic coats of arms representing the noble lineage of the knights, but devices which each knight designed himself to express his purpose ["labour"] . . . the device or impresa is nothing else than a symbolic representation of a purpose, a wish, a line of conduct (impresa is what one intends to *imprendere*, i.e. to undertake) by means of a motto and a picture which reciprocally interpret each other. Thus Thaisa, asked by her father to "entertain / The labour of each knight in his device", is reading in the devices not only the knight's artistic accomplishments but also the various lines of conduct each knight sees himself following in the attempt to win her hand . . . the devices show their conception of that love.' See also Young, pp. 453–4: 'Each knight's page would . . . present his knight's impresa – that is to say, his personal motto and accompanying emblematic picture specially composed for the occasion and designed to express the intentions, aspirations, and state of mind of its bearer.' H. Green,

Shakespeare and the Emblem Writers, 1870, deals fully with the sources of the mottos found in this scene. Shakespeare himself received 40 shillings in gold for composing an impresa for the entry into Whitehall tiltyard of Francis Manners, the Earl of Rutland, in connection with the celebrations on James I's accession day. See Young, p. 456 and Scott-Giles, p. 20. Compare Marlowe's *Edward II* 2.2.11–28, in which Mortimer and Lancaster describe their impresas and mottos.

    2.2.28 *Pue per doleera kee per forsa* Like Elton John's 'word in Spanish', Q's weird collection of syllables has caused much innocent perplexity especially to editors. The meaning of the Second Knight's impresa is not at issue ('More by gentleness rather than by force'). But what Thaisa reads, according to Q, is neither Spanish nor Italian: in Spanish, the tag would have to read something like 'Mas por dulzura que por fuerza'; in Italian, 'Più per dolcezza che per forza'. Clearly, Q cannot be converted to either without violence, though the Italian is closer. It seems best to recognise here one of Shakespeare's linguistic jokes: the theatrical opportunity offered by Thaisa's uncertainty of the language should not be overlooked. All the other mottos are in Latin; this one, she's not sure of. It could be staged thus: 'The motto thus, in [pause, doubtfully] Spanish'; she has a game stab at it, to which Simonides could return a quizzical shrug, 'eh?' (since he declines to attempt a translation). Whether any such staging is adopted (it was in both the BBC and Stratford 1986), it seems preferable to stay with Q than attempt linguistic correction. See also Textual Analysis, p. 206.

    3.2.85–6 the rough . . . music None of the meanings given for 'rough' in *OED* defines the word precisely apt to this present context. The following are close: 6a, of language or expression, harsh or passionate; 8, of remedies, strong, powerful; 11, of sounds, harsh, discordant (citing this example); 13a, of diction or style, rugged (there is a probable parallel with Prospero's 'rough magic', *Temp.* 5.1.50). Yet the sense seems clear: Cerimon wants not soothing, sweet music, but stimulating music, music that will penetrate Thaisa's coma. One of Dowland's consorts for viols would fit the bill. From classical times onwards, music was believed to hold various restorative and animating powers: Robert Burton declared that music is a 'a most *forcible medicine . . . a roaring-meg . . . to revive the languishing soul* [our italics] . . . affecting not only the ears, but the very arteries, the vital and animal spirits, it erects the mind, and makes it nimble . . . the spirits about the heart take in that trembling and dancing air into the body, are moved together, and stirred up with it . . . the mind, as some suppose, harmonically composed, is roused up at the tunes of music' (*The Anatomy of Melancholy*, ed. Holbrook Jackson, 1932, Second Partition, pp. 115–16). Compare *Lear* 4.7.24. For the role of music in the play, see Introduction, pp. 71–3.

    5.1.29–30 You may, but bootless. / In your sight, he will not speak to any An emendation is necessary, but difficult. Q uncorrected reads 'You may, but bootlesse. Is your sight see, will not speake to any, yet let me obtaine my wish.' The press-corrector altered 'sight see, will' to 'sight, hee will', but neglected to give 'yet let me obtaine my wish' to Lysimachus (which would have required re-setting the next three lines); he also left 'bootlesse. Is' unaltered, which cannot be right either. The usual emendation made here is Collier's: 'You may; / But bootless is your sight; he will not speak / To any.' One of the problems in deciding how to emend is that, as usual, Hellicanus is not quite answering the question he has been asked. Can Lysimachus see Pericles? Well, yes, but he will not speak, says Hellicanus. Lysimachus, however, had not asked if he could *speak* to Pericles. If all Lysimachus wants is to look at Pericles, his sight of him will not be bootless, and Collier's emendation fails. (Of course, Lysimachus does want to talk to Pericles, but that is another matter.) It seems clear that the press-corrector, reading over the lines, perceived that they failed to make sense; but his one alteration does not make sense out of them either: presumably he was emending by inspiration, rather than by consultation of copy. Visually the most striking thing in the first line is the full stop and ensuing capital. We think it more likely that these should be left alone, even if it means a substantive emendation ('In' for 'Is'). Hellicanus' reply still makes incomplete sense, but that is typical of Hellicanus' style in the play. It is obvious that the copy hereabouts was seriously disturbed: the incorrect assignment of the lines to the two speakers (not corrected in proof) is another sign of unusual corruption.

    5.1.150–2 But . . . no fairy / Motion? Although Q's reading looks plausible, there is no record in *OED* of 'motion' as a verb meaning anything other than 'to move a motion' before the eighteenth century. An emendation is thus necessary, and though editors have rung the changes, the simplest and best is just to shift the question mark. Paraphrased: 'Are you really human? Do you have life in you, or are you an illusion whose movement is created by enchantment?' Two meanings must be kept active in the word 'motion': movement and puppet. Marina has declared (99) that she was 'mortally brought forth' yet Pericles still fears that he is 'mocked . . . by some incensèd god' (140) who has sent him a supernaturally controlled creature, a kind of automaton or puppet, as the courtiers in *Temp.* are controlled by Ariel (4.1.39, 'Incite them to quick motion'): both meanings, of movement and puppet at the control of a supernatural agent, are implied. C. S. Lewis, in his unfinished story 'After Ten Years' refers to the classical concept of the *eidolon*, a fantasmal creature fashioned to resemble a real person (see 'Notes, to "After Ten Years"' by Roger Lancelyn Green, in *The Dark Tower and Other Stories*, 1977, p. 156). Compare *TGV* 2.1.94–5, 'O excellent motion! O exceeding puppet!', also *WT* 4.3.96–7, *MV* 5.1.61, 'But in his motion like an angel sings'. For the association of the heroine with a fairy, see *Cym.* 3.7.41. Like Pericles here, Alonso in *Temp.* 5.1.111–14 responds to Prospero's appearance in similar terms of disbelief, 'Whe'er thou beest he or no, / Or some enchanted trifle to abuse me / . . . Thy pulse / Beats as of flesh and blood.'

5.1.218 SD, 223 'The music of the spheres', the heavenly harmony that the planets make in tracing their orbits, voices singing the praises of God, was a common medieval idea. How represented in Shakespeare's theatre, we cannot say; but the type of music usually associated with celestial music by the Elizabethans was played by a consort of recorders (see Long, p. 47). The most ingenious recent theatrical solution was Stratford 1986's: the eerily beautiful and disembodied tones of the glass harp, or 'arpa armonica' which Goethe called 'das Herzblut der Welt'. That no one else hears the music of the spheres is dramatically appropriate, for it is only Pericles, having completed his arduous spiritual journey, who is now allowed (because the music of the spheres was said to be inaudible by human ears) an epiphany as symbolised by the heavenly music. That the audience is allowed to hear it with him is a sharing of a dramatic experience of the most intense and intimate kind. Compare *MV* 5.1.60–5, 'There's not the smallest orb which thou behold'st / But in his motion like an angel sings, / Still quiring to the young-ey'd cherubins; / Such harmony is in immortal souls, / But whilst this muddy vesture of decay / Doth grossly close it in, we cannot hear it.' See Introduction, pp. 71–3, for a discussion of the importance of music in the play.

5.1.231 SD.2 DIANA *descends from the heavens* Shakespeare's treatment of this episode goes beyond what he found in the sources. In both *CA* and *PPA* the vision follows the marriage of Pericles' daughter. In neither source does Diana herself appear; in *CA* the vision is referred to only as 'The hie god' (1797) and the 'avision' (1809) who tells Apollonius to recount only the relevant part of his story (1805–7), 'That in the temple amongest all / His fortune, as it is befalle, / Touchyng his doughter, and his wife'. In *PPA* an angel appears in Apollonius' sleep and tells him 'to declare all his adventures, whatsoever had befallen him from his youth unto that present day' (p. 471). Clearly, Shakespeare decided, in theatrical terms, to 'top' the immensely powerful recognition scene with a visually elaborate conclusion, a 'theophany' (manifestation of a god). Since Diana is one of the regent gods in the play, she is appropriate for the vision. Similar theophanies occur in *Cym.* 5.4.92 ff. where Jupiter appears to Posthumus in a vision and *Temp.* 4.1.74, the descent of Juno. The entrance in *Cym.* is quite specific: 'JUPITER *descends in thunder and lightning, sitting upon an eagle: he throws a thunderbolt*'. The direction in Q *Pericles* simply reads 'Diana' without specifing how her entrance was managed; but as the Oxford editors remark, the usual Shakespearean practice was to have a god's entrance from above, either on the balcony or, more spectacularly, as a descent in a throne from the 'heavens'. There is no evidence in the text, then, to justify our direction, but the parallel uses of spectacle in *Cym.* and *Temp.* offer strong clues for the management of the present scene, enough to justify the direction (in line with our policy of attempting throughout the play to keep the probable original staging in mind when introducing directions). See illustration 11, p. 40, for a reconstruction. Inigo Jones's design of a theophany in Aurelian Townsend's *Tempe Restored* is reproduced in Allardyce Nicoll, *Stuart Masques*, 1938, p. 94.

TEXTUAL ANALYSIS

There is no solution to the problems of *Pericles*.   Philip Edwards

On this encouraging note, we begin our account of the textual origins of *Pericles*, which are, appropriately, surrounded in mist and fog. On 20 May 1608 the respectable bookseller Edward Blount entered 'A booke called. *The booke of PERICLES prynce of Tyre*' in the Stationers' Register, thereby asserting copyright in it.[1] The phrasing of the entry ('A booke called. *The booke*') strongly suggests that Blount had access to the official 'book' (prompt-book) of the play. However, he did not go on to publish it.

Instead, in the same year, there appeared a mysterious little black-letter quarto entitled *The Painfull Aduentures of Pericles Prince of Tyre* (STC 25638.5). This very rare book[2] declares on its title page that it is 'the true History of the Play of *Pericles*, as it was lately presented by the worthy and ancient Poet *John Gower*', a claim reiterated at the end of the Argument on A3ʳ: 'Onely intreating the Reader to receive this Historie in the same maner as it was under the habite of auncient *Gower* the famous English Poet, by the Kings Maiesties Players excellently presented'. *PA* retells the story of the play, with considerable additional material, and much variation from the text subsequently published. The Periclean fog extends to the author of this novella, George Wilkins.[3]

In 1609 a quarto purporting to be the text of the play finally appeared, published by Henry Gosson, not by Blount, and printed by two printers, William White and Thomas Creede (STC 22334).[4] The title page is elaborate: it reads, 'THE LATE, And much admired Play, Called Pericles, Prince of Tyre. With the true Relation of the whole Historie, aduentures, and fortunes of the said Prince: As also, The no lesse

---

[1] Arber, III, 378. Blount also entered *Antony and Cleopatra* the same day, but did not publish it either. It was not unheard of for a bookseller or printer to make what was called a 'staying' entry, that is, one intended to prevent anyone else from publishing the book. How effective this procedure was is debatable.

[2] Only two copies survive, one in the Zürich Zentralbibliothek, the other (lacking the dedication) in the British Library. It was not entered on the Stationers' Register (adding to the confusion, STC wrongly lists for it Blount's entry for the play, though this error was corrected in the addenda and corrigenda, III, 316).

[3] For a fuller discussion, see Introduction, pp. 8–15.

[4] Blount's licence was not transferred to Gosson: an irregular, but not unique circumstance. Greg, in his *Bibliography of the English Printed Drama*, 4 vols., 1939–59, identified the work of White; the identification of Creede as the other printer was made by Peter Blayney ('The prevalence of shared printing in the early seventeenth century', *PBSA* 67 (1973), 437–42). The first quarto survives in nine copies, located in the British Library, the Bodleian Library (Oxford), Trinity College, Cambridge, the Shakespeare Centre (Stratford-upon-Avon), the Folger Library (Washington, D.C.), the Huntington Library (San Marino, California), the Boston Public Library, and the Elizabethan Club of Yale University. One copy is in private hands. The principal copy used in preparation of this edition was that in the British Library. The Oxford facsimile, ed. W. W. Greg, 1940, is made from the Malone copy in the Bodleian, a copy disfigured by many pencilled 'corrections' of the quarto's punctuation. Greg gives a list of these in his preface, but they remain traps for the unwary. Like most play-texts of the period, Q1 is proof-variant, but none of the corrections seem to imply consultation of copy. See Hoeniger, p. xxxviii for details.

strange, and worthy accidents, in the Birth and Life, of his Daughter *MARIANA* [*sic*]. As it hath been diuers and sundry times acted by his Maiesties Seruants, at the Globe on the Banck-side. By William [two ornaments] Shakespeare. [Block] Imprinted at London for *Henry Gosson*, and are to be sold at the signe of the Sunne in Pater-noster row, &c. 1609.' There is nothing about the title page to suggest that the quarto was a work of piracy, or in any way seriously irregular (though to be sure the misprint of Marina's name does not inspire confidence).

This quarto was reprinted no fewer than five times (see List of Abbreviations, pp. *x-xi*),[1] good evidence both of its popularity as a printed book (obviously) and presumably as a stage-play. The next relevant fact is that the collected edition of Shakespeare's plays, published by Blount and others and printed by Jaggard, the First Folio of 1623, does not include *Pericles*. Two reasons are usually advanced to explain this: firstly, because it was written in collaboration (examined and dismissed in the Introduction, 'Authorship', pp. 8–15). Secondly, and even more difficult to credit, is the view that it was excluded because its only known text was 'bad'.

If this were so, it would mean that the company had lost the 'book'[2] of one of its most popular plays of the period, and had not troubled to replace it (scarcely conceivable). It would also argue a delicacy and scrupulousness on the parts of Heminge and Condell difficult to reconcile with the actual (rather than the advertised) state of the texts in the Folio. While it is true that at least two 'bad quartos' of Shakespearean plays (*Romeo and Juliet* and *Hamlet*) were promptly replaced (perhaps at the company's instigation) by quartos based on authorial manuscripts, a lot of text of doubtful authenticity is to be found in the Folio. The fact that the King's Men did not have a different version of *Pericles* published to supersede Gosson's suggests they were not unduly concerned by the quarto of 1609 or its successors.

The long and the short of it is that we do not know why *Pericles* was excluded from the Folio. A stronger possibility than those hitherto discussed is that Heminge and Condell were unable to obtain the right to print, which at the time of the Folio's publication was in the possession of Thomas Pavier, the bookseller who had tried to publish a 'collected' Shakespeare by putting out several quartos together in 1619 with falsely dated title pages. *Pericles* was one of these.[3] The initial entry of the play in 1608, followed by Blount's failure to have it printed, suggests that something had gone amiss; what, we cannot usefully conjecture. The play eventually appeared in the Third Folio of 1663–4, and also in the Fourth and in Rowe's editions, but was dropped by Pope; it has been included in most collected editions of Shakespeare since Malone's *Supplement* to Steevens in 1780 (see List of Abbreviations, p. *x*).

All these rather strange features of the play's publication-history have bothered

---

[1] Each edition was reprinted from its predecessor, with the exception that Q6 seems to have made some use of Q4 as well as Q5. In editorial jargon, therefore, they are 'derivative' texts, without authority.

[2] That is, the prompt-book, containing the licence of the Master of the Revels, without which (in theory) a play could not be performed.

[3] Oxford admits inability to obtain permission to print as a possible cause for the exclusion of *Love's Labour's Won* ('Possibly the copyright belonged to a recalcitrant stationer, unwilling to relinquish it to the Folio syndicate') and accepts it as the reason for the near-omission of *Troilus and Cressida* (*Companion*, p. 71), but does not consider the possibility of a refusal for *Pericles*' absence.

scholars, especially when taken in conjunction with another aspect thereof: that the first quarto has many textual problems. The two chief difficulties are first, verse is more often than not printed as prose, especially towards the end of the play; earlier, prose had been set as verse, and there are also passages set as verse where the lineation seems very improbable. Secondly, there are many readings in the text that cannot be right, many more that are suspect and, on a lower level, there is a lot of very peculiar spelling and punctuation. Collectively, these defects reveal a level of textual corruption far and away above the norm one would expect in a Shakespearean quarto printed from a reliable manuscript.

If not a reliable manuscript, what other possibilities are there? Though scholars are rightly cautious about attempting any too-rigid categorisation, it is fairly safe to say that the script of the average Elizabethan/Jacobean play seems to have gone through the following stages. Ignoring the dramatist's notes and rough drafts, there must at some point have been an effectively complete draft of the play, which the author normally seems to have read to the company for approval.[1] This draft is called the 'foul papers', a term used at the time to distinguish this state of the text from the 'fair copy'. A fair copy might be made by the author himself, or by a professional scrivener. Its purpose was twofold. First, all plays had to be submitted to the Master of the Revels for their performance-licence, and it is clear that the Master expected a fair copy. Secondly, the company would need an official 'book' of the play, from which the actors' parts would be transcribed, and which would record such adaptations and corrections to the foul papers as had been determined upon in the process of production.

One must not be hasty to generalise here, for there is no surviving complete manuscript of the foul-papers stage of a professional play,[2] and while quite a number of prompt-books survive, there are hardly enough, especially from the early Jacobean period, to make positive declarations that *all* such manuscripts shared certain features. Another legitimate class of manuscript, of which there are several survivors from the period, was the presentation copy (again, either authorial or scribal) given to a patron or friend.[3] Any of these three classes of manuscript could be given or sold to a printer as copy for a printed edition,[4] and though there would be differences among these

---

[1] See G. E. Bentley, *The Profession of Dramatist in Shakespeare's Time*, 1971, pp. 76–9.

[2] Sir Walter Greg, in his survey of the surviving dramatic MSS. (*Dramatic Documents from the Elizabethan Playhouses*, 2 vols., 1931), did not identify any as being foul papers. However, it is true that the *additions* to *Sir Thomas More* are foul; and Greg by the time he published *The Shakespeare First Folio*, 1955, had come to think that the MS. of Heywood's *The Captives* was foul papers. We are not persuaded of the latter. In 1985 a fragment of the foul papers of an unknown Jacobean play was discovered among Sir John Coke's papers at Melbourne Hall in Derbyshire. See the editors' 'The Melbourne Manuscript and John Webster' (*Studies in Bibliography* 41 (1988), 1–32). Trevor Howard-Hill has described some foul papers of a play written in a provincial centre, by John Newdigate of Arbury. See 'Boccaccio, *Ghismonda*, and its foul papers, *Glausamond*' (*Renaissance Papers 1980* (1981), 19–28). This is a thin harvest indeed.

[3] Not all plays were published in printed form, or not thus published shortly ofter the first performance. In any event, there seems to have been still something of a cachet in receiving a MS. copy. A special case of this class of MSS. is that of notorious or banned plays, such as Middleton's *A Game at Chess*.

[4] Obviously, an acting company would not dispose of its 'book' of a play still in repertory, perhaps not even subsequently. But if desired a transcript of the book could be made for the printer.

manuscripts, each could be claimed to represent some legitimate aspect of the play's text.

Early this century, A. W. Pollard was the principal definer of a class of Shakespearean printed plays which seemed by their imperfections hardly to be credited as deriving from any of these legitimate manuscripts. Spurred by the sinister phrase in the preface to the First Folio, that there existed 'diuerse stolne, and surreptitious copies, maimed, and deformed by the frauds and stealths of iniurious impostors' (which the Folio was going to remedy with its better texts), Pollard classified the quartos into 'good' and 'bad', the good being derived from authoritative sources, the bad, not. The quarto of *Pericles* was one that was promptly dubbed 'bad'.

As to what makes a quarto 'bad': by mid-century it was generally accepted that a 'bad' text was based on a 'memorial reconstruction' of part or all of the play, that is, that someone's *memory* of what the script said intervenes in the chain of transmission. One obvious way such a reconstruction might occur would be for one or more actors who had performed in the play to write down all he/they could recall of it. It was further presumed that the purpose of this activity was larceny, to sell a popular play to an unscrupulous publisher and thereby make a little extra money.

This scenario never gained universal assent,[1] and has been much challenged in recent years.[2] For instance, it is now widely held that the first quarto of *King Lear*, far from being 'bad', actually was printed from Shakespeare's foul papers, and the version of the play that appears in the Folio constitutes a revised text.[3] So the wheel turns; the common view of these 'bad' quartos in the nineteenth century was that they were rough drafts or early versions of some kind. It is not necessary to debate this new–old opinion here; only to say that in our opinion some texts, such as the bizarre first quarto of *Hamlet*, remain virtually impossible to explain except by some version of the memorial theory. However, of all the Shakespearean quartos that have commonly been regarded as 'bad', only one lacks the independent check of a different text in the Folio: that one is *Pericles*. Therefore, before joining in the rush to declare the quarto of *Pericles* 'bad', it is necessary to examine sceptically the evidence brought forward for so classing it.

---

[1] One of its doughtiest opponents was Hardin Craig, whose mature views are to be found in his *A New Look at Shakespeare's Quartos*, 1961.

[2] Steven Urkowitz, for instance, has turned his aggressive and acerbic manner to the question: see for instance 'Reconsidering the relationship of quarto and Folio texts of *Richard III*' (*ELR* 16 (1986), 442–66) and ' "If I mistake in those foundations which I build upon": Peter Alexander's textual analysis of *Henry VI Parts 2 and 3*' (*ELR* 18 (1988), 230–56). A better-balanced reappraisal is Paul Werstine's 'Narratives about printed Shakespeare texts: "foul papers" and "bad quartos" ', *SQ* 41.1 (Spring 1990), 65–86, which rightly points out the undesirable binarism Pollard's terminology compels: 'if a critic represents a quarto (like that of *King Lear*) as being not very "good," it immediately is threatened with becoming "bad"; and even those who now wish to eliminate altogether the category of "bad" quarto have become trapped by Pollard's binarism into arguing that all the formerly "bad" quartos must be reassessed as "good" ' (pp. 65–6). It is true that what Werstine calls Pollard's 'narratives' about the genesis of these texts, memorial reconstruction in particular, seemed such a neat solution to the problem of variant texts that for many scholars it came to seem *proven*. Of course it is not, but then neither is the theory of evolution.

[3] An obstinate minority of scholars continues to reject the 'two-text *Lear*': see, for instance, Robert Clare, ' "Who is it that can tell me who I am?": the theory of authorial revision between the quarto and Folio texts of *King Lear*', *The Library*, Sixth Series, 17 (March 1995), 34–59.

The clearest account of the signs that scholars seek for to identify such a text is probably still Patrick's.[1] He argues that memorial contamination will show up in a variety of identifiable ways; his two primary categories are *shifting* (or transposition) of words within a line, or in adjacent lines, or from one speech to another, and *substitutions*, where a synonym is substituted for the word in the text. Anyone who has had anything to do with the theatre will know how normal all this is, but two examples from our own experience will conveniently illustrate the point. A good student actor with an accurate memory, playing Fitzdottrel in Jonson's *The Devil is an Ass* at the McMaster Summer Drama Festival in 1993, delivered himself of the following line in 2.1: 'I swear, when I have my millions else, I will depose you, and make another lady duchess.' The text from which the actor learned his lines read: 'I swear, when I have my millions else, I'll make another duchess' (353–4). In 2.3 another of his speeches to his wife ends 'I could now find i' my very heart to make another lady duchess and depose you' (18–19). The presence of the phrase 'I will depose you' in his earlier speech is instantly explained. It is a classic instance of shifting. An error of shifting which in turn caused the other kind of memorial error (substitution) occurred in the 1979 RSC production of *Richard III* when, instead of 'And brief, good mother, for I am in haste' (4.4.167), Alan Howard said 'And hasty, mother, [pause] for I soon must go.' Substitution includes another classic kind of memorial contamination, namely gag: words or phrases invented by the actor. ('Let those that play your clowns speak no more than is set down for them', warns Hamlet primly, but all clowns do, and so do serious actors).

Patrick's categorisation of the kinds of memorial error needs further to be divided into two other principal classes. There is the *transient* error, that committed by an actor as a result of a temporary difficulty with his part. Howard's was obviously of this class: having on this one occasion got 'hasty' in the wrong place, he paused just long enough to invent (substitute) a different set of words to end the line. Our Fitzdottrel's error was of the other kind: one where the actor had memorised an incorrect version of his line. Now, the transient error in Elizabethan drama would normally leave no trace in any text of the play. But a memorised error could do so, if the actor wrote down, or dictated, his part as he remembered it. These errors could then become perpetuated in a printed text, should that actor's script become the printer's copy.

For memorial error to be *proven* in a text, there must be cases in which the suspect text is *demonstrably a corruption of another*. Synonyms alone are not enough: there must be a persuasive direction of change, from better to worse.[2] A conclusive demonstration may not be possible, but at any event, to attempt such a demonstration two texts are

[1] David Lyall Patrick, *The Textual History of Richard III*, 1936. Since we wrote these pages, there has appeared Laurie E. Maguire's book, *Shakespearean Suspect Texts: The 'Bad' Quartos and Their Contexts*, 1996, which attempts to undertake a complete, systematic survey and analysis of the 'bad quartos'. Although we do not agree with all her conclusions, her opinion (pp. 294–5) that the only justification for considering *Pericles* 'bad' is what she calls 'wrecked verse' (i.e. the lineation problem) is encouraging.

[2] The two examples we have cited obviously do not fall into this category. So although they were in fact memorial errors, if they had occurred as variants in early printed texts, neither could have been convincingly cited as proof of memorial contamination.

obviously required. The lack of another substantive text against which that of Q1 *Pericles* can be tested is a grave, probably insuperable, obstacle to any attempt either to prove or disprove that it is memorially contaminated.

The first scholar to make an extended attempt to establish a memorial element in Q1 *Pericles* was Philip Edwards, and his long article on the subject is still of the first importance.[1] Briefly, he rests his case for Q's being a memorial text on three factors: some repetition of phrases from speech to speech, and what looks like some gag; the peculiarities of the mislineation; and the poor quality of the verse in the first two acts.

Edwards gives three instances of repetition,[2] of which we will repeat one (since the others are identical in nature). At 5.1.101 Pericles declares 'I am great with woe, and shall deliver weeping.' Some 50 lines later, Marina echoes this, saying 'as my good nurse / Lychorida hath oft delivered weeping'. Now in most memorial texts, as in the example from *The Devil is an Ass* above, transposition usually occurs when an actor shifts bits of his own lines from one speech to another. Naturally, if Q1 *Pericles* were indeed memorially reconstructed by an actor or actors, this would leave no trace: a bit of text has moved from there to here, and left no evidence of its passing. But it is true that actors occasionally will be so struck by a colleague's line that they (unconsciously) borrow it for themselves. Perhaps Marina borrows Pericles' phrase thus, or vice versa. But a mere three such 'repetitions' in a play are not going to prove anything. Edwards says 'Certainly we seem to have here the tricks of memory rather than the workings of the law of association in a dramatist's mind', but is the 'seeming' as 'certain' as his Irishism proposes? Hardly so.[3]

On the other hand, there is indeed a lot of what looks like gag in *Pericles*: the inmates of the brothel are very fond of the phrase 'come your ways' (but this may be part of their 'low' characterisation); Dioniza in 4.1 is addicted to beginning a sentence with 'Come', and in 3.1 we find Pericles saying 'O how, Lychorida', 'Now Lychorida', 'How? How Lychorida?' and 'O Lychorida' in quick succession (6, 14, 18, and 64). However, if an actor is prone to gag it is likely to be evident throughout his part. Yet Dioniza elsewhere does not begin her sentences thus; neither is Pericles' mannerism in 3.1 found in the rest of the play. This would suggest that the usual mechanisms proposed for memorial reconstruction will not explain adequately these aspects of the text of *Pericles*.

What other explanations are possible? Until G. I. Duthie's magisterial study of the texts of *King Lear*, it was widely assumed that a play could have been taken down during performance in shorthand. However, Duthie showed that the various systems of 'brachigraphy' available at the time were inadequate for such a task, and his findings

---

[1] 'An approach to the problem of *Pericles*', *S.Sur.* 5 (1952), 25–49.
[2] Edwards, p. 28.
[3] Consider the case of John Webster's *The White Devil*, whose text is almost certainly set from foul papers. In 1.2.182 Camillo says 'Didst thou not mark the jeast of the silke-worme?' and three lines later Flamineo observes 'thou intanglest thy self in thine own worke like a silke-worme'. Authors can echo themselves too. See also Introduction, pp. 36–51. Oxford adds a few more 'repetitions': the Oxford editors regard Simonides' 'A pretty moral' (2.2.45) as 'suspicious' because Pericles uses the same phrase of the Fishermen (2.1.33) (*Companion* p. 567); but since Simonides was not on stage to hear Pericles' observation (he would almost certainly have been in the tire-chamber), no mechanism for its borrowing suggests itself.

remain uncontroverted.[1] Nonetheless, Edwards founded his theory of the text on the belief that a reporter or reporters with some knowledge of the play, supplemented by some surreptitious shorthand, could produce a version of the text which would be consistent with the kinds of error and confusion found in *Pericles*. His principal argument for thinking that this might have occurred is to be found in the vagaries of the lineation, and credit is due to Edwards for perceiving the relevance thereto of the work of the three compositors.

His identification of the compositors (as modified by Hoeniger, Jackson, and Blayney) is that Compositor X, who worked for White, set gatherings A and C–E (that is, the first scene up to line 160, and 1.4.91–3.3.30). Compositors Y and Z, working for Creede, divided the rest of the book up between them as follows: Y set B1^r–2^v, F1^r–3^r, F4^v, G1^r–2^v and H3^r–I2^r; Compositor Z set B3^r–4^v, F3^v–4^r, G3^r–H2^v and I2^v–3^v.[2] It is evident that all three compositors were in their various degrees competent to recognise verse and to set it, for they all do so (after some initial hesitations) in the first four gatherings.

However, in the *middle* of gathering E this orderly setting goes haywire, more or less from the beginning of 3.2. It is true that Compositor X seemed to be beginning to get the hang of it again by the end of the scene, but his involvement in the book ends at that point (at the end of gathering E), and the layout of the copy seems to have left both Y and Z flummoxed: both of them set about 80 per cent of the verse as prose.

It is very difficult to explain this difference between the two halves of the play except by supposing it a manifestation of some major alteration in the copy. Edwards believed that it meant that everything from 3.2 on was written as prose. No sane author would do so, which seems to strengthen the case for a reporter; but other possibilities are suggested by examination of surviving theatrical MSS., some of which are so written that distinctions between prose and verse are not at all easy to make. Edwards also believed that it meant that two scribes had written the MS., which is certainly possible, but not inevitable. Edwards also maintained that the reported text was produced by two reporters of different abilities: the first two acts, he says, 'seem to give us the attempt of some versifier, working from his memory or from notes, to rebuild a play by a more competent writer' (p. 37); the remainder of the play was written by a reporter who knew the text better but had no skill at, or interest in, metrics. This rather elaborate theory exceeds the facts, and on the whole has not worn well.

Edwards's theory is strongest on the fact that even when the lineation in the first two acts goes awry, it is relatively easy to restore it; but from 3.2 on, 'even where [editors] succeed in fitting a speech into a structure of ten-syllable lines, the regularity so gained does not carry with it the reader's conviction that this is a poet's way of handling the rhythmic units of his verse' (p. 38). This, alas, is true: the reader consulting the collation of this edition will find that though Malone is the editor most

[1] George Ian Duthie, *Elizabethan Shorthand and the First Quarto of King Lear*, 1949.
[2] Hoeniger's investigations for the Arden edition show that White's compositor set by formes, while Creede's men set consecutive batches of four pages. The fact that the printing was shared is not unusual; the fact that the two shops adopted different methods of dealing with the manuscript suggests that there was nothing about it that enforced a particular kind of treatment by the master-printer and his workmen.

frequently cited for relineation, many other names appear, and in many more cases we have not felt persuaded by any previous solution, and 'gone it alone' (without much conviction, really, that what we are offering is *right* as distinct from different, we hope a little better, than our predecessors' guesses). In other words, do what one will, much of Q1, though obviously 'poetic', cannot be arranged convincingly into what looks like Jacobean blank verse, even the much freer blank verse that Shakespeare wrote in the later phase of his career. However, curiously, the problem is basically a visual rather than an auditory one, in that the verse (in anyone's lineation) sounds convincing on the stage; it just looks odd on the printed page.

Edwards's other conclusion, that the 'versifier' of the first two acts was none other than George Wilkins, is much less persuasive.[1] That Wilkins had seen the play seems beyond dispute, because of the parallels between it and *PA*, but there is no evidence to connect Wilkins with both texts unless one accepts the theory that Wilkins was co-author of the play. Even if that were the case, a reporter is *still* required to account for the *differences* between the play and the novella, the things the play gets 'wrong' which the novella allegedly 'makes clear', the tangles in the sense, and the 'humdrum' verse. All these are less serious than Edwards believed: he was almost driven to believe the Q text worse than it is in order to justify his conviction of Shakespeare's presence in the latter part of the play. (After all, the presumption goes, why would the greatest dramatic poet of this or any other age work in collaboration with someone who couldn't write sense? The text *must* have been messed about by a reporter.)

Since Edwards's article, there has been only one major new discussion of the text of the play: Taylor's separately published exposition of his theory, which became the basis of the Oxford Shakespeare's text.[2] Unfortunately, Taylor merely accepts, rather than reassesses, the memorial theory; his main purpose is to demolish Edwards's two-reporter theory, and to promote his own guess concerning the origins of the manuscript. The best points he makes against Edwards are, first, that the lineation differences are not as extreme as Edwards had supposed. 'The rather primitive, end-stopped, regular verse (often rhymed) of the first two acts would have been much easier to align correctly than the fluid and variable verse of Shakespeare's late style' (p. 195). It is certainly a shame that Compositor X's work ends so early in this part of the play, since he seemed to be capable of making reasonably good sense of it. It is anomalous in Edwards's theory, Taylor observes, that amidst the otherwise chaotic lineation in the second part of the play, Gower's verse is mainly correctly lined, and inexplicable that the breakdown in lineation occurs in 3.2, rather than in 3.1, at the point where, so the general opinion goes, the play's poetic style changes. Finally, and perhaps most tellingly, a point first made by Ernst Schanzer:[3] if (as Edwards maintained) the second reporter had a better recall of the play than the first, the number of verbal echoes of the play in *PA* should increase whereas in fact the contrary is the case.

---

[1] Edwards indeed abandons this fanciful theory in his Penguin edition.
[2] Gary Taylor, 'The transmission of *Pericles*', *PBSA* 80 (1986), 193–217.
[3] In his edition of *Pericles* for the Signet Shakespeare.

As for the source of the report, Taylor proposes that the boy-actor who, he believes, doubled the parts of Lychorida and Marina, was principally responsible, aided perhaps by one of the hired men who played one of the Fishermen in 2.1, and a copy of Gower's 'part'. This tissue of fancy need detain us but briefly since it is supported by the merest gossamer threads of inference. While it is true, as Taylor declares, that 'critics have for centuries' agreed that 3.1 and 5.1 are 'superior', that superiority is in terms of literary style, not textual reliability: both have major cruces in them, and 5.1 is a worst-case scenario as far as lineation is concerned. They thus make doubtful choices as scenes that demonstrate that the reporter must have been a player in them.

Another method of making such a determination would be to choose the scenes that (by consensus) have attracted the least emendation: by that criterion, some of the early scenes such as 1.1, or the brothel scenes, have a better claim. But even accepting 3.1 and 5.1, Taylor's suggestions bristle with difficulty. Would a boy playing such a major role as Marina have been asked to double? Taylor's point, that with doubling the play can be performed by three boys, is true but irrelevant, since in 1607 the company undoubtedly had more than three boy-actors. Most of his other speculations are equally ill-founded.

Many critics have complained of what they take to be deficiencies in the Q text of 4.5, when Marina confronts Lysimachus in the brothel. In particular, there are two difficulties: first, is Lysimachus indeed intent on lechery when he arrives, or should we take at face value his protestation that he came 'with no ill intent' at the end of the scene; and second, it is odd that Marina says so little to him to change his mind before he declares 'I did not think / Thou couldst have spoke so well, ne'er dreamed thou couldst.' The point is that *PA* elaborates on both these subjects in its own pedestrian way. Yet if Marina had been the source of the report, it is highly improbable that the text of one of her own scenes should have such major lacunae.

To overcome these difficulties, Taylor finds himself obliged to defend Q against *PA*, which he does to such good effect that it makes one wish he had done so for the entire play. On the first point, for instance, he writes:

The expansive moralizing in *PA* is, as others have noted, entirely characteristic of Wilkins, so in itself the mere presence of such additional matter in *PA* is not reliable evidence of a serious lacuna in Q. The presumption that such a lacuna exists arises from impatience with the ambiguity of Q. Does Lysimachus begin the scene as a lecher, or not? In Wilkins he clearly does so; in Q he appears to be equally immoral, but at the end claims, unconvincingly, that he intended no ill. It does not seem to me that such ambiguity as we find in Q here is untypical of Shakespeare; nor does the palpably unconvincing character of Lysimachus' excuse demonstrate that the text is corrupt.   (p. 202)

Likewise, Taylor's demolition of Edwards's argument about Marina's 'eloquence' (p. 206) is clear and entirely persuasive. What this all shows, actually, is precisely the dangers critics fall into when they use Wilkins as a weapon against the play, as Edwards did here and elsewhere, and equally, how the play-text's supposed defects can be plausibly defended. However, Taylor does not supply any clear explanation of why, by his own theory, Wilkins here is both so wide of what is in Q *and worse than* Q.[1]

No matter what theory is adopted, the textual scenarios are dismayingly intricate.[2] Their intricacy does not mean that they are wrong, of course, for complex events did occur in the composition and transmission of dramatic scripts at the time. It would be a bold scholar who would claim that if *Sir Thomas More* had in fact been completed, performed, and printed, and the manuscript lost, it would be possible to reconstruct from any printed edition just how complicated the play's genesis, as revealed by the manuscript, really was. Nonetheless, it makes sense to apply Occam's razor where possible.

First, although it is not imperative to accept Edwards's view that two scribes wrote the manuscript that found its way into Henry Gosson's hands, *some* change in the MS. must be admitted to account for the collapse of the verse lineation. It would not be unreasonable to suppose that the MS. was of mixed nature. If the *Sir Thomas More* scene is really in Shakespeare's hand,[3] then although his verse was clearly and regularly lined, like most of his contemporaries he did not begin his verse lines with a capital letter. This could make it relatively easy for a compositor to mistake prose for verse, and possible, though much less likely, to set verse as prose. However, *Sir Thomas More* is something of a special case; a piece of patchwork inserted into a pre-existing manuscript in an attempt to get it past the censor. It would be unwise to generalise from it.

The problem remains: while it is not hard to invoke normal compositorial misprisions to account for the prose set as verse, and the verse mislineations up to 3.2, the rest of the play, with its acres of verse set either as prose or else lamentably mislined, is a more intractable difficulty. However, if one presumes a mixed copy, that of the first part of the play perhaps transcribed from foul papers, the second half being in much fouler condition, there is no absolute need to postulate two scribes; though there is no difficulty either, if the transcription of the first half was done by a hand other than the author's.

Secondly, how strong (really) is the case for the MS.'s being a report? As we have seen, the kinds of evidence depended upon in other allegedly memorial Shakespearean texts cannot be found in *Pericles*. The primary evidence then is the mistakes and the lineation.

One kind of error much sought after in allegedly memorial texts is the 'auditory error': that where the scribe has copied down what he thought he heard, but because he didn't understand it, makes nonsense of it. The most seeming-plausible example of

---

[1] In Oxford, Taylor now explains the differences between the play and Wilkins by equally hypothetical censorship (*Companion*, p. 559).

[2] For example, Hoeniger's: that John Day and George Wilkins (and perhaps a third dramatist) in 1607 decided to make a play out of the Apollonius/Pericles legend; that Shakespeare became interested in their venture and took it over, and thence via Edwards's two reporters we get the quarto.

[3] The most famous thing about this manuscript is the three pages written by 'Hand D' which are widely believed to be in Shakespeare's handwriting. See *Shakespeare's Hand in The Play of Sir Thomas More*, by Alfred Pollard *et al.*, 1923, and, for a more modern survey of the evidence, T. H. Howard-Hill, ed.: *Shakespeare and Sir Thomas More: Essays on the Play and its Shakespearean Interest*, 1989. The point being made here, however, relates to the amazingly complex genesis and development of this playscript by a variety of authors and scribes.

this in *Pericles* is 2.2.27–8, which reads in Q 'The motto thus in Spanish. *Pue Per doleera kee per forsa.*' Editors have assumed that the reporter was doing his best with an unfamiliar language. But an alternative explanation of the text is possible (see Supplementary Note to 2.2.28) and so this 'auditory error' joins other such where it has proved possible to defend what at first seemed an obvious corruption.[1] And obvious corruptions are what must be sought; since an actor, trying to recapture a line which he recalls imperfectly, will not set down nonsense, but something that makes sense of a kind, even if it is not what was in his part. We do not believe that *any* of the mistakes in Q1 *Pericles* (i.e. those readings which we have been obliged to emend) compels the memorial explanation: the usual errors of misreading a difficult script or compositorial error are adequate to explain them.

On the other hand, there are in *Pericles* errors which have seemed to other editors besides ourselves more characteristic of foul-papers copy than of memorial failure. The real problem with this assertion is the scarcity of hard evidence concerning foul papers.[2] Many of the alleged signs of foul-papers copy are unreliable. For example, ambiguity in stage directions (e.g. 2.4.16, which in Q reads '*Enter two or three Lords*') was long held to be a sign of a pre-production document. Unfortunately, examination of surviving prompt-books proves this not to be the case. Likewise, confusion or inconsistency in speech headings is no longer thought to be a reliable indication of foul-papers copy. Both are likely to be found in foul papers, but it is clear that both could survive into a prompt-book. What is left? Perhaps not enough to carry conviction. One may continue to assume that any major textual inconsistencies may be a sign of foul papers;[3] irregular spelling or punctuation that survived the compositor another; and irregular lineation (perhaps).

A few specific examples may help. Consider the following (4.1.4–6), which in Q (set as prose) reads 'Let not conscience which is but cold, in flaming, thy loue bosome, enflame too nicelie,' – lines which make little sense as they stand. But with a little remedial punctuation they yield good sense:

> Let not conscience,
> Which is but cold in flaming, thy love-bosom
> Inflame too nicely;[4]

Errors such as 2.0.11, 'Is still at *Tharstill*', or 3.3.0.1, '*Enter Pericles Atharsus*', are characteristic not of memorial mistakes, but of compositorial inattention. Many other 'errors' which editors, bewitched by their theory of memorial reconstruction, see as corruption, turn out to be explicable.[5]

---

[1] See *King Lear* 4.6.158–9: the Folio reads 'a Dogg's obey'd in Office'; Q1 reads 'a dogge, so bade in office'. Duthie, Greg, and others all assumed the Q reading to be an error of hearing. W. J. B. Owen first pointed out that it is also an easy *misreading* (for 'a dogges obaide': *N&Q* 194 (April 1949), 141–2); Oxford adopts a version of Owen's conjecture, without acknowledgement.

[2] See p. 199, n. 2.

[3] A case could be made in *Pericles* for considering the crux at 3.3.28–9 to be such an inconsistency. How it would have been resolved in production, no one can say.

[4] C. J. Sisson, *New Readings in Shakespeare*, 1961, II, 296 cites this example.

[5] See notes to 1.2.25, 1.3.26, 1.4.40, 3.0.6, 3.1.74, 4.0.31–3, 4.4.48, 5.1.42–3, 5.1.137, 5.1.251, 5.2.2 for some examples. There are many more.

Turning now to the lineation, we find that the closest parallel to the situation in *Pericles* is that in the first quarto of *King Lear*, where what should be about 500 lines of verse are set as prose, and over 600 lines set as verse are mislined. It will not do, as Oxford does, to blame Nicholas Okes, the printer, for this: 'by contrast with Quarto *Lear* (set by one printer who had never before attempted a play, and whose later play quartos often contain significant quantities of similar mislineation), Quarto *Pericles* was set by two experienced printers'.[1] *Printers* were not responsible for lineation, *compositors* were, and the experience or otherwise of the compositors who worked for White and Creede on *Pericles*, or for Okes on *Lear*, is not known for certain.[2]

Taken as a whole, then, Q1 *Pericles* seems to us to manifest reliably far fewer of the stigmata of memorial reconstruction than recent editors have assumed. A better approach might be to consider which printed texts in the Shakespeare 'canon' Q1 *Pericles* most resembles. The answer, clearly, is the first ('Pide Bull') quarto of *King Lear*, which has a similar error-rate, similar gross mistakes, and a similar amount of mislineation. If the memorial theory can be abandoned for Q1 *King Lear*, there is no compelling reason to retain it for *Pericles*.

Our conclusion then is that the copy for Q1 *Pericles* probably resembled the copy for Q1 *Lear* more closely than any other document, in that it seems to have been based on very primitive, and perhaps not homogeneous, foul papers. It is surely possible that the first half of the play, with its deliberate use of rhyme and more formal constructions, was easier for the compositors to line than the latter half, where Shakespeare wrote his more usual late-period free verse. It is equally possible that the first half of the play was transcribed from the foul papers, the second not, and that this accounts for the differences in treatment of lineation. There is not sufficient evidence to decide between the two hypotheses. In practice it has made little difference: in this edition, the memorial explanation has been entirely rejected, and the errors in Q attributed either to misreading by a scribe or by a compositor or both, without necessarily attempting to determine which.

What then should be done about *PA*? That there is a connection between it and *Pericles* is not in doubt. *PA* is, to borrow a more recent term, 'the book of the film' of the stage-play. All recent editors, recognising this, have mined *PA* for details about staging, and even for chunks of text when it seemed apparent to them that something had gone badly awry in the quarto. This edition does not follow suit, and it is necessary

---

[1] *Companion*, p. 556. Oxford evasively omits mention of the mislineation of Q *Lear* in its discussion of that text, p. 510.

[2] Even Peter Blayney, despite what is undoubtedly the most comprehensive bibliographical study ever attempted of a single book, has not identified the compositors of Q *Lear* for certain. His conclusion is that Compositor B was perhaps still an apprentice who had served two-and-a-quarter years, but may have become a journeyman by this time, and that Compositor C was an apprentice of eight months' standing, while Okes himself had been a master-printer for only eight months at the time *Lear* was set. Yet he concedes he cannot be absolutely certain whether there were two or three compositors (p. 167), and his observations on the experience of the compositors go no farther than: 'The general level of competence shown by [Compositor] B in dealing with the combined problems of the copy and the type-shortage may perhaps suggest inexperience with dramatic copy' (p. 186). See Peter W. M. Blayney, *The Texts of King Lear and their Origins*, vol. I: *Nicholas Okes and the First Quarto*, 1982, chapter 5, 'The Compositors', pp. 151–87.

to explain why. The only reason for doing so would be that the text of the play is so corrupt that any source, however unreliable, might be used in an attempt to make sense of it. Since we are convinced that this view of Q1 *Pericles* is wrong, we have more reason to hesitate before admitting anything from *PA*. We accept that Wilkins was, in *PA*, conflating his *recollections* of the play as performed with the account of the tale of Apollonius of Tyre as retold by Laurence Twine (see Introduction, 'Sources', pp. 6–8). We agree that there are many 'verse-fossils' embedded in the prose of *PA* (that is, lines that would make passable blank, or rhyming, verse if so set out). Editors have also commended *PA* for 'making sense' out of 1.3, and for explaining the reference to Pericles' music (2.5.25), among other information that may have a bearing on how the play was staged. But then again it may not: we are less enthusiastic about these and other alleged revelations. It is equally possible that they are additions by Wilkins, 'improvements' to the staged play, added to his novella to make it more interesting or lively.

It must be stressed that *PA* is unique: the only attempt in the period to present a popular play in prose narrative. We thus have nothing to compare it with, no idea, really, of its author's philosophy, motivation, or principles. These days the practice is common enough, but as those who misguidedly purchased the book of (say) the film of *Star Wars* found out to their cost, ill-written prose fiction is not the same as a highly professional, lively enacted scene. The fiction usually includes material not in the film, especially explanations of motivation and emotions; on the other hand, the film's effect is all too often uncapturable in language (not that the author of that series was any Shakespeare). But then, neither was Wilkins. Much of *PA* is flat, stale, and unprofit-able; much of it clearly has little relationship to the stage-play (the long introductory chapter describing Antiochus' violent seduction of his daughter, for instance).

There is absolutely no reason for thinking it a *reliable* report of the play, and to accept its information is a counsel of desperation forced upon the editor who believes that the text of *Pericles* is irremediably corrupt. Such an edition is the Oxford, which carried the belief of the editors (Gary Taylor and MacDonald P. Jackson) that *PA* is essentially *more reliable than Q* to extraordinary extremes, re-writing its text as the fancy took them, and for trivial reasons. A few examples will make it clear how their theories led them into emendation that can only be called reckless.

In the brothel scenes, for instance, Taylor and Jackson emend the 'thousand pieces' the Pirates have demanded of Boult (4.2.40) to 'a hundred Sestercies' on the grounds that this is the reading in both Twine and *PA*, and comment 'A reporter might easily have substituted Q's less specific phrase; there seems little reason for Shakespeare to abandon his source in such a detail.' The agreement between Twine and *PA* is actually grounds for caution, rather than the reverse; and Q's phrase is not less specific (the editors must not have checked its meaning in *OED*); as for their editorial assurance concerning Shakespeare's treatment of his sources, we can only say we don't share it. A little earlier, the Pander's phrase 'there's two [of the wenches] unwholesome a' conscience' (4.2.17) Taylor and Jackson emend (following Malone) to 'they're too', dismissing the Q reading as 'an easy aural error'. But there's *nothing wrong* with Q's phrase; surely it is highly injudicious to campaign against intelligible readings just because they *might* be corrupt? Yet the Oxford editors do so over and over again: they omit the Bawd's 'Boult's returned' (4.2.74) on the grounds that 'memorial texts often enough substitute dialogue for action, and vice-versa', an uncomfortably sweeping generalisation. Likewise at 5.1.157 they replace Q's 'delivered' with 'recounted', observing that Edwards first 'stigmatized this repetition' as a memorial corruption, without apparently noticing just how much repetition there is, and how dramatically important it is, in this scene. Sometimes Taylor and Jackson find themselves going through strange contortions, as when they are obliged to invent a highly complicated pair of theories to enable the edition to get rid of Marina's epitaph in 4.4 (which by their own basic theory derives from MS.) so as to print *PA*'s version. All these misjudgements and meddlings originate in the memorial theory, and show its dangers more clearly than any description on our parts.

Our view is that *PA* may be drawn upon occasionally and cautiously for information about staging details (which are never fully documented in any Elizabethan/Jacobean play-text), but that as a rule it should be regarded as no more reliable than any other memorial text: whatever the truth about the play-text, *PA* is most certainly a 'bad quarto' – that is, it is based on Wilkins's recollection of the play as performed: all authorities agree he did not have a text of the play to hand when writing *PA*. We believe that editors who have been seduced by the Memorial Caper and the Wilkins Connection have come up with worse texts than they need have. It would be a bold textual critic who would attempt a theoretical justification of mending one putatively 'bad' text by the application of another, demonstrably bad, yet this is exactly what the Wilkinsisers, in their different degrees, have done. The texts of both *Pericles* and *PA* bear partial witness to an event (the production of the play) now irrecoverably lost. That of *Pericles* is a witness to an event still in the future (the produced play), that of *PA* a (bad) witness to an event in the past. To conflate the two is likely to produce *contaminatio*: picking out the things where *both* texts report the event incorrectly, Q1 *Pericles* because it is based on a pre-production document, *PA* because it is a memorial reconstruction.[1]

Most editors of plays today would prefer to edit a text based on production, rather than a pre-production document derived from foul papers (a significant change in editorial policy since about 1970). Lacking that option, we have decided to edit the text of the quarto of *Pericles*: just that, and nothing more, defending its readings where we can do so; emending them (in common with so many of our illustrious predecessors) when we cannot, and where either a previous editor or our own wits have suggested a defensible emendation; leaving well alone in cases where no emendation meets the tests of plausibility and intelligibility. We (obviously) make no claim that this is *Pericles* as Shakespeare's company staged it. Q1's witness to that event is patently incomplete and unreliable. But we think that this text provides a more honest basis for an attempt to re-create *Pericles* in our own time (either on the stage or for a reader) than any text stuffed with indigestible chunks of Wilkins's memories.

[1] The elaborate series of improbable stage directions that Oxford prints out of *PA* is an example.

READING LIST

This list comprises a small selection of reference and critical works which may serve as a guide to those who wish to undertake a further study of the play.

Arthos, J. '*Pericles, Prince of Tyre*: a study in the dramatic use of romantic narrative', *SQ* 4 (1953), 257–70

Bentley, G. E. *The Profession of Dramatist in Shakespeare's Time*, 1971

Brockbank, J. P. '*Pericles* and the dream of immortality', *S.Sur.* 24 (1971), 105–16

Brown, John Russell and Harris, Bernard (eds.). *Later Shakespeare*, Stratford-upon-Avon Studies 8, 1966

Bullough, Geoffrey (ed.). *Narrative and Dramatic Sources of Shakespeare*, 8 vols., VI, 1966

Csengeri, Karen. 'William Shakespeare, sole author of *Pericles*', *English Studies* (1990), 230–43

Edwards, Philip. 'An approach to the problem of *Pericles*', *S.Sur.* 5 (1952), 25–49

Ellacombe, Henry. *The Plant-Lore and Garden-Craft of Shakespeare*, 1884

Ewbank, Inga-Stina. '"My name is Marina": the language of recognition', in Philip Edwards *et al.* (eds.), *Shakespeare's Styles: Essays in Honour of Kenneth Muir*, 1980

Falconer, Alexander Frederick. *Shakespeare and the Sea*, 1964

Farmer, John and Henley, W. E. *A Dictionary of Slang and Colloquial English*, 1905

Felperin, Howard. *Shakespearean Romance*, 1972
    'Shakespeare's Miracle Play', *SQ* 18 (1967), 363–74

Flower, Annette C. 'Disguise and identity in *Pericles, Prince of Tyre*', *SQ* 26 (1975), 30–41

Freeman, Rosemary. *English Emblem Books*, 1948

Frye, Northrop. *Anatomy of Criticism*, 1957
    A Natural Perspective: The Development of Shakespearean Comedy and Romance, 1965

Gesner, Carol. *Shakespeare and the Greek Romance: A Study of Origins*, 1970

Goolden, P. 'Antiochus's riddle in Gower and Shakespeare', *RES* n.s. 6 (1955), 245–51

Gower, John. *Confessio Amantis*, Book VIII in *The Complete Works of John Gower*, III, ed. G. Macaulay, 1901

Green, Henry. *Shakespeare and the Emblem Writers*, 1870

Greg, Sir Walter. *Dramatic Documents from the Elizabethan Playhouses*, 2 vols., 1931

Hartwig, Joan. *Shakespeare's Tragicomic Vision*, 1972

Hillman, Richard. 'Shakespeare's Gower and Gower's Shakespeare: the larger debt of *Pericles*', *SQ* 36 (1985), 427–37

Hoeniger, F. David. 'Gower and Shakespeare in *Pericles*', *SQ* 33 (1982), 461–79
Holland, Peter. *Shakespeare and the Contemporary English Stage*, 1996
Hope, Jonathan. *The Authorship of Shakespeare's Plays: A Socio-Linguistic Study*, 1994
Kay, Carol McGinnis and Jacobs, Henry E. (eds.). *Shakespeare's Romances Reconsidered*, 1978
Jackson, MacD. P. 'George Wilkins and the first two acts of *Pericles*: new evidence from function words', *Literary and Linguistic Computing* 6 (1991), 155–63
    'Rhyming in *Pericles*: more evidence of dual authorship', *Studies in Bibliography*, 1993, 239–49
Knight, G. Wilson. *The Crown of Life*, [1947] 1948
    Shakespeare and Religion, 1967
    The Shakespearian Tempest, 1953
Lake, D. J. 'Rhymes in *Pericles*', *N&Q* 214 (1969), 139–43; and other articles on related topics in the same journal: 214 (1969), 288–91; 215 (1970), 135–41
Leiter, Samuel L. (ed.). *Shakespeare Around the Globe: A Guide to Notable Postwar Revivals*, 1986
Long, John Henderson. *Shakespeare's Use of Music: The Final Comedies*, 1961
Mehl, Dieter. *The Elizabethan Dumb Show: The History of a Dramatic Convention*, [1964] 1965
Musgrove, S. 'The first quarto of *Pericles* reconsidered' *SQ* 29 (1978), 389–406
Nelson, Thomas Allen. *Shakespeare's Comic Theory: A Study of Art and Artifice in the Last Plays*, 1972
Ness, Frederick William. *The Use of Rhyme in Shakespeare's Plays*, 1941
Nosworthy, J. M. 'Music and its function in the romances of Shakespeare', *S.Sur.* 11 (1958), 60–9
Pafford, J. H. P. (ed.). *The Winter's Tale*, 1963
Palmer, D. J. (ed.). *Shakespeare's Later Comedies: An Anthology of Modern Criticism*, 1971
Peterson, Douglas L. *Time, Tide and Tempest: A Study of Shakespeare's Romances*, 1973
Pettet, E. C. *Shakespeare and the Romance Tradition*, 1949
Prior, Roger. 'The life of George Wilkins', *S.Sur.* 25 (1972), 137–52
Sams, Eric. 'The painful misadventures of *Pericles* Acts I and II', *N&Q* 236 (1991) 67–70
Scott-Giles, C. W. *Shakespeare's Heraldry*, 1971
Smith, Hallett. *Shakespeare's Romances: A Study of Some Ways of the Imagination*, 1972
Smith, W. M. A. 'The authorship of *Pericles*: new evidence for Wilkins', *Literary and Linguistic Computing* 2 (1987), 221–30; and a series of articles on this topic in *Computers and the Humanities* 22 (1988), 23–41; 23 (1989), 113–29; 24 (1990), 295–300
Smyth, Albert H. *Shakespeare's Pericles and Apollonius of Tyre*, 1898
Taylor, Gary. 'The transmission of *Pericles*', *PBSA*, 80 (1986), 193–217
Tillyard, E. M. W. *Shakespeare's Last Plays*, 1958

Traversi, Derek. *Shakespeare: The Last Phase*, 1955

Uphaus, Robert W. *Beyond Tragedy: Structure and Experience in Shakespeare's Romances*, 1981

Waters, David W. *The Art of Navigation in England in Elizabethan and Early Stuart Times*, 1958

Welsh, Andrew. 'Heritage in *Pericles*', in Richard Tobias *et al.* (eds.), *Shakespeare's Late Plays: Essays in Honour of Charles Crow*, 1974

Werstine, Paul. 'Narratives about printed Shakespeare texts: "foul papers" and "bad quartos"', *SQ* 41 (1990), 65–86

White, R. S. *'Let Wonder Seem Familiar': Endings in Shakespeare's Romance Vision*, 1985

Wood, James O. 'The running image in *Pericles*', *Shakespeare Studies* 5 (1969), 240–52

Young, Alan R. 'A note on the tournament impresas in *Pericles*', *SQ* 36 (1985), 453–56